Select Material for Property I

Aspen Custom Publishing Series

Select Material for Property I

Curated by
John Infranca

Suffolk University Law School

Selected pages from

Property Law, Sixth Edition
by Joseph William Singer, Bethany R. Berger, Nestor M. Davidson and Eduardo
Moisés Peñalver

Property Law
by D. Benjamin Barros and Anna P. Hemingway

Cases and Text on Property, Sixth Edition
by Susan Fletcher French and Gerald Korngold

Wolters Kluwer

Wolters Kluwer serves customers worldwide with CCH, Aspen Publishers, and Kluwer Law International products. (www.wolterskluwerlb.com)

No part of this publication may be reproduced or transmitted in any form or by any means, electronic or mechanical, including photocopy, recording, or utilized by any information storage or retrieval system, without written permission from the publisher. For information about permissions or to request permissions online, visit us at www.wolterskluwerlb.com, or a written request may be faxed to our permissions department at 212-771-0803.

To contact Customer Service, e-mail customer.service@wolterskluwer.com, call 1-800-234-1660, fax 1-800-901-9075, or mail correspondence to:

Wolters Kluwer
Attn: Order Department
PO Box 990
Frederick, MD 21705

Printed in the United States of America.

1 2 3 4 5 6 7 8 9 0

978-1-4548-7055-5

SUMMARY OF CONTENTS

CONTENTS

CHAPTER 3

INTELLECTUAL PROPERTY/PROPERTY
IN THE PERSON   135

> D. Benjamin Barros and Anna P. Hemingway, *Property Law* and Joseph William Singer,
> Bethany R. Berger, Nestor M. Davidson and Eduardo Moisés Peñalver, *Property Law*, 6E

CHAPTER 4

ESTATES AND FUTURE INTERESTS   167

D. Benjamin Barros and Anna P. Hemingway, *Property Law* and Joseph William Singer,
Bethany R. Berger, Nestor M. Davidson and Eduardo Moisés Peñalver, *Property Law*, 6E

CHAPTER 5

CONCURRENT OWNERSHIP   233

D. Benjamin Barros and Anna P. Hemingway, *Property Law* and Joseph William Singer,
Bethany R. Berger, Nestor M. Davidson and Eduardo Moisés Peñalver, *Property Law*, 6E

ACKNOWLEDGMENTS

Permission to reprint the following is gratefully acknowledged:

Strahilevitz, Lior Jacob. Information Asymmetries and the Rights to Exclude, 104 Mich. L. R. 1835 (2006). Reprinted by permission of the author.

Tom the Dancing Bug cartoon, "Harvey Richards: Lawyer for Children." TOM THE DANCING BUG © 2013 Ruben Bolling. Reprinted with permission of UNIVERSAL UCLICK. All rights reserved.

Waldman, Carl. maps from *Atlas of the North American Indian* (3d ed. 2009). Reprinted by permission.

CHAPTER
1

Introduction

A.   A GUIDE TO THE BOOK

Organization of the Book

The book is organized around six broad themes. In Part One, we introduce a basic framework for understanding the balance of rights, limitations, and duties inherent in ownership, using the example of tensions between the right to exclude and the right of access. We then address the primary justifications that have traditionally been invoked to justify property rights, including sovereignty, reward for labor, distributive justice, efficiency, recognition of relationships, possession, and personhood. Part Two explores the outer boundaries of ownership by examining how the legal system mediates a variety of resources other than real estate and personal goods, notably ideas, culture, human beings, and human bodies. Many of the most important doctrines in property law focus on relationships between neighbors and Part Three explores adverse possession, nuisance, zoning, and private agreements between owners (called servitudes) as examples. In Part Four, we explore the myriad ways the law allows property to be divided and shared, both concurrently and over time. These forms of ownership in common include concurrent tenancies, family property, corporate and other entity property, leaseholds, as well as the complex system of estates and future interests we have inherited from early English law. Part Five explores two fundamental aspects of the market for real estate, the role of property law and property lawyers in sales and financing and the importance of antidiscrimination law. Finally, the book concludes in Part Six with two chapters that highlight the fundamental tension between the role of the state in both defining and defending property rights. The constitutional law of property, including equal protection, due process, and takings, is a fitting way to return to the themes explored throughout these materials. In all of this, we seek to present a contemporary introduction to the law of property, focusing on various pressing issues of current concern as well as the basic rules governing the property system.

What Is Property?

Property rights concern relations among people regarding control of valued resources. Property law gives owners the power to control things, and it does this

1

by placing duties on non-owners. For example, owners have the right to exclude non-owners from their property; this right imposes a duty on others not to enter property without the owner's consent. Property rights are relational; ownership is not just power over things but entails relations among people. This is true not only of the right to exclude but of the privilege to use property. An owner who operates a business on a particular parcel may benefit the community by creating jobs and providing needed services, and she may harm the community by increasing traffic or causing pollution. Development of a subdivision may affect drainage patterns and cause flooding on neighboring land. Property use makes others vulnerable to the effects of that use, for better or for worse. Power over things is actually power over people.

Property rights are *not absolute*. The recognition and exercise of a property right in one person often affects and may even conflict with the personal or property rights of others. To give one person an absolute legal entitlement would mean that others could not exercise similar entitlements. Property rights are therefore limited to ensure that property use and ownership do not unreasonably harm the legitimate, legally protected personal or property interests of others. The duty to exercise property rights in a manner compatible with the legal rights of others means that *owners have obligations as well as rights*.

Owners of property generally possess a *bundle of entitlements*. The most important are the privilege to use the property, the right to exclude others, the power to transfer title to the property, and immunity from having the property taken or damaged without their consent. These entitlements may be disaggregated—an owner can give up some of the sticks in the bundle while keeping others. Landlords, for example, grant tenants the right to possess their property in exchange for periodic rental payments while retaining the right to regain possession at the end of the leasehold. Because property rights are limited to protect the legitimate interests of others and because owners have the power to disaggregate property rights, entitlements in a particular piece of property are more often shared than unitary. It is almost always the case that more than one person will have something to say about the use of a particular piece of property. Property law therefore cannot be reduced to the rules that determine ownership; rather, it comprises rules that allocate particular entitlements and define their scope.

Property is owned in a *variety of forms*. An infinite number of bundles of rights can be created from the sticks in the bundle that comprise full ownership. However, some bundles are widely used and they comprise the basic forms or models of ownership. Some forms are used by individuals while others are used by couples (married or unmarried) or families. Other forms are used by groups of unrelated owners. Differences exist between forms that give owners management powers and those that separate ownership from management. Further distinctions exist between residential and commercial property and between nonprofit organizations and for-profit businesses. Within each of these categories are multiple subcategories, such as the distinction between partnerships and corporations or between male-female couples and same-sex couples. Particular models of property ownership have been created for different social contexts and types of property. Each model has a different way of bundling and dispersing the rights and obligations of ownership among various persons. Understanding property requires knowledge both of the individual sticks in the bundle of property rights and the characteristic bundles that characterize particular ownership forms.

Property is a *system* as well as an *entitlement*. A property right is a legal entitlement granted to an individual or entity but the extent of the legal right is partly determined by rules designed to ensure that the property system functions effectively and fairly. Many property law rules are geared not to protecting individual entitlements, but to ensuring that the environment in which those rights are exercised is one that maximizes the benefits of property ownership for everyone and is compatible with the norms underlying a free and democratic society. Some rules promote efficiency, such as the rules that facilitate the smooth operation of the real estate market. Other rules promote fairness or distributive justice, such as the fair housing laws that prohibit owners from denying access to property on the basis of race, sex, religion, or disability.

Tensions Within the Property System

In 1990, roughly a year after his nation was freed from Soviet domination, the foreign minister of Czechoslovakia, Jiri Dienstbier, commented that "[i]t was easier to make a revolution than to write 600 to 800 laws to create a market economy."[1] If anything, he understated the case. Each of the basic property entitlements is limited to ensure that the exercise of a property right by one person is compatible with the property and personal rights of others. The construction of a property system requires property law to adjudicate characteristic core tensions in the system.

Right to exclude versus right of access.   It is often said that the most fundamental right associated with property ownership is the right to exclude non-owners from the property. If the right to exclude were unlimited, owners could exclude non-owners based on race or religion. Although at one time owners were empowered (and in some states required) to do this, current law prohibits discrimination on the basis of race, sex, national origin, religion, or disability in public accommodations, housing, and employment. Although individuals are free to choose whom to invite to their homes for dinner, market actors are regulated to ensure that access to property is available without regard to invidious discrimination. Property therefore entails a tension between privacy and free association norms on one side and equality norms on the other. Sometimes the right of access will take precedence over the right to exclude. The tension between these claims is one that property law must resolve.

Privilege to use versus security from harm.   Owners are generally free to use their property as they wish, but they are not free to harm their neighbors' property substantially and unreasonably. A factory that emits pollutants into the air may be regulated to prevent the use of its property in ways that will destroy the individual property rights of others and common resources in air and water. Many uses of property impose "externalities" or spillover effects on other owners and on the community as a whole. Because owners are legally entitled to have their own property protected from pollutants dispatched to their property by others, owners' freedom to use their property is limited to ensure that their property use does not cause such unreasonable negative externalities.

---

1. William Echikson, *Euphoria Dies Down in Czechoslovakia*, Wall St. J., Sept. 18, 1990, at A-26, 1990 WL-WSJ 56114.

Power to transfer versus powers of ownership.   Owners are generally free to transfer their property to whomever they wish, on whatever terms they want. Freedom of disposition gives them the power to sell it, give it away, or write a will identifying who will get it when they die. They are also free to contract with others to transfer particular sticks in the bundle of sticks comprising full ownership to others while keeping the rest for themselves. Owners may even place conditions on the use of property when they sell it, limiting what future owners may do with it. They may, for example, limit the property to residential purposes by including a restriction in the deed limiting the property to such uses. Although owners are free to disaggregate property rights in various ways, and to impose particular restrictions on the use and ownership of land, that freedom is not unlimited. Owners are not allowed to impose conditions that violate public policy or that unduly infringe on the liberty interests of future owners. For example, an owner could not impose an enforceable condition that all future owners agree to vote for the Democratic candidate for president; this condition infringes on the liberty of future owners and wrongfully attempts to tie ownership of the land to membership in a particular political party. Nor are owners allowed to limit the sale of the property to persons of a particular race. Similarly, restrictions limiting the transfer of property will ordinarily not be enforced, both to protect the freedom of owners to move and to promote the efficient transfer of property in the marketplace. The freedom of an owner to restrict the future use or disposition of property must be curtailed to protect the freedom of future owners to use their property as they wish. The law limits freedom of contract and freedom of disposition to ensure that owners have sufficient powers over the property they own.

Immunity from loss versus power to acquire.   Property owners have the right not to have their property taken or damaged by others against their will. However, it is often lawful to interfere with the property interests of others. For example, an owner who builds a house on a vacant lot may block a view enjoyed by the neighbor for many years. A new company may put a prior company out of business or reduce its profits through competition. Property rights must be limited to ensure that others can exercise similar rights in acquiring and using property. In addition, immunity from forced seizure or loss of property rights is not absolute when the needs of the community take precedence. To construct a new public highway or municipal building, for example, the government may exercise its eminent power to take private property for public uses with just compensation.

Recurring Themes

A number of important themes will recur throughout this book. They include the following:

Social context.   Social context matters in defining property rights. We have different typical models of property depending on whether it is owned individually or jointly, among family members or non-family members, by a private or a governmental entity, devoted to profitable or charitable purposes, for residential or commercial purposes, open to public use or limited to private use.

Formal versus informal sources of rights.   Property rights generally have their source in some formal grant, such as a deed, a will, a lease, a contract, or a government grant. However, property rights also arise informally, by an oral promise, a course of conduct, actual possession, a family relationship, an oral gift, longstanding reliance, and social customs and norms. Many of the basic rules of property law concern contests between formal and informal sources of property rights. While the law usually insists on formality to create property rights, it often protects informally created expectations over formally created ones. Determining when expectations based on informal arrangements should prevail over formal ones is a central issue in property law.

The alienability dilemma.   It is a fundamental tenet of the property law system that property should be "alienable," meaning that it should be transferable from one person to another. Transferability allows a market to function and enables efficient transactions and property use to occur. It also promotes individual autonomy by allowing owners to sell or give away property when they please on terms they have chosen. This suggests that the law should allow owners to disaggregate property rights as they please. However, if owners are allowed to disaggregate property rights at will, it may be difficult to reconsolidate those rights. If property is burdened by obsolete restrictions, it may be expensive or impossible to get rid of them. Similarly, if property is disaggregated among too many owners, transaction costs may block agreements to reconsolidate the interests and make the property useable for current needs. The property may therefore be rendered inalienable.

Many rules of property law limit contractual freedom to ensure that particular bundles of property rights are consolidated in the same person—the "owner." Consolidating power in an "owner" ensures that resources can be used for current purposes and current needs and allows property to be freely transferred in the marketplace. We therefore face a tension between promoting alienability by consolidating rights in owners and promoting alienability by allowing owners to disaggregate their rights into unique bundles constructed by them.

Contractual freedom and minimum standards.   Individuals want to be free to develop human relationships without having government dictate the terms of their association with others. Having the ability to rearrange property rights to create desirable packages of entitlements will help enable various relationships to flourish. However, there are also bounds to what is acceptable; this is why the law imposes certain minimum standards on contractual relationships. For example, although landlords are entitled to evict residential tenants who do not pay rent, the law in almost every state requires landlords to use court eviction proceedings to dispossess defaulting tenants. These proceedings give tenants a chance to contest the landlord's possessory claim and to have time to find a new place to live, rather than having their belongings tossed on the street and being dispossessed overnight. These limitations on free contract protect basic norms of fair dealing and promote the justified expectations of individuals who enter market transactions.

Social welfare.   Granting owners power over property ensures that they can obtain resources to satisfy human needs. It also promotes social welfare by encouraging productive activity and by granting security to those who invest in economic projects. Clear property rights facilitate exchange and lower the costs of transactions by clarifying who owns what. At the same time, owners may use their property in socially harmful ways, and clear property rights may promote harmful, as well as beneficial, actions. Property rights must be limited to ensure that conflicting uses are accommodated to minimize the costs of desirable development on other owners and on the community. Moreover, rigid property rights may inhibit bargaining rather than facilitate it by granting owners the power to act unreasonably, thereby encouraging litigation to clarify the limits on the owner's entitlements. Reasonableness requirements, while less predictable than clear rules, may promote efficient bargaining by encouraging competing claimants to compromise in ways that minimize the costs of property use on others. We need to design rules of ownership and transfer that promote efficiency and social welfare by decreasing the costs of using and obtaining property while maximizing its benefits both to individual owners and to society as a whole.

Justified expectations. In a famous phrase, Jeremy Bentham wrote that "[p]roperty is nothing but a basis of expectation; the expectation of deriving certain advantages from a thing which we are said to possess, in consequence of the relation in which we stand towards it."[2] Owners justifiably expect to use their own property for their own purposes and to transfer it on terms chosen by them. However, because the property use often affects others, it must be limited to protect the expectations of others. Property law protects justified expectations. A central function of property law is to determine what the parties' actual expectations are and when they are, and are not, justified.

Distributive justice. Property rights are the legal form of wealth. Wealth takes many forms, including the right to control tangible assets, such as land and buildings, and intangible assets, such as stocks that give the holder the right to control and derive profit from a business enterprise. In fact, any legal entitlement that benefits the right holder may be viewed as a species of property. The rules of property law, like the rules of contract, family, and tax law, play an enormous role in determining the distribution of both wealth and income.

How well is property dispersed in the United States? One expert has noted that "[b]y several measurements, the United States in the late twentieth century led all other major industrial countries in the gap dividing the upper fifth of the population from the lower—in the disparity between top and bottom."[3]

One indicator of the distribution of property is income. Since 1967, income distribution has become increasingly unequal in the United States. In 2011, the Census Bureau reported that the share of total income going to the top fifth of American households increased from 43.6 percent in 1967 to 51.1 percent in 2011.[4] Within the top fifth of the population, the bulk of this increase was

---

2. 1 Jeremy Bentham, *Theory of Legislation* 137 (Boston: Weeks, Jordan & Co., R. Hildreth trans. 1840).

3. Kevin Phillips, *The Politics of Rich and Poor: Wealth and the American Electorate in the Reagan Aftermath* 8 (1990).

4. Data in this section come from Carmen DeNavas-Walt, Bernadette D. Proctor & Jessica C. Smith, U.S. Census Bureau, *Income, Poverty, and Health Insurance Coverage in the United States: 2011* (Sept. 2012), *available at http://www.census.gov/prod/2012pubs/p60-236.pdf.* Data for 2010 come from U.S. Census Bureau, *Facts for Features: American Indian and Alaska Native Heritage Month: November 2011*, CB11-FF.22 (Nov. 2011), *available at http://www.census.gov/newsroom/releases/archives/facts_for_features_special_editions/cb11-ff22.html.*

obtained by those at the very top. A 2010 white paper showed that between 1982 and 2006, the real incomes of the top 1 percent of families rose 127 percent, whereas the bottom 80 percent of families saw increases of only 13 percent or less in real income.[5]

The distribution of income also varies according to race, gender, and age. The median income of households in the United States was $50,054 in 2011; half of all households received more and half less than that amount. However, differences are substantial along racial lines. While the median income of white, non-Hispanic families was $55,412 in 2011, the median income for African American households was only $32,229 and that of Latino households was $38,624. The median household income of American Indians and Native Alaskan households in 2010 was $35,062.

Poverty is similarly unequally distributed by race. While 15 percent of all persons were poor by federal standards in 2011, only 9.8 percent of non-Hispanic whites were poor; by comparison, 27.6 percent of African Americans and 25.3 percent of Latinos fell below the poverty line. Data from 2010 show that 28.4 percent of American Indians and Native Alaskans were poor by official standards.

Although the gap in incomes between men and women has narrowed over the last quarter-century, men still earn more than women on average. In 2011, men who worked full time earned an average of $48,202 while women who worked full time earned only $37,118, or 77 percent of male earnings.

Children are more likely to be poor than adults, and some children are very likely to be poor. Although 13.5 percent of the population fell below the poverty line in 2011, 21.9 percent of children did so; moreover, 38.8 percent of African American children and 34.1 percent of Hispanic children were living in poverty. Children who live in households without an adult male are extremely likely to be poor. While only 6.2 percent of children in families of married couples were poor in 2011, 31.2 percent of children living in female-headed households were poor. More than half of all children under six living in female-headed households (57.2 percent) were poor. Although 23.8 percent of white, non-Hispanic, female-headed households were poor, 42.3 percent of African American, female-headed households and 44 percent of Hispanic, female-headed households were poor. While the median income of married couples was $74,130, the median income of female-headed households was only $33,637, and the median income of male-headed households was $49,567.

Inequalities of both income and wealth are somewhat alleviated by transfer payments in the form of public assistance. Until the 1970s, elderly persons were more likely to be poor than the non-elderly. By 1990, however, the poverty rate for persons over 65 was less than that for the rest of the population, and relatively few elderly persons are among the homeless and extremely poor. This change in the position of the elderly was the result of public spending in the form of Social Security pensions, Medicare, and housing subsidies.[6] In 2011, the poverty rate for those 65 and older was 8.7 percent compared to 13.7 percent for those between 18 and 64.[7]

---

5. Edward N. Wolff, *Recent Trends in Household Wealth in the United States: Rising Debt and the Middle-Class Squeeze—An Update to 2007*, 14 (Levy Economics Institute Working Paper No. 589, Mar. 2010), *available at http://www.levyinstitute.org/pubs/wp_589.pdf.*

6. Peter H. Rossi, *Down and Out in America: The Origins of Homelessness* 193 (1989).

7. U.S. Census Bureau, *Income, Poverty, and Health Insurance Coverage, supra* note 4.

Wealth data show even greater inequality than income data. Far more than income, wealth determines financial security and economic prospects in the United States.[8] In 2007, the top 1 percent of U.S. households owned 34.6 percent of U.S. family net wealth while the top 5 percent owned well over half of all net wealth (62 percent). The top quintile owned 86 percent of wealth while the bottom 40 percent of the population owned 2 percent of net wealth.[9] The racial disparities are equally stark. In 2011, the median net worth of African American households was only 5.7 percent that of non-Hispanic white households, while the median net worth of Hispanic households was only 6.9 percent.[10] These racial disparities are essentially unchanged since 1983.[11] The 2008 recession and uneven recovery exacerbated wealth inequality. Declines in jobs and property values hit the primary sources of wealth for most Americans. Wealthy Americans, however, have a greater proportion of their assets invested in financial markets. The rebound in financial markets and sluggish recovery in jobs and home values meant that although 93 percent of households saw their net worth decline between 2009 and 2011, the top 7 percent saw their net worth rise significantly.[12]

Individual versus shared ownership. Property may be owned and controlled by individuals; the history of the development of land law in England, for example, may be described as a shift from control over property by feudal lords and family inheritance restrictions to control by individual owners. But shared ownership continues to characterize property, perhaps increasingly so. In marriages and other intimate relationships, for example, ownership of homes and bank accounts is typically in the name of both partners. The assets of Americans, moreover, increasingly consist of investments in corporate stocks and ownership of condominiums or other common interest developments, both forms of property in which ownership and control are shared with many individuals. In addition, because ownership rights affect others, both statutory and common law recognize rights in the community to control property to some degree. The recognition of shared rights in property may differ in different cultures and legal systems. Compared to U.S. property law, for example, continental European systems may do more to recognize and facilitate common ownership, while English and Scottish legal systems recognize greater rights in the community to traverse and enjoy private lands.[13]

One persistent conflict between shared and individualist conceptions of property concerns American Indian nations, the original possessors of land in the United States. With more than 550 federally recognized tribes and scores of

---

8. Alfred Gottschalck, Marina Vornovytskyy & Adam Smith, U.S. Census Bureau, *Household Wealth in the U.S.: 2000 to 2011* (2013).

9. Wolff, *supra* note 5 (analyzing 2007 census data). *See also* Marco Cagetti & Mariacristina De Nardi, *Wealth Inequality: Data and Models* (Federal Reserve Bank of Chicago Working Paper No. 2005-10, Aug. 17, 2005), *available at http://papers.ssrn.com/sol3/papers.cfm?abstract_id=838325*; Lisa A. Keister, *Wealth in America* 64 (2000); Kevin Phillips, *supra* note 3, at 1-13.

10. U.S. Census Bureau, *Median Value of Assets for Households, by Type of Asset Owned and Other Selected Characteristics: 2011* (2013), *available at http://www.census.gov/people/wealth/*.

11. *Wolff, supra* note 5 (providing historical data).

12. Richard Fry & Paul Taylor, Pew Research Center, *An Uneven Recovery, 2009-2011: A Rise in Wealth for the Wealthy, Declines for the Lower 93%* (2013), *available at http://www.pewsocialtrends.org/2013/04/23/a-rise-in-wealth-for-the-wealthydeclines-for-the-lower-93*.

13. *See* Michael Heller & Hanoch Dagan, *The Liberal Commons,* 110 Yale L.J. 549, 610-611 (2001); John A. Lovett, *Progressive Property in Action: The Land Reform (Scotland) Act 2003,* 89 Neb. L. Rev. 739 (2011); Jerry L. Anderson, *Britain's Right to Roam: Redefining the Landowner's Bundle of Sticks,* 19 Geo. Intl. Envtl. L. Rev. 375 (2007).

unrecognized tribes, it is difficult to generalize about American Indian land use systems, either in the past or the present. Nonetheless, many Native peoples recognized shared and community ownership more explicitly than did European American settlers. Native individuals and families did own property and land was bought and sold, but indigenous property systems often had a robust concept of shared use rights. While a particular family might use a piece of land to plant crops, for example, this would not preclude other tribal members from entering or gathering nonagricultural food on such lands. Much land, moreover, was considered to be owned by a tribe in common, and open to hunting, fishing, or the like by the tribe as a whole. (Note, however, that this sense of shared rights is not so different from rights of villagers to graze on common or uncultivated lands in early England, discussed in Chapter 8 [Joseph William Singer, Bethany R. Berger, Nestor M. Davidson and Eduardo Moisés Peñalver, Property Law, 6th ed., (2014)], §2.1, or the "right to roam" on unfenced land recognized for much of American history, discussed in Chapter 1 [Joseph William Singer, Bethany R. Berger, Nestor M. Davidson and Eduardo Moisés Peñalver, Property Law, 6th ed., (2014)], §1.)

More radically, for most indigenous peoples, land was not fungible—it could not simply be replaced with similar land elsewhere. Rather, specific areas were deeply connected to the history and spiritual identity of a tribe. For many Native peoples even today, particular areas may be "the source of spiritual origins and sustaining myth which in turn provides a landscape of cultural and emotional meaning. The land often determines the values of the human landscape."[14] The community, therefore, could not be excluded from such areas without doing violence to the tribe and its identity. These differences in emphasis on shared versus individual rights in U.S. and Indian property systems were the source of much conflict, as well as repeated efforts by the federal government to inculcate a love of individual property as a tool to encourage tribal assimilation and dissolution.[15]

Normative Approaches

How should courts and legislatures adjudicate conflicting property claims? Various approaches can be used to conceptualize property rights and to adjudicate conflicts among property claimants.[16] Here is a brief description of the most common approaches.[17]

---

14. Frank Pommersheim, *The Reservation as Place: A South Dakota Essay*, 34 S.D. L. Rev. 246, 250 (1989); *see also* Rebecca Tsosie, *Land, Culture and Community: Reflections on Native Sovereignty and Property in America*, 34 Ind. L. Rev. 1291, 1302-1303 (2001).

15. *See, e.g.,* Chapter 15 [Joseph William Singer, Bethany R. Berger, Nestor M. Davidson and Eduardo Moisés Peñalver, Property Law, 6th ed., (2014)], §5.1 (cases and materials on the allotment policy, through which the United States forcibly divided tribal land among individual households).

16. For collections of scholarly approaches to property, *see Perspectives on Property Law* (Robert C. Ellickson, Carol M. Rose & Bruce A. Ackerman eds. 3d ed. 2002); *A Property Anthology* (Richard H. Chused ed. 2d ed. 1997).

17. Many, if not most, scholars combine various approaches. *See, e.g.,* Stephen R. Munzer, *A Theory of Property* (1990) (adopting a pluralist perspective including justice and equality, desert based on labor, and utility and efficiency); Carol M. Rose, *Property and Persuasion: Essays on the History, Theory, and Rhetoric of Ownership* (1994) (combining economic analysis, justice-based arguments, and feminist legal theory); Joseph William Singer, *Entitlement: The Paradoxes of Property* (2000) (using both justice and utilitarian considerations, as well as narrative theory, feminism, critical race theory, and critical legal studies).

Positivism and legal realism.   Positivist theories identify law with the "commands of the sovereign" or the rules promulgated by authoritative government officials for reasons of public policy.[18] Those rules may be intended to protect individual rights, promote the general welfare, increase social wealth, or maximize social utility. Judges are therefore directed to apply the law, as promulgated by authoritative government lawmakers, and to exercise discretion where there are gaps, conflicts, or ambiguities in the law while respecting the need for consistency with the letter and spirit of preexisting laws. Jeremy Bentham wrote that the "idea of property consists in an established expectation . . . of being able to draw . . . an advantage from the thing possessed."[19] He believed that "this expectation, this persuasion, can only be the work of law. It is only through the protection of law that I am able to inclose a field, and to give myself up to its cultivation with the sure though distant hope of harvest . . . . "[20] Property exists to the extent the law will protect it. "Property and law are born together, and die together. Before laws were made there was no property; take away laws, and property ceases."[21]

Positivists separate law and morals; they emphasize that, although moral judgments may underlie rules of law, they are not fully or consistently enforced by legal sanctions. Positivism was adopted by Progressive-era judges and scholars such as Oliver Wendell Holmes, who suggested analyzing legal rules in the way a "bad man" would. Such a person would not be interested in the moral content of the law but would simply want to predict what legal sanctions would be imposed on him if he engaged in prohibited conduct.[22] This approach was adopted by legal realist scholars of the 1920s and 1930s such as Karl Llewellyn, who argued that the law is what officials will do in resolving disputes.[23]

All lawyers are positivists in some sense because the job of advising clients necessarily entails identifying the rules of law that have been explicitly or implicitly adopted by authoritative lawmakers and predicting how those rules will be applied to the client's situation. Judges may also see their jobs as the enforcement of existing law and leave the job of amending law to legislatures. On the other hand, determining whether an existing rule was intended to apply to a particular situation requires judgment, as well as techniques of *statutory interpretation* and analysis of *precedent*, and a conception about the proper role of courts in the lawmaking process.

Justice and fairness.   Positivism has been criticized by scholars who argue that ambiguities in existing laws must be filled in by judges, and that judges should not exercise untrammeled discretion in doing so. Rather, they should interpret gaps, conflicts, and ambiguities in the law in a manner that protects individual rights, promotes fairness, or ensures justice.

Rights theorists attempt to identify individual interests that are so important from a moral point of view that they not only deserve legal protection but may count as "trumps" that override more general considerations of

---

18. John Austin, *Lectures of Jurisprudence* (1861-1863); H.L.A. Hart, *The Concept of Law* (1961).
19. Bentham, *supra* note 2, at 138.
20. *Id.*
21. *Id.* at 139.
22. *See* Oliver Wendell Holmes, *The Path of the Law*, 8 Harv. L. Rev. 1 (1894).
23. Karl Llewellyn, *The Bramble Bush* (1930).

public policy by which competing interests are balanced against each other. Such individual rights cannot legitimately be sacrificed for the good of the community.[24] Some *natural rights* theorists argue that rights have roots in the nature of human beings or that they are natural in the sense that people who think about human relationships from a rational and moral point of view are bound to understand particular individual interests as fundamental.[25] Other scholars, building on Immanuel Kant, ask whether a claim that an interest should be protected could be *universalized* such that every person in similar circumstances would be entitled to similar protection. Still others build on the *social contract* tradition begun by John Locke and Thomas Hobbes and ask whether individuals would choose to protect certain interests if they had to come to agreement in a suitably defined decision-making context. John Rawls, for example, asks what principles of justice would be adopted by individuals who did not know morally irrelevant facts about themselves, such as their race or sex.[26]

Some theorists focus on *desert.* John Locke argued that labor is the foundation of property. "Whatsoever then he removes out of the state that nature has provided and left it in, he has mixed his labor with, and joined to it something that is his own, and thereby makes it his property."[27] Other theorists focus on the role that property rights play in developing individual *autonomy.*[28] Hegel believed that property was a way that human beings constituted themselves as people by extending their will to manipulate the objects of the external world.[29] Professor Margaret Jane Radin, for example, has argued that "to be a *person* . . . an individual needs some control over resources in the external environment."[30] She distinguishes between forms of property that are important for the meaning they have to individuals (personal property such as a wedding ring) and property that is important solely because it can be used in exchange (fungible property such as money and investments).[31]

Other scholars focus on satisfying *human needs* or ensuring *distributive justice.* Nancy Fraser has argued that an important way to think about property rights is to focus on the ways we define people's needs and the ways in which the legal system does or does not meet those needs.[32] Frank Michelman has similarly argued that a system of private property requires, by its very nature, that property be widely dispersed. If all property were owned by one person, that person would be a dictator. Private property implies wide availability. It therefore entails a

---

24. Ronald Dworkin, *Law's Empire* (1986); Ronald Dworkin, *Taking Rights Seriously* (1978); Charles Fried, *Right and Wrong* (1978); Allan Gewirth, *The Community of Rights* (1996); Jeremy Waldron, *The Right to Private Property* (1998).

25. *See* Robert Nozick, *Anarchy, State, and Utopia* (1974); Judith Jarvis Thompson, *The Realm of Rights* (1990).

26. John Rawls, *A Theory of Justice* (1971). *See also* Thomas M. Scanlon, *What We Owe Each Other* (1998).

27. John Locke, *Second Treatise of Government* 17-18 (Bobbs-Merrill ed. 1952) (originally published in 1960).

28. Richard A. Epstein, *Simple Rules for a Complex World* 53-70 (1995).

29. Georg Wilhelm Friedrich Hegel, *Philosophy of Right* 40-41 (T. Knox trans. 1942).

30. Margaret Jane Radin, *Property and Personhood,* 34 Stan. L. Rev. 957 (1982).

31. Margaret Jane Radin, *Market-Inalienability,* 100 Harv. L. Rev. 1849 (1987). *See also* Margaret Jane Radin, *Contested Commodities: The Trouble with Trade in Sex, Children, Body Parts, and Other Things* (1996); Margaret Jane Radin, *Reinterpreting Property* (1993).

32. Nancy Fraser, *Unruly Practices, Power, Discourse, and Gender in Contemporary Social Theory* (1989).

compromise between the principle of protecting possession and promoting widespread distribution.[33]

Utilitarianism, social welfare, and efficiency.   Utilitarians focus on the *consequences* of alternative legal rules. They compare the costs and benefits of alternative property rules or institutions with the goal of adopting rules that will maximize *social utility* or *welfare*. Some scholars in the law and economics school of thought measure social utility by the concept of economic *efficiency*. Efficiency theorists measure costs and benefits by reference to what people are willing and able to pay for entitlements, given their resources.[34]

Individual property rights are thought to increase efficiency by encouraging productive activity and by granting security to those who invest in economic projects. Clear property rights also facilitate exchange by clarifying who owns what. They therefore create incentives to use resources efficiently.[35] On the other hand, Carol Rose has argued that clear definitions of property rights may be overly rigid, upsetting settled expectations and reliance interests.[36] This is why property rights are often defined by flexible standards, such as a reasonableness requirement, that adjust the relations of the parties to achieve a fair and efficient result. Rose has also argued that common ownership is sometimes the most efficient way to manage property.[37] Frank Michelman and Duncan Kennedy have also argued that efficiency requires a mixture of private property, sharing, and deregulation.[38] Cass Sunstein has noted that preferences are partially shaped by law and that cognitive biases may affect individuals' perceptions of their preferences.[39]

Social relations.   Social relations approaches analyze property rights as relations among persons regarding control of valued resources. Legal rights are correlative; every legal entitlement in an individual implies a correlative vulnerability in someone else, and every entitlement is limited by the competing rights of others.[40] This analysis was developed by pragmatic legal scholars—called "legal realists"—from the 1920s through the 1930s. Property rights are interpreted as delegations of sovereign power to individuals by the state; these rights should therefore be defined to accommodate the conflicting interests of social actors.[41] Current social relations theorists have broadened the scope of this analysis by examining the role property rights play in structuring social

---

33. Frank Michelman, *Possession and Distribution in the Constitutional Idea of Property*, 72 Iowa L. Rev. 1319 (1987). *See also* Waldron, *supra* note 24.

34. *See generally* Richard A. Posner, *Economic Analysis and Law* (7th ed. 2007); Steven Shavell, *Foundations of Economic Analysis of Law* (2004).

35. Shavell, *supra* note 34, at 11-23. *See also* Garrett Hardin, *The Tragedy of the Commons*, reprinted in *Economic Foundations of Property Law* 4 (Bruce Ackerman ed. 1975); Harold Demsetz, *Toward a Theory of Property Rights*, 57 Am. Econ. Rev. 347 (1967).

36. Carol Rose, *Crystals and Mud in Property Law*, 40 Stan. L. Rev. 577 (1988).

37. Carol Rose, *The Comedy of the Commons: Customs, Commerce, and Inherently Public Property*, 53 U. Chi. L. Rev. 711 (1986). *See also* Frank Michelman, *Ethics, Economics, and the Law of Property*, 24 Nomos: Ethics, Economics, and the Law 3 (1982) (arguing that the institution of property, by its nature, requires a large amount of cooperative activity).

38. Duncan Kennedy & Frank Michelman, *Are Property and Contract Efficient?*, 8 Hofstra L. Rev. 711 (1980).

39. Cass R. Sunstein, *Free Markets and Social Justice* (1997).

40. Wesley Hohfield, *Some Fundamental Legal Conception as Applied in Judicial Reasoning*, 28 Yale L.J. 16 (1913).

41. Walter Wheeler Cook, *Privileges of Labor Unions in the Struggle for Life*, 27 Yale L.J. 779 (1918); Robert Hale, *Bargaining, Duress, and Economic Liberty*, 43 Colum. L. Rev. 603 (1943); Morris Cohen, *Property and Sovereignty*, 13 Cornell L.Q. 8 (1927).

relations and the ways in which social relations shape access to property.[42] These approaches include feminist legal theory, critical race theory, critical legal studies, communitarianism, law and society, deconstruction and cultural studies.

Feminists such as Martha Minow argue that our identities, values, and needs are developed in relation to and in connection with others. The legal system relies on implicit conceptions of social relations and often implicitly treats certain groups or individuals as the norm and others as the exception. She argues that we must become conscious of the ways those underlying assumptions function in both social relations and the legal system.[43] Elizabeth V. Spelman similarly analyzes the implicit assumptions underlying conceptions of human relations. In particular, she focuses on the role that race, class, and gender play in shaping the concepts with which we understand human relations.[44]

These new insights have permeated recent discussions of property law. Property has traditionally been associated with the idea of autonomy within boundaries; for example, we assume that people are generally free to do what they like within the borders of their land. Yet Jennifer Nedelsky has argued that "[w]hat makes human autonomy possible is not isolation but relationship" with others.[45] She proposes that we replace the idea of *boundary* as the central metaphor for property rights with the idea of *relationships*.[46] Social relations approaches assume that people are situated in a complicated network of relationships with others, from relations among strangers, to relations among neighbors, to continuing relations in the market, to intimate relations in the family. Moreover, many of the legal developments of the twentieth century can be described as recognition of obligations that emerge over time out of relationships of interdependence.[47] The relational approach shifts our attention from asking who the owner is to the question of what relationships have been established.[48]

Feminists[49] and critical race theorists have explored the relationship between race, sex, and property.[50] Patricia Williams has written eloquently about the social meaning of race and gender and their relation to power and to property law.[51] Keith Aoki has described the thinking that led to the alien land laws that denied property ownership to Japanese immigrants and provided the precursor to internment during World War II.[52] Alice Kessler-Harris and many other

---

42. Gregory S. Alexander, *Commodity and Propriety: Competing Visions of Property in American Legal Thought, 1776-1970* (1997); C. Edwin Baker, *Property and Its Relation to Constitutionally Protected Liberty*, 134 U. Pa. L. Rev. 741 (1986).

43. Martha Minow, *Making All the Difference: Inclusion, Exclusion, and American Law* (1990).

44. Elizabeth V. Spelman, *Inessential Woman: Problems of Exclusion in Feminist Thought* (1989).

45. Jennifer Nedelsky, *Law, Boundaries, and the Bounded Self*, 30 Representations 162, 169 (1990).

46. *Id.* at 171-184. *See also* Jennifer Nedelsky, *Reconceiving Rights as Relationships*, 1 Rev. Const. Studies/Revue d'etudes Constitionelles 1 (1993); Singer, *supra* note 17.

47. Roberto Mangabeira Unger, *The Critical Legal Studies Movement* 83-84 (1983).

48. Joseph William Singer, *The Reliance Interest in Property*, 40 Stan L. Rev. 611, 657 (1988).

49. Martha Albertson Fineman, *The Illusion of Equality: The Rhetoric and Reality of Divorce Reform* (1991); Vicki Schultz, *Life's Work*, 100 Colum. L. Rev. 1881 (2000); Reva B. Siegel, *Home as Work: The First Women's Rights Claim Concerning Wives' Household Labor, 1850-1880*, 103 Yale L.J. 1073, 1077 (1994); Reva B. Siegel, *The Modernization of Marital Status Law: Adjudicating Wives' Rights to Earnings, (1860-1930)*, 82 Geo. L.J. 2127 (1994); Joan Williams, *Unbending Gender: Why Family and Work Conflict and What to Do About It* (2000).

50. *Critical Race Theory: The Cutting Edge* (Richard Delgado ed. 1995).

51. Patricia Williams, *Fetal Fictions: An Exploration of Property Archetypes in Racial and Gendered Contexts*, 42 Fla. L. Rev. 81 (1990).

52. Keith Aoki, *No Right to Own? The Early Twentieth-Century "Alien Land Laws" as a Prelude to Internment*, 40 B.C. L. Rev. 37 (1998).

scholars have explored the social factors that determine the unequal wages paid to women and men as well as the relation between those factors and the distribution of property and power based on gender.[53]

Critical legal theorists have explored tensions or contradictions within property theory and law and used marginalized doctrines to argue for reform of property rules and institutions.[54] Communitarians and environmentalists emphasize the importance of community life as well as individual rights and argue that individuals have obligations as well as rights.[55] Law and society theorists investigate the "law in practice" rather than the "law on the books" to determine what norms actually govern behavior in the real world with respect to property.[56] Other scholars have used deconstruction, poststructuralism, or cultural theory to explore the unconscious assumptions underlying property law.[57]

Human flourishing.   In recent years, some property theorists have begun to turn to the Aristotelian idea of human flourishing.[58] Human flourishing theories of property are self-consciously pluralist in their normative outlook. Like utilitarian theory, they view property as an institution that (like other legal institutions) ought to be structured to promote human well-being. Unlike utilitarianism, they understand well-being as comprised of a plurality of goods that are both objectively valuable and not fully commensurable with one another. These include goods like health, practical reason, sociability, personhood, and autonomy. These theorists draw on prior work by economists and philosophers in the Aristotelian tradition, such as Amartya Sen and Martha Nussbaum.[59]

Libertarian and progressive approaches to property.   Property is not only an intensely interesting subject but also an intensely debated one. As much or more than another subject typically covered in the first year of law school, property law is likely to elicit disagreement between libertarians who hope to minimize government regulation of property and progressives who hope to promote more equal opportunities to acquire property. The text will incorporate explicit considerations of these alternative perspectives, as well as the contrast between approaches focused on the normative idea of economic efficiency and approaches focused on norms of liberty, fairness, justice, and democracy. Those who would like background reading may look to Richard Epstein's books and the articles of Eric Claeys[60] for excellent introductions to the libertarian

---

53. Alice Kessler-Harris, *A Woman's Wage* (1990).

54. Singer, *supra* note 17.

55. Mary Ann Glendon, *Rights Talk* (1991); Avishai Margalit, *The Decent Society* (1998); Jedediah Purdy, *For Common Things: Irony, Trust, and Commitment in America Today* (1999).

56. Robert C. Ellickson, *Order Without Law: How Neighbors Settle Disputes* (1991).

57. Jeanne Lorraine Schroeder, *The Vestal and the Fasces: Hegel, Lacan, Property, and the Feminine* (1998).

58. *See* Gregory S. Alexander & Eduardo Moisés Peñalver, *An Introduction to Property Theory*, ch. 5 (2012).

59. *See, e.g.*, Martha C. Nussbaum, *Women and Human Development* (2000); Amartya Sen, *Development as Freedom* (1999); Amartya Sen, *Commodities and Capabilities* (1985).

60. *Compare* Epstein, *supra* note 28; Richard Epstein, *Takings: Private Property and the Power of Eminent Domain* (1985). Although he is a natural rights theorist and eschews the libertarian label, Professor Eric Claeys has written extensively, and in a sophisticated manner, in a vein that seeks to limit government interference with the rights of owners. *See, e.g.*, Eric R. Claeys, *Virtue and Rights in American Property Law*, 94 Cornell L. Rev. 889 (2009); Eric R. Claeys, *Takings, Regulations, and Natural Property Rights*, 88 Cornell L. Rev. 1549, 1669-1671 (2003).

perspective and to the recent Symposium in the Cornell Law Review for an introduction to the progressive approach.[61]

B. HOW TO BRIEF A CASE AND PREPARE FOR CLASS

Sources of Law

Legal rules are promulgated by a wide variety of government bodies in a hier-
archical scheme. The major sources of law in that system include the following:

1. United States Constitution.   The federal Constitution is the fundamental
law of the land. It was adopted by state constitutional conventions, whose members were elected by (a small subset of) the people.[62] Constitutional amendments are generally passed by Congress and ratified by state legislatures. The
Constitution determines the structure of the federal government, including the
relations among the executive, legislative, and judicial branches of the federal
government, and the relations between the federal government and the state
governments. It also defines the powers of the federal government and limits the
powers of both the federal government and the states to protect individual
rights, including property rights and other rights such as freedom of speech,
freedom from unreasonable searches and seizures, equal protection of the laws,
and due process.

2. Federal statutes.   Legislation is passed by the Congress of the United
States and ratified by the president, or passed over the president's veto. Federal
statutes address a wide variety of matters relating to property law; examples
include the *Fair Housing Act of 1968,* the *Civil Rights Act of 1964,* the Internal Revenue Code, the *Sherman Antitrust Act,* and the *Worker Adjustment and Retraining
Notification Act of 1988.*

3. Administrative regulations.   Congress may pass legislation creating
administrative agencies, such as the Environmental Protection Agency, the
Equal Employment Opportunity Commission, the Federal Trade Commission,
or the Internal Revenue Service; these agencies may have the power to promulgate regulations in a particular field (environmental protection, employment
discrimination, or tax law).

4. State constitutions.   Each state has its own constitution defining the
structure of state government and defining certain fundamental individual
rights against the state. In some instances, state constitutions grant greater

---

61. Symposium: *Property and Obligation,* 94 Cornell L. Rev. 743 (2009), *including* Gregory S.
Alexander, Eduardo Moisés Peñalver, Joseph William Singer & Laura S. Underkuffler, *A Statement of
Progressive Property,* 94 Cornell L. Rev. 743 (2009); Gregory S. Alexander, *The Social-Obligation Norm in
American Property Law,* 94 Cornell L. Rev. 745 (2009); Eduardo Moisés Peñalver, *Land Virtues,* 94 Cor-
nell L. Rev. 821 (2009).

62. It is important to note that when the United States Constitution was adopted in 1789, the
voting population in the 13 states excluded women, African American men, American Indians, and
white men who owned less than a certain amount of property.

protection to individual rights than does the federal constitution. For example, a search by the police that is allowed under the fourth amendment to the U.S. Constitution may be prohibited under the New Jersey constitution. Although state constitutions may not grant citizens less protection than provided by the federal constitution, they may grant their citizens more protection by going further than the U.S. Constitution in limiting the power of state officials.

5. State statutes.   State statutes are passed by state legislatures with the consent of the governor (or by a supermajority vote over the governor's veto). Many state statutes deal with property law matters such as landlord-tenant legislation, recording acts, civil rights statutes, and regulation of family property on divorce.

6. State administrative regulations.   State legislatures, like the federal Congress, may create administrative agencies that have the power to promulgate regulations in limited fields of law. The Massachusetts legislature, for example, has created a Building Code Commission endowed with the power to promulgate and enforce regulations on building construction and materials to protect the public from unsafe structures.

7. Common law.   In the absence of any controlling statute or regulation, state courts adjudicate civil disputes by promulgating or applying rules of law. Judicial opinions explain and justify the rules adopted by judges to adjudicate civil disputes. During the first year of law school, most courses focus on common law rules and the process of common law decision making by judges, but property law is as much a statutory and regulatory topic as it is a product of common law decision making.

8. Local ordinances and bylaws.   State legislatures delegate to local governments such as counties, cities, and towns the power to promulgate ordinances or bylaws in limited areas of law, including zoning, rent control, schools, traffic, and parking.

Lawyers' Skills

In reading materials and in preparing for class, you should keep in mind three basic tasks that lawyers perform.

1. Counseling.   In advising clients, lawyers perform a variety of roles. First, they answer clients' questions about their legal rights. They do so by looking up the law in statutes, regulations, and judicial opinions. In so doing, they may or may not find legal rules that specifically address the question they need to answer. In either case, lawyers must predict how the courts would rule on the question if they had the opportunity to do so. This requires lawyers to make educated judgments about how prior case law will be applied to new fact situations. Second, lawyers counsel clients on how to conform their conduct to the dictates of the law and how to achieve their goals in a lawful manner. Third, lawyers draft legal documents for clients, including leases, deeds, purchase and sale agreements, bond documents, and employment contracts. Fourth, lawyers negotiate with other parties or their attorneys to settle disputes or to make deals.

2. Advocacy.   If a dispute cannot be resolved amicably, one of the parties— called the "plaintiff"—may bring a lawsuit against the other party—called the "defendant"—claiming that the defendant engaged in wrongful conduct that violated the plaintiff's legal rights. To prevail in such a lawsuit, the plaintiff must be able to (a) prove in court by testimony, documentation, or other admissible evidence that the defendant engaged in the wrongful conduct and that the conduct caused the plaintiff's harm, and (b) demonstrate that the defendant's conduct violates a legally protected interest guaranteed to the plaintiff in a way that violates the plaintiff's legal rights. The parties will normally hire attorneys to conduct the lawsuit. Lawyers argue before judges about what the legal rules are governing the dispute. Sometimes the rules in force are clear. Often, however, the rule governing a particular situation is not clear. The rules contain numerous gaps, conflicts and ambiguities, and lawyers are experts in using the open texture of the law to develop plausible competing arguments about alternative possible rules of law to govern the situation. The attorneys for each side engage in advocacy of alternative possible rules of law, both in written arguments called "briefs" and in oral arguments before judges. In these settings, lawyers attempt to persuade judges to interpret existing rules or to create new legal rules in ways that favor their clients' interests. Lawyers must therefore learn the kinds of arguments judges find persuasive in interpreting and in modernizing the rules in force. Lawyers may also represent clients before legislative committees considering the passage of legislation.

3. Decision making.   Finally, it is important to remember that the judges who decide cases are also lawyers. Their role is to adjudicate the cases before them by choosing the applicable legal rules to govern the dispute and others like it in the future. Similarly, legislatures promulgate statutes regulating conduct and resolving conflicts among competing interests. It is also important for you as a participant in the legal system to develop your own views about the wisdom and justice of our legal institutions and rules. Legal education teaches us to consider both sides of important contested questions of law before reaching a judgment about the proper outcome of the dispute. This does not mean we should be indifferent to what those outcomes are or that we should not criticize the rules in force. Your ability to argue for and against a position does not mean that you cannot make up your mind or present persuasive arguments to justify the result you reach; it means simply that your judgment about right and wrong should be true to the complexity of your own moral beliefs and that it is important to recognize what is lost, as well as what is gained, by any choice.

Reading Cases

Rules of law.   In researching the law, attorneys might (1) find a rule of law that clearly defines the parties' respective rights; (2) find no rule of law directly on point (a gap in the law); (3) find a rule of law that does not clearly answer the question (an ambiguity in an existing rule); or (4) find two or more rules of law that arguably govern the dispute (a conflict among possibly applicable rules). Moreover, attorneys might find rules of law applying to situations that are arguably analogous to the case at hand. Lawyers find and exploit the gaps, conflicts, and ambiguities in the law to attempt to define the law in ways that benefit their clients.

In preparing for class, you should try to identify the rule of law—the general principle—each side in the case would like the court to promulgate. Ask yourself: What rule of law did the plaintiff urge the court to adopt? What rule of law did the defendant urge the court to adopt?

This is harder than it seems. Sometimes the parties' proposed rules of law are described in the judicial opinion, sometimes not. In either event, you must ask whether it would be wise to argue for a broad rule of law or a narrow one. For example, one might argue for a broad, rather vague, rule of law: "Non-owners are privileged to enter property when their activity will further a significant public policy." Or one might argue for a narrow rule of law, tied very closely to the facts of the case: "Lawyers and physicians working for agencies funded by the federal government may enter property to give professional assistance to migrant farmworkers." Similarly, an owner might argue for a broad rule of law granting owners the right to exclude non-owners under all circumstances, or she might argue for a narrower rule granting owners the right to exclude non-owners only if the owner can show just cause. It is up to you to identify the different ways each side might have framed its proposed rules of law.

Arguments

After identifying possible rules of law for each side, you should ask what arguments the parties might have given to justify adopting their proposed rules, as well as what arguments they could have given against the rule proposed by the other side. These arguments should include considerations about the fairness of the proposed rules to the parties: Which rule better protects individual rights? You should also consider the social consequences of the competing rules: Which rule better promotes the general welfare?

Briefing Cases

In preparing for class, at least at the beginning, you should brief your cases. This means writing an outline of the important elements of the decision. These elements include the following.

1. Facts.   Who did what to whom? What is the relationship between the parties? What is the wrongful conduct the plaintiff claims the defendant engaged in, and how did it harm the plaintiff? What is the dispute between the parties about?

2. Procedural history.   How did the courts below rule on the case? First, how did the trial court resolve the matter? Who won, and why? Did the party who lost in the trial court appeal an adverse ruling of law to an intermediate appellate court? If so, how did the appellate court rule, and why? Did one of the parties appeal the result in the appellate court to the state supreme court? What court issued the opinion you are reading—the state supreme court or some lower court? (Note that because cases in this and other casebooks have been edited, some portion of the procedural history may be omitted from the text reprinted in the book.)

3. Relief sought and judgment.   What relief did the plaintiff seek? Did she ask for (a) a declaration of her rights (a declaratory judgment); (b) an injunction ordering the defendant to act or not to act in certain ways; or (c) damages to compensate the plaintiff for the harm? What was the judgment of the court issuing the opinion you are reading? Did it grant a declaratory judgment, issue an injunction, or order the payment of damages? Did it remand the case to a lower court for further proceedings, such as a new trial?

4. Legal question, or rule choice.   What is the legal question or questions the court resolved? To answer this, you should determine what rule of law the plaintiff favored and what rule of law the defendant favored. What different legal rules did the court consider? What rules should it have considered? What rule of law would you propose if you were the plaintiff's attorney? The defendant's attorney?

5. Arguments and counterarguments.   Place yourself in the position of the plaintiff's lawyer. What arguments would you give to persuade the court to adopt the rule of law favored by your client, and what arguments can you give against the rule of law favored by the defendant? Next, place yourself in the position of the defendant's lawyer. What arguments would you give to persuade the court to adopt the rule of law favored by your client, and what arguments can you give against the rule of law favored by the plaintiff?

a. Precedential arguments.   These arguments appeal to existing rules of law. You may argue that an ambiguous rule of law—such as a rule creating a reasonableness standard of conduct—entitles your client to win. You may also argue that one of two conflicting rules of law governs the fact situation in your case or that a rule of law applies by analogy. To do either of these things, you must argue that a prior case establishes a principle of law that governs a situation that is identical—or sufficiently similar—to the case at hand such that the policies or principles that underlie and justify the earlier decision are applicable to the current case. Under these circumstances, you can argue that the prior case establishes a precedent that applies to your case. The lawyer on the other side will argue that the case at hand is different in important ways from the prior case and that because of those differences, the policies and principles underlying the earlier case do not apply to the case at hand. When the rule of law in the prior case does not apply to the case at hand, we say the lawyer has distinguished the precedent. What rules have you learned that can be applied either directly or by analogy to govern this case?

b. Statutory interpretation.   The rights of the parties may be governed by a federal or state statute that regulates their conduct. Judges must interpret ambiguities in those statutes by reference to (1) the language of the statute; and (2) the legislative intent behind the statute, which may be elucidated by reference to the policies and purposes the legislation was intended to serve. How can you persuade the judge that your proposed interpretation of the statutory language or purposes best accords with the intent of the legislature? What counterarguments will the attorney on the other side make to answer your claims?

c. Policy arguments.   These arguments appeal to a variety of considerations, including (1) fairness, individual and group rights, and justice in social relationships; and (2) the social consequences of alternative rules such that the choice of rules promotes social utility, efficiency, or the general welfare. What reasons can you give to persuade the judge that your proposed rule promotes both justice and social welfare? What counterarguments will the attorney on the other side make to answer your claims?

6. Holding.   What rule of law did the court adopt, and how did it apply to the case? In identifying the holding of the case, it is important to consider several possibilities. Try to describe the rule of law in as broad a fashion as possible by (a) identifying a general category or a broad range of situations to which the rule would apply, and/or (b) appealing to general principles such as foreseeability, reasonableness, or promotion of alienability. Then try to describe the rule of law in as narrow a fashion as possible so as to limit the application of the rule to a narrow range of circumstances by (a) identifying the specific facts of the case as necessary to application of the rule, and/or (b) appealing to specific, rather than general, principles. For example, a possible broad holding of a case is that owners have an absolute right to exclude non-owners from their property unless the owner's act of exclusion violates public policy. An alternative narrow holding would be that owners of property open to the general public for business purposes have a right to exclude non-owners from their property unless those non-owners are engaging in expressive political activity that does not interfere with the operation of the business.

7. Reasoning of the court and criticism of that reasoning.   What reasons did the court give for deciding the case the way it did? What problems can you find with the court's reasoning? Do you agree or disagree?

Reading Statutes and Regulations

Statutory interpretation can be the subject of entire law school courses, but it is important to become comfortable from the outset with statutory and regulatory language. This is because a great deal of legal practice involves statutory or regulatory questions that have not necessarily been ruled on by the courts.

There are examples of statutes and regulations throughout this book. The task in reading these legal texts is different than briefing cases for class discussion. The goal is to come to class with a broad-brush understanding of how the relevant statute or regulation works. As you prepare, pay attention to the details of the language and the structure of the text, note the kinds of issues the statute or regulation covers (and does not), what explicit exceptions or exemptions are set out, how the various parts of the text relate to each other, and ambiguities the language creates. It can be hard to master statutory or regulatory language in the absence of a specific conflict or question, but the basic exercise of careful reading will soon come naturally.

CHAPTER

2

Acquisition of Property

A. AN INTRODUCTION TO THE LAW OF OWNERSHIP

We begin our study of property law with an introduction to the law of ownership. What does it mean to own something? The U.S. legal tradition recognizes four classic "incidents" of ownership—possession, use, alienation, and exclusion. By "incidents" we mean rights that a property owner has in an object. In this context, "alienation" means the transfer (by sale or gift) of property. If I own a home I typically have the right to possess the home, use the home, alienate the home, and exclude others from the home.

Our first chapter focuses on the concept of possession. The chapter ends with a discussion of exclusion, and we will discuss alienation and use at points throughout the book. Possession is especially important in the law of personal property, which raises a preliminary issue: What is "personal property"?

- *Real property* is ownership of land and things, like buildings, that are physically attached to the land.
- *Personal property* is ownership of everything else.

The distinction between real property and personal property can be a bit blurry in some circumstances. If you are wondering whether your dishwasher is real property or personal property, wait until we get to the law of fixtures later in the course (hint—as the definition of real property suggests, the answer to this question will turn on whether the dishwasher is physically attached to your house). The definition of personal property is very broad and includes some intangible interests—like intellectual property and contract rights. We will discuss intangible property in a few discrete places, but our focus in this book largely is on the ownership of tangible objects.

Note that real property is defined as the *ownership* of land and things attached to the land and that personal property is defined as the *ownership* of everything else. In our everyday language, we might refer to our car or our house as our "property." We often do the same thing as lawyers, and we will do so sometimes in this book. At times, however, we will need to be more precise. We will often need to keep in mind that our focus is on the legal ownership rights in objects, not the objects themselves.

1. *Possession Part I—The Law of Personal Property*

"Possession is very strong; rather more than nine points of the law."
                    —Lord Mansfield, *Corporation of Kingston-upon-Hull v. Horner,*
                                                    98 Eng. Rep. 807, 815 (1774)

Possession is one of the incidents of ownership, and as Lord Mansfield suggested, it can be very important for legal issues involving property. As we will
soon see, however, possession can be a very slippery topic. We will have to
explore the answers to two separate questions: (1) what, exactly, does "possession" mean?, and (2) what is the legal significance of having possession of an
object?

Possession plays a central role in many legal rules relating to the ownership of
personal property. The law of personal property therefore is a good place to start
in our exploration of the concept of possession. For now, we will focus on the
ownership of objects that are not real property—cars, computers, wedding rings,
paintings, footballs, etc. For many objects like this, there are circumstances
where possession is very clear. If I'm holding a football tightly in my hands, for
example, we can say that I have possession of the football. As you have probably
seen in watching a football game, though, there are far more ambiguous possession scenarios. If a receiver might have been juggling the ball while going out of
bounds, the referee is likely to spend some time looking at instant replay trying
to figure out whether the receiver had possession of the ball.

a. The Rule of Capture

Our first case involves a question of possession of a different object—a fox.
This classic case is at the beginning of most Property textbooks. On one level,
the case has to do with the law of ownership of wild animals. On another, more
important, level, the case has to do with possession. As you read the opinions in
the case, keep our two primary questions in mind. What concept of possession
does each judge use (even if they sometimes use words other than "possession")?
And what legal significance does each judge place on a person being in possession of an object?

> Items of personal property are sometimes referred to as *chattels.* The word
> *chattel* derives from the Anglo-French word for cattle. This is not surprising,
> because cattle were very important items of personal property in the
> Middle Ages.

There is a lot going on in this case. The language is a bit antiquated, but work
your way through it to identify the reasons that the judges give to support their
opinions. What facts did they think were relevant? What did the different legal
authorities that they cited have to say? What policies did they think were important in this context? To give you a sense of the level of detail that is necessary to
have a good understanding of the case, here are two questions to answer as you
work through the case: (a) What would the majority have to say about ownership

of a wild animal that was caught in a trap? (b) What does the dissent have to say about the distinction between pursuit with large hounds compared to pursuit with beagles?

PIERSON V. POST

Supreme Court of New York, 1805 3. Cai. R. 175, 2 Am. Dec. 264

This was an action of trespass on the case commenced in a justice's court, by the present defendant against the now plaintiff.

The declaration stated that Post, being in possession of certain dogs and hounds under his command, did, "upon a certain wild and uninhabited, unpossessed and waste land, called the beach, find and start one of those noxious beasts called a fox," and whilst there hunting, chasing and pursuing the same with his dogs and hounds, and when in view thereof, Pierson, well knowing the fox was so hunted and pursued, did, in the sight of Post, to prevent his catching the same, kill and carry it off. A verdict having been rendered for the plaintiff below, the defendant there sued out a *certiorari*, and now assigned for error, that the declaration and the matters therein contained were not sufficient in law to maintain an action.

TOMPKINS, J. delivered the opinion of the court. This cause comes before us on a return to a *certiorari* directed to one of the justices of Queens county.

The question submitted by the counsel in this cause for our determination is, whether *Lodowick Post*, by the pursuit with his hounds in the manner alleged in his declaration, acquired such a right to, or property in, the fox, as will sustain an action against *Pierson* for killing and taking him away?

The cause was argued with much ability by the counsel on both sides, and presents for our decision a novel and nice question. It is admitted that a fox is an animal *fer natur*, and that property in such animals is acquired by occupancy only. These admissions narrow the discussion to the simple question of what acts amount to occupancy, applied to acquiring right to wild animals?

If we have recourse to the ancient writers upon general principles of law, the judgment below is obviously erroneous. *Justinian's Institutes,* lib. 2. tit. 1. s. 13. and *Fleta,* lib. 3. c. 2. p. 175. adopt the principle, that pursuit alone vests no property or right in the huntsman; and that even pursuit, accompanied with wounding, is equally ineffectual for that purpose, unless the animal be actually taken. The same principle is recognised by *Bracton,* lib. 2. c. 1. p. 8.

PERSONAL PROPERTY CAUSES OF ACTION

You will see a variety of causes of action (i.e., legal claims brought by the plaintiff) in our personal property cases. Here is an overview of the most common personal property causes of action:

Conversion/Trover: An action for damages for the wrongful possession or destruction of personal property. If I take your watch and refuse to give it back, you can bring an action for conversion against me. Similarly, if I destroy your watch, you can sue me for conversion. The remedy for conversion is money damages. *Conversion* is the contemporary name for this

REMEDIES

claim; *trover* is a more antiquated name that you are more likely to see in older cases.

Replevin: An action for the return of property wrongfully possessed by the defendant. If I take your watch and refuse to give it back, you can sue me for replevin to force me to give it back. The remedy for replevin is a court order forcing the return of the property.

Trespass to Chattels: An action for damage to personal property. If I borrow your watch and damage it, you can sue me for trespass to chattels. The typical remedy for trespass to chattels is money damages.

Puffendorf, lib. 4. c. 6. s. 2. and 10. defines occupancy of beasts *fer natur,* to be the actual corporal possession of them, and *Bynkershoek* is cited as coinciding in this definition. It is indeed with hesitation that *Puffendorf* affirms that a wild beast mortally wounded, or greatly maimed, cannot be fairly intercepted by another, whilst the pursuit of the person inflicting the wound continues. The foregoing authorities are decisive to show that mere pursuit gave *Post* no legal right to the fox, but that he became the property of *Pierson,* who intercepted and killed him.

It therefore only remains to inquire whether there are any contrary principles, or authorities, to be found in other books, which ought to induce a different decision. Most of the cases which have occurred in *England,* relating to property in wild animals, have either been discussed and decided upon the principles of their positive statute regulations, or have arisen between the huntsman and the owner of the land upon which beasts *fer natur* have been apprehended; the former claiming them by title of occupancy, and the latter *ratione soli.* Little satisfactory aid can, therefore, be derived from the *English* reporters.

Barbeyrac, in his notes on *Puffendorf,* does not accede to the definition of occupancy by the latter, but, on the contrary, affirms, that actual bodily seizure is not, in all cases, necessary to constitute possession of wild animals. He does not, however, *describe* the acts which, according to his ideas, will amount to an appropriation of such animals to private use, so as to exclude the claims of all other persons, by title of occupancy, to the same animals; and he is far from averring that pursuit alone is sufficient for that purpose. To a certain extent, and as far as *Barbeyrac* appears to me to go, his objections to *Puffendorf's* definition of occupancy are reasonable and correct. That is to say, that actual bodily seizure is not indispensable to acquire right to, or possession of, wild beasts; but that, on the contrary, the mortal wounding of such beasts, by one not abandoning his pursuit, may, with the utmost propriety, be deemed possession of him; since, thereby, the pursuer manifests an unequivocal intention of appropriating the animal to his individual use, has deprived him of his natural liberty, and brought him within his certain control. So also, encompassing and securing such animals with nets and toils, or otherwise intercepting them in such a manner as to deprive them of their natural liberty, and render escape impossible, may justly be deemed to give possession of them to those persons who, by their industry and labour, have used such means of apprehending them. *Barbeyrac* seems to have adopted, and had in view in his notes, the more accurate opinion of *Grotius,* with respect to occupancy. . . . The case now under consideration is one of mere pursuit, and presents no circumstances or acts which can bring it within the definition of occupancy by *Puffendorf,* or *Grotius,* or the ideas of *Barbeyrac* upon that subject. . . .

We are the more readily inclined to confine possession or occupancy of beasts *fer natur*, within the limits prescribed by the learned authors above cited, for the sake of certainty, and preserving peace and order in society. If the first seeing, starting, or pursuing such animals, without having so wounded, circumvented or ensnared them, so as to deprive them of their natural liberty, and subject them to the control of their pursuer, should afford the basis of actions against others for intercepting and killing them, it would prove a fertile source of quarrels and litigation.

However uncourteous or unkind the conduct of *Pierson* towards *Post,* in this instance, may have been, yet his act was productive of no injury or damage for which a legal remedy can be applied. We are of opinion the judgment below was erroneous, and ought to be reversed.

LIVINGSTON, J. My opinion differs from that of the court. Of six exceptions, taken to the proceedings below, all are abandoned except the third, which reduces the controversy to a single question.

Whether a person who, with his own hounds, starts and hunts a fox on waste and uninhabited ground, and is on the point of seizing his prey, acquires such an interest in the animal, as to have a right of action against another, who in view of the huntsman and his dogs in full pursuit, and with knowledge of the chase, shall kill and carry him away?

This is a knotty point, and should have been submitted to the arbitration of sportsmen, without poring over *Justinian, Fleta, Bracton, Puffendorf, Locke, Barbeyrac,* or *Blackstone,* all of whom have been cited; they would have had no difficulty in coming to a prompt and correct conclusion. In a court thus constituted, the skin and carcass of poor *reynard* would have been properly disposed of, and a precedent set, interfering with no usage or custom which the experience of ages has sanctioned, and which must be so well known to every votary of *Diana.* But the parties have referred the question to our judgment, and we must dispose of it as well as we can, from the partial lights we possess, leaving to a higher tribunal, the correction of any mistake which we may be so unfortunate as to make. By the pleadings it is admitted that a fox is a "wild and noxious beast." Both parties have regarded him, as the law of nations does a pirate, "*hostem humani generis,*" [an enemy of humanity] and although "*de mortuis nil nisi bonum,*" [do not speak ill of the dead] be a maxim of our profession, the memory of the deceased has not been spared. His depredations on farmers and on barn yards, have not been forgotten; and to put him to death wherever found, is allowed to be meritorious, and of public benefit. Hence it follows, that our decision should have in view the greatest possible encouragement to the destruction of an animal, so cunning and ruthless in his career. But who would keep a pack of hounds; or what gentleman, at the sound of the horn, and at peep of day, would mount his steed, and for hours together, "*sub jove frigido,*" [under the cold sky] or a vertical sun, pursue the windings of this wily quadruped, if, just as night came on, and his stratagems and strength were nearly exhausted, a saucy intruder, who had not shared in the honours or labours of the chase, were permitted to come in at the death, and bear away in triumph the object of pursuit? Whatever *Justinian* may have thought of the matter, it must be recollected that his code was compiled many hundred years ago, and it would be very hard indeed, at the distance of so many centuries, not to have a right to establish a rule for ourselves. In his day, we read of no order of men who made it a business, in the language of the declaration in this cause, "with hounds and dogs to find, start, pursue, hunt, and chase," these animals, and that, too, without any other motive than the preservation of *Roman* poultry; if this diversion had been then in fashion, the lawyers who composed his institutes, would have taken care not to pass it by, without suitable encouragement. If any thing, therefore, in the digests or pandects shall appear to militate against the defendant in error, who, on this occasion, was the foxhunter, we have only to say *tempora mutantur* [times have changed]; and if men themselves change with the times, why should not laws also undergo an alteration?

It may be expected, however, by the learned counsel, that more particular notice be taken of their authorities. I have examined them all, and feel great difficulty in determining, whether to acquire dominion over a thing, before in common, it be sufficient that we barely see it, or know where it is, or wish for it, or make a declaration of our will respecting it; or whether, in the case of wild beasts, setting a trap, or lying in wait, or starting, or pursuing, be enough; or if an actual wounding, or killing, or bodily tact and occupation be necessary. Writers on general law, who have favoured us with their speculations on these points, differ on them all; but, great as is the diversity of sentiment among them, some conclusion must be adopted on the question immediately before us. After mature deliberation, I embrace that of *Barbeyrac*, as the most rational, and least liable to objection. If at liberty, we might imitate the courtesy of a certain emperor, who, to avoid giving offence to the advocates of any of these different doctrines, adopted a middle course, and by ingenious distinctions, rendered it difficult to say (as often happens after a fierce and angry contest) to whom the palm of victory belonged. He ordained, that if a beast be followed with *large dogs and hounds,* he shall belong to the hunter, not to the chance occupant; and in like manner, if he be killed or wounded with a lance or sword; but if chased with *beagles only,* then he passed to the captor, not to the first pursuer. If slain with a dart, a sling, or a bow, he fell to the hunter, if still in chase, and not to him who might afterwards find and seize him.

Now, as we are without any municipal regulations of our own, and the pursuit here, for aught that appears on the case, being with dogs and hounds of *imperial stature,* we are at liberty to adopt one of the provisions just cited, which comports also with the learned conclusion of *Barbeyrac,* that property in animals *fer natur* may be acquired without bodily touch or manucaption, provided the pursuer be within reach, or have a *reasonable* prospect (which certainly existed here) of taking, what he has *thus* discovered an intention of converting to his own use.

When we reflect also that the interest of our husbandmen, the most useful of men in any community, will be advanced by the destruction of a beast so pernicious and incorrigible, we cannot greatly err, in saying, that a pursuit like the present, through waste and unoccupied lands, and which must inevitably and speedily have terminated in corporal possession, or bodily *seisin,* confers such a right to the object of it, as to make any one a wrongdoer, who shall interfere and shoulder the spoil. The *justice's* judgment ought, therefore, in my opinion, to be affirmed.

Judgment of reversal.

THE TRAGEDY OF THE COMMONS

In this chapter, we will examine a number of theoretical justifications for the protection of private property. The capture of wild animals provides us with a good context to examine one theoretical justification: private property prevents the overconsumption of resources.

The rule of capture gives ownership of a previously unowned resource to the first person to gain possession of that resource. It is easy to see that this rule might lead to the overconsumption of a resource. For example, ocean fisheries tend to operate on a rule of capture basis. Today, large factory fishing vessels have become so efficient at capturing fish that many fishing stocks have collapsed. The overconsumption of ocean fish is an example of the *tragedy of the commons*, which takes its name from a famous article: Garrett Hardin, *The Tragedy of the Commons*, 162 Science 1243 (1968). "Commons" refers to resources that are unowned or subject to communal, as opposed to private, ownership. In a tragedy of the commons scenario, people acting in their rational self-interest will overconsume a resource that is unowned. If I am fishing in the ocean, I have an incentive to capture all the fish I can, even if I know that the rate of capture is unsustainable. I might want to leave some fish behind to protect the fish population, but if I refrain from capturing the fish, then you or someone else might come along and capture them. Because there is nothing preventing other people from capturing as many fish as possible, I have an incentive to capture as many as I can now.

A key problem with protecting ocean fisheries is that no one owns the sea or the fish. In other words, an absence of property rights is arguably the cause of the problem. For example, imagine that I own a large pond that contains fish. Because I own the pond, I can prevent you and anyone else from fishing there. I therefore don't have to worry about anyone else capturing the fish I leave behind. In these circumstances, it is in my interest to consume the fish on a sustainable basis. If I refrain from capturing some fish now, I will benefit later. Note the contrast with the ocean fisheries example, where if I refrain from capturing now, I likely will not benefit later because you or someone else will come along and capture the fish I leave behind. These examples illustrate that private property can help prevent the overconsumption of resources and solve the problem of the tragedy of the commons.

We do not mean to suggest here that private ownership is a solution to all overconsumption problems, or that common ownership structures inevitably collapse into tragedy of the commons scenarios. Rather, we are simply noting that solving tragedy of the commons problems is frequently used as a theoretical justification of private ownership of natural resources. There is a tremendous amount of scholarship on this issue, much of it centered on the work of Nobel Memorial Prize in Economic Sciences winner Elinor Ostrom. In some of her most important work, Ostrom argued that in certain circumstances common ownership of a resource will not lead to tragedy. *See, e.g.,* Elinor Ostrom, *Governing the Commons: The Evolution of Institutions for Collective Action* (1990).

NOTES AND QUESTIONS

1. *The Cited Authorities.* Because of a lack of case law on point, both the majority and dissenting opinions reference a series of treatises for authority. *Justinian's Institutes* was a famous Roman law treatise. Barbeyrac, Bynkershoek, Grotius, and Pufendorf were European civil law scholars. *Fleta* was an early treatise on English law. John Locke was an important English political philosopher; his work on Property is discussed later in this chapter. William Blackstone was the author of the tremendously influential *Commentaries on the Laws of England* (1765-1769).

2. *Possession of a Football.* We mentioned possession of a football in the text preceding *Pierson v. Post.* National Football League Rule 3, Section 2, Article 7 states that "A player is in possession when he is in firm grip and control of the ball inbounds." How does this definition compare to the court's definition of possession in *Pierson?*

3. *The Rule of Capture and First Possession.* The rule of capture states that a person gains ownership of a previously unowned wild animal by capturing or gaining possession of it. More broadly, the rule of capture applies (at least arguably) to other fugitive resources—that is, resources that move around on their own. The rule of capture gives us our first exposure to *first possession,* the idea that a person gains ownership of an unowned thing by gaining possession over that thing. Because very few objects in the modern world are unowned, first possession has more theoretical importance than practical importance in modern property law. A related concept, however, is of great practical importance, and runs throughout the course. This concept is *first in time, first in right*—the idea that if I had rights to an object before you, my rights are superior to yours. We will explore this theme in some depth as we progress through the course.

4. Ratione Soli, *Constructive Possession, and Landowner Rights.* The English common-law rule of *ratione soli* gave a landowner *constructive* possession of wild animals while they were located on the landowner's property. The landowner did not have *actual* possession, because wild animals move from place to place. If a deer is on my property right now, it might wander off onto neighboring property later today. By giving me constructive possession, *ratione soli* effectively gives me the exclusive right to capture wild animals on my land. The court in *Pierson* had to rely on treatise writers because most of the prior cases were disputes between landowners and hunters that turned on *ratione soli. Pierson* is unusual and interesting because the fox was captured on property that was treated as common (i.e., not privately owned) by members of the community.

We will see the word "constructive" many times in this course, and you will see it in many other legal contexts. "Constructive" is an all-purpose legal word that means "it isn't so, but we will pretend that it is." In the *ratione soli* context, we know that the landowner does not have actual possession, but we will pretend that the landowner does have possession.

Ratione soli was not widely adopted by U.S. courts. The default rule in most states is that the hunter gets ownership of a wild animal even if it is captured on private land. The landowner can avoid this result by posting the property "no hunting" or "no trespassing." Because this posting would make the capture of a wild animal on the property wrongful, the hunter gains no rights to the animal.

5. *Further Reading.* If beginning the course with *Pierson v. Post* wasn't enough to convince you that Property professors love the case, consider this recent scholarship: Angela Fernandez, *The Lost Record of* Pierson v. Post, *The Famous Fox Case,* 27

Law & Hist. Rev. 149 (2009); Angela Fernandez, Pierson v. Post: *A Great Debate, James Kent, and the Project of Building a Learned Law for New York State,* 34 Law & Soc. Inquiry 301 (2009); Andrea McDowell, *Legal Fictions in* Pierson v. Post, 105 Mich. L. Rev. 735 (2007); Bethany Berger, *It's Not About the Fox: The Untold Story of* Pierson v. Post, 55 Duke L.J. 1089 (2006).

GHEN V. RICH

United States District Court, Massachusetts 8 Fed. 159 (D. Mass. 1881)

Nelson, D.J. This is a libel to recover the value of a fin-back whale. The libellant lives in Provincetown and the respondent in Wellfleet. The facts, as they appeared at the hearing, are as follows:

In the early spring months the easterly part of Massachusetts bay is frequented by the species of whale known as the fin-back whale. Fishermen from Province-town pursue them in open boats from the shore, and shoot them with bomb-lances fired from guns made expressly for the purpose. When killed they sink at once to the bottom, but in the course of from one to three days they rise and float on the surface. Some of them are picked up by vessels and towed into Prov-incetown. Some float ashore at high water and are left stranded on the beach as the tide recedes. Others float out to sea and are never recovered. The person who happens to find them on the beach usually sends word to Provincetown, and the owner comes to the spot and removes the blubber. The finder usually receives a small salvage for his services. Try-works are established in Province-town for trying out the oil. The business is of considerable extent, but, since it requires skill and experience, as well as some outlay of capital, and is attended with great exposure and hardship, few persons engage in it. The average yield of oil is about 20 barrels to a whale. It swims with great swiftness, and for that reason cannot be taken by the harpoon and line. Each boat's crew engaged in the busi-ness has its peculiar mark or device on its lances, and in this way it is known by whom a whale is killed.

The usage on Cape Cod, for many years, has been that the person who kills a whale in the manner and under the circumstances described, owns it, and this right has never been disputed until this case. The libellant has been engaged in this business for ten years past. On the morning of April 9, 1880, in Massachu-setts bay, near the end of Cape Cod, he shot and instantly killed with a bomb-lance the whale in question. It sunk immediately, and on the morning of the 12th was found stranded on the beach in Brewster, within the ebb and flow of the tide, by one Ellis, 17 Miles from the spot where it was killed. Instead of send-ing word to Provincetown, as is customary, Ellis advertised the whale for sale at auction, and sold it to the respondent, who shipped off the blubber and tried out the oil. The libellant heard of the finding of the whale on the morning of the 15th, and immediately sent one of his boat's crew to the place and claimed it. Neither the respondent nor Ellis knew the whale had been killed by the libellant, but they knew or might have known, if they had wished, that it had been shot and killed with a bomb-lance, by some person engaged in this species of business.

The libellant claims title to the whale under this usage. The respondent insists that this usage is invalid. It was decided . . . in Taber v. Jenny, 1 Sprague, 315, that when a whale has been killed, and is anchored and left with marks of appropriation, it is the property of the captors; and if it is afterwards found, still anchored, by another ship, there is no usage or principle of law by which the property of the original captors is diverted, even though the whale may have dragged from its anchorage. The learned judge says:

> "When the whale had been killed and taken possession of by the boat of the Hillman, (the first taker,) it became the property of the owners of that ship, and all was done which was then practicable in order to secure it. They left it anchored, with unequivocal marks of appropriation."

In Bartlett v. Budd, 1 Low. 223, the facts were these: The first officer of the libellant's ship killed a whale in the Okhotsk sea, anchored it, attached a waif to the body, and then left it and went ashore at some distance for the night. The next morning the boats of the respondent's ship found the whale adrift, the anchor not holding, the cable coiled round the body, and no waif or irons attached to it. Judge Lowell held that, as the libellants had killed and taken actual possession of the whale, the ownership vested in them. In his opinion the learned judge says:

> "A whale, being ferae naturae, does not become property until a firm possession has been established by the taker. But when such possession has become firm and complete, the right of property is clear, and has all the characteristics of property."

He doubted whether a usage set up but not proved by the respondents, that a whale found adrift in the ocean is the property of the finder, unless the first taker should appear and claim it before it is cut in, would be valid, and remarked that "there would be great difficulty in upholding a custom that should take the property of A. and give it to B., under so very short and uncertain a substitute for the statute of limitations, and one so open to fraud and deceit." Both the cases cited were decided without reference to usage, upon the ground that the property had been acquired by the first taker by actual possession and appropriation.

In Swift v. Gifford, 2 Low, 110, Judge Lowell decided that a custom among whalemen in the Arctic seas, that the iron holds the whale was reasonable and valid. In that case a boat's crew from the respondent's ship pursued and struck a whale in the Arctic ocean, and the harpoon and the line attached to it remained in the whale, but did not remain fast to the boat. A boat's crew from the libellant's ship continued the pursuit and captured the whale, and the master of the respondent's ship claimed it on the spot. It was held by the learned judge that the whale belonged to the respondents. It was said by Judge Sprague, in Bourne v. Ashley, an unprinted case referred to by Judge Lowell in Swift v. Gifford, that the usage for the first iron, whether attached to the boat or not, to hold the whale was fully established; and he added that, although local usages of a particular port ought not to be allowed to set aside the general maritime law, this objection did not apply to a custom which embraced an entire business, and had been concurred in for a long time by every one engaged in the trade.

In Swift v. Gifford, Judge Lowell also said:

"The rule of law invoked in this case is one of very limited application. The whale fishery is the only branch of industry of any importance in which it is likely to be much used, and if a usage is found to prevail generally in that business, it will not be open to the objection that it is likely to disturb the general understanding of mankind by the interposition of an arbitrary exception."

I see no reason why the usage proved in this case is not as reasonable as that sustained in the cases cited. Its application must necessarily be extremely limited, and can affect but a few persons. It has been recognized and acquiesced in for many years. It requires in the first taker the only act of appropriation that is possible in the nature of the case. Unless it is sustained, this branch of industry must necessarily cease, for no person would engage in it if the fruits of his labor could be appropriated by any chance finder. It gives reasonable salvage for securing or reporting the property. That the rule works well in practice is shown by the extent of the industry which has grown up under it, and the general acquiescence of a whole community interested to dispute it. It is by no means clear that without regard to usage the common law would not reach the same result. That seems to be the effect of the decisions in Taber v. Jenny and Bartlett v. Budd. If the fisherman does all that is possible to do to make the animal his own, that would seem to be sufficient. Such a rule might well be applied in the interest of trade, there being no usage or custom to the contrary. Holmes, Com. Law, 217. But be that as it may, I hold the usage to be valid, and that the property in the whale was in the libellant.

The rule of damages is the market value of the oil obtained from the whale, less the cost of trying it out and preparing it for the market, with interest on the amount so ascertained from the date of conversion. As the question is new and important, and the suit is contested on both sides, more for the purpose of having it settled than for the amount involved, I shall give no costs.

Decree for libellant for $71.05, without costs.

NOTES AND QUESTIONS

1. Libellant is the name used for the plaintiff in cases in admiralty, which are largely within the exclusive jurisdiction of the federal courts.

2. Note the court's use of custom as the source of law. Was it more appropriate to use custom in this case than in *Pierson v. Post?*

MORE ABOUT WILD ANIMALS

As we have seen, a person can establish ownership of a wild animal by killing it and taking it into his or her possession. What happens if the animal is captured alive and later escapes? There is a surprising amount of litigation on this question involving animals from sea lions to parrots. Blackstone, quoted in *Mullett v. Bradley* (below), says: "These animals [*ferae naturae*] are no longer the property of a man than while they continue in his keeping or actual possession; but if at any time they regain their natural liberty, his property instantly ceases; unless they have *animus revertendi*,[7] which is only to be known by their usual custom of returning." Does this statement explain the following cases? If not, what other

---

7. This means a disposition to return.—Eds.

principles are at work? What factors should be taken into account in resolving these competing claims?

In *C.B. Wiley v. Baker*, 597 S.W.2d 3 (Tex. Civ. App. 1980), the owner of a game farm sued to recover the value of an elk that escaped, remained out of range of the farm owner's tranquilizing rifle, and was shot by the defendant a month later. The elk was not native to the area. The court held for the defendant. In *Mullett v. Bradley*, 53 N.Y.S. 781 (Sup. Ct. 1898), a sea lion captured by the plaintiff in the Pacific Ocean for a marine display escaped from a small island in the New York harbor. The defendant bought it from a fisherman who had found it a couple of weeks later about 70 miles from New York. Sea lions are not normally found in the Atlantic Ocean. The plaintiff learned that the defendant had the sea lion about a year later and sued for its value. The defendant won. In *E.A. Stephens & Co. v. Albers*, 256 P.2d 15 (Colo. 1927), a valuable nonnative silver fox escaped from the plaintiff's breeding ranch and was shot by a farmer who found it prowling around his chicken house. The farmer sold the pelt to the defendant, a fur-buying company. Although it was clear from the pelt that the fox had been shot (rather than poisoned or crushed as was usual with ranch-bred fox killed for their pelts), the pelt did have tattoos in the ears. The plaintiff won. In *Conti v. ASPCA*, 353 N.Y.S. 288 (Sup. Ct. 1974), Chester, a parrot used by the ASPCA (American Society for the Prevention of Cruelty to Animals) in educational exhibitions escaped. A few days later, the plaintiff befriended a parrot who had flown into his yard. When he called the ASPCA for advice on caring for the parrot, the ASPCA claimed it was theirs and took it back. The ASPCA won.

POPOV V. HAYASHI
2002 WL 31833731 (Cal. Super.)

McCarthy, J.

In 1927, Babe Ruth hit sixty home runs. That record stood for thirty four years until Roger Maris broke it in 1961 with sixty one home runs. Mark McGwire hit seventy in 1998. On October 7, 2001, at PacBell Park in San Francisco, Barry Bonds hit number seventy three. That accomplishment set a record which, in all probability, will remain un-broken for years into the future.

The event was widely anticipated and received a great deal of attention. The ball that found itself at the receiving end of Mr. Bond's bat garnered some of that attention. Baseball fans in general, and especially people at the game, understood the importance of the ball. It was worth a great deal of money[4] and whoever caught it would bask, for a brief period of time, in the reflected fame of Mr. Bonds.

With that in mind, many people who attended the game came prepared for the possibility that a record setting ball would be hit in their direction. Among this group were plaintiff Alex Popov and defendant Patrick Hayashi. They were unacquainted at the time. Both men brought baseball gloves, which they anticipated using if the ball came within their reach.

Barry Bonds came to bat in the first inning. With nobody on base and a full count, Bonds swung at a slow knuckleball. He connected. The ball sailed over

---

4. It has been suggested that the ball might sell for something in excess of $1,000,000.

the right-field fence and into the arcade. When the seventy-third home run ball went into the arcade, it landed in the upper portion of the webbing of a softball glove worn by Alex Popov. While the glove stopped the trajectory of the ball, it is not at all clear that the ball was secure. Popov had to reach for the ball and in doing so, may have lost his balance.

Even as the ball was going into his glove, a crowd of people began to engulf Mr. Popov. He was tackled and thrown to the ground while still in the process of attempting to complete the catch. Some people intentionally descended on him for the purpose of taking the ball away, while others were involuntarily forced to the ground by the momentum of the crowd.

Eventually, Mr. Popov was buried face down on the ground under several layers of people. At one point he had trouble breathing. Mr. Popov was grabbed, hit and kicked. People reached underneath him in the area of his glove. Neither the tape nor the testimony is sufficient to establish which individual members of the crowd were responsible for the assaults on Mr. Popov.

The videotape clearly establishes that this was an out of control mob, engaged in violent, illegal behavior. Although some witnesses testified in a manner inconsistent with this finding, their testimony is specifically rejected as being false on a material point. At some point the ball left his glove and ended up on the ground. It is impossible to establish the exact point in time that this occurred or what caused it to occur.

Mr. Hayashi was standing near Mr. Popov when the ball came into the stands. He, like Mr. Popov, was involuntarily forced to the ground. He committed no wrongful act. While on the ground he saw the loose ball. He picked it up, rose to his feet and put it in his pocket.

We will never know if Mr. Popov would have been able to retain control of the ball had the crowd not interfered with his efforts to do so. Resolution of that question is the work of a psychic, not a judge

The deciding question in this case . . . is whether Mr. Popov achieved possession or the right to possession as he attempted to catch and hold on to the ball.

The parties have agreed to a starting point for the legal analysis. Prior to the time the ball was hit, it was possessed and owned by Major League Baseball. At the time it was hit it became intentionally abandoned property. The first person who came in possession of the ball became its new owner.

The parties fundamentally disagree about the definition of possession. In order to assist the court in resolving this disagreement, four distinguished law professors participated in a forum to discuss the legal definition of possession. The professors also disagreed.

The disagreement is understandable. Although the term possession appears repeatedly throughout the law, its definition varies depending on the context in which it is used. Various courts have condemned the term as vague and meaningless.

While there is a degree of ambiguity built into the term possession, that ambiguity exists for a purpose. Courts are often called upon to resolve conflicting claims of possession in the context of commercial disputes. A stable economic environment requires rules of conduct which are understandable and consistent with the fundamental customs and practices of the industry they regulate. Without that, rules will be difficult to enforce and economic instability will result. Because each industry has different customs and practices, a single definition of possession cannot be applied to different industries without creating havoc.

[S]ome cases recognize possession even before absolute dominion and control is achieved. Those cases require the actor to be actively and ably engaged in efforts to establish complete control. Moreover, such efforts must be significant and they must be reasonably calculated to result in unequivocal dominion and control at some point in the near future.

This rule is applied in cases involving the hunting or fishing of wild animals or the salvage of sunken vessels.

These rules are contextual in nature. They are crafted in response to the unique nature of the conduct they seek to regulate. Moreover, they are influenced by the custom and practice of each industry. The reason that absolute dominion and control is not required to establish possession in the cases cited by Mr. Popov is that such a rule would be unworkable and unreasonable. The "nature and situation" of the property at issue does not immediately lend itself to unequivocal dominion and control. It is impossible to wrap ones arms around a whale, a fleeing fox or a sunken ship.

The opposite is true of a baseball hit into the stands of a stadium. Not only is it physically possible for a person to acquire unequivocal dominion and control of an abandoned baseball, but fans generally expect a claimant to have accomplished as much. The custom and practice of the stands creates a reasonable expectation that a person will achieve full control of a ball before claiming possession. There is no reason for the legal rule to be inconsistent with that expectation.

The central tenant of [the] Rule [advocated by Professor Brian Gray] is that the actor must retain control of the ball after incidental contact with people and things. Mr. Popov has not established by a preponderance of the evidence that he would have retained control of the ball after all momentum ceased and after any incidental contact with people or objects. Consequently, he did not achieve full possession.

That finding, however, does not resolve the case. The reason we do not know whether Mr. Popov would have retained control of the ball is not because of incidental contact. It is because he was attacked. His efforts to establish possession were interrupted by the collective assault of a band of wrongdoers.

As a matter of fundamental fairness, Mr. Popov should have had the opportunity to try to complete his catch unimpeded by unlawful activity. To hold otherwise would be to allow the result in this case to be dictated by violence. That will not happen.

A court sitting in equity has the authority to fashion rules and remedies designed to achieve fundamental fairness. Consistent with this principle, the court adopts the following rule. Where an actor undertakes significant but incomplete steps to achieve possession of a piece of abandoned personal property and the effort is interrupted by the unlawful acts of others, the actor has a legally cognizable pre-possessory interest in the property. That pre-possessory interest constitutes a qualified right to possession which can support a cause of action for conversion.

[T]his does not, however, address the interests of Mr. Hayashi. Mr. Hayashi was not a wrongdoer. He was a victim of the same bandits that attacked Mr. Popov. The difference is that he was able to extract himself from their assault and move to the side of the road. It was there that he discovered the loose ball. When he picked up and put it in his pocket he attained unequivocal dominion and control.

If Mr. Popov had achieved complete possession before Mr. Hayashi got the ball, those actions would not have divested Mr. Popov of any rights, nor would they have created any rights to which Mr. Hayashi could lay claim. Mr. Popov, however, was able to establish only a qualified pre-possessory interest in the ball. That interest does not establish a full right to possession that is protected from a subsequent legitimate claim.

An award of the ball to Mr. Popov would be unfair to Mr. Hayashi. It would be premised on the assumption that Mr. Popov would have caught the ball. That assumption is not supported by the facts. An award of the ball to Mr. Hayashi would unfairly penalize Mr. Popov. It would be based on the assumption that Mr. Popov would have dropped the ball. That conclusion is also unsupported by the facts.

Both men have a superior claim to the ball as against all the world. Each man has a claim of equal dignity as to the other. We are, therefore, left with something of a dilemma. Thankfully, there is a middle ground.

The concept of equitable division was fully explored in a law review article authored by Professor R.H. Helmholz in the December 1983 edition of the Fordham Law Review. As Helmholz points out, it is useful in that it "provides an equitable way to resolve competing claims which are equally strong." Moreover, "[i]t comports with what one instinctively feels to be fair."

Mr. Hayashi's claim is compromised by Mr. Popov's pre-possessory interest. Mr. Popov cannot demonstrate full control. Albeit for different reasons, they stand before the court in exactly the same legal position as did the five boys [in *Keron v. Cashman*, 33 A. 1055 (N.J. 1896), who found an old sock and played with the sock together until it broke open, spilling out $775. Here, as in *Keron*, Popov and Hayashi's] legal claims are of equal quality and they are equally entitled to the ball.

The court therefore declares that both plaintiff and defendant have an equal and undivided interest in the ball. Plaintiff's cause of action for conversion is sustained only as to his equal and undivided interest. In order to effectuate this ruling, the ball must be sold and the proceeds divided equally between the parties.

NOTES AND QUESTIONS

1. Aftermath.   The full story of the battle for Barry Bonds's home run ball is captured in the documentary *Up for Grabs*. The ball ultimately sold only for $450,000, far less than was expected. (The same collector had purchased Mark McGwire's record-breaking ball for $3.2 million in 1999.) Popov's lawyer later sued Popov for his attorneys' fees, which he claimed at an hourly rate amounted to $473,000. Hayashi, who was an engineering student at the time of the suit, had retained his attorney on a contingency basis and so did not have a legal bill that dwarfed his gains. David Kravets, *Lawyer Sues Client Who Caught Bond's Ball: Fan Owes $473,000*, National Journal (Canada), July 9, 2003.

2. Custom.   Ownership of the ball was only up for grabs because the original owner, Major League Baseball, had a policy of intentionally abandoning any balls hit into the stands. Major League Baseball only provides balls in games that are likely to have record-breaking hits, but home teams provide balls for other games and universally follow the same fan-friendly policy. This policy has been a matter of custom and practice for more than 60 years. Could a ball club reverse this policy? In 2001, Raphael Vasquez caught Mike Piazza's three-hundredth career home run and gave it to his six-year old daughter, Denise. Mets security guards surrounded the father and daughter and forced them to give up the ball, apparently because Piazza wanted it as a souvenir. Could Vasquez successfully sue the ball club?

What about balls that stay in the field? In 2004, backup Boston Red Sox first baseman Doug Mientkiewicz caught the ball that won the World Series for the team, breaking the "curse of the Bambino" of Red Sox lore. When he kept the ball, the Red Sox sued, claiming that Mientkiewicz's possession was only the result of his employment for the team. Who should win? Does it matter that the stadium was owned by the St. Louis Cardinals, which also supplied the ball? The suit was ultimately settled with the agreement that the ball would go to the National Baseball Hall of Fame. For more on ball ownership, *see* Paul Finkelman, *Fugitive Baseballs and Abandoned Property: Who Owns the Home Run Ball?*, 23 Cardozo L. Rev. 1609 (2002). For its surprisingly complicated tax consequences, *see* Andrew Appleby, *Ball Busters: How the IRS Should Tax Record-Setting Baseballs and Other Found Property Under the Treasure Trove Regulation*, 33 Vt. L. Rev. 43 (2008).

3. Constructive possession.   What would have happened had Popov been able to prove that he got the ball firmly in his glove and was walking away, but the "gang of bandits" subsequently made him lose it? He would win against Hayashi. This illustrates that the doctrine of acquisition by possession does not require continual possession, but rather clear marking of ownership without abandonment of the property. Major League Baseball having abandoned the ball, once Popov had reduced it to his possession it remained in his constructive possession, and he could claim it against all others.

4. Equitable division.   Scholars have advocated equitable division resolutions to different categories of cases. A 2007 article advocates their use in the case of what the authors call "windfalls," gains or losses that neither party could reasonably predict, so that the possibility of the windfall would not change the behavior of either party. In such cases, they assert, equitable division is efficient, because a normally risk-averse person would ex ante choose the equal division remedy as insurance against total loss; it is more just because it does not place the unforeseen loss entirely on any one party; and it furthers judicial integrity because it does not force courts into judicial contortions to justify choosing one party or the other. *See* Gideon Parchomovsky, Peter Siegelman & Steve Thel, *Of Equal Wrongs and Half Rights*, 82 N.Y.U. L. Rev. 738 (2007). Is this correct? If it is, why aren't split-the-difference remedies more common?

b. Capture of Natural Resources

The law of capture has also been applied to disputes over ownership of oil and gas as well as water. How is an oil pool beneath your and your neighbor's land like a wild animal? How is it different? What about the water in a stream that flows past your land and your neighbor's? How do these similarities and differences affect the legal tests that should govern ownership of these resources? The materials below consider the rule of capture and oil and gas; rights and duties regarding water are covered in Chapter 7 [Joseph William Singer, Bethany R. Berger, Nestor M. Davidson and Eduardo Moisés Peñalver, Property Law, 6th ed., (2014)], § 8.

ELLIFF V. TEXON DRILLING CO.
210 S.W.2d 558 (Tex. 1948)

A.J. FOLLEY, Justice.

This is a suit by the petitioners, Mrs. Mabel Elliff, Frank Elliff, and Charles C. Elliff, against the respondents, Texon Drilling Company, a Texas corporation, Texon Royalty Company, a Texas corporation, Texon Royalty Company, a Delaware corporation, and John L. Sullivan, for damages resulting from a "blowout" gas well drilled by respondents in the Agua Dulce Field in Nueces County.

The petitioners owned the surface and certain royalty interests in 3054.9 acres of land in Nueces County, upon which there was a producing well known as Elliff No. 1. They owned all the mineral estate underlying the west 1500 acres of the tract, and an undivided one-half interest in the mineral estate underlying the east 1554.9 acres. Both tracts were subject to oil and gas leases, and therefore their royalty interest in the west 1500 acres was one-eighth of the oil or gas, and in the east 1554.9 acres was one-sixteenth of the oil and gas.

It was alleged that these lands overlaid approximately fifty per cent of a huge reservoir of gas and distillate and that the remainder of the reservoir was under the lands owned by Mrs. Clara Driscoll, adjoining the lands of petitioners on the east. Prior to November 1936, respondents were engaged in the drilling of Driscoll-Sevier No. 2 as an offset well at a location 466 feet east of petitioners' east line. On the date stated, when respondents had reached a depth of approximately 6838 feet, the well blew out, caught fire and cratered. Attempts to control it were unsuccessful, and huge quantities of gas, distillate and some oil were blown into the air, dissipating large quantities from the reservoir into which the offset well was drilled. When the Driscoll-Sevier No. 2 well blew out, the fissure or opening in the ground around the well gradually increased until it enveloped and destroyed Elliff No. 1. The latter well also blew out, cratered, caught fire and burned for several years. Two water wells on petitioners' land became involved in the cratering and each of them blew out. Certain damages also resulted to the surface of petitioners' lands and to their cattle thereon. The cratering process and the eruption continued until large quantities of gas and distillate were drained from under petitioners' land and escaped into the air, all of which was alleged to be the direct and proximate result of the negligence of respondents in permitting their well to blow out. The extent of the emissions from the Driscoll-Sevier No. 2 and Elliff No. 1, and the two water wells on petitioners' lands, was shown at various times during the several years between the blowout in November 1936, and the time of the trial in June 1946. There was also expert testimony from petroleum engineers showing the extent of the losses from the underground reservoir, which computations extended from the date of the blowout only up to June 1938. It was indicated that it was not feasible to calculate the losses subsequent thereto, although lesser emissions of gas continued even up to the time of the trial. All the evidence with reference to the damages included all losses from the reservoir beneath petitioners' land without regard to whether they were wasted and dissipated from above the Driscoll land or from petitioners' land.

The jury found that respondents were negligent in failing to use drilling mud of sufficient weight in drilling their well, and that such negligence was the proximate cause of the well blowing out.

On the findings of the jury the trial court rendered judgment for petitioners for $154,518.19, which included $148,548.19 for the gas and distillate, and $5970 for damages to the land and cattle. The Court of Civil Appeals reversed the judgment and remanded the cause.

The reversal by the Court of Civil Appeals rests [on the ground] that since substantially all of the gas and distillate which was drained from under petitioners' lands was lost through respondents' blowout well, petitioners could not recover because under the law of capture they had lost all property rights in the gas or distillate which had migrated from their lands.

[T]he sole question [is] whether the law of capture absolves respondents of any liability for the negligent waste or destruction of petitioners' gas and distillate, though substantially all of such waste or destruction occurred after the minerals had been drained from beneath petitioners' lands.

In the more recent trend of the decisions of our state, with the growth and development of scientific knowledge of oil and gas, it is now recognized "that when a[n] oil field has been fairly tested and developed, experts can determine approximately the amount of oil and gas in place in a common pool, and can also equitably determine the amount of oil and gas recoverable by the owner of each tract of land under certain operating conditions." *Brown v. Humble Oil & Refining Co.*, 83 S.W.2d 935, 940 (Tex. 1935).

In our state the landowner is regarded as having absolute title in severalty to the oil and gas in place beneath his land. The only qualification of that rule of ownership is that it must be considered in connection with the law of capture and is subject to police regulations. The oil and gas beneath the soil are considered a part of the realty. Each owner of land owns separately, distinctly and exclusively all the oil and gas under his land and is accorded the usual remedies against trespassers who appropriate the minerals or destroy their market value.

The conflict in the decisions of the various states with reference to the character of ownership is traceable to some extent to the divergent views entertained by the courts, particularly in the earlier cases, as to the nature and migratory character of oil and gas in the soil. In the absence of common law precedent, and owing to the lack of scientific information as to the movement of these minerals, some of the courts have sought by analogy to compare oil and gas to other types of property such as wild animals, birds, subterranean waters and other migratory things, with reference to which the common law had established rules denying any character of ownership prior to capture. However, as was said by Professor A.W. Walker, Jr., of the School of Law of the University of Texas: "There is no oil or gas producing state today which follows the wild-animal analogy to its logical conclusion that the landowner has no property interest in the oil and gas in place." 16 Tex. L. Rev. 370, 371. In the light of modern scientific knowledge these early analogies have been disproven, and courts generally have come to recognize that oil and gas, as commonly found in underground reservoirs, are securely entrapped in a static condition in the original pool, and, ordinarily, so remain until disturbed by penetrations from the surface. It is further established, nevertheless, that these minerals will migrate across property lines towards any low pressure area created by production from the common pool. This migratory character of oil and gas has given rise to the so-called rule or law of capture. That rule simply is that the owner of a tract of land acquires title to the oil or gas which he produces from wells on his land, though part of the oil or gas may have migrated from adjoining lands. He may thus appropriate the oil and gas that have flowed from adjacent lands without the consent of the owner of those lands, and without incurring liability to him for drainage. The non-liability is based upon the theory that after the drainage the title or property interest of the former owner is gone. This rule, at first blush, would seem to conflict with the view of absolute ownership of the minerals in place, but it was otherwise decided in the early case of *Stephens County v. Mid-Kansas Oil & Gas Co.*, 254 S.W. 290 (Tex. 1923). Mr. Justice Greenwood there stated, 254 S.W. at 292: "The objection lacks substantial foundation that gas or oil in a certain tract of land cannot be owned in place, because subject to appropriation, without the consent of the owner of the tract, through drainage from wells on adjacent lands. If the owners of adjacent lands have the right to appropriate, without liability, the gas and oil underlying their neighbor's land, then their neighbor has the correlative right to appropriate, through like methods of drainage, the gas and oil underlying the tracts adjacent to his own."

Thus it is seen that, notwithstanding the fact that oil and gas beneath the surface are subject both to capture and administrative regulation, the fundamental rule of absolute ownership of the minerals in place is not affected in our state. In recognition of such ownership, our courts, in decisions involving well-spacing regulations of our Railroad Commission, have frequently announced the sound view that each landowner should be afforded the opportunity to produce his fair share of the recoverable oil and gas beneath his land, which is but another way of recognizing the existence of correlative rights between the various landowners over a common reservoir of oil or gas.

It must be conceded that under the law of capture there is no liability for reasonable and legitimate drainage from the common pool. The landowner is privileged to sink as many wells as he desires upon his tract of land and extract therefrom and appropriate all the oil and gas that he may produce, so long as he operates within the spirit and purpose of conservation statutes and orders of the Railroad Commission. These laws and regulations are designed to afford each owner a reasonable opportunity to produce his proportionate part of the oil and gas from the entire pool and to prevent operating practices injurious to the common reservoir. In this manner, if all operators exercise the same degree of skill and diligence, each owner will recover in most instances his fair share of the oil and gas. This reasonable opportunity to produce his fair share of the oil and gas is the landowner's common law right under our theory of absolute ownership of the minerals in place. But from the very nature of this theory the right of each land holder is qualified, and is limited to legitimate operations. Each owner whose land overlies the basin has a like interest, and each must of necessity exercise his right with some regard to the rights of others. No owner should be permitted to carry on his operations in reckless or lawless irresponsibility, but must submit to such limitations as are necessary to enable each to get his own.

While we are cognizant of the fact that there is a certain amount of reasonable and necessary waste incident to the production of oil and gas to which the nonliability rule must also apply, we do not think this immunity should be extended so as to include the negligent waste or destruction of the oil and gas.

In 85 A.L.R. 1156, . . . the annotator states: " . . . The fact that the owner of the land has a right to take and to use gas and oil, even to the diminution or exhaustion of the supply under his neighbor's land, does not give him the right to waste the gas. His property in the gas underlying his land consists of the right to appropriate the same, and permitting the gas to escape into the air is not an appropriation thereof in the proper sense of the term."

In like manner, the negligent waste and destruction of petitioners' gas and distillate was neither a legitimate drainage of the minerals from beneath their lands nor a lawful or reasonable appropriation of them. Consequently, the petitioners did not lose their right, title and interest in them under the law of capture. At the time of their removal they belonged to petitioners, and their wrongful dissipation deprived these owners of the right and opportunity to produce them. That right is forever lost, the same cannot be restored, and petitioners are without an adequate legal remedy unless we allow a recovery under the same common law which governs other actions for damages and under which the property rights in oil and gas are vested. This remedy should not be denied.

In common with others who are familiar with the nature of oil and gas and the risks involved in their production, the respondents had knowledge that a failure to use due care in drilling their well might result in a blowout with the consequent waste and dissipation of the oil, gas and distillate from the common reservoir. In the conduct of one's business or in the use and exploitation of one's property, the law imposes upon all persons the duty to exercise ordinary care to avoid injury or damage to the property of others. Thus under the common law, and independent of the conservation statutes, the respondents were legally bound to use due care to avoid the negligent waste or destruction of the minerals imbedded in petitioners' oil and gas-bearing strata. This common-law duty the respondents failed to discharge. For that omission they should be required to respond in such damages as will reasonably compensate the injured parties for the loss sustained as the proximate result of the negligent conduct. The fact that the major portion of the gas and distillate escaped from the well on respondents' premises is immaterial. Irrespective of the opening from which the minerals escaped, they belonged to the petitioners and the loss was the same. They would not have been dissipated at any opening except for the wrongful conduct of the respondents. Being responsible for the loss they are in no position to deny liability because the gas and distillate did not escape through the surface of petitioners' lands.

We are therefore of the opinion the Court of Civil Appeals erred in holding that under the law of capture the petitioners cannot recover for the damages resulting from the wrongful drainage of the gas and distillate from beneath their lands.

NOTES AND QUESTIONS

Continuing impact of the rule of capture in oil and gas production. Although oil and gas production are subject to extensive regulation to prevent waste and protect the environment, the rule of capture generally remains the law. *See Browning Oil Co., Inc. v. Luecke,* 38 S.W.3d 625 (Tex. Ct. App. 2000); 6 *Thompson* *on Real Property, Second Thomas Editions* § 49.02. Is the rule fair? Does it promote or inhibit investment in producing oil and gas? The effect of the rule has been diminished by the correlative rights recognized in cases like *Elliff* as well as spacing and drilling regulations designed to conserve the resource. In some situations, these regulations may involve *compulsory unitization,* or coordination between all surface owners to ensure maximum recovery from the common pool. *Thompson, supra,* at § 49.02(d).

Problems

1. Plaintiff Corporation invests $1 million in exploring for oil on its property. After it discovers oil and begins to extract it for sale, its neighboring landowner, Defendant Corporation, begins to do likewise. Because the oil is part of a common pool underlying the neighboring pieces of property, the defendant is able to extract oil from the same pool discovered by the plaintiff. Defendant's costs are much less than plaintiff's because it does not have to undergo the expense of searching for the oil. This gives the defendant a competitive advantage. Plaintiff sues defendant, asking for an injunction ordering defendant to stop exploiting oil discovered by plaintiff's investment and labor. Defendant claims a right to extract oil from beneath its own property.

    a. As plaintiff's attorney, what rule of law would you advocate that the court adopt? How would you justify that rule in terms of both fairness and social utility?

    b. As defendant's attorney, what rule of law would you advocate that the court adopt? How would you justify that rule in terms of both fairness and social utility?

    c. As the judge deciding the case, what rule of law would you adopt, and why?

2. The Exxon Valdez ran aground off the coast of Alaska in 1989, resulting in one of the largest oil spills in United States history. A lawsuit was filed against Exxon representing a class of tens of thousands of individuals who made their livelihood through commercial and subsistence fishing in the area. *Exxon Valdez v. Hazelwood,* 270 F.3d 1215 (9th Cir. 2001). The suit sought damages for the destruction of the fish supply. Use *Pierson v. Post* and *Elliff v. Texon* to argue for the plaintiffs or the defendants.

c.   Possession and the Presumption of Title

In the earlier cases, capture *creates* title to the property. But possession, even without evidence of capture or how the possession arose, may also create a presumption of legal title that will continue unless rebutted. Why does the law create this presumption? What functions does it serve? See the next case.

WILLCOX V. STROUP
467 F.3d 409 (4th Cir. 2006)

J. HARVIE WILKINSON III, Circuit Judge.

[Plaintiff Thomas Law Willcox found 444 documents from the administrations of two governors of South Carolina during the Civil War in a shopping bag in a closet at his late stepmother's home. The documents concern Confederate military reports, correspondence, and telegrams between various Confederate generals, officers, servicemen, and government officials, and related materials and have an appraised value of $2.4 million. Willcox allowed the papers to be microfilmed for the state archives. When he tried to sell the papers, Rodger Stroup, director of the South Carolina Department of Archives and History, obtained a temporary restraining order preventing the sale. Willcox then sued Stroup and the State of South Carolina for a declaratory judgment that he owned the papers.]

The papers seem to have come into Willcox's family through his great-great-uncle, Confederate Major General Evander McIver Law, who most likely came into possession of them during the February 1865 attack on the South Carolina capital by Union General William Tecumseh Sherman. On February 15, 1865, in anticipation of imminent attack, Governor A.G. Magrath declared martial law in Columbia and appointed General Law the Provost Marshal of the city. On February 16, 1865, a large number of State archives and records were removed from Columbia for safekeeping. On February 17, 1865, General Law was relieved of his duties as Provost Marshal, and General Sherman took control of Columbia. The parties submit no direct evidence of how General Law came into possession of the papers, nor is there any suggestion that he did so illegally.

On February 16, 1896, General Law wrote a letter to a New York book dealer regarding the sale of some letters which, both parties agree, appear to belong to the collection at issue here. By the 1940s, Mrs. Annie J. Storm, the granddaughter of General Law, was in possession of the papers and attempted to sell them to both the University of North Carolina at Chapel Hill ("UNC") and the South Caroliniana Library of the University of South Carolina. Mrs. Storm described the documents as "original State House papers entrusted to [her] grandfather at the time of the surrender." No sale resulted, but the papers were placed on microfilm at the Southern Historical Collection at UNC.

No evidence has been submitted of the papers' movements between the time of the Storm correspondence and plaintiff Willcox's discovery more than fifty years later. The point for present purposes is simply that, while the precise route by which Civil War-era gubernatorial papers arrived in a shopping bag in Thomas Law Willcox's stepmother's closet remains a mystery, it appears that the papers have been in the possession of the Law and Willcox families for over one hundred and forty years.

The exceptional nature of the papers in dispute—their early vintage, their unknown history—presents issues distinct from those of the typical personal property case. Without the benefit of clear chain of title, evidence of original ownership, eyewitness testimony, and any number of documentary aids usually helpful in the determination of ownership, the court must utilize the legal tools that remain at its disposal. In this situation, tenets of the common law that usually remain in the background of ownership determinations come to the forefront, their logic and utility revealed anew.

That possession is nine-tenths of the law is a truism hardly bearing repetition. The importance of possession gave rise to the principle that "[p]ossession of property is indicia of ownership, and a rebuttable presumption exists that those in possession of property are rightly in possession." 73 C.J.S. *Property* § 70 (2004).

The common law has long recognized that "actual possession is, prima facie, evidence of a legal title in the possessor." William Blackstone, 2 *Commentaries* *196. *See, e.g.,* Edward Coke, 1 *Commentary upon Littleton* 6.b. (19th ed. 1832) (strong presumption of ownership created by "continuall and quiet possession"); *Jeffries v. Great W. Ry. Co.* (1856) 119 Eng. Rep. 680 (K.B.) ("[T]he presumption of law is that the person who has possession has the property.").

This presumption has been a feature of American law almost since its inception. "Undoubtedly," noted the Supreme Court, "if a person be found in possession . . . it is prima facie evidence of his ownership." *Ricard v. Williams,* 20 U.S. 59, 105 (1822). Almost eighty years later, the Court reaffirmed, "If there be no evidence to the contrary, proof of possession, at least under a color of right, is sufficient proof of title." *Bradshaw v. Ashley,* 180 U.S. 59, 63 (1901). In this case, the possession of the Law and Willcox families triggers the presumption of their ownership of the papers.

The . . . unusual circumstances of this case . . . provide a notable illustration of why such a presumption exists in the first place.

First and foremost, the presumption operates to resolve otherwise impenetrable difficulties. Where neither party can establish title by a preponderance of the evidence, the presumption cuts the Gordian knot, determining ownership in favor of the possessor. This case shows the need for such a default rule. It presents questions the answers to which remain a mystery. Little is known of the papers' whereabouts, status, or movements from their creation to their acquisition by General Law. There is no evidence of how General Law acquired the papers. Not even the chain of possession within the Law and Willcox families has yet been determined with any certainty. In fact, in over one hundred and forty years of existence, these papers have apparently surfaced in the historical record only three times: in General Law's 1896 correspondence, in Annie Storm's 1940's correspondence, and in the current litigation.

This case thus poses questions which we are ill equipped to answer. Fortunately, however, the common law reveals its usefulness even in the acknowledgment of its limitations. The presumption of ownership from possession locates the parties' burdens. Where the party not in possession is able to establish superior title by satisfactory evidence, the presumption gives way in favor of this evidence. But where no such evidence is produced—where, as here, the events at issue are impossible to reconstruct—the presumption recognizes and averts the possibility of a court's presiding over a historical goose chase.

Second, the presumption of ownership in the possessor promotes stability. The presumption of ownership from possession is one of an array of legal principles designed to this end. The presumption means that, absent proof to the contrary, settled distributions and expectations will continue undisturbed. Even where evidence overcomes the presumption, other principles work to protect settled expectations, including the statute of limitations, the doctrine of adverse possession, and equitable defenses such as laches, staleness, abandonment, and waiver.

Such principles, working in concert, favor status-quo distributions over great upsets in property rights. At the most basic level, this fosters "the policy of protecting the public peace against violence and disorder." *See Sabariego v. Maverick,* 124 U.S. 261, 297 (1888). In contemporary commercial society, it protects the expectations of those in possession, thus encouraging them to make improvements that increase social wealth. *See, e.g.,* Richard A. Posner, *Economic Analysis of*

Law 80-84 (6th ed. 2003); Thomas W. Merrill & Henry E. Smith, *What Happened to Property in Law and Economics?*, 111 Yale L.J. 357, 398 (2001) ("[T]he refined problems of concern in advanced economies exist at the apex of a pyramid, the base of which consists of the security of property rights."). Without rules such as the presumption of ownership, whether public or private, such valuable goals would give way to uncertainty.

In this case, the resulting confusion is not difficult to imagine. If the State were not required to defeat the presumption in order to gain title, a whole system of archival practice could be thrown into question. The State could claim ownership of other papers of Governors Pickens and Bonham held by the Library of Congress and Duke University, as well as papers of other South Carolina governors currently at institutions other than the State Archives. The result would be immense litigation over papers held by private owners, universities, historical societies, and federal depositories. It would upset settled archival arrangements and the expectations of institutions and historical scholars alike. Disregard of possession as presumptive evidence of ownership would throw the whole of this important area into turmoil.

Finally, while it has never been the practice of federal courts to ignore the law in favor of equitable considerations, it is worth noting that the employment of the presumption in this case in no way frustrates the public interest. Here, private possession does not shut the papers off from access by scholars or, indeed, by the interested public. They have been available for study for decades on microfilm at the University of North Carolina at Chapel Hill, and through the permission of plaintiff Willcox the South Carolina Department of Archives and History now also has a copy on microfilm. The papers are thus freely available for perusal and study regardless of who owns the originals. And, of course, if the State values possession of the original documents, it may acquire them on the open market.

In short, the common law, through the presumption of ownership in the possessor, resolves otherwise insoluble historical puzzles in favor of longstanding distributions and long-held expectations. Such a rule both protects the private interests of longtime possessors and increases social utility. Of course, this presumption will not always cut in one direction. In many instances, the State will possess the papers, and it will then be entitled to the strong presumption that the private party claims here. In this case, however, where the Law and Willcox families have been in possession for well over a century, the presumption favors plaintiff Willcox.

Having recognized the presumption in favor of Willcox's ownership, the court must consider whether the State has rebutted this presumption. In this case, the State has been unable to provide such evidence. There is no documentary evidence of the State's title, nor is there evidence of its recent possession. While there is no suggestion that the Law and Willcox families are bona fide purchasers, since no purchase was involved, there is also no indication that they acquired the papers in bad faith. In any case, the State's burden may not be met by challenging the sufficiency of the possessor's title but only by proving the superior strength of its claim.

Given the insufficient factual evidence, the State's remaining argument for ownership is that, under the law at the time of the documents' creation (1860-64) or their acquisition by General Law (1865), they were public property. South

Carolina law of the relevant time period provides no basis for the State's claim of ownership.

[T]he practice in South Carolina accords with common law practice more generally. Presidential papers, for example, were considered private property from the time of George Washington, who following his second term removed his papers to Mount Vernon and bequeathed them in his will to his nephew, Supreme Court Justice Bushrod Washington. *See Nixon v. United States,* 978 F.2d 1269, 1278 (D.C. Cir. 1992). Jefferson, Madison, and Monroe also bequeathed their papers as private property by will. *See id.* When Congress first provided public funding for presidential libraries, such libraries depended upon former presidents to deposit their papers voluntarily. *See Presidential Libraries Act of 1955,* Pub. L. No. 84-373, 69 Stat. 695 (*codified as amended* at 44 U.S.C. § 2112 (2000)).

For Congress to change this private ownership regime required a law prospectively granting the United States "complete ownership, possession, and control" of official presidential records. *See Presidential Records Act of 1978,* 44 U.S.C. § 2201 *et seq.* (implementing process for archiving records and making them publicly available as soon as possible, subject to exceptions for confidential and privileged materials). A previous l aw, the *Presidential Records and Materials Preservation Act of 1974,* Pub. L. 93-526, 88 Stat. 1695, which exerted federal control over former President Nixon's papers in the wake of the Watergate scandal, was determined to have effected a per se taking of President Nixon's property interest in his papers. *See Nixon,* 978 F.2d at 1284.

We conclude that the State has failed to establish that South Carolina law at the relevant time treated gubernatorial papers as public property. This conclusion leaves the State with no basis upon which to rebut the strong presumption of possession in the Law and Willcox families and no basis upon which to claim title superior to that of plaintiff Willcox.

d.   Finding

Imagine that you are walking down the street and notice a valuable watch on the sidewalk. You pick it up. What rights do you have as the finder of the watch?

In a found property scenario, we have several potential characters. First, we have the *true owner* of the watch. Second, we have the *finder.* Third, we have a potential *subsequent possessor* of the found item. For example, after finding the watch you leave it with a jeweler to have it valued. The jeweler is a subsequent possessor compared to the finder. Fourth, we have the owner of the location—in this context, often called the *owner of the locus*—where the item was found. For example, if we change our scenario a bit, and you now find the watch on my front lawn, I might have some claim to the watch as the owner of the locus.

We will begin with a classic case that sheds light on the respective rights of the first three characters—the true owner, the finder, and a subsequent possessor. We will return shortly to the owner of the locus.

ARMORY V. DELAMIRIE
King's Bench, 1722 1 Strange 505

The plaintiff being a chimney sweeper's boy found a jewel and carried it to the defendant's shop (who was a goldsmith) to know what it was, and delivered it into the hands of the apprentice, who under the pretence of weighing it, took out the stones, and calling to the master to let him know it came to three half-pence, the master offered the boy the money, who refused to take it, and insisted to have the thing again; whereupon the apprentice delivered him back the socket without the stones. And now in trover against the master these points were ruled:

1. That the finder of a jewel, though he does not by such finding acquire an absolute property or ownership, yet he has such a property as will enable him to keep it against all but the rightful owner, and consequently may maintain trover.
2. That the action well lay against the master, who gives a credit to his apprentice, and is answerable for his neglect.
3. As to the value of the jewel several of the trade were examined to prove what a jewel of the finest water that would fit in the socket would be worth; and the Chief Justice (Pratt) directed the jury, that unless the defendant did produce the jewel, and shew it not to be of the finest water, they should presume the strongest against him, and make the value of the best jewels the measure of their damages, which they accordingly did.

NOTE

1. *Armory v. Delamirie* establishes two simple finding rules. First, the true owner always wins. This rule is ironclad and holds in all circumstances. "Finders keepers, losers weepers" might be the law on the playground, but nowhere else.

Second, the finder wins against everyone except the true owner. This rule applies broadly, but requires two caveats. First, as we will discuss further below, the finder might lose against the owner of the locus. Second, the finder might lose against a prior possessor who is not the true owner. Here is an example. Alice is the true owner of a necklace. She loses it, and Becky finds it. Becky then manages to lose the necklace herself, and Carol later finds it. As the true owner, Alice would win against either Becky or Carol. But say that Becky and Carol get into a dispute over ownership of the necklace. As a prior possessor, Becky will win against Carol. So we should modify our rule to state that a *finder wins against everyone except the true owner and any prior possessor.* (Again, we have left the owner of the locus out of the picture.)

FIRST IN TIME   Both of these rules are straightforward applications of the principle of first in time, first in right. The true owner is first in time as compared to any subsequent finder. Becky was first in time as compared to Carol, so Becky would win in a dispute between Becky and Carol. This is another example of the concept of relatively of title that we first encountered in our discussion of bailments—Becky may have superior rights as compared to one person (Carol) but inferior rights as compared to another (the true owner).

It is a good thing that the law of the playground is not the law of the courts.

So far, we have established that (a) true owners always win in finding cases, and (b) a finder wins against subsequent possessors of the property. In *Armory v. Delamirie*, however, one party was notably absent—the owner of the premises where the object was found. The owner of the premises has a strong intuitive claim to a found object—if a chimney sweep found a jewel in your house, you would probably feel that you had a good claim to it. Disputes between a finder and the owner of the premises turn on a number of factors, as discussed in our next two cases.

BENJAMIN V. LINDNER AVIATION, INC.

Supreme Court of Iowa, 1995 534 N.W.2d 400

TERNUS, Justice.

Appellant, Heath Benjamin, found over $18,000 in currency inside the wing of an airplane. At the time of this discovery, appellee, State Central Bank, owned the plane and it was being serviced by appellee, Lindner Aviation, Inc. All three parties claimed the money as against the true owner. After a bench trial, the district court held that the currency was mislaid property and belonged to the owner of the plane. The court awarded a finder's fee to Benjamin. Benjamin appealed and Lindner Aviation and State Central Bank cross-appealed. We reverse on the bank's cross-appeal and otherwise affirm the judgment of the district court.

[The following summary appears in the original opinion as Section IV; it is presented out of order to introduce concepts implicit in the early part of the opinion.—Ed.]

I. Classification of Found Property

Under the common law, there are four categories of found property: (1) abandoned property, (2) lost property, (3) mislaid property, and (4) treasure trove. *Ritz*, 467 N.W.2d at 269. The rights of a finder of property depend on how the found property is classified. *Id.* at 268-69.

A. *Abandoned property.* Property is abandoned when the owner no longer wants to possess it. *Cf. Pearson v. City of Guttenberg*, 245 N.W.2d 519, 529 (Iowa 1976) (considering abandonment of real estate). Abandonment is shown by proof that the owner intends to abandon the property and has voluntarily relinquished all right, title and interest in the property. *Ritz*, 467 N.W.2d at 269; 1 Am.Jur.2d *Abandoned Property* §§ 11-14, at 15-20. Abandoned property belongs to the finder of the property against all others, including the former owner. *Ritz*, 467 N.W.2d at 269.

B. *Lost property.* "Property is lost when the owner unintentionally and involuntarily parts with its possession and does not know where it is." *Id.* (citing *Eldridge v. Herman*, 291 N.W.2d 319, 323 (Iowa 1980)); *accord* 1 Am.Jur.2d *Abandoned Property* § 4, at 9-10. Stolen property found by someone who did not participate in the theft is lost property. *Flood*, 218 Iowa at 905, 253 N.W. at 513; 1 Am.Jur.2d *Abandoned Property* § 5, at 11. Under chapter 644, lost property becomes the property of the finder once the statutory procedures are followed and the owner makes no claim within twelve months. Iowa Code § 644.11 (1991).

C. *Mislaid property.* Mislaid property is voluntarily put in a certain place by the owner who then overlooks or forgets where the property is. *Ritz*, 467 N.W.2d at 269. It differs from lost property in that the owner voluntarily and intentionally places mislaid property in the location where it is eventually found by another. 1 Am.Jur.2d *Abandoned Property* § 10, at 14. In contrast, property is not considered lost unless the owner parts with it involuntarily. *Ritz*, 467 N.W.2d at 269; 1 Am.Jur.2d *Abandoned Property* § 10, at 14; *see Hill v. Schrunk*, 207 Or. 71, 292 P.2d 141, 143 (1956) (carefully concealed currency was mislaid property, not lost property).

The finder of mislaid property acquires no rights to the property. 1 Am.Jur.2d *Abandoned Property* § 24, at 30. The right of possession of mislaid property belongs to the owner of the premises upon which the property is found, as against all persons other than the true owner. *Ritz*, 467 N.W.2d at 269.

D. *Treasure trove.* Treasure trove consists of coins or currency concealed by the owner. *Id.* It includes an element of antiquity. *Id.* To be classified as treasure trove, the property must have been hidden or concealed for such a length of time that the owner is probably dead or undiscoverable. *Id.*; 1 Am.Jur.2d

Abandoned Property § 8, at 13. Treasure trove belongs to the finder as against all but the true owner. *Zornes*, 223 Iowa at 1145, 274 N.W. at 879.

II. Background Facts and Proceedings

In April of 1992, State Central Bank became the owner of an airplane when the bank repossessed it from its prior owner who had defaulted on a loan. In August of that year, the bank took the plane to Lindner Aviation for a routine annual inspection. Benjamin worked for Lindner Aviation and did the inspection.

As part of the inspection, Benjamin removed panels from the underside of the wings. Although these panels were to be removed annually as part of the routine inspection, a couple of the screws holding the panel on the left wing were so rusty that Benjamin had to use a drill to remove them. Benjamin testified that the panel probably had not been removed for several years.

Inside the left wing Benjamin discovered two packets approximately four inches high and wrapped in aluminum foil. He removed the packets from the wing and took off the foil wrapping. Inside the foil was paper currency, tied in string and wrapped in handkerchiefs. The currency was predominately twenty-dollar bills with mint dates before the 1960s, primarily in the 1950s. The money smelled musty.

Benjamin took one packet to his jeep and then reported what he had found to his supervisor, offering to divide the money with him. However, the supervisor reported the discovery to the owner of Lindner Aviation, William Engle. Engle insisted that they contact the authorities and he called the Department of Criminal Investigation. The money was eventually turned over to the Keokuk police department.

Two days later, Benjamin filed an affidavit with the county auditor claiming that he was the finder of the currency under the provisions of Iowa Code chapter 644 (1991). Lindner Aviation and the bank also filed claims to the money. The notices required by chapter 644 were published and posted. *See* Iowa Code § 644.8 (1991). No one came forward within twelve months claiming to be the true owner of the money. *See id.* § 644.11 (if true owner does not claim property within twelve months, the right to the property vests in the finder).

[Chapter 644 was moved to Chapter 556F in a 1995 revision of the Iowa Code. The relevant provisions of the code are as follows:

§ 556F.7 (formerly § 644.7)
If the owner is unknown, the finder shall, within five days after finding the property, take the money, bank notes, and a description of any other property to the county sheriff of the county or the chief of police of the city in which the property was found, and provide an affidavit describing the property, the time when and place where the property was found, and attesting that no alteration has been made in the appearance of the property since the finding. The sheriff or chief of police shall send a copy of the affidavit to the county auditor who shall enter a description of the property and the value of the property, as nearly as the auditor can determine it, in the auditor's lost property book, together with the copy of the affidavit of the finder.

§ 556F.8 (formerly § 644.8)
The finder of the lost goods, money, bank notes, or other things shall give written notice of the finding of the property. The notice shall contain an accurate

description of the property and a statement as to the time when and place where the same was found, and the post-office address of the finder. The notice shall:

1. Be posted at the door of the courthouse in the county in which the property was found or at the city hall or police station if found within a city and in one other of the most public places in the county; and
2. If the property found exceeds forty dollars in value, the notice shall be published once each week for three consecutive weeks in some newspaper published in and having general circulation in the county.

I.C.A. § 556F.11 (formerly § 644.11)
If no person appears to claim and prove ownership to said goods, money, bank notes, or other things within twelve months of the date when proof of said publication and posting is filed in the office of the county auditor, the right to such property shall irrevocably vest in said finder.

I.C.A. § 556F.13 (formerly § 644.13)
As a reward . . . for finding lost goods, money, bank notes, and other things, before restitution of the property or proceeds thereof shall be made, the finder shall be entitled to ten percent upon the value thereof . . . .]

Benjamin filed this declaratory judgment action against Lindner Aviation and the bank to establish his right to the property. The parties tried the case to the court. The district court held that chapter 644 applies only to "lost" property and the money here was mislaid property. The court awarded the money to the bank, holding that it was entitled to possession of the money to the exclusion of all but the true owner. The court also held that Benjamin was a "finder" within the meaning of chapter 644 and awarded him a ten percent finder's fee. *See id.* § 644.13 (a finder of lost property is entitled to ten percent of the value of the lost property as a reward).

Benjamin appealed. He claims that chapter 644 governs the disposition of all found property and any common law distinctions between various types of found property are no longer valid. He asserts alternatively that even under the common law classes of found property, he is entitled to the money he discovered. He claims that the trial court should have found that the property was treasure trove or was lost or abandoned rather than mislaid, thereby entitling the finder to the property.

The bank and Lindner Aviation cross-appealed. Lindner Aviation claims that if the money is mislaid property, it is entitled to the money as the owner of the premises on which the money was found, the hangar where the plane was parked. It argues in the alternative that it is the finder, not Benjamin, because Benjamin discovered the money during his work for Lindner Aviation. The bank asserts in its cross-appeal that it owns the premises where the money was found—the airplane—and that no one is entitled to a finder's fee because chapter 644 does not apply to mislaid property.

III. Standard of Review

This case was tried as an ordinary proceeding at law. Therefore, the standard of review is for correction of errors at law. Iowa R.App.P. 4; *Kuehl v. Freeman Bros.*

Agency, Inc., 521 N.W.2d 714, 717 (Iowa 1994); *Eldridge v. Herman*, 291 N.W.2d 319, 321 (Iowa 1980).

Whether the money found by Benjamin was treasure trove or was mislaid, abandoned or lost property is a fact question. 1 Am.Jur.2d *Abandoned, Lost, and Unclaimed Property* § 41, at 49 (2d ed. 1994) (hereinafter "1 Am.Jur.2d *Abandoned Property*"); *cf. Bennett v. Bowers*, 238 Iowa 702, 706, 28 N.W.2d 618, 620 (1947) (whether realty has been abandoned is a question of fact); *Roberson v. Ellis*, 58 Or. 219, 114 P. 100, 103 (1911) (whether money was hidden long enough to be classified as treasure trove was a fact question for the jury). Therefore, the trial court's finding that the money was mislaid is binding on us if supported by substantial evidence. Iowa R.App.P. 14(f)(1); *see Eldridge*, 291 N.W.2d at 323 (affirming trial court's finding that property was lost property because supported by substantial evidence).

IV. Does Chapter 644 Supersede the Common Law Classifications of Found Property?

Benjamin argues that chapter 644 governs the rights of finders of property and abrogates the common law distinctions between types of found property. As he points out, lost property statutes are intended "to encourage and facilitate the return of property to the true owner, and then to reward a finder for his honesty if the property remains unclaimed." *Paset v. Old Orchard Bank & Trust Co.*, 62 Ill.-App.3d 534, 19 Ill.Dec. 389, 393, 378 N.E.2d 1264, 1268 (1978) (interpreting a statute similar to chapter 644); *accord Flood v. City Nat'l Bank*, 218 Iowa 898, 908, 253 N.W. 509, 514 (1934), *cert. denied*, 298 U.S. 666, 56 S.Ct. 749, 80 L.Ed. 1390 (1936) (public policy reflected in lost property statute is "to provide a reward to the finder of lost goods"); *Willsmore v. Township of Oceola*, 106 Mich.App. 671, 308 N.W.2d 796, 804 (1981) (lost goods act "provides protection to the finder, a reasonable method of uniting goods with their true owner, and a plan which benefits the people of the state through their local governments").[2] These goals, Benjamin argues, can best be achieved by applying such statutes to all types of found property.

The Michigan Court of Appeals had an additional reason in *Willsmore* to apply the Michigan statute to all classes of discovered property. The Michigan court noted that the common law distinctions between categories of found property were embraced in Michigan after the enactment of its lost property statute. *Willsmore*, 308 N.W.2d at 803. Based on this fact, the Michigan court concluded that the legislature could not have intended to reflect in the term "lost property" distinctions not then in existence. *Id.* However, the Michigan court did not address the fact that the common law distinctions were first developed in England, before the enactment of most states' lost property statutes. *See Goodard v. Winchell*, 86 Iowa 71, 52 N.W. 1124 (1892) (citing to English common law); *Hurley v. City of Niagara Falls*, 30 A.D.2d 89, 289 N.Y.S.2d 889, 891 (1968) (stating that common law principles relating to lost property were established as early as 1722).

---

2. The Michigan statute had two provisions lacking in the Iowa lost property statute. The Michigan law provided for registration of a find in a central location so that the true owner could locate the goods with ease. *Willsmore*, 308 N.W.2d at 803. It also required notice to potential true owners. *Id.* Because Iowa's statute has no central registry and requires only posting and publication of notice, Iowa's law does not accomplish as well the goal of reuniting property with its true owner. Finally, under the Michigan statute, the local government obtains one half the value of the goods. *Id.* Iowa's law does not include this public benefit.

Although a few courts have adopted an expansive view of lost property statutes, we think Iowa law is to the contrary. In 1937, we quoted and affirmed a trial court ruling that "the old law of treasure trove is not merged in the statutory law of chapter 515, 1935 Code of Iowa." *Zornes v. Bowen*, 223 Iowa 1141, 1145, 274 N.W. 877, 879 (1937). Chapter 515 of the 1935 Iowa Code was eventually renumbered as chapter 644. The relevant sections of chapter 644 are unchanged since our 1937 decision. As recently as 1991, we stated that "[t]he rights of finders of property vary according to the characterization of the property found." *Ritz v. Selma United Methodist Church*, 467 N.W.2d 266, 268 (Iowa 1991). We went on to define and apply the common law classifications of found property in deciding the rights of the parties. *Id.* at 269. As our prior cases show, we have continued to use the common law distinctions between classes of found property despite the legislature's enactment of chapter 644 and its predecessors.

The legislature has had many opportunities since our decision in *Zornes* to amend the statute so that it clearly applies to all types of found property. However, it has not done so. When the legislature leaves a statute unchanged after the supreme court has interpreted it, we presume the legislature has acquiesced in our interpretation. *State v. Sheffey*, 234 N.W.2d 92, 97 (Iowa 1975). Therefore, we presume here that the legislature approves of our application of chapter 644 to lost property only. Consequently, we hold that chapter 644 does not abrogate the common law classifications of found property. We note this position is consistent with that taken by most jurisdictions. *See, e.g., Bishop v. Ellsworth*, 91 Ill.App.2d 386, 234 N.E.2d 49, 51 (1968) (holding lost property statute does not apply to abandoned or mislaid property); *Foster v. Fidelity Safe Deposit Co.*, 264 Mo. 89, 174 S.W. 376, 379 (1915) (refusing to apply lost property statute to property that would not be considered lost under the common law); *Sovern v. Yoran*, 16 Or. 269, 20 P. 100, 105 (1888) (same); *Zech v. Accola*, 253 Wis. 80, 33 N.W.2d 232, 235 (1948) (concluding that if legislature had intended to include treasure trove within lost property statute, it would have specifically mentioned treasure trove).

In summary, chapter 644 applies only if the property discovered can be categorized as "lost" property as that term is defined under the common law. Thus, the trial court correctly looked to the common law classifications of found property to decide who had the right to the money discovered here.

[Section IV of the opinion is reproduced above]

V. Is There Substantial Evidence to Support the Trial Court's Finding that the Money Found by Benjamin Was Mislaid?

We think there was substantial evidence to find that the currency discovered by Benjamin was mislaid property. In the *Eldridge* case, we examined the location where the money was found as a factor in determining whether the money was lost property. *Eldridge*, 291 N.W.2d at 323; *accord* 1 Am.Jur.2d *Abandoned Property* § 6, at 11-12 ("The place where money or property claimed as lost is found is an important factor in the determination of the question of whether it was lost or only mislaid."). Similarly, in *Ritz*, we considered the manner in which the money had been secreted in deciding that it had not been abandoned. *Ritz*, 467 N.W.2d at 269.

The place where Benjamin found the money and the manner in which it was hidden are also important here. The bills were carefully tied and wrapped and then concealed in a location that was accessible only by removing screws and a panel. These circumstances support an inference that the money was placed there intentionally. This inference supports the conclusion that the money was mislaid. *Jackson v. Steinberg*, 186 Or. 129, 200 P.2d 376, 378 (1948) (fact that $800 in currency was found concealed beneath the paper lining of a dresser indicates that money was intentionally concealed with intention of reclaiming it; therefore, property was mislaid, not lost); *Schley v. Couch*, 155 Tex. 195, 284 S.W.2d 333, 336 (1955) (holding that money found buried under garage floor was mislaid property as a matter of law because circumstances showed that money was placed there deliberately and court presumed that owner had either forgotten where he hid the money or had died before retrieving it).

The same facts that support the trial court's conclusion that the money was mislaid prevent us from ruling as a matter of law that the property was lost. Property is not considered lost unless considering the place where and the conditions under which the property is found, there is an inference that the property was left there unintentionally. 1 Am.Jur.2d *Abandoned Property* § 6, at 12; *see Sovern*, 20 P. at 105 (holding that coins found in a jar under a wooden floor of a barn were not lost property because the circumstances showed that the money was hidden there intentionally); *see Farrare v. City of Pasco*, 68 Wash.App. 459, 843 P.2d 1082, 1084 (1993) (where currency was deliberately concealed, it cannot be characterized as lost property). Contrary to Benjamin's position the circumstances here do not support a conclusion that the money was placed in the wing of the airplane unintentionally. Additionally, as the trial court concluded, there was no evidence suggesting that the money was placed in the wing by someone other than the owner of the money and that its location was unknown to the owner. For these reasons, we reject Benjamin's argument that the trial court was obligated to find that the currency Benjamin discovered was lost property.

We also reject Benjamin's assertion that as a matter of law this money was abandoned property. Both logic and common sense suggest that it is unlikely someone would voluntarily part with over $18,000 with the intention of terminating his ownership. The location where this money was found is much more consistent with the conclusion that the owner of the property was placing the money there for safekeeping. *See Ritz*, 467 N.W.2d at 269 (property not abandoned where money was buried in jars and tin cans, indicating a desire by the owner to preserve it); *Jackson*, 200 P.2d at 378 (because currency was concealed intentionally and deliberately, the bills could not be regarded as abandoned property); 1 Am.Jur.2d *Abandoned Property* § 13, at 17 (where property is concealed in such a way that the concealment appears intentional and deliberate, there can be no abandonment). We will not presume that an owner has abandoned his property when his conduct is consistent with a continued claim to the property. *Linscomb v. Goodyear Tire & Rubber Co.*, 199 F.2d 431, 435 (8th Cir.1952) (applying Missouri law); *Hoffman Management Corp. v. S.L.C. of N. Am., Inc.*, 800 S.W.2d 755, 762 (Mo.Ct.App.1990); *Foulke v. New York Consolidated R.R.*, 228 N.Y. 269, 127 N.E. 237, 238 (1920); 1 Am.Jur.2d *Abandoned Property* §§ 14, 42, at 20, 49; *cf. Bennett*, 238 Iowa at 706, 28 N.W.2d at 620 (stating that there is no presumption that real property is abandoned). Therefore, we cannot rule that the district court erred in failing to find that the currency discovered by Benjamin was abandoned property.

Finally, we also conclude that the trial court was not obligated to decide that this money was treasure trove. Based on the dates of the currency, the money was no older than thirty-five years. The mint dates, the musty odor and the rusty condition of a few of the panel screws indicate that the money may have been hidden for some time. However, there was no evidence of the age of the airplane or the date of its last inspection. These facts may have shown that the money was concealed for a much shorter period of time.

Moreover, it is also significant that the airplane had a well-documented ownership history. The record reveals that there were only two owners of the plane prior to the bank. One was the person from whom the bank repossessed the plane; the other was the original purchaser of the plane when it was manufactured. Nevertheless, there is no indication that Benjamin or any other party attempted to locate and notify the prior owners of the plane, which could very possibly have led to the identification of the true owner of the money. Under these circumstances, we cannot say as a matter of law that the money meets the antiquity requirement or that it is probable that the owner of the money is not discoverable.

We think the district court had substantial evidence to support its finding that the money found by Benjamin was mislaid. The circumstances of its concealment and the location where it was found support inferences that the owner intentionally placed the money there and intended to retain ownership. We are bound by this factual finding.

VI. Is the Airplane or the Hangar the "Premises" Where the Money was Discovered?

Because the money discovered by Benjamin was properly found to be mislaid property, it belongs to the owner of the premises where it was found. Mislaid property is entrusted to the owner of the premises where it is found rather than the finder of the property because it is assumed that the true owner may eventually recall where he has placed his property and return there to reclaim it. *Willsmore*, 308 N.W.2d at 802; *Foster*, 174 S.W. at 378; *Foulke*, 127 N.E. at 238-39.

We think that the premises where the money was found is the airplane, not Lindner Aviation's hangar where the airplane happened to be parked when the money was discovered. The policy behind giving ownership of mislaid property to the owner of the premises where the property was mislaid supports this conclusion. If the true owner of the money attempts to locate it, he would initially look for the plane; it is unlikely he would begin his search by contacting businesses where the airplane might have been inspected. Therefore, we affirm the trial court's judgment that the bank, as the owner of the plane, has the right to possession of the property as against all but the true owner.[4]

VII. Is Benjamin Entitled to a Finder's Fee?

Benjamin claims that if he is not entitled to the money, he should be paid a ten percent finder's fee under section 644.13. The problem with this claim is that only the finder of "lost goods, money, bank notes, and other things" is rewarded with a finder's fee under chapter 644. Iowa Code § 644.13 (1991). Because the property found by Benjamin was mislaid property, not lost property, section

---

4. Some jurisdictions require that one in possession of mislaid property use ordinary care to return the property to its owner. E.g., *Kimbrough v. Giant Food Inc.*, 26 Md.App. 640, 339 A.2d 688, 696 (1975); *see generally* 1 Am.Jur.2d *Abandoned Property* § 24, at 31-32.

644.13 does not apply here. The trial court erred in awarding Benjamin a finder's fee.

VIII. Summary

We conclude that the district court's finding that the money discovered by Benjamin was mislaid property is supported by substantial evidence. Therefore, we affirm the district court's judgment that the bank has the right to the money as against all but the true owner. This decision makes it unnecessary to decide whether Benjamin or Lindner Aviation was the finder of the property. We reverse the court's decision awarding a finder's fee to Benjamin.

AFFIRMED IN PART; REVERSED IN PART.

All justices concur except HARRIS, SNELL, and ANDREASEN, JJ., who dissent.

SNELL, Justice (dissenting).

I respectfully dissent.

The life of the law is logic, it has been said. *See Davis v. Aiken*, 111 Ga.App. 505, 142 S.E.2d 112, 119 (1965) (quoting Sir Edward Coke). If so, it should be applied here.

The majority quotes with approval the general rule that whether money found is treasure trove, mislaid, abandoned, or lost property is a fact question. 1 Am.Jur.2d *Abandoned, Lost, and Unclaimed Property* § 41, at 49 (2d ed. 1994). In deciding a fact question, we are to consider the facts as known and all reasonable inferences to be drawn from them. *Wright v. Thompson*, 254 Iowa 342, 347, 117 N.W.2d 520, 523 (1962). Thus does logic, reason, and common sense enter in.

After considering the four categories of found money, the majority decides that Benjamin found mislaid money. The result is that the bank gets all the money; Benjamin, the finder, gets nothing. Apart from the obvious unfairness in result, I believe this conclusion fails to come from logical analysis.

Mislaid property is property voluntarily put in a certain place by the owner who then overlooks or forgets where the property is. *Ritz v. Selma United Methodist Church*, 467 N.W.2d 266, 268 (Iowa 1991). The property here consisted of two packets of paper currency totalling $18,910, three to four inches high, wrapped in aluminum foil. Inside the foil, the paper currency, predominantly twenty dollar bills, was tied with string and wrapped in handkerchiefs. Most of the mint dates were in the 1950s with one dated 1934. These packets were found in the left wing of the Mooney airplane after Benjamin removed a panel held in by rusty screws.

These facts satisfy the requirement that the property was voluntarily put in a certain place by the owner. But the second test for determining that property is mislaid is that the owner "overlooks or forgets where the property is." *See Ritz*, 467 N.W.2d at 269. I do not believe that the facts, logic, or common sense lead to a finding that this requirement is met. It is not likely or reasonable to suppose that a person would secrete $18,000 in an airplane wing and then forget where it was.

Cases cited by the majority contrasting "mislaid" property and "lost" property are appropriate for a comparison of these principles but do not foreclose other considerations. After finding the money, Benjamin proceeded to give written notice of finding the property as prescribed in Iowa Code chapter 644 (1993), "Lost Property." As set out in section 556F.8, notices were posted on the court-house door and in three other public places in the county. In addition, notice was published once each week for three consecutive weeks in a newspaper of general circulation in the county. Also, affidavits of publication were filed with the county auditor who then had them published as part of the board of supervi-sors' proceedings. Iowa Code § 556F.9. After twelve months, if no person appears to claim and prove ownership of the property, the right to the property rests irrevocably in the finder. Iowa Code § 556F.11.

The purpose of this type of legal notice is to give people the opportunity to assert a claim if they have one. *See, e.g., Neeley v. Murchison*, 815 F.2d 345, 347 (5th Cir.1987). If no claim is made, the law presumes there is none or for whatever reason it is not asserted. Thus, a failure to make a claim after legal notice is given is a bar to a claim made thereafter. *See, e.g., Tulsa Professional Collection Servs., Inc. v. Pope*, 485 U.S. 478, 481, 108 S.Ct. 1340, 1343, 99 L.Ed.2d 565, 572-73 (1988).

Benjamin followed the law in giving legal notice of finding property. None of the parties dispute this. The suggestion that Benjamin should have initiated a further search for the true owner is not a requirement of the law, is therefore irrelevant, and in no way diminishes Benjamin's rights as finder.

The scenario unfolded in this case convinces me that the money found in the airplane wing was abandoned. Property is abandoned when the owner no longer wants to possess it. *See Ritz*, 467 N.W.2d at 269; *Pearson v. City of Guttenberg*, 245 N.W.2d 519, 529 (Iowa 1976). The money had been there for years, possibly thirty. No owner had claimed it in that time. No claim was made by the owner after legally prescribed notice was given that it had been found. Thereafter, logic and the law support a finding that the owner has voluntarily relinquished all right, title, and interest in the property. Whether the money was abandoned due to its connection to illegal drug trafficking or is otherwise contraband property is a matter for speculation. In any event, abandonment by the true owner has legally occurred and been established.

I would hold that Benjamin is legally entitled to the entire amount of money that he found in the airplane wing as the owner of abandoned property.

HARRIS and ANDREASEN, JJ., join this dissent.

QUESTIONS

1. Leaving aside the question of whether the state legislature acquiesced over time, do you agree with the Iowa Supreme Court's interpretation of the Iowa statute? Why/why not? What do you think was the purpose behind the statute? Is the Iowa Supreme Court's interpretation consistent with this purpose?

2. The dissent argues that the property at issue was abandoned. Do you agree?

NOTES

1. *Lost, Mislaid, Abandoned, and Treasure Trove.* The common-law categories described in *Benjamin v. Lindner Aviation* are still applied (unmodified by any

statute) in many jurisdictions throughout the United States. The typical summary of the common-law rule is that, as between the finder and the owner of the locus, lost and abandoned property go to the finder, while mislaid property goes to the owner of the locus. Treasure trove also typically goes to the finder, though, as we will see in the next case, the law is not as uniform on this particular point.

> The distinctions between the lost, mislaid, and abandoned turn on possession. Unlike our prior possession-based issues, however, the distinctions turn on how the object left the true owner's possession, rather than how the object came into the true owner's possession.

The lost-mislaid distinction is best understood through examples. Imagine that you are walking down the street and your keys fall out of your pocket. Your keys are lost, because they left your possession involuntarily. Now imagine that you put your watch down on a table and later forget where it is. Your watch is mislaid, because you voluntarily placed it on the table, but later forgot where you put it. One justification for giving mislaid property to the owner of the locus is that the true owner is more likely to retrace her steps with mislaid property than with lost property. Giving ownership to the owner of the locus therefore makes it more likely that the true owner will be able to get her property back. Do you agree with this reasoning?

Note two things about the category of abandoned property. First, abandonment is a question of intent—for property to be abandoned, the true owner must intend to relinquish ownership. Second, as a result, the finder of abandoned property will win even against the true owner. Abandoned property is therefore an exception to our general rule that the true owner will always win.

The legal rules for lost, mislaid, and abandoned property are relatively clear in the abstract, but it can be hard to determine which category should be applied to a given found object. The majority and dissenting opinions in *Benjamin* provide a good example. It often is possible to come up with plausible stories about how the object got to the location where it was found that would allow us to fit the object into more than one category. One potential problem with legal rules that are this vague is that they provide little guidance to courts. Indeed, it is easy to imagine a court deciding which of the claimants (the finder and the owner of the locus) has a more sympathetic claim and then constructing an argument to justify placing the object into a category that will reach the court's desired result. Whether this kind of decisionmaking would be good or bad raises deep questions about legal theory. Generally speaking, however, we want our legal rules to be specific enough to lead to predictable outcomes.

2. *Contraband.* As suggested by the dissent, there is one other category of property that might have been relevant in *Benjamin*. *Contraband* is typically defined by statute to be property used in certain crimes, or the proceeds gained from crimes. Contraband is usually subject to seizure by the state. If the state cannot prove that the property is contraband, ownership of the property will turn on the finding rules that we have been discussing. *See State v. $281,420.00 in United States Currency*, 312 S.W.3d 547 (Tex. 2010).

CORLISS V. WENNER

Idaho Court of Appeals, 2001 34 P.3d 1100

SCHWARTZMAN, Chief Judge.

Gregory Corliss appeals from the district court's orders granting summary judgment in favor of Jann Wenner on the right to possess ninety-six gold coins unearthed by Anderson and Corliss on Wenner's property . . . . [Wenner is the co-founder and publisher of *Rolling Stone* magazine.—Ed.]. We affirm.

I. FACTUAL AND PROCEDURAL BACKGROUND

A. THE GOLD COINS

In the fall of 1996, Jann Wenner hired Anderson Asphalt Paving to construct a driveway on his ranch in Blaine County. Larry Anderson, the owner of Anderson Asphalt Paving, and his employee, Gregory Corliss, were excavating soil for the driveway when they unearthed a glass jar containing paper wrapped rolls of gold coins. Anderson and Corliss collected, cleaned, and inventoried the gold pieces dating from 1857 to 1914.[1] The coins themselves weighed about four pounds. Anderson and Corliss agreed to split the gold coins between themselves, with Anderson retaining possession of all the coins. At some point Anderson and Corliss argued over ownership of the coins and Anderson fired Corliss. Anderson later gave possession of the coins to Wenner in exchange for indemnification on any claim Corliss might have against him regarding the coins.

Corliss sued Anderson and Wenner for possession of some or all of the coins. Wenner, defending both himself and Anderson, filed a motion for summary judgment. The facts, except whether Corliss found all or just some of the gold coins without Anderson's help, are not in dispute. All parties agree that the coins were unearthed during excavation by Anderson and Corliss for a driveway on Wenner's ranch, that the coins had been protected in paper tube rolls and buried in a glass jar estimated to be about seventy years old. Following a hearing on Wenner's motion for summary judgment, the district court declined to grant the motion and allowed approximately five months for additional discovery. Six months later the court held a status conference at which counsel for Wenner and Anderson asked the court to rule on Wenner's motion and counsel for Corliss did not object. No new facts were offered.

The district court then entered a memorandum decision stating that the "finders keepers" rule of treasure trove had not been previously adopted in Idaho, that it was not a part of the common law of England incorporated into Idaho law at the time of statehood by statute, and that the coins, having been carefully concealed for safekeeping, fit within the legal classification of mislaid property, to which the right of possession goes to the land owner. Alternatively, the court ruled that the coins, like the topsoil being excavated, were a part of the property owned by Wenner and that Anderson and Corliss were merely Wenner's employees. Corliss appeals. . . .

---

1. Of the ninety-six coins gathered up by Anderson and Corliss, there were thirty-six five-dollar gold pieces with mint dates ranging from 1857 to 1909, twenty-two ten-dollar gold pieces dating from 1882 to 1910, and thirty-eight twenty-dollar gold pieces dating from 1870 to 1914. Corliss claimed the value of the coins was in excess of $30,000 and at oral argument offered a value of between $500,000 and $1,000,000. Counsel for Wenner countered that the value of the coins was between $25,000 and $30,000. There is no independent appraisal of the coins in the record.

II. Standard of Review

Summary judgment is proper only when there is no genuine issue of material fact and the moving party is entitled to judgment as a matter of law. I.R.C.P. 56(c); *Dunham v. Hackney Airpark, Inc.*, 133 Idaho 613, 616, 990 P.2d 1224, 1227 (Ct.App.1999) (citing *Edwards v. Conchemco, Inc.*, 111 Idaho 851, 852, 727 P.2d 1279, 1280 (Ct.App.1986)). In order to determine whether judgment should be entered as a matter of law, the trial court must review the pleadings, depositions, affidavits, and admissions on file. I.R.C.P. 56(c).

In general, a party opposing summary judgment is entitled to favorable inferences from the underlying facts. *See Tolmie Farms v. J.R. Simplot Co., Inc.*, 124 Idaho 607, 609, 862 P.2d 299, 301 (1993). In this case, we note that none of the parties requested a jury trial, thus the court was to be the trier of fact. Furthermore, at a status conference, held after allowing the completion of discovery into the antiquity of the coins, counsel for Wenner and Anderson stated that the case was ready for summary judgment. Counsel for Corliss stated that he had nothing to add to the record. "When the evidentiary facts are not disputed and the judge rather than the jury will be the ultimate trier of fact, the judge may draw the inferences he or she deems most probable since the judge alone would be responsible for drawing such inferences from the same facts at trial." *Dunham*, 133 Idaho at 616, 990 P.2d at 1227. Therefore, the court in this case was entitled to draw all reasonable inferences from the facts presented.

III. Law Applicable to Determining the Rightful Possessor of the Gold Coins

A. STANDARD APPLICABLE TO REVIEW OF THE DISTRICT COURT'S CHOICE OF LAW

This is a case of first impression in Idaho, the central issue being the proper rule to apply in characterizing the gold coins found by Corliss and Anderson on Wenner's property. The major distinctions between characterizations of found property turn on questions of fact, i.e., an analysis of the facts and circumstances in an effort to divine the intent of the true owner at the time he or she parted with the property. *See generally* 1 Am.Jur.2d *Abandoned, Lost and Unclaimed Property* §§ 1-14 (1994). The material facts and circumstances surrounding the discovery of the gold coins are not in dispute. However, the characterization of that property, in light of these facts, is a question of law over which we exercise free review. *Schley v. Couch*, 155 Tex. 195, 284 S.W.2d 333, 336 (1955) (While the character of property is determined from all the facts and circumstances in the particular case of the property found, the choice among categories of found property is a question of law.); *see also Batra v. Batra*, 135 Idaho 388, 392, 17 P.3d 889, 893 (Ct.App.2001) (The characterization of an asset as separate or community, in light of the facts found, is a question of law.). With these principles in mind we now discuss, in turn, the choice of categories applicable to the district court's characterization of the gold coins found by Anderson and Corliss, recognizing that the choice of characterization of found property determines its rightful possessor as between the finder and landowner.

B. CHOICE OF CATEGORIES

At common law all found property is generally categorized in one of five ways. *See Benjamin v. Lindner Aviation, Inc.*, 534 N.W.2d 400 (Iowa 1995); *see also*

36A C.J.S. *Finding Lost Goods* § 5 (1961); 1 Am.Jur.2d, *Abandoned, Lost, Etc.,* § 10 (1994). Those categories are:

- Abandoned Property—that which the owner has discarded or voluntarily forsaken with the intention of terminating his ownership, but without vesting ownership in any other person. *Terry v. Lock,* 343 Ark. 452, 37 S.W.3d 202, 206 (2001);
- Lost Property—that property which the owner has involuntarily and unintentionally parted with through neglect, carelessness, or inadvertence and does not know the whereabouts. Id; *Ritz v. Selma United Methodist Church,* 467 N.W.2d 266 (Iowa 1991);
- Mislaid Property—that which the owner has intentionally set down in a place where he can again resort to it, and then forgets where he put it. *Terry,* 37 S.W.3d at 206;
- Treasure Trove—a category exclusively for gold or silver in coin, plate, bullion, and sometimes its paper money equivalents, found concealed in the earth or in a house or other private place. *Id.* Treasure trove carries with it the thought of antiquity, i.e., that the treasure has been concealed for so long as to indicate that the owner is probably dead or unknown. 1 Am.Jur.2d *Abandoned, Lost, Etc.,* § 8 (1994);
- Embedded Property—that personal property which has become a part of the natural earth, such as pottery, the sunken wreck of a steamship, or a rotted-away sack of gold-bearing quartz rock buried or partially buried in the ground. *See Chance v. Certain Artifacts Found and Salvaged from the Nashville,* 606 F.Supp. 801 (S.D.Ga.1984); *Ferguson v. Ray,* 44 Or. 557, 77 P. 600 (1904).

Under these doctrines, the finder of lost or abandoned property and treasure trove acquires a right to possess the property against the entire world but the rightful owner regardless of the place of finding. *Terry,* 37 S.W.3d at 206. The finder of mislaid property is required to turn it over to the owner of the premises who has the duty to safeguard the property for the true owner. *Id.* Possession of embedded property goes to owner of the land on which the property was found. *Allred v. Biegel,* 240 Mo.App. 818, 219 S.W.2d 665 (1949) (citing *Elwes v. Brigg Gas Co.,* 33 Ch. D. 562 (Eng.1886)); 1 Am.Jur.2d *Abandoned, Lost, Etc.,* § 29.

One of the major distinctions between these various categories is that only lost property necessarily involves an element of involuntariness. *Campbell v. Cochran,* 416 A.2d 211, 221 (Del.Super.Ct.1980). The four remaining categories involve voluntary and intentional acts by the true owner in placing the property where another eventually finds it. *Id.* However, treasure trove, despite not being lost or abandoned property, is treated as such in that the right to possession is recognized to be in the finder rather than the premises owner.

C. DISCUSSION AND ANALYSIS

On appeal, Corliss argues that the district court should have interpreted the undisputed facts and circumstances surrounding the placement of the coins in the ground to indicate that the gold coins were either lost, abandoned, or treasure trove. Wenner argues that the property was properly categorized as either embedded or mislaid property.

As with most accidentally discovered buried treasure, the history of the original ownership of the coins is shrouded in mystery and obscured by time. The coins had been wrapped in paper, like coins from a bank, and buried in a glass jar, apparently for safekeeping. Based on these circumstances, the district court determined that the coins were not abandoned because the condition in which the coins were found evidenced an intent to keep them safe, not an intent to voluntarily relinquish all possessory interest in them. The district court also implicitly rejected the notion that the coins were lost, noting that the coins were secreted with care in a specific place to protect them from the elements and from other people until such time as the original owner might return for them. There is no indication that the coins came to be buried through neglect, carelessness, or inadvertence. Accordingly, the district court properly concluded, as a matter of law, that the coins were neither lost nor abandoned.

The district court then determined that the modern trend favored characterizing the coins as property either embedded in the earth or mislaid—under which the right of possession goes to the landowner—rather than treasure trove—under which the right of possession goes to the finder. Although accepted by a number of states prior to 1950, the modern trend since then, as illustrated by decisions of the state and federal courts, is decidedly against recognizing the "finders keepers" rule of treasure trove. *See, e.g., Klein v. Unidentified, Wrecked & Abandoned Sailing Vessel,* 758 F.2d 1511 (11th Cir.1985) (treasure and artifacts from a sunken sailing ship properly characterized as embedded property); *Ritz,* 467 N.W.2d 266 (silver coins and currency dated prior to 1910 and 1928 gold certificates buried in cans and jars under a garage floor classified as mislaid property); *Morgan v. Wiser,* 711 S.W.2d 220 (Tenn.Ct.App.1985) (gold coins found buried in an iron pot properly characterized as embedded property).

Corliss argues that the district court erred in deciding that the law of treasure trove should not apply in Idaho. However, the doctrine of treasure trove has never been adopted in this state. Idaho Code § 73-116 provides: "[t]he common law of England, so far as it is not repugnant to, or inconsistent with, the constitution or laws of the United States, in all cases not provided for in these compiled laws, is the rule of decision in all courts of this state." Nevertheless, the history of the "finders keepers" rule was not a part of the common law of England at the time the colonies gained their independence. Rather, the doctrine of treasure trove was created to determine a rightful possessor of buried Roman treasures discovered in feudal times. *See* Leeanna Izuel, *Property Owner's Constructive Possession of Treasure Trove: Rethinking the Finders Keepers Rule,* 38 U.C.L.A. L.Rev. 1659, 1666-67 (1991). And while the common law initially awarded the treasure to the finder, the crown, as early as the year 1130, exercised its royal prerogative to take such property for itself. *Id.* Only after the American colonies gained their independence from England did some states grant possession of treasure trove to the finder. *Id.* Thus, it does not appear that the "finders keepers" rule of treasure trove was a part of the common law of England as defined by Idaho Code § 73-116. We hold that the district court correctly determined that I.C. § 73-116 does not require the treasure trove doctrine to be adopted in Idaho.

Additionally, we conclude that the rule of treasure trove is of dubious heritage and misunderstood application, inconsistent with our values and traditions. The danger of adopting the doctrine of treasure trove is laid out in *Morgan,* 711 S.W.2d at 222-23:

[We] find the rule with respect to treasure-trove to be out of harmony with modern notions of fair play. The common-law rule of treasure-trove invites trespassers to roam at large over the property of others with their metal detecting devices and to dig wherever such devices tell them property might be found. If the discovery happens to fit the definition of treasure-trove, the trespasser may claim it as his own. To paraphrase another court: The mind refuses consent to the proposition that one may go upon the lands of another and dig up and take away anything he discovers there which does not belong to the owner of the land. [citation omitted]

The invitation to trespassers inherent in the rule with respect to treasure-trove is repugnant to the common law rules dealing with trespassers in general. The common-law made a trespass an actionable wrong without the necessity of showing any damage therefrom. Because a trespass often involved a breach of the peace and because the law was designed to keep the peace, the common law dealt severely with trespassers.

. . .

Recognizing the validity of the idea that the discouragement of trespassers contributes to the preservation of the peace in the community, we think this state should not follow the common law rule with respect to treasure-trove. Rather, we adopt the rule suggested in the concurring opinion in *Schley v. Couch*, [. . .] which we restate as follows:

Where property is found embedded in the soil under circumstances repelling the idea that it has been lost, the finder acquires no title thereto, for the presumption is that the possession of the article found is in the owner of the locus in quo.

Land ownership includes control over crops on the land, buildings and appurtenances, soils, and minerals buried under those soils. The average Idaho landowner would expect to have a possessory interest in any object uncovered on his or her property. And certainly the notion that a trespassing treasure hunter, or a hired handyman or employee, could or might have greater possessory rights than a landowner in objects uncovered on his or her property runs counter to the reasonable expectations of present-day land ownership.[2]

There is no reason for a special rule for gold and silver coins, bullion, or plate as opposed to other property. Insofar as personal property (money and the like) buried or secreted on privately owned realty is concerned, the distinctions between treasure trove, lost property, and mislaid property are anachronistic and of little value. The principle point of such distinctions is the intent of the true owner which, absent some written declaration indicating such, is obscured in the mists of time and subject to a great deal of speculation.[3]

By holding that property classed as treasure trove (gold or silver coins, bullion, plate) in other jurisdictions is classed in Idaho as personal property embedded in the soil, subject to the same limitations as mislaid property, possession will be awarded to the owner of the soil as a matter of law. Thus, we craft a simple and reasonable solution to the problem, discourage trespass, and avoid the risk of speculating about the true owner's intent when attempting to infer such from the manner and circumstances in which an object is found. Additionally, the true owner, if any, will have the opportunity to recover the property.

---

2. We note that nothing would prevent a would-be treasure hunter or hired builder or excavator from contracting some type of arrangement where the right of possession is shared or purchased outright.

3. As one commentator has wryly noted, "The old rule of treasure trove may make good theater, but it's poor law, and its death can come none to[*sic*] soon." Richard B. Cunningham, *The Slow Death of the Treasure Trove*, Archaeology (Feb. 7, 2000).

D. CONCLUSION

We hold that the owner of the land has constructive possession of all personal property secreted in, on or under his or her land. Accordingly, we adopt the district court's reasoning and conclusion melding the law of mislaid property with that of embedded property and conclude, as a matter of law, that the landowner is entitled to possession to the exclusion of all but the true owner, absence a contract between the landowner and finder. . . .

NOTES

1. *Treasure Trove vs. Embedded.* As the court explained in *Corliss,* there is a tension between the treasure trove and embedded categories. The two overlap to a significant degree, and reach opposite results—treasure trove goes to the finder, while embedded property goes to the owner of the locus. Based on the discussion in *Corliss,* what do you think is the right approach and why? Don't limit yourself to the two existing categories. If you were going to set up the rules on the ownership of buried treasure, what would you do?

2. *Other Relevant Factors.* In addition to the lost/mislaid/abandoned/treasure trove/embedded classifications, disputes between the finder and the owner of the premises where the object was found might also turn, at least in part, on these other issues:

a. Was the finder on the property in some kind of inferior legal position to the owner of the premises? Some of the court's reasoning in *Corliss* suggests that a finder who is a trespasser might have a harder time winning than a finder who was on the property as an invited guest. Similarly, a finder who is on the property as an employee or other agent of the owner of the premises might have a relatively weaker claim to found property. Indeed, the holding in *Corliss v. Wenner* could have been based on the alternative ground that Corliss and Anderson were working as Wenner's agents.

b. Was the property found in a public or private part of the premises? The owner of a shop, for example, might have a stronger expectation that they would be entitled to property found in the private areas of the premises than to property found in the areas open to the public.

c. Was the finder honest? Courts always like honesty. In the leading English case of *Hannah v. Peel,* [1945] K.B. 509, the court seemed impressed that the finder had been honest and turned the found property over to the police.

3. *The True Owner Always Wins.* Don't forget about the true owner, who will win against both the finder and the owner of the premises. In one recent case, a contractor named Bob Kitts found $182,000 in Depression-era currency hidden in a wall. Kitts and the owner of the house, Amanda Reece, couldn't agree on how to split the money, and the dispute between the two ended up in court. Press coverage of the lawsuit drew claims from the heirs of a former owner of the house, who purportedly was the true owner of the money. Some of the money disappeared, and no one ended up happy. *See* "Found: $182,000 and a Lot of Grief," *Washington Post* (Nov. 9, 2008), *http://www.washingtonpost.com/wp-dyn/content/article/2008/11/08/AR2008110802248.html.*

Problems

In each of the following fact patterns, apply the common-law categories described in *Benjamin* and *Corliss* and presume that the jurisdiction does not have any applicable statutes. Explanatory answers can be found on page 1029.

1. Cindy's Cinful Chocolates is a retail store owned by Cindy Wu. One day Paul Prescott was shopping in Cindy's store when he noticed a backpack on the floor by the door. Paul picked up the backpack and showed it to Cindy, asking if she knew whose it was. Cindy didn't know. Thinking he'd find some identification of the owner, Paul opened the backpack. It turned out that it was full of bundles of new $20 bills, $15,300 worth in all. The true owner was never identified, and Paul and Cindy soon ended up in a dispute over ownership of the money. Which one of them has a better claim? Would your answer change if the money had been found in a small envelope, rather than in a backpack? How about if the money was found in a small envelope, but the envelope was found on the counter, rather than the floor?

2. One day, Ryan Gual was walking in a small park. The park was located on land owned by Theresa Simmons, who allowed the public to access the park. Ryan was walking along a path when he noticed a small gully that appeared to have been created by a recent rainstorm. He saw a glint of metal and when looking closer noticed a gold ring set with diamonds sitting on the dirt in the gully. He picked it up and brought it to a jeweler. The jeweler cleaned the ring, which was very dirty, and said that it was more than a hundred years old. Theresa heard through the grapevine about Ryan's find, and now the two are in a dispute about ownership of the ring. Which one of them has a better claim?

e. Finding Remedies and the Rule of Capture, Again

All of the finder versus owner of the locus cases we have seen so far have led to all-or-nothing results—either the finder wins or the owner of the locus wins. There are other possible ways of resolving these disputes. One is suggested in *Benjamin v. Lindner Aviation*, where the Iowa statute provided that a finder would get a 10 percent reward before the property was returned to the true owner. A similar system could be made between finders and the owner of the locus. Having a rule where the finder gets something would, among other things, encourage finders to be honest.

The possibility of sharing the value of the found object raises a larger point about how we approach legal issues. In our adversary legal system, disputes are typically framed in terms of which of two (or more) parties should win on any given issue. Sometimes we might be better off if instead we ask a different question. Rather than ask "who should win, A or B?," we might ask "what is the best resolution of this dispute?" This more abstract question might lead us to think more about the best outcome and would give us more options than the binary choice between giving all or nothing to A and B. Our next case illustrates the potential strengths and weaknesses of this alternative approach. It also includes a sophisticated discussion of our primary topic, possession.

f.   Gifts of Personal Property

ENGAGEMENT RINGS

What happens to an engagement ring if the engagement is later broken off? Engagement rings are often viewed as a type of conditional gift—that is, a gift intended to be permanent on the happening of a condition, here, marriage. In some jurisdictions, the ring must be returned if the recipient was responsible for calling off the marriage, but need not be returned if the donor was responsible for breaking the engagement. Other states have adopted a no-fault rule, where the ring must be returned regardless of who was responsible. *See* Elaine Marie Tomko, *Rights in Respect of Engagement and Courtship Presents When Marriage Does Not Ensue*, 44 A.L.R.5th 1 (1996).

Our next case involves the gift of a painting. To give you the background needed to fully understand the case, we need to introduce the concept of present and future interests in property. We will cover this topic in depth in the next chapter. For now, you need to know that we can split ownership of property over time, with one person owning the present interest and another person owning the future interest. (As we will see, there can be multiple owners of present and future interests; for now, we will focus on one present interest holder and one future interest holder.) The owner of the present interest has all of the rights of possession, use, and exclusion that we typically associate with the ownership of property. The future interest holder will not have any of these rights until the present interest expires.

One type of present interest is a life estate. As its name implies, a life estate lasts for the present interest holder's life and expires at the present interest holder's death. The owner of property could convey the property "to Father for life, then to Son." In this conveyance, Father has a life estate, and Son has a type of future interest called a remainder. Father will be the present owner of the property during his life. He will have all of the rights to possess, use, and exclude that we typically associate with property ownership. (The right to alienate is a little bit more complicated—we will leave that discussion to our next chapter.) During Father's life, Son will have no present rights in the property. When Father dies, Son will then become the present owner of the property and will have the attendant rights of possession, use, and exclusion.

You might have a host of questions about how present and future interests work. Hold on to those questions until we get to our chapter on present and future interests. One thing that you need to know now is that future interests are property interests that exist at the time of creation. In our example above, Son's remainder interest existed from the time the conveyance was made. The remainder interest will become possessory, giving Son all of the basic rights of ownership, later when Father dies. But the future interest itself was created at the time of conveyance.

Understanding that future interests exist at the time of conveyance is crucial to understanding our next case. Like our example, the case involves a father and son. The father already owned the item that he gave to his son. The father wanted to keep possession of the item during his life, so his conveyance took this form: "to myself for life, then to my son." As we have been discussing, the son's future interest existed at the time the father made the gift. We already know that there is an important distinction between gifts made during life and gifts made at death. Because the future interest is created at the time of conveyance, when the father is alive, the gift of the future interest is an *inter vivos* gift. It may help you understand the case to remember that a valid *inter vivos* gift is irrevocable. If the father's conveyance of "to myself for life, then to my son" meets all of the elements of a valid *inter vivos* gift, then the father can't later change his mind and retract the gift.

GRUEN V. GRUEN

New York Court of Appeals, 1986 496 N.E.2d 869

SIMONS, Judge. Plaintiff commenced this action seeking a declaration that he is the rightful owner of a painting which he alleges his father, now deceased, gave to him. He concedes that he has never had possession of the painting but asserts that his father made a valid gift of the title in 1963 reserving a life estate for himself. His father retained possession of the painting until he died in 1980. Defendant, plaintiff's stepmother, has the painting now and has refused plaintiff's requests that she turn it over to him. She contends that the purported gift was testamentary in nature and invalid insofar as the formalities of a will were not met or, alternatively, that a donor may not make a valid inter vivos gift of a chattel and retain a life estate with a complete right of possession. Following a seven-day nonjury trial, Special Term found that plaintiff had failed to establish any of the elements of an inter vivos gift and that in any event an attempt by a donor to retain a present possessory life estate in a chattel invalidated a purported gift of it. The Appellate Division held that a valid gift may be made reserving a life estate and, finding the elements of a gift established in this case, it reversed and remitted the matter for a determination of value (104 A.D.2d 171, 488 N.Y.S.2d 401). That determination has now been made and defendant appeals directly to this court, pursuant to CPLR 5601(d), from the subsequent final judgment entered in Supreme Court awarding plaintiff $2,500,000 in damages representing the value of the painting, plus interest. We now affirm.

The subject of the dispute is a work entitled "Schloss Kammer am Attersee II" painted by a noted Austrian modernist, Gustav Klimt. It was purchased by plaintiff's father, Victor Gruen, in 1959 for $8,000. On April 1, 1963 the elder Gruen, a successful architect with offices and residences in both New York City and Los Angeles during most of the time involved in this action, wrote a letter to plaintiff, then an undergraduate student at Harvard, stating that he was giving him the Klimt painting for his birthday but that he wished to retain the possession of it for his lifetime. This letter is not in evidence, apparently because plaintiff destroyed it on instructions from his father. Two other letters were received, however, one dated May 22, 1963 and the other April 1, 1963. Both had been dictated by Victor Gruen and sent together to plaintiff on or about May 22, 1963. The letter dated May 22, 1963 reads as follows:

Dear Michael:

I wrote you at the time of your birthday about the gift of the painting by Klimt.

Now my lawyer tells me that because of the existing tax laws, it was wrong to mention in that letter that I want to use the painting as long as I live. Though I still want to use it, this should not appear in the letter. I am enclosing, therefore, a new letter and I ask you to send the old one back to me so that it can be destroyed.

I know this is all very silly, but the lawyer and our accountant insist that they must have in their possession copies of a letter which will serve the purpose of making it possible for you, once I die, to get this picture without having to pay inheritance taxes on it.

Love,
s/Victor

Enclosed with this letter was a substitute gift letter, dated April 1, 1963, which stated:

Dear Michael:

The 21st birthday, being an important event in life, should be celebrated accordingly. I therefore wish to give you as a present the oil painting by Gustav Klimt of Schloss Kammer which now hangs in the New York living room. You know that Lazette and I bought it some 5 or 6 years ago, and you always told us how much you liked it.

Happy birthday again.

Love,
s/Victor

Plaintiff never took possession of the painting nor did he seek to do so. Except for a brief period between 1964 and 1965 when it was on loan to art exhibits and when restoration work was performed on it, the painting remained in his father's possession, moving with him from New York City to Beverly Hills and finally to Vienna, Austria, where Victor Gruen died on February 14, 1980. Following Victor's death plaintiff requested possession of the Klimt painting and when defendant refused, he commenced this action.

The issues framed for appeal are whether a valid inter vivos gift of a chattel may be made where the donor has reserved a life estate in the chattel and the donee never has had physical possession of it before the donor's death and, if it may, which factual findings on the elements of a valid inter vivos gift more nearly comport with the weight of the evidence in this case, those of Special Term or those of the Appellate Division. The latter issue requires application of two general rules. First, to make a valid inter vivos gift there must exist the intent on the part of the donor to make a present transfer; delivery of the gift, either actual or constructive to the donee; and acceptance by the donee (*Matter of Szabo*, 10 N.Y.2d 94, 98, 217 N.Y.S.2d 593, 176 N.E.2d 395; *Matter of Kelly*, 285 N.Y. 139, 150, 33 N.E.2d 62 [dissenting in part opn]; *Matter of Van Alstyne*, 207 N.Y. 298, 306, 100 N.E. 802; *Beaver v. Beaver*, 117 N.Y. 421, 428, 22 N.E. 940). Second, the proponent of a gift has the burden of proving each of these elements by clear and convincing evidence (*Matter of Kelley, supra*, 285 N.Y. at p. 150, 33 N.E.2d 62; *Matter of Abramowitz*, 38 A.D.2d 387, 389-390, 329 N.Y.S.2d 932, *affd. on opn.* 32 N.Y.2d 654, 342 N.Y.S.2d 855, 295 N.E.2d 654).

DONATIVE INTENT

There is an important distinction between the intent with which an inter vivos gift is made and the intent to make a gift by will. An inter vivos gift requires that the donor intend to make an irrevocable present transfer of ownership; if the intention is to make a testamentary disposition effective only after death, the gift is invalid unless made by will (*see, McCarthy v. Pieret*, 281 N.Y. 407, 409, 24 N.E.2d 102; *Gannon v. McGuire*, 160 N.Y. 476, 481, 55 N.E. 7; *Martin v. Funk*, 75 N.Y. 134, 137-138).

Defendant contends that the trial court was correct in finding that Victor did not intend to transfer any present interest in the painting to plaintiff in 1963 but only expressed an intention that plaintiff was to get the painting upon his death. The evidence is all but conclusive, however, that Victor intended to transfer ownership of the painting to plaintiff in 1963 but to retain a life estate in it and that he did, therefore, effectively transfer a remainder interest in the painting to plaintiff at that time. Although the original letter was not in evidence, testimony of its contents was received along with the substitute gift letter and its covering letter dated May 22, 1963. The three letters should be considered together as a single instrument (*see, Matter of Brandreth*, 169 N.Y. 437, 440, 62 N.E. 563) and when they are they unambiguously establish that Victor Gruen intended to make a present gift of title to the painting at that time. But there was other evidence for after 1963 Victor made several statements orally and in writing indicating that he had previously given plaintiff the painting and that plaintiff owned it. Victor Gruen retained possession of the property, insured it, allowed others to exhibit it and made necessary repairs to it but those acts are not inconsistent with his retention of a life estate. Furthermore, whatever probative value could be attached to his statement that he had bequeathed the painting to his heirs, made 16 years later when he prepared an export license application so that he could take the painting out of Austria, is negated by the overwhelming evidence that he intended a present transfer of title in 1963. Victor's failure to file a gift tax return on the transaction was partially explained by allegedly erroneous legal advice he received, and while that omission sometimes may indicate that the donor had no intention of making a present gift, it does not necessarily do so and it is not dispositive in this case.

Defendant contends that even if a present gift was intended, Victor's reservation of a lifetime interest in the painting defeated it. She relies on a statement from *Young v. Young*, 80 N.Y. 422 that "'[a]ny gift of chattels which expressly reserves the use of the property to the donor for a certain period, or . . . as long as the donor shall live, is ineffectual'" (*id.*, at p. 436, quoting 2 Schouler, *Personal Property*, at 118). The statement was dictum, however, and the holding of the court was limited to a determination that an attempted gift of bonds in which the donor reserved the interest for life failed because there had been no delivery of the gift, either actual or constructive (*see, id.*, at p. 434; *see also, Speelman v. Pascal*, 10 N.Y.2d 313, 319-320, 222 N.Y.S.2d 324, 178 N.E.2d 723). The court expressly left undecided the question "whether a remainder in a chattel may be created and given by a donor by carving out a life estate for himself and transferring the remainder" (*Young v. Young, supra*, at p. 440). We answered part of that question in *Matter of Brandreth* (169 N.Y. 437, 441-442, 62 N.E. 563, *supra*) when we held that "[in] this state a life estate and remainder can be created in a chattel or a fund the same as in real property." The case did not require us to decide whether there could be a valid gift of the remainder.

Defendant recognizes that a valid inter vivos gift of a remainder interest can be made not only of real property but also of such intangibles as stocks and bonds. Indeed, several of the cases she cites so hold. That being so, it is difficult to perceive any legal basis for the distinction she urges which would permit gifts of remainder interests in those properties but not of remainder interests in chattels such as the Klimt painting here. The only reason suggested is that the gift of a chattel must include a present right to possession. The application of *Brandreth* to permit a gift of the remainder in this case, however, is consistent with the distinction, well recognized in the law of gifts as well as in real property law, between ownership and possession or enjoyment (*see, Speelman v. Pascal,* 10 N.Y.2d 313, 318, 222 N.Y.S.2d 324, 178 N.E.2d 723, *supra; McCarthy v. Pieret,* 281 N.Y. 407, 409-411, 24 N.E.2d 102, *supra; Matter of Brandreth,* 169 N.Y. 437, 442, 62 N.E. 563, *supra*). Insofar as some of our cases purport to require that the donor intend to transfer both title and possession immediately to have a valid inter vivos gift (*see, Gannon v. McGuire,* 160 N.Y. 476, 481, 55 N.E. 7, *supra; Young v. Young,* 80 N.Y. 422, 430, *supra*), they state the rule too broadly and confuse the effectiveness of a gift with the transfer of the possession of the subject of that gift. The correct test is "'whether the maker intended the [gift] to have *no effect* until after the maker's death, or whether he intended it to transfer *some present interest*'" (*McCarthy v. Pieret,* 281 N.Y. 407, 409, 24 N.E.2d 102, *supra* [emphasis added]; *see also,* 25 N.Y.Jur., Gifts, § 14, at 156-157). As long as the evidence establishes an intent to make a present and irrevocable transfer of title or the right of ownership, there is a present transfer of some interest and the gift is effective immediately (see, *Matter of Brady,* 228 App. Div. 56, 60, 239 N.Y.S. 5, *affd. no opn.* 254 N.Y. 590, 173 N.E. 879; *In re Sussman's Estate,* 125 N.Y.S.2d 584, 589-591, *affd. no opn.* 283 App. Div. 1051, 134 N.Y.S.2d 586, *Matter of Valentine,* 122 Misc. 486, 489, 204 N.Y.S. 284; Brown, *Personal Property* § 48, at 133-136 [2d ed]; 25 N.Y.Jur., Gifts, § 30, at 173-174; *see also, Farmers' Loan & Trust Co. v. Winthrop,* 238 N.Y. 477, 485-486, 144 N.E. 686). Thus, in *Speelman v. Pascal* (*supra*), we held valid a gift of a percentage of the future royalties to the play "My Fair Lady" before the play even existed. There, as in this case, the donee received title or the right of ownership to some property immediately upon the making of the gift but possession or enjoyment of the subject of the gift was postponed to some future time.

Defendant suggests that allowing a donor to make a present gift of a remainder with the reservation of a life estate will lead courts to effectuate otherwise invalid testamentary dispositions of property. The two have entirely different characteristics, however, which make them distinguishable. Once the gift is made it is irrevocable and the donor is limited to the rights of a life tenant not an owner. Moreover, with the gift of a remainder title vests immediately in the donee and any possession is postponed until the donor's death whereas under a will neither title nor possession vests immediately. Finally, the postponement of enjoyment of the gift is produced by the express terms of the gift not by the nature of the instrument as it is with a will (*see, Robb v. Washington & Jefferson Coll.,* 185 N.Y. 485, 493, 78 N.E. 359).

DELIVERY

In order to have a valid inter vivos gift, there must be a delivery of the gift, either by a physical delivery of the subject of the gift or a constructive or symbolic delivery such as by an instrument of gift, sufficient to divest the donor of dominion and control over the property (*see, Matter of Szabo,* 10 N.Y.2d 94, 98-99, 217 N.Y.S.2d 593, 176 N.E.2d 395, *supra; Speelman v. Pascal,* 10 N.Y.2d 313, 318-320, 222 N.Y.S.2d 324, 178 N.E.2d 723, *supra; Beaver v. Beaver,* 117 N.Y. 421, 428-429, 22 N.E. 940, *supra; Matter of Cohn,* 187 App. Div. 392, 395, 176 N.Y.S.2d 225). As the statement of the rule suggests, the requirement of delivery is not rigid or inflexible, but is to be applied in light of its purpose to avoid mistakes by donors and fraudulent claims by donees (*see, Matter of Van Alstyne,* 207 N.Y. 298, 308, 100 N.E. 802, *supra; Matter of Cohn, supra,* 187 App. Div. at pp. 395-396, 176 N.Y.S.2d 255; Mechem, *Requirement of Delivery in Gifts of Chattels and of Choses in Actions Evidenced by Commercial Instruments,* 21 Ill. L. Rev. 341, 348-349). Accordingly, what is sufficient to constitute delivery "must be tailored to suit the circumstances of the case" (*Matter of Szabo, supra,* 10 N.Y.2d at p. 98, 217 N.Y.S.2d 593, 176 N.E.2d 395). The rule requires that "'[t]he delivery necessary to consummate a gift must be as perfect as the nature of the property and the circumstances and surroundings of the parties will reasonably permit'" (*id.; Vincent v. Rix,* 248 N.Y. 76, 83, 161 N.E. 425; *Matter of Van Alstyne, supra,* 207 N.Y. at p. 309, 100 N.E. 802; *see, Beaver v. Beaver, supra,* 117 N.Y. at p. 428, 22 N.E. 940).

Defendant contends that when a tangible piece of personal property such as a painting is the subject of a gift, physical delivery of the painting itself is the best form of delivery and should be required. Here, of course, we have only delivery of Victor Gruen's letters which serve as instruments of gift. Defendant's statement of the rule as applied may be generally true, but it ignores the fact that what Victor Gruen gave plaintiff was not all rights to the Klimt painting, but only title to it with no right of possession until his death. Under these circumstances, it would be illogical for the law to require the donor to part with possession of the painting when that is exactly what he intends to retain.

Nor is there any reason to require a donor making a gift of a remainder interest in a chattel to physically deliver the chattel into the donee's hands only to have the donee redeliver it to the donor. As the facts of this case demonstrate, such a requirement could impose practical burdens on the parties to the gift while serving the delivery requirement poorly. Thus, in order to accomplish this type of delivery the parties would have been required to travel to New York for the symbolic transfer and redelivery of the Klimt painting which was hanging on the wall of Victor Gruen's Manhattan apartment. Defendant suggests that such a requirement would be stronger evidence of a completed gift, but in the absence of witnesses to the event or any written confirmation of the gift it would provide less protection against fraudulent claims than have the written instruments of gift delivered in this case.

ACCEPTANCE

Acceptance by the donee is essential to the validity of an inter vivos gift, but when a gift is of value to the donee, as it is here, the law will presume an acceptance on his part (*Matter of Kelsey,* 26 N.Y.2d 792, 309 N.Y.S.2d 219, 257 N.E.2d 663, *affg. on opn. at* 29 A.D.2d 450, 456, 289 N.Y.S.2d 314; *Beaver v. Beaver,* 117 N.Y. 421, 429, 22 N.E. 940, *supra*). Plaintiff did not rely on this presumption alone but also presented clear and convincing proof of his acceptance of a remainder interest in the Klimt painting by evidence that he had made several contemporaneous statements acknowledging the gift to his friends and associates, even showing some of them his father's gift letter, and that he had retained both letters for over 17 years to verify the gift after his father died. Defendant relied exclusively on affidavits filed by plaintiff in a matrimonial action with his former wife, in which plaintiff failed to list his interest in the painting as an asset. These affidavits were made over 10 years after acceptance was complete and they do not even approach the evidence in *Matter of Kelly* (285 N.Y. 139, 148-149, 33 N.E.2d 62 [dissenting in part opn.], *supra*) where the donee, immediately upon delivery of a diamond ring, rejected it as "too flashy." We agree with the Appellate Division that interpretation of the affidavit was too speculative to support a finding of rejection and overcome the substantial showing of acceptance by plaintiff.

Accordingly, the judgment appealed from and the order of the Appellate Division brought up for review should be affirmed, with costs.

NOTES AND QUESTIONS

1. Make sure that you understand the court's analysis of each of the elements of a valid *inter vivos* gift. In particular, be sure that you do not misunderstand the holding of the case. *Gruen does not* stand for the proposition that it is possible to make a valid *inter vivos* gift of a painting by giving the donee a written document stating that "I want you to have this painting when I die." Be sure that you understand why.

2. As you think about the court's discussion of the delivery element, keep two questions in mind. First, is there any practical way of making a delivery of a future interest other than symbolically? Second, if Victor had wanted to make an outright gift of the painting, rather than reserving a life estate for himself, could he have satisfied the delivery requirement symbolically? For this second question, you may want to review our discussion of the delivery element from the beginning of this section.

3. Make a note to come back and reread *Gruen* again after you have finished our chapter on present and future interests in property, especially if you are not completely confident in your understanding of the case now.

4. After the litigation was complete, Michael sold the painting at auction in 1987 for $5.3 million. It sold in the late 1990s for $23.5 million and is currently housed in the Galleria Nazionale d'Arte Moderna in Rome, Italy.

Problems

Consider whether a valid *inter vivos* gift was made in each of the following scenarios. Explanatory answers can be found on page 1031.

1. Maurice Eto was crossing Main Street one day last month when he was struck by a car. Maurice was very seriously injured, and as the ambulance was taking him away, Maurice said to Sally, one of the paramedics, "I think I'm dying— here, I want you to have this ring." With that, he slipped the ring off his finger and handed it to Sally. Maurice recovered a few months later and now wants his ring back. Sally refused to return it, so Maurice has brought an action for replevin against her.

2. Theresa Spencer had a pretty good life. She did very well for herself in business and owned a number of classic cars. Last March, Theresa decided to give her 1973 Jaguar XKE to her oldest daughter Holly for Holly's 25th birthday.

Theresa gave Holly a card on her birthday that said in part "In honor of your 25th birthday, I hereby give you my 1973 Jag." Before Theresa could drive the car to Holly's house or give Holly the keys, Theresa was killed when she wrapped her Bentley around a telephone poll. Theresa left all of her personal property to the Symphony, and her executor has refused to let Holly have the Jaguar. As a result, Holly has brought a suit against the executor for possession of the car. In your answer, use the common-law rules of gifts that we have been studying and presume that the jurisdiction does not require ownership of cars to be transferred by written title.

3. Nick Kasisa was very close to his granddaughter Katie. Nick knew that Katie was very attached to a Tiffany lamp that he had in his living room. One day, Nick said to Katie, "Here, take the lamp and use it for now. You will own it when I die." Katie took the lamp and kept it in her apartment. Nick died recently, and left all his property to his son Mark. Mark and Katie never got along, and they are now in a dispute about ownership of the lamp.

B. COMPETING JUSTIFICATIONS FOR PROPERTY RIGHTS

Property serves many policy goals, and parties justify their claims with many arguments. Some of the core justifications for property claims include sovereign allocation of rights; efficiency or social welfare maximization; distributive justice or equality; settled expectations; labor and investment; and possession or occupancy of the property. You will see courts and litigants invoking various arguments along these lines throughout the materials in this book. In arguing for and evaluating legal claims, lawyers need to be able to identify and employ these arguments to support their legal assertions. This chapter provides an introduction to some of these justifications.

Justifications may point in different directions: one could argue that the first to occupy the property is not the one who will use it most efficiently, for example, or that the government-sanctioned distribution is unequal and therefore unjust. Different justifications may also support each other: awarding rights to the current possessor might encourage investment in the property; or correcting distributive inequalities may facilitate full and efficient use. Some may argue that particular justifications are more compelling than others. Today, for example, much scholarship focuses on economic efficiency, while early American common law placed more emphasis on protecting established expectations. But almost everyone recognizes multiple justifications for property rights. Although the sections below are divided among different kinds of arguments for property rights, you will see litigants and courts making multiple arguments within each section.

1. Property and Sovereignty

Property and sovereignty are inextricably linked. First, property is the product of sovereignty: without authoritative enforcement of rights to things—without, that is, a sovereign—many argue that there is no property. Second, property in effect delegates sovereign rights to owners—by creating control over use of valuable resources, property gives owners legal control over other individuals. Morris Cohen, *Property and Sovereignty*, 13 Cornell L.Q. 8 (1928).

What justifies sovereign power to allocate and set rules for control of valuable resources? What if there is conflict over which sovereign has that authority? What if the rules set by the sovereign violate justice, equality, efficiency, or expectations founded on other sources? As you will see, while sovereign allocation is a powerful source of property rights, governmental actors (whether judicial, legislative, or executive) sometimes enforce rights acquired in violation of official rules.

a.   United States and American Indian Sovereignty

In the United States, all land held by non-Indians theoretically can be traced to title ultimately derived from the U.S. government or a prior colonial power, which in turn obtained title from an American Indian nation. In the mid-fifteenth century, an estimated five to ten million native inhabitants occupied the land mass that is now the United States. By a process of cultural extermination and diseases such as measles and smallpox, the population of American Indians shrank to about 200,000 by 1910. Louise Erdrich notes that this "is proportionately as if the population of the United States were to decrease from its present level to the population of Cleveland." Louise Erdrich, *Where I Ought to Be: A Writer's Sense of Place*, N.Y. Times Book Rev., July 28, 1985, at 1, 23.

European nations colonizing the Americas initially distributed the land without regard to Indian property rights. Asserting divine authority, they granted charters to the Americas from sea to sea and pole to pole. But in North America, both colonial and British law soon required Indian consent to acquire rights in Indian lands. This "consent" was often coerced, forged, or misunderstood. Land acquisition created intense conflict, both between American Indian nations and settlers and among the settlers themselves, who disagreed both about whether a government could regulate their acquisition of Indian land and which government could do so.

Johnson v. M'Intosh, 21 U.S. (8 Wheat.) 543 (1823), involves a conflict between non-Indians over the acquisition of Indian land. The plaintiffs claimed to have obtained title directly from the Illinois and Piankeshaw Indians. The defendant was later granted title by the United States after the government entered into treaties with a number of Indian tribes. In adjudicating this dispute, the Supreme Court had the unenviable task of justifying the process by which American Indian nations were robbed of their ancestral lands. At the same time, Chief Justice John Marshall's opinion provided the basis for substantial legal protection of Indian possessions. How well did the Chief Justice do in attempting to reconcile the demands of justice and power?

JOHNSON V. M'INTOSH
21 U.S. 543 (1823)

[Joshua Johnson and Thomas Graham sued to eject William M'Intosh from certain lands in Illinois. Johnson and Graham claimed the lands by purchase from the Piankeshaw Indians, and M'Intosh claimed it under a grant from the United States. The parties stipulated to the following facts.

The lands were within those that the King of England had originally granted the Virginia Company in 1609. At the time of the grant this territory was "held, occupied, and possessed, in full sovereignty, by various independent tribes or nations of Indians, who were the sovereigns of their respective portions of the territory, and the absolute owners and proprietors of the soil." In 1624, the Virginia Company was dissolved, and it and its lands became the British colony of Virginia.

On October 7, 1763, the King of England issued the Royal Proclamation, reserving for the Indians all lands west of the Appalachians, and forbidding British subjects from purchasing or settling on any of those lands. In 1773, chiefs of the Illinois Nation sold William Murray and others two tracts of land west of the Appalachians for 24,000 dollars. The lands were within the limits of Virginia, east of the Mississippi and northwest of the Ohio Rivers. In 1775, certain chiefs of the Piankeshaw Nation sold Louis Viviat and others lands in the same area for $31,000.

In 1776, the colony of Virginia declared its independence from Great Britain. In 1779, the new State of Virginia decreed that it had the sole right to purchase lands from the Indians within its territory, and that any past or future purchases by individuals from the Indians were void. In 1783, Virginia conveyed all its lands northwest of the Ohio River to the United States. The lands ultimately became part of the State of Illinois. In 1803 and 1809 treaties, the United States acquired parts of the same territory previously purchased by Murray and Viviat from various Indian tribes. In 1818, the United States sold 11,560 acres of this territory to William M'Intosh.

Joshua Johnson and Thomas J. Graham inherited a portion of the lands purchased from the Piankeshaw in 1775 from one of the original private grantees. Neither they nor any of the grantees claiming under the 1773 and 1775 sales had ever had actual possession of the lands. The private grantees had, between 1781 and 1816, repeatedly petitioned the Congress of the United States to acknowledge and confirm their title to those lands without success.]

On the part of the plaintiffs, it was contended,

1. That . . . the Piankeshaw Indians were the owners of the lands in dispute, at the time of executing the deed of October 10th, 1775, and had power to sell. But as the United States had [later] purchased the same lands of the same Indians, both parties claim from the same source. [The Indian] title by occupancy is to be respected, as much as that of an individual, obtained by the same right, in a civilized state. The circumstance, that the members of the society held in common, did not affect the strength of their title by occupancy. In short, all, or nearly all, the lands in the United States, is holden under purchases from the Indian nations; and the only question in this case must be, whether it be competent to individuals to make such purchases, or whether that be the exclusive prerogative of government.

2. That the British king's proclamation of October 7th, 1763, could not affect this right of the Indians to sell; because they were not British subjects, nor in any manner bound by the authority of the British government, legislative or executive. And, because, even admitting them to be British subjects, absolutely, or sub modo, they were still proprietors of the soil, and could not be devested of their

rights of property, or any of its incidents, by a mere act of the executive government, such as this proclamation.

3. That the proclamation of 1763 could not restrain the purchasers under these deeds from purchasing. [T]he establishment of a government establishes a system of laws, and excludes the power of legislating by proclamation. The proclamation could not have the force of law within the chartered limits of Virginia. A proclamation, that no person should purchase land in England or Canada, would be clearly void.

4. That the act of Assembly of Virginia, passed in May, 1779, cannot affect the right of the plaintiffs, and others claiming under these deeds; because, on general principles, and by the constitution of Virginia, the legislature was not competent to take away private, vested rights, or appropriate private property to public use, under the circumstances of this case.

On the part of the defendants, it was insisted, that the uniform understanding and practice of European nations, and the settled law, as laid down by the tribunals of civilized states, denied the right of the Indians to be considered as independent communities, having a permanent property in the soil, capable of alienation to private individuals. They remain in a state of nature, and have never been admitted into the general society of nations. Even if it should be admitted that the Indians were originally an independent people, they have ceased to be so. A nation that has passed under the dominion of another, is no longer a sovereign state. The same treaties and negotiations, before referred to, show their dependent condition. Or, if it be admitted that they are now independent and foreign states, the title of the plaintiffs would still be invalid: as grantees from the Indians, they must take according to their laws of property, and as Indian subjects. The law of every dominion affects all persons and property situate within it; and the Indians never had any idea of individual property in lands. It cannot be said that the lands conveyed were disjoined from their dominion; because the grantees could not take the sovereignty and eminent domain to themselves.

. . . By the law of nature, [American Indians] had not acquired a fixed property capable of being transferred. The measure of property acquired by occupancy is determined, according to the law of nature, by the extent of men's wants, and their capacity of using it to supply them. It is a violation of the rights of others to exclude them from the use of what we do not want, and they have an occasion for. Upon this principle the North American Indians could have acquired no proprietary interest in the vast tracts of territory which they wandered over; and their right to the lands on which they hunted, could not be considered as superior to that which is acquired to the sea by fishing in it. The use in the one case, as well as the other, is not exclusive. According to every theory of property, the Indians had no individual rights to land; nor had they any collectively, or in their national capacity; for the lands occupied by each tribe were not used by them in such a manner as to prevent their being appropriated by a people of cultivators. All the proprietary rights of civilized nations on this continent are founded on this principle. . . .

Mr. Chief Justice JOHN MARSHALL delivered the opinion of the Court.

The plaintiffs in this cause claim the land, in their declaration mentioned, under two grants, purporting to be made, the first in 1773, and the last in 1775, by the chiefs of certain Indian tribes, constituting the Illinois and the Piankeshaw nations; and the question is, whether this title can be recognized in the Courts of the United States?

The facts, as stated in the case agreed, show the authority of the chiefs who executed this conveyance, so far as it could be given by their own people; and likewise show, that the particular tribes for whom these chiefs acted were in rightful possession of the land they sold. The inquiry, therefore, is, in a great measure, confined to the power of Indians to give, and of private individuals to receive, a title which can be sustained in the Courts of this country.

As the right of society, to prescribe those rules by which property may be acquired and preserved is not, and cannot be drawn into question; as the title to lands, especially, is and must be admitted to depend entirely on the law of the nation in which they lie; it will be necessary, in pursuing this inquiry, to examine, not singly those principles of abstract justice, which the Creator of all things has impressed on the mind of his creature man, and which are admitted to regulate, in a great degree, the rights of civilized nations, whose perfect independence is acknowledged; but those principles also which our own government has adopted in the particular case, and given us as the rule for our decision.

On the discovery of this immense continent, the great nations of Europe were eager to appropriate to themselves so much of it as they could respectively acquire. Its vast extent offered an ample field to the ambition and enterprise of all; and the character and religion of its inhabitants afforded an apology for considering them as a people over whom the superior genius of Europe might claim an ascendency. The potentates of the old world found no difficulty in convincing themselves that they made ample compensation to the inhabitants of the new, by bestowing on them civilization and Christianity, in exchange for unlimited independence. But, as they were all in pursuit of nearly the same object, it was necessary, in order to avoid conflicting settlements, and consequent war with each other, to establish a principle, which all should acknowledge as the law by which the right of acquisition, which they all asserted, should be regulated as between themselves. This principle was, that discovery gave title to the government by whose subjects, or by whose authority, it was made, against all other European governments, which title might be consummated by possession.

The exclusion of all other Europeans, necessarily gave to the nation making the discovery the sole right of acquiring the soil from the natives, and establishing settlements upon it. It was a right with which no Europeans could interfere. It was a right which all asserted for themselves, and to the assertion of which, by others, all assented.

Those relations which were to exist between the discoverer and the natives, were to be regulated by themselves. The rights thus acquired being exclusive, no other power could interpose between them.

In the establishment of these relations, the rights of the original inhabitants were, in no instance, entirely disregarded; but were necessarily, to a considerable extent, impaired. They were admitted to be the rightful occupants of the soil, with a legal as well as just claim to retain possession of it, and to use it according to their own discretion; but their rights to complete sovereignty, as independent nations, were necessarily diminished, and their power to dispose of the soil at their own will, to whomsoever they pleased, was denied by the original fundamental principle, that discovery gave exclusive title to those who made it.

While the different nations of Europe respected the right of the natives, as occupants, they asserted the ultimate dominion to be in themselves; and claimed and exercised, as a consequence of this ultimate dominion, a power to grant the soil, while yet in possession of the natives. These grants have been understood by all, to convey a title to the grantees, subject only to the Indian right of occupancy.

The history of America, from its discovery to the present day, proves, we think, the universal recognition of these principles.

No one of the powers of Europe gave its full assent to this principle, more unequivocally than England. The documents upon this subject are ample and complete. So early as the year 1496, her monarch granted a commission to the Cabots, to discover countries then unknown to Christian people, and to take possession of them in the name of the king of England. Two years afterwards, Cabot proceeded on this voyage, and discovered the continent of North America, along which he sailed as far south as Virginia. To this discovery the English trace their title.

[A]ll the nations of Europe, who have acquired territory on this continent, have asserted in themselves, and have recognized in others, the exclusive right of the discoverer to appropriate the lands occupied by the Indians. Have the American States rejected or adopted this principle?

By the treaty which concluded the war of our revolution, Great Britain relinquished all claim, not only to the government, but to the "propriety and territorial rights of the United States," whose boundaries were fixed in the second article. By this treaty, the powers of government, and the right to soil, which had previously been in Great Britain, passed definitively to these States. We had before taken possession of them, by declaring independence; but neither the declaration of independence, nor the treaty confirming it, could give us more than that which we before possessed, or to which Great Britain was before entitled. It has never been doubted, that either the United States, or the several States, had a clear title to all the lands within the boundary lines described in the treaty, subject only to the Indian right of occupancy, and that the exclusive power to extinguish that right, was vested in that government which might constitutionally exercise it.

The States, having within their chartered limits different portions of territory covered by Indians, ceded that territory, generally, to the United States, on conditions expressed in their deeds of cession, which demonstrate the opinion, that they ceded the soil as well as jurisdiction, and that in doing so, they granted a productive fund to the government of the Union. The lands in controversy lay within the chartered limits of Virginia, and were ceded with the whole country northwest of the river Ohio.

The ceded territory was occupied by numerous and warlike tribes of Indians; but the exclusive right of the United States to extinguish their title, and to grant the soil, has never, we believe, been doubted.

The magnificent purchase of Louisiana, was the purchase from France of a country almost entirely occupied by numerous tribes of Indians, who are in fact independent. Yet, any attempt of others to intrude into that country, would be considered as an aggression which would justify war.

Our late acquisitions from Spain are of the same character; and the negotiations which preceded those acquisitions, recognize and elucidate the principle which has been received as the foundation of all European title in America.

The United States, then, have unequivocally acceded to that great and broad rule by which its civilized inhabitants now hold this country. They hold, and assert in themselves, the title by which it was acquired. They maintain, as all others have maintained, that discovery gave an exclusive right to extinguish the Indian title of occupancy, either by purchase or by conquest; and gave also a right to such a degree of sovereignty, as the circumstances of the people would allow them to exercise.

The power now possessed by the government of the United States to grant lands, resided, while we were colonies, in the crown, or its grantees. The validity of the titles given by either has never been questioned in our Courts. It has been exercised uniformly over territory in possession of the Indians. The existence of this power must negative the existence of any right which may conflict with, and control it. An absolute title to lands cannot exist, at the same time, in different persons, or in different governments. An absolute, must be an exclusive title, or at least a title which excludes all others not compatible with it. All our institutions recognise the absolute title of the crown, subject only to the Indian right of occupancy, and recognise the absolute title of the crown to extinguish that right. This is incompatible with an absolute and complete title in the Indians.

We will not enter into the controversy, whether agriculturists, merchants, and manufacturers, have a right, on abstract principles, to expel hunters from the territory they possess, or to contract their limits. Conquest gives a title which the Courts of the conqueror cannot deny, whatever the private and speculative opinions of individuals may be, respecting the original justice of the claim which has been successfully asserted. The British government, which was then our government, and whose rights have passed to the United States, asserted title to all the lands occupied by Indians, within the chartered limits of the British colonies. It asserted also a limited sovereignty over them, and the exclusive right of extinguishing the title which occupancy gave to them. These claims have been maintained and established as far west as the river Mississippi, by the sword. The title to a vast portion of the lands we now hold, originates in them. It is not for the Courts of this country to question the validity of this title, or to sustain one which is incompatible with it.

Although we do not mean to engage in the defence of those principles which Europeans have applied to Indian title, they may, we think, find some excuse, if not justification, in the character and habits of the people whose rights have been wrested from them.

The title by conquest is acquired and maintained by force. The conqueror prescribes its limits. Humanity, however, acting on public opinion, has established, as a general rule, that the conquered shall not be wantonly oppressed, and that their condition shall remain as eligible as is compatible with the objects of the conquest. Most usually, they are incorporated with the victorious nation, and become subjects or citizens of the government with which they are connected. The new and old members of the society mingle with each other; the distinction between them is gradually lost, and they make one people. Where this incorporation is practicable, humanity demands, and a wise policy requires, that the rights of the conquered to property should remain unimpaired; that the new subjects should be governed as equitably as the old, and that confidence in their security should gradually banish the painful sense of being separated from their ancient connexions, and united by force to strangers.

When the conquest is complete, and the conquered inhabitants can be blended with the conquerors, or safely governed as a distinct people, public opinion, which not even the conqueror can disregard, imposes these restraints upon him; and he cannot neglect them without injury to his fame, and hazard to his power.

But the tribes of Indians inhabiting this country were fierce savages, whose occupation was war, and whose subsistence was drawn chiefly from the forest. To leave them in possession of their country, was to leave the country a wilderness; to govern them as a distinct people, was impossible, because they were as brave and as high spirited as they were fierce, and were ready to repel by arms every attempt on their independence.

What was the inevitable consequence of this state of things? The Europeans were under the necessity either of abandoning the country, and relinquishing their pompous claims to it, or of enforcing those claims by the sword, and by the adoption of principles adapted to the condition of a people with whom it was impossible to mix, and who could not be governed as a distinct society, or of remaining in their neighbourhood, and exposing themselves and their families to the perpetual hazard of being massacred.

Frequent and bloody wars, in which the whites were not always the aggressors, unavoidably ensued. European policy, numbers, and skill, prevailed. As the white population advanced, that of the Indians necessarily receded. The country in the immediate neighbourhood of agriculturists became unfit for them. The game fled into thicker and more unbroken forests, and the Indians followed. The soil, to which the crown originally claimed title, being no longer occupied by its ancient inhabitants, was parcelled out according to the will of the sovereign power, and taken possession of by persons who claimed immediately from the crown, or mediately, through its grantees or deputies.

That law which regulates, and ought to regulate in general, the relations between the conqueror and conquered, was incapable of application to a people under such circumstances. The resort to some new and different rule, better adapted to the actual state of things, was unavoidable. Every rule which can be suggested will be found to be attended with great difficulty.

However extravagant the pretension of converting the discovery of an inhabited country into conquest may appear; if the principle has been asserted in the first instance, and afterwards sustained; if a country has been acquired and held under it; if the property of the great mass of the community originates in it, it becomes the law of the land, and cannot be questioned. So, too, with respect to the concomitant principle, that the Indian inhabitants are to be considered merely as occupants, to be protected, indeed, while in peace, in the possession of their lands, but to be deemed incapable of transferring the absolute title to others. However this restriction may be opposed to natural right, and to the usages of civilized nations, yet, if it be indispensable to that system under which the country has been settled, and be adapted to the actual condition of the two people, it may, perhaps, be supported by reason, and certainly cannot be rejected by Courts of justice.

. . . The absolute ultimate title has been considered as acquired by discovery, subject only to the Indian title of occupancy, which title the discoverers possessed the exclusive right of acquiring. Such a right is no more incompatible with a seisin in fee, than a lease for years, and might as effectually bar an ejectment.

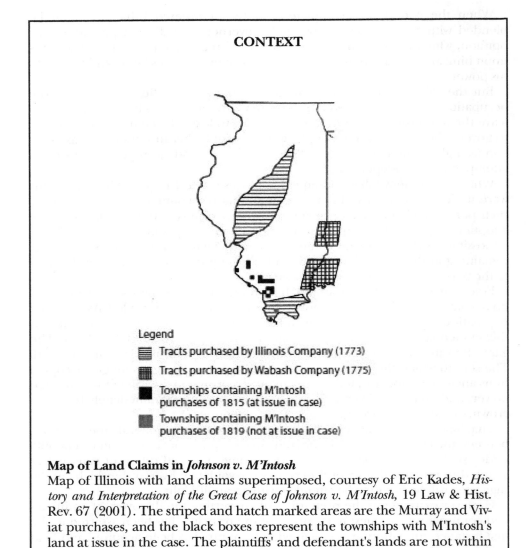

CONTEXT

Legend

▤ Tracts purchased by Illinois Company (1773)

▦ Tracts purchased by Wabash Company (1775)

■ Townships containing M'Intosh
purchases of 1815 (at issue in case)

▩ Townships containing M'Intosh
purchases of 1819 (not at issue in case)

Map of Land Claims in *Johnson v. M'Intosh*
Map of Illinois with land claims superimposed, courtesy of Eric Kades, *History and Interpretation of the Great Case of Johnson v. M'Intosh*, 19 Law & Hist. Rev. 67 (2001). The striped and hatch marked areas are the Murray and Viviat purchases, and the black boxes represent the townships with M'Intosh's land at issue in the case. The plaintiffs' and defendant's lands are not within 50 miles of each other (the gray box at the tip of Illinois includes M'Intosh land not challenged in the case). Why then did they pursue the claim?

Another view has been taken of this question, which deserves to be considered. The title of the crown, whatever it might be, could be acquired only by a conveyance from the crown. If an individual might extinguish the Indian title for his own benefit, or, in other words, might purchase it, still he could acquire only that title. Admitting their power to change their laws or usages, so far as to allow an individual to separate a portion of their lands from the common stock, and hold it in severalty, still it is a part of their territory, and is held under them, by a title dependent on their laws. The grant derives its efficacy from their will; and, if they choose to resume it, and make a different disposition of the land, the Courts of the United States cannot interpose for the protection of the title. The person who purchases lands from the Indians, within their territory, incorporates himself with them, so far as respects the property purchased; holds their title under their protection, and subject to their laws. If they annul the grant, we know of no tribunal which can revise and set aside the proceeding. We know of no principle which can distinguish this case from a grant made to a native Indian, authorizing him to hold a particular tract of land in severalty.

As such a grant could not separate the Indian from his nation, nor give a title which our Courts could distinguish from the title of his tribe, as it might still be conquered from, or ceded by his tribe, we can perceive no legal principle which will authorize a Court to say, that different consequences are attached to this purchase, because it was made by a stranger. By the treaties concluded between the United States and the Indian nations, whose title the plaintiffs claim, the country comprehending the lands in controversy has been ceded to the United States, without any reservation of their title. These nations had been at war with the United States, and had an unquestionable right to annul any grant they had made to American citizens. Their cession of the country, without a reservation of this land, affords a fair presumption, that they considered it as of no validity. They ceded to the United States this very property, after having used it in common with other lands, as their own, from the date of their deeds to the time of cession; and the attempt now made, is to set up their title against that of the United States.

It has never been contended, that the Indian title amounted to nothing. Their right of possession has never been questioned. The claim of government extends to the complete ultimate title, charged with this right of possession, and to the exclusive power of acquiring that right.

After bestowing on this subject a degree of attention which was more required by the magnitude of the interest in litigation, and the able and elaborate arguments of the bar, than by its intrinsic difficulty, the Court is decidedly of opinion, that the plaintiffs do not exhibit a title which can be sustained in the Courts of the United States.

NOTES AND QUESTIONS

1. Role of doctrine of discovery.   What was the purpose of the doctrine of discovery according to Justice Marshall? To whom did it apply?

2. Indian property rights under doctrine.   What property rights did Indian nations have under the doctrine? What rights do they lack? Imagine, for example, that a non-Indian individual without federal consent forced an Indian off her land. Does the Indian have a cause of action to remove him? *See Fellows v. Blacksmith*, 60 U.S. 366 (1856) (deciding whether non-Indian state grantees have right to forcibly dispossess Seneca Indian landowners).

3. United States property rights under doctrine.   What rights did the United States get in Indian lands under the doctrine of discovery? What property rights did they lack? Imagine, for example, that the United States grants an individual a right to lands subject to the Indian title of occupancy. What has to happen before the individual can legally move onto the land and start farming?

4. The courts of the conqueror.   At the beginning of the opinion, the court reporter summarizes the arguments made by the parties. Note that the opinion does not adopt either of these arguments. Instead, Justice Marshall declared, "Conquest gives a title which the Courts of the conqueror cannot deny, whatever the private and speculative opinions of individuals may be, respecting the original justice of the claim which has been successfully asserted." What does this mean? Can you tell what Justice Marshall's "private and speculative opinion" is of the original justice of the loss of Indian property rights through the doctrine of discovery?

5. Role of public opinion. Justice Marshall states that "[h]umanity" has established "as a general rule" that the property rights of a conquered people remain unchanged after conquest, declaring that "public opinion, which not even the conqueror can disregard, imposes these restraints upon him; and he cannot neglect them without injury to his fame, and hazard to his power." In *United States v. Percheman*, 32 U.S. 51 (1833), the Supreme Court followed this rule in interpreting various laws to validate titles to private citizens granted by Spain before the United States acquired Florida. Chief Justice Marshall's opinion explained, "The modern usage of nations, which has become law, would be violated; that sense of justice and of right which is acknowledged and felt by the whole civilized world would be outraged, if private property should be generally confiscated, and private rights annulled." *Percheman* at 86-87. Why does public opinion limit governmental actions? What are the costs to a government of ignoring public opinion? Why did the general rule not apply to Indian lands?

6. Later Supreme Court statements on Indian land. *Johnson v. M'Intosh* was among the earliest of many Supreme Court statements regarding Indian land. In 1831, Justice Marshall described the discovery doctrine in these words: "The extravagant and absurd idea, that the feeble settlements made on the sea coast, or the companies under whom they were made, acquired legitimate power by them to govern the people, or occupy the lands from sea to sea, did not enter the mind of any man. [All they gained] was the exclusive right of purchasing such lands as the natives were willing to sell." *Worcester v. Georgia*, 31 U.S. 515, 544-545 (1831). In 1835, the Court stated that "it [is] a settled principle, that [American Indians'] right of occupancy is considered as sacred as the fee simple of the whites." *Mitchel v. United States*, 34 U.S. 711, 746 (1835). Are these statements consistent with *Johnson v. M'Intosh*?

In *Tee-Hit-Ton Indians v. United States*, 348 U.S. 272 (1955), the Supreme Court rejected a claim by Alaska Native tribes against the United States for compensation for millions of acres of land. The Court held that although the fifth amendment provides that property shall not be taken without just compensation, U.S. Const., amdt. V, the Constitution did not protect tribal property unless the federal government had formally affirmed title to the land. The Court claimed to base its holding on "the rule derived from *Johnson v. M'Intosh* that the taking by the United States of unrecognized Indian title is not compensable under the Fifth Amendment":

> The line of cases adjudicating Indian rights on American soil leads to the conclusion that Indian occupancy, not specifically recognized as ownership by action authorized by Congress, may be extinguished by the Government without compensation. Every American schoolboy knows that the savage tribes of this continent were deprived of their ancestral ranges by force and that, even when the Indians ceded millions of acres by treaty in return for blankets, food and trinkets, it was not a sale but the conquerors' will that deprived them of their land.

In the light of the history of Indian relations in this Nation, no other course would meet the problem of the growth of the United States. Our conclusion does not uphold harshness as against tenderness toward the Indians, but it leaves with Congress, where it belongs, the policy of Indian gratuities for the termination of Indian occupancy of Government-owned land rather than making compensation for its value a rigid constitutional principle.

In 1884 and 1900, laws for the acquisition and settlement of the Alaska Territory, the United States had provided that the Indians "shall not be disturbed in the possession of any lands actually in their use or occupation or now claimed by them," but the Court found these laws did not recognize any property rights in the Alaska Natives, but simply reserved the question for another day. Therefore the Alaska Natives had no legal protection—besides the "Indian gratuities" Congress was willing to provide—for the acquisition of the lands they had occupied for centuries. Is *Tee-Hit-Ton* consistent with *Johnson*?

b.   Competing Justifications for Property Rights

Johnson v. M'Intosh, together with the arguments of the parties at the beginning of the opinion, is a rich source of competing justifications for property rights. To help you spot and evaluate these arguments in the rest of the book, let's trace some of these competing justifications. (Note, however, that *Johnson* has been the subject of perhaps hundreds of articles and multiple full-length books: the list below is necessarily incomplete.)

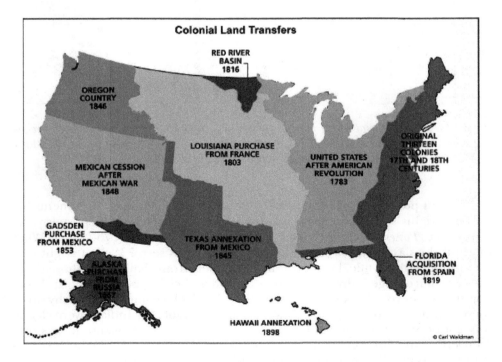

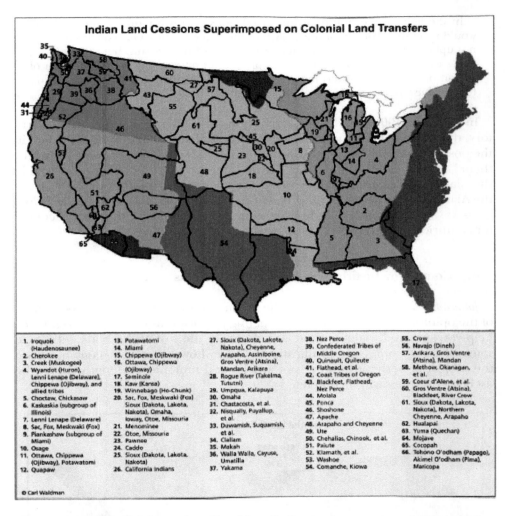

By superimposing official transfers of land from Indian nations over transfers from foreign nations, one can see that the United States recognized the need for consent from both. Maps by Carl Waldman, superimposed by Mira Singer.

1. First possession or occupancy. One of the most common arguments for property rights is that one is the first possessor or occupier of the property. *See* Carol Rose, *Possession as the Origin of Property,* 52 U. Chi. L. Rev. 73 (1985). What interests does a rule according title to first possessors serve? Well, it might prevent disputes about title, by preventing latecomers from challenging those there first, and encourage individuals to quickly find and claim useful property. What objections can you think of to these justifications? More importantly, why don't these arguments work in *Johnson?* As the plaintiffs argue, the Indians were clearly the first occupants of the land in question. Justice Marshall acknowledges that "converting the discovery of an inhabited country into conquest" is an "extravagant pretension." So why don't the Indians have full property rights?

2. Labor and investment. The defendants counter that the Indians never acquired property rights because as hunters rather than farmers, "the lands occupied by each tribe were not used by them in such a manner as to prevent their being appropriated by a people of cultivators." Does this mean I can demand my neighbor's land if I intend to farm it, while he simply occasionally picnics on it? Recent scholarship shows that in fact Indians had transformed the North American landscape by their work before non-Indians arrived; and as the facts stipulate, neither of the parties in *Johnson* had ever set foot on the land. Regardless, Justice Marshall rejects that as a basis for deciding the case as well, saying, "We will not enter into the controversy, whether agriculturists, merchants, and manufacturers, have a right, on abstract principles, to expel hunters from the territory they possess, or to contract their limits."

3. Efficiency and maximization of social welfare. The farmers over hunters argument is also an efficiency argument that the farmers maximize overall social welfare by engaging in the most productive use of the land. Marshall's opinion does not turn on this argument, but he acknowledges it with his statement that part of the "excuse" for the discovery doctrine is that "[t]o leave [the Indians] in possession of their country, was to leave the country a wilderness." Two central tenets in efficiency-based arguments for property rules are (1) that property rights should be protected, to "assure to the cultivator the fruits of his industry," and so encourage productive labor, and (2) that property should be freely alienable because "[e]very alienation imports advantage" by transferring property from one who values it less to one who values it more. Jeremy Bentham, *Principles of the Civil Code*, chs. 3 & 19 (1802). Can you think of challenges to these principles? Does the rule in *Johnson* further these principles?

4. Distributive justice. The defendants also raise a distributive justice argument, by claiming that the Indians do not have property rights in their lands because "[i]t is a violation of the rights of others to exclude them from the use of what we do not want, and they have occasion for." The desire to prevent gross inequality and ensure distribution to those in great need has also been influential in American law and policy, influencing, for example, the passage of the *Homestead Act* in 1862, and the *Social Security Act* in 1934. Thomas Jefferson urged James Madison in 1785, "I am conscious that an equal division of property is impracticable. But the consequences of this enormous inequality producing so much misery to the bulk of mankind, legislators cannot invent too many devices for subdividing property." Does inequality justify redistribution of property? Under which circumstances, if any?

5. Sovereign authority or might makes right? That brings us back to Marshall's central point: the discovery doctrine is the law because the government in charge said so, and the government has to have the power to say who can acquire property rights and how. One could see this as a simple statement that property arises from law: in order to prevent constant insecurity of property rights and to facilitate transfers, we have agreed to governmental rules regarding what property rights are and how they are acquired. To settle a vast continent, and prevent settlers from getting the United States into wars it could not handle, the government needed authority over when Indian land was acquired and how.

For the Indians, however, the doctrine that they lacked rights to transfer their land based on the decree of foreigners who had never set foot on that land must have felt like a subtly different rule: that property rights are created by and favor those in power. U.S. history provides other support for such a perception. African slaves not only were property, but were prevented from owning property. *See, e.g., Graves v. Allan,* 52 Ky. 190 (Ky. App. 1852). *But see* Dylan C. Penningroth, *The Claims of Kinfolk: African American Property and Community in the Nineteenth-Century South* (2003) (describing the well-established ownership networks slaves developed with the consent of their masters). Married women's property became that of their husbands until the late nineteenth century. *See* Chapter 9 [Joseph William Singer, Bethany R. Berger, Nestor M. Davidson and Eduardo Moisés Peñalver, Property Law, 6th ed., (2014)], Section 5.D.1.b; Reva Siegel, *Home as Work: The First Women's Rights Claims Concerning Wives' Household Labor: 1850-1880,* Yale L.J. 1073, 1082 (1994) ("[A] wife negotiated marriage as a dependent: without property or the legal prerogative to earn it."). And "immigrants ineligible for citizenship," a category that included almost all Asian immigrants until well into the twentieth century, were prevented from owning property up and down the West Coast and in many other states. See Keith Aoki, *No Right to Own? The Early Twentieth-Century "Alien Land Laws" as a Prelude to Internment,* 40 B.C. L. Rev. 37 (1998); Rose Cuison Villazor, *Oyama v. California: At the Intersection of Property, Race, and Citizenship,* 87 Wash. U. L. Rev. 979 (2010). At the same time, these laws clashed with another fundamental precept of property: that the system works better when everyone can participate in property ownership.

c.   Past Wrongs, Present Remedies: Modern Indian Land Claims

In 1790, the year after the U.S. Constitution was ratified, Congress codified the prohibition on purchasing Indian land without federal consent. The *Trade and Intercourse Act,* also called the *Nonintercourse Act,* remains in effect with slight amendments today:

> No purchase, grant, lease, or other conveyance of lands, or of any title or claim thereto, from any Indian nation or tribe of Indians, shall be of any validity in law or equity, unless the same be made by treaty or convention entered into pursuant to the Constitution.

25 U.S.C. § 177. Despite the statute, both states and private parties continued to acquire Indian land without federal consent. New York, for example, purchased most of the treaty lands of the Iroquois Nations of the Haudenosaunee Confederacy. Federal officials urged New York to comply with the *Nonintercourse Act,* but the state ignored them. Rather than enforcing the restriction, the United States tried to convince the tribes to exchange their remaining land for lands west of the Mississippi River. Although the tribes challenged the state purchases (including by arguing that they were fraudulent), procedural obstacles made it difficult for tribes to sue the states directly. State law prohibited tribes from bringing suit regarding Indian lands except through state-appointed guardians. Until 1875, federal courts lacked general jurisdiction to review questions of federal law. Even after 1875, state sovereign immunity barred suits against the state to acquire their lands. *See* Robert N. Clinton & Margaret Tobey Hotopp, *Judicial Enforcement of the*

Federal Restraints on the Alienation of Indian Land: The Origins of the Indian Land Claims, 31 Me. L. Rev. 17 (1979-1980); Joseph William Singer, *Nine-Tenths of the Law: Title, Possession & Sacred Obligations*, 38 Conn. L. Rev. 605 (2006). In the meantime, non-Indians bought and sold the acquired lands, cities and towns developed, and homes and businesses were built. The federal treaties guaranteeing the land to the Iroquois Nations seemed a thing of the past.

In 1966, however, the United States enacted a statute allowing tribes to bring actions against third parties in federal court without federal consent. In 1969, the Oneida Indian Nation of New York sued Oneida County seeking rent for occupation between 1968 and 1969 of 100,000 acres of land. The United States had guaranteed the land to the Oneidas in a 1794 treaty, but New York purchased the treaty land in 1795. In 1974, the Supreme Court held that the *Nonintercourse Act* granted the tribes a federal common law right to sue for violations of the act. *Oneida Indian Nation v. County of Oneida*, 414 U.S. 661 (1974) (*Oneida I*). On remand, the district court and court of appeals held that the 1795 purchase was void, and ordered the county to pay rent for the land. *Oneida Indian Nation v. Oneida County*, 719 F.2d 525 (2d Cir. 1983). The Supreme Court affirmed the decision, holding that no federal statute of limitations barred the tribal claims. *County of Oneida v. Oneida Indian Nation*, 470 U.S. 226 (1985) (*Oneida II*).

While this litigation was pending, the Oneidas brought an additional claim for possession of all of their original treaty land. Over the course of the 1970s, other tribes in New York, Maine, Massachusetts, Rhode Island, and Connecticut, brought *Nonintercourse Act* claims challenging state and private acquisitions of their land. Some of these claims were defeated or delayed by arguments that the plaintiffs were not really Indian tribes. Other claims were settled, usually with agreements that the tribe would cede most of its original land in exchange for the guarantee of some publicly owned lands as a reservation and funds to purchase additional reservation lands from willing sellers in a specified area. *E.g., Rhode Island Indian Claims Settlement Act*, 25 U.S.C. § 1701 et seq.; *Maine Indian Claims Settlement Act*, 25 U.S.C. § 1721 et seq.; *Mashantucket Pequot Indian Claims Settlement Act*, 25 U.S.C.A. § 1751 et seq.; *Mohegan Nation (Connecticut) Land Claims Settlement Act*, 25 U.S.C. § 1755 et seq. In order to secure the settlements, the tribes also agreed to significant state jurisdiction over the new lands.

But New York and the Iroquois Nations never settled. The ongoing litigation created concern among landowners, who feared ejectmentalso *specific acts*[ipri][/ipri][sec]ejectment[/sec]",4,0,2> from the land, and hostility against the tribes. Signs reading "no sovereign nation, no reservation" appeared along county roads. In 1999, in a case concerning land claims by the Cayuga Indian Nation, the U.S. district court held that the parties could not join private landowners to the litigation or seek to eject them, finding that such a remedy was impossible given the passage of time. *Cayuga Indian Nation of New York v. Cuomo*, 1999 U.S. Dist. LEXIS 10579 (N.D.N.Y. 1999). The district judge found that "the loss of their homeland has had an immeasurable impact upon the Cayuga culture and Cayuga society as a whole," *id.* at *77, and that the tribes had continuously tried to get back the land but that the "systems which theoretically should have assisted the Cayugas seemingly thwarted their efforts." *Id.* at *77 & *83. Nevertheless, ejectmentalso *specific acts*[ipri][/ipri][sec]ejectment[/sec]",4,0,2> of private landowners would "potentially displace literally thousands of private landowners and several public landowners" and would "prove all too vividly the old axiom: 'Two wrongs don't make a right.' " *Id.* at *90-*91; *see also Oneida Indian*

Nation of N.Y. v. County of Oneida, 199 F.R.D. 61 (N.D.N.Y. 2000). In a later opinion, the court awarded the Cayuga Indian Nation approximately $247 million in damages for the lost rental value of their land, *Cayuga Indian Nation of New York v. Pataki*, 165 F. Supp. 2d 266 (N.D.N.Y. 2002), *rev'd*, 413 F.3d 266 (2d Cir. 2005), but, as you will see, the Second Circuit later held the Cayuga could not claim even that.

As the legal battle continued, the Oneida Indian Nation of New York bought back some of the lands within the boundaries laid out by its 1794 treaty with the United States. It began to operate businesses on the lands, arguing that because the treaty had never been legally terminated, the lands were part of a reservation and free from state taxation. The district court and Second Circuit agreed, but Supreme Court reversed. *Sherrill v. Oneida Indian Nation of New York*, 544 U.S. 197 (2005), held that laches, acquiescence, and impossibility barred the claim to freedom from state jurisdiction.

Laches is an equitable doctrine barring actions by those whose unreasonable delay in suing has resulted in prejudice to their opponents in defending the claim. *See* Kathryn E. Fort, *The New Laches: Creating Title Where None Existed*, 16 Geo. Mason L. Rev. 357 (2009). The Court did not discuss whether the Oneidas could have brought the suit earlier, or find that the passage of time would prejudice the defendants. Nevertheless, it held, laches applied because the state and counties had long exercised sovereignty over the territory, the Oneida Indian Nation had acquiesced in this state of affairs, and it would be disruptive now to alter the jurisdiction with respect to these parcels of land. The Second Circuit has applied the *Sherrill* decision to other ongoing land claims, reversing the aforementioned damages award in favor of the Cayugas as barred by laches as well. *Cayuga Indian Nation v. Pataki*, 413 F.3d 266 (2d Cir. 2005); *see also Oneida Indian Nation of N.Y. v. County of Oneida*, 617 F.3d 114 (2d Cir. 2010).

NOTES AND QUESTIONS

1. No one today argues that unauthorized state acquisitions of tribal lands were legal in 1795, and few still argue that they were justified at the time. But uncorrected injustice in allocations of property often leads to justifiable expectations by those who later purchase and improve the lands. How should these conflicting expectations—between Indian nations deprived of their homelands and those who later built homes and towns on those lands—be resolved? Do you agree with Judge McCurn that while states may be held liable today for the illegal acquisition of land, private landowners cannot be? Do you agree with the Supreme Court that even when tribes purchase land within their treaty boundaries from private sellers, it is too disruptive for tribes to assert immunity from state jurisdiction on those lands?

2. Many nations face the conflict between past injustice and present land possession. In South Africa, for example, apartheid segregated the races and concentrated all political and economic power in a white minority until the 1990s. Even after the formal end of apartheid in 1994, the same white minority owned most of the productive land in the country. Although the country began a voluntary land distribution program, the program stalled because funds that might have been used to pay landowners were necessary for other social and economic programs. In addition, the existing landowners, who could take advantage of economies of scale and had far more capital and experience, were often more productive farmers. In the meantime, some landless black South Africans left desperately overcrowded townships to occupy lands they believed were unowned, or at least unneeded by their owners. *See* Sharon LaFraniere & Michael Wines, *Africa Quandary: Whites' Land v. the Landlessness of Blacks*, N.Y. Times, Jan. 6, 2004, at A-1.

In one case, over 40,000 squatters moved onto a portion of the Modderklip-Boerdery farm, building a makeshift town with thousands of shacks and streets. Although the lower courts granted Modderklip-Boerdery an order of eviction, when the residents refused to leave voluntarily, the sheriff demanded that Modderklip-Boerdery provide a deposit of 1.8 million rand (about 200,000 dollars) to cover the costs of the security firm the sheriff would need to hire to assist with the removal. The owner appealed, and the Supreme Court of Appeal of South Africa held that because government enforcement of property rights is an essential part of property, denying enforcement was therefore the equivalent of a taking of property. Eviction without provision of alternate housing, however, would violate the right to housing provided by the South African Constitution. The court found that Modderklip-Boerdery was entitled to damages for the loss of the land, and that the squatters were entitled to stay until the state provided them with other housing. *Modder East Squatters v. Modderklip Boerdery (PTY), Ltd.*, 2004 (8) BCLR 821 (SCA) (S. Afr.). How should the government respond to such conflicts? What are the potential costs of different courses of action?

C.   ADVERSE POSSESSION

Imagine that you own property in a remote rural area. You have not visited the property in many years. One day you decide to drive out to see the property, and you discover that someone is living there. We will call this person the Adverse Possessor. After asking around, you find out that the Adverse Possessor has been on your property for the past 20 years. If the circumstances are right, the Adverse Possessor might have acquired title to your property by adverse possession. In other words, you might not own the property anymore.

Adverse possession is a product of the statute of limitations. When the Adverse Possessor first entered your property, you could have brought an action for trespass or ejectment to kick the person off. If enough time has passed, the statute of limitations might have run on your action against the Adverse Possessor. Because you cannot bring an action to get the Adverse Possessor off of your property, title passes from you to the Adverse Possessor.

Each state's statute of limitations will set the time for bringing an action for trespass or ejectment. In most states, this time period will be somewhere in the range of 10-21 years. Although adverse possession is rooted in the statute of limitations, the actual operation of the doctrine involves a number of elements that have been developed by the common-law courts. You will see the elements of adverse possession stated in various different ways, and each has its complexities. Here are the basics:

1. The adverse possessor must make an *actual entry giving exclusive possession.* The entry by the adverse possessor starts the statute of limitations clock running.

We have talked a lot about the idea of possession already and know that it involves intent and control. So the adverse possessor must intend to possess the property and must exert some degree of control over it. As we suggested at the outset of this unit, thinking about adverse possession will give us an opportunity to think about how we demonstrate possession of real property.

2. The adverse possession must be *open and notorious.* The adverse possessor can't hide the possession. If the adverse possessor uses the property in the same way as a typical owner, then this element will typically be met. (Note here the connection between possession and use.) There are exceptions, though, as we will see in both the *Marengo Cave* and *Mannillo v. Gorski* cases.

3. The adverse possession must be *adverse and under a claim of right.* This element goes to the adverse possessor's state of mind. There are three possible approaches to this element: (a) The "objective standard" holds that the adverse possessor's state of mind is irrelevant. (b) The "good-faith" standard requires that the adverse possessor honestly believe that the adverse possessor owned the property. In other words, this standard requires the adverse possession to have been the result of an honest mistake. (c) The "bad faith" or "aggressive trespasser" standard requires that the adverse possessor know that the property was owned by someone else. In other words, this standard requires the adverse possession to have been motivated by a conscious desire to acquire someone else's property. *See* Margaret Jane Radin, *Time, Possession, and Alienation,* 64 Wash. U. L.Q. 739, 746-747 (1986). We will consider these alternatives in *Mannillo v. Gorski.*

4. The adverse possession must be *continuous for the statutory period.* This element requires that the statutory time period be met. This seemingly simple issue can be very complex, as we will see in *Howard v. Kunto.*

As we mentioned, these basic elements of adverse possession can be stated in different ways by different courts. We begin with the classic *Marengo Cave* case. As you will see, the court in *Marengo Cave* organizes the adverse possession elements slightly differently than we have, but we think it will be fairly easy for you to fit the court's analysis into our framework. This classic case involves a dispute about a claim of adverse possession of part of a cave. It is an excellent introduction to the concept of adverse possession, and because it involves a claim of adverse possession of something underground, it gives us a very good opportunity to think in detail about the open and notorious element.

THE *AD COLEUM* DOCTRINE

Under the *ad coleum* doctrine, the owner of the surface also owns the airspace above and the subsurface below. The doctrine takes its name from the Latin maxim *cuius est solum, eius est usque ad coelum et ad inferos*—whoever owns the soil owns all the way to heaven and to hell. Taken literally, the surface owner would own from the center of the earth to the edge of space. In practice, the scope of ownership is not so broad. Surface owners do own some airspace above their land, but upward ownership is limited to the extent that it would interfere with air travel. *See United States v. Causby,* 328 U.S. 256 (1946). Downward ownership of the subsurface might also be limited. *See* John G. Sprankling, *Owning the Center of the Earth,* 55 U.C.L.A. L. Rev. 979 (2008). This said, our default position is that the surface owner will own minerals and other natural resources located below the surface.

The surface owner will also own caves below the surface. This is only our default position, however, because subsurface ownership can be separated from surface ownership. For example, the surface owner could transfer the right to extract subsurface minerals to a mining company. The process of separating mineral ownership from surface ownership is often called *severance*—a term you will see in the *Marengo Cave* case. Similarly, the surface owner can transfer some air rights. For example, in some circumstances, the right to build a tower above a particular piece of land can be transferred from the owner of the surface to a different person.

MARENGO CAVE CO. V. ROSS
Supreme Court of Indiana, 1937 212 Ind. 624, 10 N.E.2d 917

ROLL, Judge. Appellee and appellant were the owners of adjoining land in Crawford county, Ind. On appellant's land was located the opening to a subterranean cavity known as "Marengo Cave." This cave extended under a considerable portion of appellant's land, and the southeastern portion thereof extended under lands owned by appellee. This action arose out of a dispute as to the ownership of that part of the cave that extended under appellee's land. Appellant was claiming title to all the cave and davities, including that portion underlying appellee's land. Appellee instituted this action to quiet his title as by a general denial and filed a cross-complaint by a general denial and filed a crosscomplaint wherein he sought to quiet its title to all the cave, including that portion underlying appellee's land. There was a trial by jury which returned a verdict for the appellee. Appellant filed its motion for a new trial which was overruled by the court, and this the only error assigned on appeal. Appellant assigns as grounds for a new trial that the verdict of the jury is not sustained by sufficient evidence, and is contrary to law. These are the only grounds urged for a reversal of this cause.

The facts as shown by the record are substantially as follows: In 1883 one Stewart owned the real estate now owned by appellant, and in September of that year some young people who were upon that land discovered what afterwards proved to be the entrance to the cavern since known as Marengo Cave, this entrance being approximately 700 feet from the boundary line between the lands now owned by appellant and appellee, and the only entrance to said cave. Within a week after discovery of the cave, it was explored, and the fact of its existence received wide publicity through newspaper articles, and otherwise. Shortly thereafter the then owner of the real estate upon which the entrance was located took complete possession of the entire cave as now occupied by appellant and used for exhibition purposes, and began to charge an admission fee to those who desired to enter and view the cave, and to exclude therefrom those who were unwilling to pay for admission. This practice continued from 1883, except in some few instances when persons were permitted by the persons claiming to own said cave to enter same without payment of the usual required fee, and during the following years the successive owners of the land upon which the entrance to the cave was located, advertised the existence of said cave through newspapers, magazines, posters, and otherwise, in order to attract visitors thereto; also made improvements within the cave, including the building of concrete walks, and concrete steps where there was a difference in elevation of said cavern, widened and heightened portions of passageways; had available and furnished guides, all in order to make the cave more easily accessibly to visitors desiring to view the same; and continuously, during all this time, without asking or obtaining consent from any one, but claiming a right so to do, held and possessed said subterranean passages constituting said cave, excluding therefrom the "whole world," except such persons as entered after paying admission for the privilege of so doing, or by permission.

Appellee has lived in the vicinity of said cave since 1903, and purchased the real estate which he now owns in 1908. He first visited the cave in 1895, paying an admission fee for the privilege, and has visited said cave several times since. He has never, at any time, occupied or been in possession of any of the subterranean passages or cavities of which the cave consists, and the possession and use of the cave by those who have done so has never interfered with his use and enjoyment of the lands owned by him. For a period of approximately 25 years prior to the time appellee purchased his land, and for a period of 21 years afterwards, exclusive possession of the cave has been held by appellant, its immediate and remote grantors.

The cave, as such, has never been listed for taxation separately from the real estate wherein it is located, and the owners of the respective tracts of land have paid the taxes assessed against said tracts.

A part of said cave at the time of its discovery and exploration extended beneath real estate now owned by appellee, but this fact was not ascertained until the year 1932, when the boundary line between the respective tracts through the cave was established by means of a survey made by a civil engineer pursuant to an order of court entered in this cause. Previous to this survey neither of the parties to this appeal, nor any of their predecessors in title, knew that any part of the cave was in fact beneath the surface of a portion of the land now owned by appellee. Possession of the cave was taken and held by appellant's remote and immediate grantors, improvements made, and control exercised, with the belief on the part of such grantors that the entire cave as it was explored and held was under the surface of lands owned by them. There is no evidence of and dispute as to ownership of the cave, or any portion thereof, prior to the time when in 1929 appellee requested a survey, which was approximately 46 years after discovery of the cave and the exercise of complete dominion thereover by appellant and its predecessors in title.

It is appellant's contention that it has a fee-simple title to all of the cave; that it owns that part underlying appellee's land by adverse possession. Section 2-602, Burns' Ann.St.1933, section 61, Baldwin's Ind.St.1934, provides as follows: "The following actions shall be commenced within the periods herein prescribed after the cause of action has accrued, and not afterward: . . . Sixth. Upon contracts in writing other than those for the payment of money, on judgments of courts of record, and for the recovery of the possession of real estate, within twenty (20) years."

It will be noted that appellee nor his predecessors in title had never effected a severance of the cave from the surface estate. Therefore the title of the appellee extends from the surface to the center but actual possession is confined to the surface. Appellee and his immediate and remote grantors have been in possession of the land and estate here in question at all times, unless it can be said that the possession of the cave by appellant as shown by the evidence above set out has met all the requirements of the law relating to the acquisition of land by adverse possession. A record title may be defeated by adverse possession. All the authorities agree that, before the owner of the legal title can be deprived of his land by another's possession, through the operation of the statute of limitation, the possession must have been actual, visible, notorious, exclusive, under claim of ownership and hostile to the owner of the legal title and to the world at large (except only the government), and continuous for the full period prescribed by the statute. The rule is not always stated in exactly the same words in the many cases dealing with the subject of adverse possession, yet the rule is so thoroughly settled that there is no doubt as to what elements are essential to establish a title by adverse possession. *Craven v. Craven* (1913) 181 Ind. 553, 103 N.E. 333, 105 N.E. 41; *Rennert v. Shirk* (1904) 163 Ind. 542, 72 N.E. 546; *Vandalia R. Co. v. Wheeler* (1914) 181 Ind. 424, 103 N.E. 1069; *Tolley v. Thomas* (1910) 46 Ind.App. 559, 93 N.E. 181; *McBeth v. Wetnight* (1914) 57 Ind.App. 47, 106 N.E. 407. Let us examine the various elements that are essential to establish title by adverse possession and apply them to the facts that are established by the undisputed facts in this case.

(1) The possession must be actual. It must be conceded that appellant in the operation of the "Marengo Cave" used not only the cavern under its own land but also that part of the cavern that underlaid appellee's land, and assumed dominion over all of it. Yet it must also be conceded that during all of the time appellee was in constructive possession, as the only constructive possession known to the law is that which inheres in the legal title and with which the owner of that title is always endowed. *Morrison v. Kelly* (1859) 22 Ill. 609, 610, 74 Am.Dec. 169; *Cook v. Clinton* (1887) 64 Mich. 309, 31 N.W. 317, 8 Am.St.Rep. 816; *Ables v. Webb* (1905) 186 Mo. 233, 85 S.W. 383, 105 Am.St.Rep. 610; 1 R.C.L. 692; 2 C.J. 51 et seq. and authorities there cited. Whether the possession was actual under the peculiar facts in this case we need not decide.

(2) The possession must be visible. The owner of land who, having notice of the fact that it is occupied by another who is claiming dominion over it, nevertheless stands by during the entire statutory period and makes no effort to eject the claimant or otherwise protect his title, ought not to be permitted, for reasons of public policy, thereafter to maintain an action for the recovery of his land. But, the authorities assert, in order that the possession of the occupying claimant may constitute notice in law, it must be visible and open to the common observer so that the owner or his agent on visiting the premises might readily see that the owner's rights are being invaded. *Holcroft v. Hunter* (1832) 3 Blackf. 147; *Towle v. Quante* (1910) 246 Ill. 568, 92 N.E. 967; *Tinker v. Bessel* (1912) 213 Mass. 74, 99 N.E. 946; *Jasperson v. Scharnikow* (1907) 150 F. 571, 80 C.C.A. 373, 15 L.R.A. (N.S.) 1178 and note. What constitutes open and visible possession has been stated in general terms, thus; it is necessary and sufficient if its nature and character is such as is calculated to apprise the world that the land is occupied and who the occupant is; *Dempsey v. Burns* (1917) 281 Ill. 644, 118 N.E. 193, and such an appropriation of the land by claimant as to apprise, or convey visible notice to the community or neighborhood in which it is situated that it is in his exclusive use and enjoyment. *Goodrich v. Mortimer* (1919) 44 Cal.App. 576, 186 P. 844. It has been declared that the disseisor "must unfurl his flag" on the land, and "keep it flying," so that the owner may see, if he will, that an enemy has invaded his domains, and planted the standard of conquest. *Robin v. Brown* (1932) 308 Pa. 123, 162 A. 161; *Willamette Real Estate Co. v. Hendrix* (1895) 28 Or. 485, 42 P. 514,

52 Am.St.Rep. 800; *People's Savings Bank v. Bufford* (1916) 90 Wash. 204, 155 P. 1068; 1 Amer.Juris. p. 865.

(3) The possession must be open and notorious. The mere possession of the land is not enough. It is knowledge, either actual or imputed, of the possession of his lands by another, claiming to own them bona fide and openly, that affects the legal owner thereof. Where there has been no actual notice, it is necessary to show that the possession of the disseisor was so open, notorious, and visible as to warrant the inference that the owner must or should have known of it. In *Philbin v. Carr* (1920) 75 Ind.App. 560, 129 N.E. 19, 29, 706, it was said: "However, in order that the possession of the occupying claimant may constitute notice in law, it must be visible and open to the common observer so that the owner or his agent on visiting the premises might readily see that the owner's rights are being invaded. In accordance with the general rule applicable to the subject of constructive notice, before possession can operate as such notice, it must be clear and unequivocal." *Holcroft v. Hunter* (1832) 3 Blackf. 147; *Towle v. Quante supra.*

And again, the possession must be notorious. It must be so conspicuous that it is generally known and talked of by the public. "It must be manifest to the community." Thus, the Appellate Court said in *Philbin v. Carr supra*, that: "Where the persons who have passed frequently over and along the premises have been unable to see any evidence of occupancy, evidently the possession has not been of the character required by the rule. The purpose of this requirement is to support the principle that a legal title will not be extinguished on flimsy and uncertain evidence. Hence, where there has been no actual notice, the possession must have been so notorious as to warrant the inference that the owner ought to have known that a stranger was asserting dominion over his land. Insidious, desultory, and fugitive acts will not serve that purpose. To have that effect the possession should be clear and satisfactory, not doubtful and equivocal." See cases there cited on page 585 of 75 Ind.App., 129 N.E. 19, 28, 706.

(4) The possession must be exclusive. It is evident that two or more persons cannot hold one tract of land adversely to each other at the same time. "It is essential that the possession of one who claims adversely must be of such an exclusive character that it will operate as an ouster of the owner of the legal title; because, in the absence of ouster the legal title draws to itself the constructive possession of the land. A possession which does not amount to an ouster or disseisin is not sufficient." *Philbin v. Carr, supra.* See cases cited on page 585 of 75 Ind.App., 129 N.E. 19, 28, 706.

The facts as set out above show that appellee and his predecessors in title have been in actual and continuous possession of his real estate since the cave was discovered in 1883. At no time were they aware that any one was trespassing upon their land. No one was claiming to be in possession of appellee's land. It is true that appellant was asserting possession of the "Marengo Cave." There would seem to be quite a difference in making claim to the "Marengo Cave," and making claim to a portion of appellee's land, even though a portion of the cave extended under appellee's land, when this latter fact was unknown to any one. The evidence on both sides of this case is to the effect that the "Marengo Cave" was thought to be altogether under the land owned by appellant, and this erroneous supposition was not revealed until a survey was made at the request of appellee and ordered by the court in this case. It seems to us that the following excerpt from *Lewey v. H. C. Frick Coke Co.* (1895) 166 Pa. 536, 31 A. 261, 263, 28

L.R.A. 283, 45 Am.St.Rep. 684, is peculiarly applicable to the situation here presented, inasmuch as we are dealing with an underground cavity. It was stated in the above case:

> "The title of the plaintiff extends from the surface to the center, but actual possession is confined to the surface. Upon the surface he must be held to know all that the most careful observation by himself and his employés could reveal, unless his ignorance is induced by the fraudulent conduct of the wrongdoer. But in the coal veins, deep down in the earth, he cannot see. Neither in person nor by his servants nor employés can he explore their recesses in seach for an intruder. If an adjoining owner goes beyond his own boundaries in the course of his mining operations, the owner on whom he enters has no means of knowledge within his reach. Nothing short of an accurate survey of the interior of his neighbor's mines would enable him to ascertain the fact. This would require the services of a competent mining engineer and his assistants, inside the mines of another, which he would have no right to insist upon. To require an owner, under such circumstances, to take notice of a trespass upon his underlying coal at the time it takes place, is to require an impossibility; and to hold that the statute begins to run at the date of the trespass is in most cases to take away the remedy of the injured party before he can know that an injury has been done him. A result so absurd and so unjust ought not to be possible. . . .
>
> "The reason for the distinction exists in the nature of things. The owner of land may be present by himself or his servants on the surface of his possessions, no matter how extensive they may be. He is for this reason held to be constructively present wherever his title extends. He cannot be present in the interior of the earth. No amount of vigilance will enable him to detect the approach of a trespasser who may be working his way through the coal seams underlying adjoining lands. His senses cannot inform him of the encroachment by such trespasser upon the coal that is hidden in the rocks under his feet. He cannot reasonably be held to be constructively present where his presence is, in the nature of things, impossible. He must learn of such a trespass by other means than such as are within his own control, and, until these come within his reach, he is necessarily ignorant of his loss. He cannot reasonably be required to act until knowledge that action is needed is possible to him."

We are not persuaded that this case falls within the rule of mistaken boundary as announced in *Rennert v. Shirk* (1904) 163 Ind. 542, 72 N.E. 546, 549, wherein this court said: "Appellant insists, however, that, if one takes and holds possession of real estate under a mistake as to where the true boundary line is, such possession cannot ripen into a title. In this state, when an owner of land, by mistake as to the boundary line of his land, takes actual, visible, and exclusive possession of another's land, and holds it as his own continuously for the statutory period of 20 years, he thereby acquires the title as against the real owner. The possession is regarded as adverse, without reference to the fact that it is based on mistake; it being prima facie sufficient that actual, visible, and exclusive possession is taken under a claim of right."

The reason for the above rule is obvious. Under such circumstances appellant was in possession of the necessary means of ascertaining the true boundary line, and to hold that a mere misapprehension on the part of appellant as to the true boundary line would nullify the well-established law on adverse possession. In that case appellee had actual, visible, notorious, and exclusive possession. The facts in the present case are far different. Here the possession of appellant was not visible. No one could see below the earth's surface and determine that appellant was trespassing upon appellee's lands. This fact could not be determined by going into the cave. Only by a survey could this fact be made known. The same undisputed facts clearly show that appellant's possession was not notorious. Not even appellant itself nor any of its remote grantors knew that any part of the "Marengo Cave" extended beyond its own boundaries, and they at no time even down to the time appellee instituted this action made any claim to appellee's lands. Appellee and his predecessors in title at all times have been in possession of the land which he is now claiming. No severance by deed or written instrument was ever made to the cave, from the surface. In the absence of a separate estate could appellant be in the exclusive possession of the cave that underlies appellee's land.

"If there is no severance, an entry upon the surface will extend downward, and draw to it a title to the underlying minerals; so that he who disseises another, and acquires title by the statute of limitations, will succeed to the estate of him upon whose possession he has entered." *Delaware & Hudson Canal Co. v. Hughes* (1897) 183 Pa. 66, 38 A. 568, 570, 38 L.R.A. 826, 63 Am.St.Rep. 743.

Even though it could be said that appellant's possession has been actual, exclusive, and continuous all these years, we would still be of the opinion that appellee has not lost his land. It has been the uniform rule in equity that the statute of limitation does not begin to run until the injured party discovers, or with reasonable diligence might have discovered, the facts constituting the injury and cause of action. Until then the owner cannot know that his possession has been invaded. Until he has knowledge, or ought to have such knowledge, he is not called upon to act, for he does not know that action in the premises is necessary and the law does not require absurd or impossible things of any one. *Lewey v. Frick Coke Co.* (1895) 166 Pa. 536, 31 A. 261, 28 L.R.A. 283, 45 Am.St.Rep. 684; *Delaware & Hudson Canal Co. v. Hughes, supra.*

In the case of *Bailey v. Glover* (1874) 21 Wall. (88 U.S.) 342, 348, 22 L.Ed. 636, the court said:

> "We also think that in suits in equity the decided weight of authority is in favor of the proposition that where the party injured by the fraud remains in ignorance of it without any fault or want of diligence or care on his part, the bar of the statute does not begin to run until the fraud is discovered, though there be no special circumstances or efforts on the part of the party committing the fraud to conceal it from the knowledge of the other party. . . .
>
> "To hold that by concealing a fraud, or by committing a fraud in a manner that it concealed itself until such time as the party committing the fraud could plead the statute of limitations to protect it, is to make the law which was designed to prevent fraud the means by which it is made successful and secure."

In *Livingston v. Rawyards* (1880) L.R. 5 App.Cas. 34, Lord Hatherly treats an underground trespass as a species of fraud. While there is no active fraud shown in this case, yet the facts come clearly within the case of *Lightner Mining Co. v. Lane* (1911) 161 Cal. 689, 120 P. 771, 776, and cases cited on page 776, Ann.Cas.1913C, 1093. The following excerpt from this opinion clearly sets forth our view:

> "In the English decisions the willful and secret taking of coal from a neighbor's mine is usually characterized as fraudulent. *Hilton v. Woods*, L.R. 4 Eq.Cas. 440;

Dean v. Thwaite, 21 Beav. 623; *Ecclesiastical Coms. v. North E. Ry. Co.,* L.R. 4, Ch.Div. 860; *Trotter v. McLean,* L.R. 13, Ch.Div. 586. Such an act, so committed, has all the substantial elements of fraud. Where one by misrepresentation induces another knowingly to part with his property, because his mind is so beclouded by the falsehood that he is unaware of the wrong done him, it is called a fraud. It is a taking of another's property without his knowledge of the fact that it is really taken from him. The ignorance in that case is produced by artifice. Where one betrays a trust and appropriates trust property to his own use, it is called a fraud. The injured party allows the other to have the possession and the opportunity to convert the property secretly, because of faith and confidence in the wrongdoer. In the case of underground mining of a neighbor's ore, nature has supplied the situation which gives the opportunity to the trespasser to take it secretly and causes the ignorance of the owner. Relying upon this ignorance, he takes an unfair advantage of his natural opportunities, and thereby clandestinely appropriates another's property while appearing to be making only a lawful use of his own. The act in its very nature constitutes the deceit which makes it a fraud."

So in the case at bar, appellant pretended to use the "Marengo Cave" as his property and all the time he was committing a trespass upon appellee's land. After 20 years of secret user, he now urges the statute of limitation, section 2-602, Burns' St.1933, section 61, Baldwin's Ind.St.1934, as a bar to appellee's action. Appellee did not know of the trespass of appellant, and had no reasonable means of discovering the fact. It is true that appellant took no active measures to prevent the discovery, except to deny appellee the right to enter the cave for the purpose of making a survey, and disclaiming any use of appellee's lands, but nature furnished the concealment, or where the wrong conceals itself. It amounts to the taking of another's property without his knowledge of the fact that it is really being taken from him. In most cases the ignorance is produced by artifice. But in this case nature has supplied the situation which gives the trespasser the opportunity to occupy the recesses on appellee's land and caused the ignorance of appellee which he now seeks to avail himself. We cannot assent to the doctrine that would enable one to trespass upon another's property through a subterranean passage and under such circumstances that the owner does not know, or by the exercise of reasonable care could not know, of such secret occupancy, for 20 years or more and by so doing obtained a fee-simple title as against the holder of the legal title. The fact that appellee had knowledge that appellant was claiming to be the owner of the "Marengo Cave," and advertised it to the general public, was no knowledge to him that it was in possession of appellee's land or any part of it. We are of the opinion that appellant's possession for 20 years or more of that part of "Marengo Cave" underlying appellee's land was not open, notorious, or exclusive, as required by the law applicable to obtaining title to land by adverse possession.

We cannot say that the evidence is not sufficient to support the verdict or that the verdict is contrary to law.

Judgment affirmed.

NOTES AND QUESTIONS

1. *Open and Notorious:* As we noted at the outset, the facts of *Marengo Cave* give us a good opportunity to think about the open and notorious element. To be

sure that you have a good handle on the court's analysis of this element, answer the following questions. Why, exactly, was the possession by the Marengo Cave Company not open and notorious? What, if anything, could the company have done differently that would have changed the outcome? What is the court's view of the purpose of the open and notorious element? The court treated visibility as a separate, but related, element. Modern courts would typically consider visibility as a subset of the open and notorious element. Do you think that considering visibility separately adds anything to the analysis?

2. *Adversity.* We will leave an in-depth discussion of the adversity element to our next case. Recall from our introductory materials that this element gets at the adverse possessor's state of mind. An adverse possessor can either have a good faith state of mind or a bad faith state of mind. Cases of good faith adverse possession involve an honest mistake—the adverse possessor thought she owned the property, but in fact did not. Cases of bad faith adverse possession involve a knowing and intentional effort to possess someone else's property. Which state of mind did the adverse possessor in *Marengo Cave* have? Do you think that it may have changed over time?

3. *The Discovery Rule and the Statute of Limitations.* Toward the end of the opinion, the court cites cases that equate underground trespass with fraud. Under the *discovery rule*, the statute of limitations period typically does not start to run in fraud cases until the victim discovers the fraud. The rule makes sense because victims cannot bring actions against the perpetrators of the fraud if they are not aware of the fraud. Can you see how an underground trespass case is similar to a fraud case, even if the underground trespasser had a good faith state of mind? More broadly, can you see how there is a similar logic behind both the discovery rule and the open and notorious element of adverse possession?

ADVERSE POSSESSION OF PERSONAL PROPERTY

Adverse possession of personal property operates in a similar way to adverse possession of real property. Over time, the statute of limitations on an action for replevin will expire, and the adverse possessor will own the personal property. The open and notorious element, however, presents a major hurdle to the adverse possessor of personal property. Imagine, for example, that you are the true owner of a painting. I currently possess the painting and have it hanging in my living room. Even though I am not doing anything to hide my possession, it is hard to see how my possession is open and notorious. It is possible, of course, to imagine the open and notorious possession of personal property. For example, if the painting was famous and was hanging in a museum open to the public, the possession of the painting might very well be open and notorious.

Perhaps the most famous case involving adverse possession of personal property is *O'Keeffe v. Snyder*, 416 A.2d 862 (N.J. 1980). *O'Keeffe* involved a dispute between Georgia O'Keeffe and a gallery owner about the ownership of three of her paintings. Using an analysis that you would find familiar from our discussion of underground trespass, the court applied the discovery rule and held that the statute of limitations clock does not run against the owner of personal property until she knows, or should have known, that the property was possessed by the putative adverse possessor.

CONSTRUCTIVE ADVERSE POSSESSION
AND COLOR OF TITLE

Legal title to property gives the owner constructive possession of that property. If, for example, you own title to Blackacre, you constructively possess Blackacre, even if you are not in actual possession of Blackacre. The court referenced this rule in *Marengo Cave*, when it noted "that during all of the time appellee was in constructive possession, as the only constructive possession known to the law is that which inheres in the legal title and with which the owner of that title is always endowed." Actual possession, however, trumps constructive possession. As a result, constructive possession does not help the owner in the adverse possession context, because the adverse possessor's actual possession will win against the owner's constructive possession.

There is one context in which constructive possession may help the adverse possessor. Typically, a successful adverse possessor will obtain ownership only of the land that she actually possessed.

> EXAMPLE 1: Imagine that Blackacre is a ten-acre parcel. If Adverse Possessor actually possesses one of the ten acres and meets all of the other elements of adverse possession, then she will own that one acre. Owner will still own the other nine acres of Blackacre that Adverse Possessor did not possess.

The exception to this general rule is when the adverse possessor takes possession under *color of title*. Color of title refers to a circumstance where the adverse possessor takes possession in reliance on some kind of written instrument that appears to give title to the property, but that is defective for some reason. The idea is that the adverse possessor has a written document—typically a deed or will—that appears to give title to the land, but the document is invalid. Perhaps the written document is a forged deed, or a will that was improperly executed. The defective document gives the adverse possessor color of title, even though it does not give actual title. The benefit of color of title is that it gives the adverse possessor constructive possession of all of the property described by the document. As a result, the adverse possessor may obtain title to all of the property described by the document, not just the property actually possessed by the adverse possessor. In jurisdictions that recognize constructive adverse possession, the adverse possessor's constructive possession under color of title will trump the owner's constructive possession as the actual title holder of the property.

> EXAMPLE 2: As with Example 1, imagine that Blackacre is a ten-acre parcel, that Adverse Possessor only possessed one of the ten acres, and that Adverse Possessor otherwise met all of the elements of adverse possession. In this example, however, Adverse Possessor has taken possession under color of title under a defective deed that describes the entire ten acres. In these circumstances, Adverse Possessor will own all ten acres—one acre that she actually possessed and nine acres that she constructively possessed.

Recall that actual possession will always trump constructive possession. The owner of the property will therefore be able to defeat the adverse possessor's constructive possession under color of title for land that the owner actually possessed.

> EXAMPLE 3: As with Examples 1 and 2, Blackacre is a ten-acre parcel, Adverse Possessor only possessed one of the ten acres, and Adverse Possessor met all of the other elements of adverse possession. As with Example 2, Adverse Possessor has take possession under color of title under a defective deed that describes all ten acres. Now, however, Owner actually possessed the other nine acres. In other words, of the ten acres, Adverse Possessor actually possessed one and Owner possessed nine. The Owner's actual possession of those nine acres will be superior to the Adverse Possessor's constructive possession of the under color of title. As a result, Adverse Possessor will only gain ownership of the one acre she actually possessed, and Owner will retain ownership of the other nine acres.

Recall that in our introduction to the elements of adverse possession, we noted that the "adverse and under a claim of right" element turned on the adverse possessor's state of mind. We also noted that there are three potential standards for this element:

a. The "objective standard" holds that the adverse possessor's state of mind is irrelevant.
b. The "good-faith" standard requires that the adverse possessor honestly believe that the adverse possessor owned the property. In other words, this standard requires the adverse possession to have been the result of an honest mistake.
c. The "bad faith" or "aggressive trespasser" standard requires that the adverse possessor know that the property was owned by someone else. In other words, this standard requires the adverse possession to have been motivated by a conscious desire to acquire someone else's property.

Our next case includes an in-depth discussion of this element. Think about how the standards discussed in the case map on to our three options. We will return to this issue in the notes after the case.

MANNILLO V. GORSKI

Supreme Court of New Jersey, 1969 255 A.2d 258

HANEMAN, J.

Plaintiffs filed a complaint in the Chancery Division seeking a mandatory and prohibitory injunction against an alleged trespass upon their lands. Defendant counterclaimed for a declaratory judgment which would adjudicate that she had gained title to the disputed premises by adverse possession under N.J.S. 2A:14-6, N.J.S.A., which provides:

"Every person having any right or title of entry into real estate shall make such entry within 20 years next after the accrual of such right or title of entry, or be barred therefrom thereafter."

After plenary trial, judgment was entered for plaintiffs. *Mannillo v. Gorski,* 100 N.J. Super. 140, 241 A.2d 276 (Ch.Div.1968). Defendant appealed to the Appellate Division. Before argument there, this Court granted defendant's motion for certification. R.R. 1:10-1a.

The facts are as follows: In 1946, defendant and her husband entered into possession of premises in Keansburg known as Lot No. 1007 in Block 42, under an agreement to purchase. Upon compliance with the terms of said agreement, the seller conveyed said lands to them on April 16, 1952. Defendant's husband thereafter died. The property consisted of a rectangular lot with a frontage of 25 feet and a depth of 100 feet. Plaintiffs are the owners of the adjacent Lot 1008 in Block 42 of like dimensions, to which they acquired title in 1953.

In the summer of 1946 Chester Gorski, one of the defendant's sons, made certain additions and changes to the defendant's house. He extended two rooms at the rear of the structure, enclosed a screened porch on the front, and put a concrete platform with steps on the west side thereof for use in connection with a side door. These steps were built to replace existing wooden steps. In addition, a concrete walk was installed from the steps to the end of the house. In 1953, defendant raised the house. In order to compensate for the resulting added height from the ground, she modified the design of the steps by extending them toward both the front and the rear of the property. She did not change their width.

Defendant admits that the steps and concrete walk encroach upon plaintiffs' lands to the extent of 15 inches. She contends, however, that she has title to said land by adverse possession. N.J.S.A. 2A:14-6, quoted above. Plaintiffs assert contrawise that defendant did not obtain title by adverse possession as her possession was not of the requisite hostile nature. They argue that to establish title by adverse possession, the entry into and continuance of possession must be accompanied by an intention to invade the rights of another in the lands, I.e., a knowing wrongful taking. They assert that, as defendant's encroachment was not accompanied by an intention to invade plaintiffs' rights in the land, but rather by the mistaken belief that she owned the land, and that therefore an essential requisite to establish title by adverse possession, I.e., an intentional tortious taking, is lacking.

The trial court concluded that defendant had clearly and convincingly proved that her possession of the 15-inch encroachment had existed for more than 20 years before the institution of this suit and that such possession was "exclusive, continuous, uninterrupted, visible, notorious and against the right and interest of the true owner." There is ample evidence to sustain this finding except as to its visible and notorious nature, of which more hereafter. However, the judge felt impelled by existing New Jersey case law, holding as argued by plaintiffs above, to deny defendant's claim and entered judgment for plaintiffs. 100 N.J. Super, at 150, 241 A.2d 276. The first issue before this Court is, therefore, whether an entry and continuance of possession under the mistaken belief that the possessor has title to the lands involved, exhibits the requisite hostile possession to sustain the obtaining of title by adverse possession.

The first detailed statement and acceptance by our then highest court, of the principle that possession as an element of title by adverse possession cannot be bottomed on mistake, is found in *Folkman v. Myers*, 93 N.J. Eq. 208, 115 A. 615 (E. & A. 1921), which embraced and followed that thesis as expressed in *Myers v. Folkman*, 89 N.J.L. 390, 99 A. 97 (Sup.Ct.1916). . . . In so doing, the former Court of Errors and Appeals aligned this State with that branch of a dichotomy which traces its genesis to *Preble v. Maine Cent. R. Co.*, 85 Me. 260, 27 A. 149, 21 L.R.A. 829 (Sup.Jud.Ct.Me.1893) and has become known as the Maine doctrine. In *Preble*, the court said at 27 A. at p. 150:

> "There is every presumption that the occupancy is in subordination to the true title, and, if the possession is claimed to be adverse, the act of the wrongdoer must be strictly construed, and the character of the possession clearly shown. *Roberts v. Richards*, 84 Me. 1, 24 Atl.Rep. 425, and authorities cited. 'The intention of the possessor to claim adversely,' says Mellen, C.J., in *Ross v. Gould, supra* (5 Me. 204), 'is an essential ingredient in disseisin.' And in *Worcester v. Lord, supra* (56 Me. 266) the court says: 'To make a disseisin in fact, there must be an intention on the part of the party assuming possession to assert title in himself.' Indeed, the authorities all agree that this intention of the occupant to claim the ownership of land not embraced in his title is a necessary element of adverse possession; and in case of occupancy by mistake beyond a line capable of being ascertained this intention to claim title to the extent of the occupancy must appear to be absolute, and not conditional; otherwise the possession will not be deemed adverse to the true owner. It must be an intention to claim title to all land within a certain boundary on the face of the earth, whether it shall eventually be found to be the correct one or not. If, for instance, one in ignorance of his actual boundaries takes and holds possession by mistake up to a certain fence beyond his limits, upon the claim and in the belief that it is the true line, with the intention to claim title, and thus, if necessary, to acquire 'title by possession' up to that fence, such possession, having the requisite duration and continuity, will ripen into title. *Hitchings v. Morrison*, 72 Me. 331, is a pertinent illustration of this principle. *See, also, Abbott v. Abbott*, 51 Me. 575; *Ricker v. Hibbard*, 73 Me. 105.
>
> If, on the other hand, a party through ignorance, inadvertence, or mistake occupies up to a given fence beyond his actual boundary, because he believes it to be the true line, but has no intention to claim title to that extent if it should be ascertained that the fence was on his neighbor's land, an indispensable element of adverse possession is wanting. In such a case the intent to claim title exists only upon the condition that the fence is on the true line. The intention is not absolute, but provisional, and the possession is not adverse."

This thesis, it is evident, rewards the possessor who entered with a premeditated and predesigned "hostility"—the intentional wrongdoer and disfavors an honest, mistaken entrant. 3 *American Law of Property* (Casner ed. 1952), § 104, pp. 773, 785; Bordwell, "Desseisin and Adverse Possession," 33 Yale L.J. 1, 154 (1923); Darling, "Adverse Possession in Boundary Cases," 19 Ore.L.Rev. 117 (1940); Sternberg, "The Element of Hostility in Adverse Possession," 6 Temp.L.Q. 206 (1932); Annotation, "Adverse possession involving ignorance or mistake as to boundaries—modern views," 80 A.L.R.2d 1171 (1961).

The other branch of the dichotomy relies upon *French v. Pearce*, 8 Conn. 439 (Sup.Ct.Conn.1831). The court said in Pearce on the question of the subjective hostility of a possessor, at pp. 442, 445-446:

"Into the recesses of his (the adverse claimant's) mind, his motives or purposes, his guilt or innocence, no enquiry is made. . . .

The very nature of the act (entry and possession) is an assertion of his own title, and the denial of the title of all others. It matters not that the possessor was mistaken, and had he been better informed, would not have entered on the land." 8 Conn. at 442, 445-446.

The Maine doctrine has been the subject of much criticism in requiring a knowing wrongful taking. The criticism of the Maine and the justification of the Connecticut branch of the dichotomy is well stated in 6 Powell, *Real Property* (1969) 1015, pp. 725-28:

"Do the facts of his possession, and of his conduct as if he were the owner, make immaterial his mistake, or does such a mistake prevent the existence of the prerequisite claim of right. The leading case holding the mistake to be of no importance was *French v. Pearce*, decided in Connecticut in 1831. . . . This viewpoint has gained increasingly widespread acceptance. The more subjectively oriented view regards the 'mistake' as necessarily preventing the existence of the required claim of right. The leading case on this position is *Preble v. Maine Central R.R.*, decided in 1893. This position is still followed in a few states. It has been strongly criticized as unsound historically, inexpedient practically, and as resulting in better treatment for a ruthless wrongdoer than for the honest landowner. . . . On the whole the law is simplified, in the direction of real justice, by a following of the Connecticut leadership on this point."

Again, 4 Tiffany, *Real Property* (3d ed. 1939), § 1159, pp. 474-475, criticizes the employment of mistake as negating hostility as follows:

" . . . Adopting this view, it is only in so far as the courts, which assert the possible materiality of the mistake, recognize a contrary presumption, of an intention on the part of the wrongful possessor not to claim title if he is mistaken as to the boundary, that the assertion of the materiality of mistake as to boundary becomes of substantial importance. That the presumption is properly in favor of the adverse or hostile character of the possession rather than against it has been previously argued, but whatever presumption in this regard may be recognized, the introduction of the element of mistake in the discussion of the question of adverse possession is, it is submitted, unnecessary and undesirable. In no case except in that of a mistake as to boundary has the element of mistake been regarded as having any significance, and there is no reason for attributing greater weight thereto when the mistake is as to the proper location of a boundary than when it is a mistake as to the title to all the land wrongfully possessed. And to introduce the element of mistake, and then limit its significance by an inquiry as to the intention which the possessor may have as to his course of action in case there should be a mistake, an intention which has ordinarily no existence whatsoever, is calculated only to cause confusion without, it is conceived, any compensating advantage."

Our Appellate Division in *Predham v. Holfester*, 32 N.J.Super. 419, 108 A.2d 458 (App.Div.1954) although acknowledging that the Maine doctrine had been severely criticized felt obliged because of Stare decisis to adhere thereto. *See also Rullis v. Jacobi*, 79 N.J.Super. 525, 528, 192 A.2d 186 (Ch.Div.1963).

We are in accord with the criticism of the Maine doctrine and favor the Connecticut doctrine for the above quoted reasons. As far as can be seen, overruling the former rule will not result in undermining any of the values which Stare decisis is intended to foster. The theory of reliance, a cornerstone of Stare decisis, is not here apt, as the problem is which of two mistaken parties is entitled to land. Realistically, the true owner does not rely upon entry of the possessor by mistake as a reason for not seeking to recover possession. Whether or not the entry is caused by mistake or intent, the same result eventuates—the true owner is ousted from possession. In either event his neglect to seek recovery of possession, within the requisite time, is in all probability the result of a lack of knowledge that he is being deprived of possession of lands to which he has title.

Accordingly, we discard the requirement that the entry and continued possession must be accompanied by a knowing intentional hostility and hold that any entry and possession for the required time which is exclusive, continuous, uninterrupted, visible and notorious, even though under mistaken claim of title, is sufficient to support a claim of title by adverse possession.

However, this conclusion is not dispositive of the matter sub judice. Of equal importance under the present factual complex, is the question of whether defendant's acts meet the necessary standard of "open and notorious" possession. It must not be forgotten that the foundation of so-called "title by adverse possession" is the failure of the true owner to commence an action for the recovery of the land involved, within the period designated by the statute of limitations. The justifications for the doctrine are aptly stated in 4 Tiffany, *Real Property* (3d ed. 1939) § 1134, p. 406 as follows:

> "The desirability of fixing, by law, a definite period within which claims to land must be asserted has been generally recognized, among the practical considerations in favor of such a policy being the prevention of the making of illegal claims after the evidence necessary to defeat them has been lost, and the interest which the community as a whole has in the security, of title. The moral justification of the policy lies in the consideration that one who has reason to know that land belonging to him is in the possession of another, and neglects, for a considerable period of time, to assert his right thereto, may properly be penalized by his preclusion from thereafter asserting such right. It is, apparently, by reason of the demerit of the true owner, rather than any supposed merit in the person who has acquired wrongful possession of the land, that this possession, if continued for the statutory period, operates to debar the former owner of all right to recover the land."

See also 5 Thompson, *Real Property* (1957 Replacement), 497.

In order to afford the true owner the opportunity to learn of the adverse claim and to protect his rights by legal action within the time specified by the statute, the adverse possession must be visible and notorious. In 4 *Tiffany, Supra* (Supp.1969, at 291), the character of possession for that purpose, is stated to be as follows:

> " . . . it must be public and based on physical facts, including known and visible lines and boundaries. Acts of dominion over the land must be so open and notorious as to put an ordinarily prudent person on notice that the land is in actual possession of another. Hence, title may never be acquired by mere possession, however long continued, which is surreptitious or secret or which is not such as will give unmistakable notice of the nature of the occupant's claim."

See also 5 *Thompson, Supra*, § 2546; 6 Powell, *Real Property*, 1013 (1969).

Generally, where possession of the land is clear and unequivocal and to such an extent as to be immediately visible, the owner may be presumed to have knowledge of the adverse occupancy. In *Foulke v. Bond*, 41 N.J.L. 527, 545 (E. & A. 1879), the court said:

> "Notoriety of the adverse claim under which possession is held, is a necessary constituent of title by adverse possession, and therefore the occupation or possession must be of that nature that the real owner is Presumed to have known that there was a possession adverse to his title, under which it was intended to make title against him." (Emphasis supplied)

However, when the encroachment of an adjoining owner is of a small area and the fact of an intrusion is not clearly and self-evidently apparent to the naked eye but requires an on-site survey for certain disclosure as in urban sections where the division line is only infrequently delineated by any monuments, natural or artificial, such a presumption is fallacious and unjustified. See concurring opinion of Judge (now Justice) Francis in *Predham v. Holfester*, 32 N.J.Super. 419, 428-429, 108 A.2d 458 (App.Div.1954). The precise location of the dividing line is then ordinarily unknown to either adjacent owner and there is nothing on the land itself to show by visual observation that a hedge, fence, wall or other structure encroaches on the neighboring land to a minor extent. Therefore, to permit a presumption of notice to arise in the case of minor border encroachments not exceeding several feet would fly in the face of reality and require the true owner to be on constant alert for possible small encroachments. The only method of certain determination would be by obtaining a survey each time the adjacent owner undertook any improvement at or near the boundary, and this would place an undue and inequitable burden upon the true owner. Accordingly we hereby hold that no presumption of knowledge arises from a minor encroachment along a common boundary. In such a case, only where the true owner has actual knowledge thereof may it be said that the possession is open and notorious.

It is conceivable that the application of the foregoing rule may in some cases result in undue hardship to the adverse possessor who under an innocent and mistaken belief of title has undertaken an extensive improvement which to some extent encroaches on an adjoining property. In that event the situation falls within the category of those cases of which *Riggle v. Skill*, 9 N.J.Super. 372, 74 A.2d 424 (Ch.Div.1950), *affirmed* 7 N.J. 268, 81 A.2d 364 (1951) is typical and equity may furnish relief. Then, if the innocent trespasser of a small portion of land adjoining a boundary line cannot without great expense remove or eliminate the encroachment, or such removal or elimination is impractical or could be accomplished only with great hardship, the true owner may be forced to convey the land so occupied upon payment of the fair value thereof without regard to whether the true owner had notice of the encroachment at its inception. Of course, such a result should eventuate only under appropriate circumstances and where no serious damage would be done to the remaining land as, for instance, by rendering the balance of the parcel unusable or no longer capable of being built upon by reason of zoning or other restrictions.

We remand the case for trial of the issues (1) whether the true owner had actual knowledge of the encroachment, (2) if not, whether plaintiffs should be obliged to convey the disputed tract to defendant, and (3) if the answer to the latter question is in the affirmative, what consideration should be paid for the conveyance. The remand, of course, contemplates further discovery and a new pretrial.

Remanded for trial in accordance with the foregoing.

NOTES

1. *Bad Faith, Good Faith, and the State of Mind Requirement.* At the outset, we asked you to think about how the state of mind standards in *Mannillo* mapped on to our three options. The Maine Doctrine matches up well with the "bad faith" or "aggressive trespass" standard, requiring the adverse possessor to have taken possession with knowledge that the property was not hers and with an intention to acquire ownership of the property. The Connecticut Doctrine, as originally articulated by the Connecticut Supreme Court in *French v. Pearce* matches up well with the "objective standard," with the court making no inquiry into the adverse possessor's state of mind. We should note, however, that a mistaken adverse possessor would win under the "good-faith" standard. Indeed, the "good-faith" standard requires the adverse possession to have been mistaken.

After having read *Mannillo*, do you have an opinion on which approach to state of mind is best? If you agree with the court's critique of the Maine/bad faith approach, which of the two remaining options—objective or good faith—would be best? A key difference between the two is that a bad faith adverse possessor would win under the objective standard but would lose under the good faith standard. We might find that the good faith standard is preferable because we do not want to reward bad faith. For example, the Colorado and New York legislatures both moved to a good faith standard after highly publicized cases involving bad faith adverse possession. *See* Jonathan Vecchi, *New York's Adverse Possession Law: An Abdication of Personal Responsibility*, 29 Touro L. Rev. 727 (2013); Geoffrey P. Anderson & David M. Pittinos, *Adverse Possession after House Bill 1148*, 37 The Colorado Lawyer 63 (Nov. 2008). On the other hand, we might prefer the objective standard because it is easier to administer. Do you see why? If not, think about how, exactly, you would prove that an adverse possessor had either good faith or bad faith.

2. *Are Minor Encroachments Open and Notorious?* The Gorskis' steps and walk encroached onto the Mannillos' land by 15 inches. Is this encroachment open and notorious? On the one hand, the steps and the walk were clearly visible to everyone. On the other hand, the fact that the steps and walk were encroaching onto the Mannillos' land was not obvious to the naked eye, and could only be established by a survey. We can call this kind of trespass, where the existence and the location of the improvement were clearly visible but the fact of encroachment onto the neighbor's property was not clearly visible, a *minor encroachment*. The court in *Mannillo* held that minor encroachments are not open and notorious unless the owner had actual knowledge that the improvements were encroaching onto her property. Most courts would probably go the other way and hold that a minor encroachment is open and notorious if the existence of the improvement is open and notorious. Which approach do you think is preferable? What does your answer say about the role and purpose of the open and notorious element and of adverse possession more generally? In this context,

you should think about how the minor encroachment fact pattern is similar to, or different from, the fact pattern presented in *Marengo Cave.*

3. *Should the Adverse Possessor Pay Compensation to the Owner?* At several points throughout this book, we will ask whether the all-or-nothing way that our legal system frames issues leads to the best results. Adverse possession gives us a good context to think about this issue. When courts consider an adverse possession case, the issue is typically framed in terms of who should win, the adverse possessor or the property owner. If the adverse possessor wins, the adverse possessor owns the property. If the property owner wins, the property owner owns the property. Perhaps it would be better to frame the issue in terms of the best result on the facts. *Mannillo* hints at an alternative to the all-or-nothing approach that courts often take by suggesting that in a minor encroachment case, the property owner might be forced to convey the encroached land to the adverse possessor in return for compensation. This raises a broader question—why don't we generally require adverse possessors to pay compensation to the true owner? If we did require compensation, would that change the way you think we should approach the elements of adverse possession in any way?   REMEDIES

Our next case, *Howard v. Kunto,* is another classic. Its peculiar facts give us the opportunity to think about both the open and notorious and continuous for the statutory period elements. The basic factual scenario of the case can be a bit confusing. Because of a surveying error, there was a mismatch between the deeds and the homes people were living in. In other words, people were living in one house, but had deeds to their next-door neighbors' house. We have illustrated the starting position as the state of affairs at Time 1. Later, to make this complicated situation even more confusing, two owners swapped deeds, leading to the state of affairs at Time 2.

Time 1:

House:		Kunto	Moyer	Howard
Deed:	Kunto	Moyer	Howard	

Time 2:

Deed:	Kunto	Howard	Moyer

Because of the surveying error, at Time 1, the Kuntos, Moyers, and Howards each had the deed to the wrong house. At Time 2, the Moyers and Howards swapped title. This gave the Moyers title to the house they were living in and gave the Howards the title to the house the Kuntos were living in. We've never found out (a) who owned the title to the Howards' house or (b) why the Howards thought that this transaction was a good idea. Whatever the Howards' motivation, the transaction led to a dispute between the Howards and the Kuntos over the house the Kuntos were living in. The Howards claimed to be owners of the house because they had the deed to the property. The Kuntos claimed to be owners of the house they were living in by adverse possession.

HOWARD V. KUNTO

Washington Court of Appeals, 1970 477 P.2d 210

PEARSON, Judge. Land surveying is an ancient art but not one free of the errors that often creep into the affairs of men. In this case, we are presented with the question of what happens when the descriptions in deeds do not fit the land the deed holders are occupying. Defendants appeal from a decree quieting title in the plaintiffs of a tract of land on the shore of Hood Canal in Mason County.

At least as long ago as 1932 the record tells us that one McCall resided in the house now occupied by the appellant-defendants, Kunto. McCall had a deed that described a 50-foot-wide parcel on the shore of Hood Canal. The error that brings this case before us is that 50 feet described in the deed is not the same 50 feet upon which McCall's house stood. Rather, the described land is an adjacent 50-foot lot directly west of that upon which the house stood. In other words, McCall's house stood on one lot and his deed described the adjacent lot. Several property owners to the west of defendants, not parties to this action, are similarly situated.

Over the years since 1946, several conveyances occurred, using the same legal description and accompanied by a transfer of possession to the succeeding occupants. The Kuntos' immediate predecessors in interest, Millers, desired to build a dock. To this end, they had a survey performed which indicated that the deed description and the physical occupation were in conformity. Several boundary stakes were placed as a result of this survey and the dock was constructed, as well as other improvements. The house as well as the others in the area continued to be used as summer recreational retreats.

The Kuntos then took possession of the disputed property under a deed from the Millers in 1959. In 1960 the respondent-plaintiffs, Howard, who held land east of that of the Kuntos, determined to convey an undivided one-half interest in their land to the Yearlys. To this end, they undertook to have a survey of the entire area made. After expending considerable effort, the surveyor retained by the Howards discovered that according to the government survey, the deed descriptions and the land occupancy of the parties did not coincide. Between the Howards and the Kuntos lay the Moyers' property. When the Howards' survey was completed, they discovered that they were the record owners of the land occupied by the Moyers and that the Moyers held record title to the land occupied by the Kuntos. Howard approached Moyer and in return for a conveyance of the land upon which the Moyers' house stood, Moyer conveyed to the Howards record title to the land upon which the Kunto house stood. Until plaintiffs Howard obtained the conveyance from Moyer in April, 1960, neither Moyer nor any of his predecessors ever asserted any right to ownership of the property actually being possessed by Kunto and his predecessors. This action was then instituted to quiet title in the Howards and Yearlys. The Kuntos appeal from a trial court decision granting this remedy.

At the time this action was commenced on August 19, 1960,[3] defendants had been in occupance of the disputed property less than a year. The trial court's

_____
3. The inordinate delay in bringing this matter to trial appears from the record to be largely inexcusable. However, neither counsel who tried the case was at fault in any way. We have intentionally declined to consider defendant's motion (probably well founded) to dismiss this case for want of prosecution (Rules of Pleading, Practice and Procedure 41.04W (1950)) for the reason that a

reason for denying their claim of adverse possession is succinctly stated in its memorandum opinion: "In this instance, defendants have failed to prove, by a preponderance of the evidence, a continuity of possession or estate to permit tacking of the adverse possession of defendants to the possession of their predecessors."

Finding of fact 6,[4] which is challenged by defendants, incorporates the above concept and additionally finds defendant's possession not to have been "continuous" because it involved only "summer occupancy."

Two issues are presented by this appeal:

(1) Is a claim of adverse possession defeated because the physical use of the premises is restricted to summer occupancy?

(2) May a person who receives record title to tract A under the mistaken belief that the has title to tract B (immediately contiguous to tract A) and who subsequently occupies tract B, for the purpose of establishing title to tract B by adverse possession, use the periods of possession of tract B by his immediate predecessors who also had record title to tract A?

In approaching both of these questions, we point out that the evidence, largely undisputed in any material sense, established that defendant or his immediate predecessors did occupy the premises, which we have called tract B, as though it was their own for far more than the 10 years as prescribed in RCW 4.16.020.[5]

We also point out that findings of fact is not challenged for its factual determinations but for the conclusions contained therein to the effect that the continuity of possession may not be established by summer occupancy, and that a predecessor's possession may not be tacked because a legal "claim of right" did not exist under the circumstances.

We start with the oft-quoted rule that:

Issues

---

new trial of the same issues would be inevitable and in light of our disposition of the case on the merits, defendants are not prejudiced by disregarding the technical grounds.

4. 'In the instant case the defendants' building was not simply over the line, but instead was built wholly upon the wrong piece of property, not the property of defendants, described in Paragraph Four (4) of the complaint herein, but on the property of plaintiffs, described in Paragraph Three of the complaint and herein. That the last three deeds in the chain of title, covering and embracing defendants' property, including defendants' deed, were executed in other states, specifically, California and Oregon. And there is no evidence of pointing out to the grantees in said three deeds, aforesaid, including defendants' deed, of any specific property, other than the property of defendants, described in their deed, and in Paragraph Four (4) of the complaint, and herein; nor of any immediate act of the grantees, including defendants, in said Three (3) deeds, aforesaid, of taking possession of any property, other than described in said three (3) deeds, aforesaid; and the testimony of husband, defendant, was unequivocally that he had no intention of possessing or holding anything other than what the deed called for; and, that there is no showing of any continuous possession by defendants or their immediate predecessors in interest, since the evidence indicates the property was in the nature, for us, as a summer occupancy, and such occupancy and use was for rather limited periods of time during comparatively short portions of the year, and was far from continuous.'

5. This statute provides:

"4.16.020 Actions to be commenced within ten years. The period prescribed in RCW 4.16.010 for the commencement of actions shall be as follows:

"Within ten years:

"Actions for the recovery of real property, or for the recovery of the possession thereof; and no action shall be maintained for such recovery unless it appears that the plaintiff, his ancestor, predecessor or grantor was seized or possessed of the premises in question within ten years before the commencement of the action."

(T)o constitute adverse possession, there must be actual possession which is *Uninterrupted*, open and notorious, hostile and exclusive, and under a *Claim of right* made in good faith for the statutory period.

(Italics ours.) *Butler v. Anderson*, 71 Wash.2d 60, 64, 426 P.2d 467, 470 (1967). *Also see Fadden v. Purvis*, 77 Wash.Dec.2d 22, 459 P.2d 385 (1969) and cases cited therein.

We reject the conclusion that summer occupancy only of a summer beach home destroys the continuity of possession required by the statute. It has become firmly established that the requisite possession requires such possession and dominion "as ordinarily marks the conduct of owners in general in holding, managing, and caring for property of like nature and condition." *Whalen v. Smith*, 183 Iowa 949, 953, 167 N.W. 646, 647 (1918). *Also see Mesher v. Connolly*, 63 Wash.2d 552, 388 P.2d 144 (1964); *Skoog v. Seymour*, 29 Wash.2d 355, 187 P.2d 304 (1947); *Butler v. Anderson, Supra; Fadden v. Purvis, Supra.*

We hold that occupancy of tract B during the summer months for more than the 10-year period by defendant and his predecessors, together with the continued existence of the improvements on the land and beach area, constituted "uninterrupted" possession within this rule. To hold otherwise is to completely ignore the nature and condition of the property. *See Fadden v. Purvis, Supra.*

We find such rule fully consonant with the legal writers on the subject. In F. Clark, *Law of Surveying and Boundaries*, § 561 (3d ed. 1959) at 565: "Continuity of possession may be established although the land is used regularly for only a certain period each year." Further, at 566:

> This rule (which permits tacking) is one of substance and not of absolute mathematical continuity, provided there is no break so as to sever two possessions. It is not necessary that the occupant should be actually upon the premises continually. If the land is occupied during the period of time during the year it is capable of use, there is sufficient continuity.

We now reach the question of tacking. The precise issue before us is novel in that none of the property occupied by defendant or his predecessors coincided with the property described in their deeds, but was contiguous.

In the typical case, which has been subject to much litigation, the party seeking to establish title by adverse possession claims more land than that described in the deed. In such cases it is clear that tacking is permitted.

In *Buchanan v. Cassell*, 53 Wash.2d 611, 614, 335 P.2d 600, 602 (1959) the Supreme Court stated:

> This state follows the rule that a purchaser may tack the adverse use of its predecessor in interest to that of his own where the land was intended to be included in the deed between them, but was mistakenly omitted from the description.

El Cerrito, Inc. v. Ryndak, 60 Wash.2d 847, 376 P.2d 528 (1962).

The general statement which appears in many of the cases is that tacking of adverse possession is permitted if the successive occupants are in "privity." *See Faubion v. Elder*, 49 Wash.2d 300, 301 P.2d 153 (1956). The deed running between the parties purporting to transfer the land possessed traditionally furnishes the privity of estate which connects the possession of the successive occupants. Plaintiff contends, and the trial court ruled, that where the deed does not describe any of the land which was occupied, the actual transfer of possession is insufficient to establish privity.

To assess the cogency of this argument and ruling, we must turn to the historical reasons for requiring privity as a necessary prerequisite to tacking the possession of several occupants. Very few, if any, of the reasons appear in the cases, nor do the cases analyze the relationships that must exist between successive possessors for tacking to be allowed. *See* W. Stoebuck, *The Law of Adverse Possession In Washington* in 35 Wash.L.Rev. 53 (1960).

The requirement of privity had its roots in the notion that a succession of trespasses, even though there was no appreciable interval between them, should not, in equity, be allowed to defeat the record title. The "claim of right," "color of title" requirement of the statutes and cases was probably derived from the early American belief that the squatter should not be able to profit by his trespass.[6]

However, it appears to this court that there is a substantial difference between the squatter or trespasser and the property purchaser, who along with several of his neighbors, as a result of an inaccurate survey or subdivision, occupies and improves property exactly 50 feet to the east of that which a survey some 30 years later demonstrates that they in fact own. It seems to us that there is also a strong public policy favoring early certainty as to the location of land ownership which enters into a proper interpretation of privity.

On the irregular perimeters of Puget Sound exact determination of land locations and boundaries is difficult and expensive. This difficulty is convincingly demonstrated in this case by the problems plaintiff's engineer encountered in attempting to locate the corners. It cannot be expected that every purchaser will or should engage a surveyor to ascertain that the beach home he is purchasing lies within the boundaries described in his deed. Such a practice is neither reasonable nor customary. Of course, 50-foot errors in descriptions are devasting where a group of adjacent owners each hold 50 feet of waterfront property.

The technical requirement of "privity" should not, we think, be used to upset the long periods of occupancy of those who in good faith received an erroneous deed description. Their "claim of right" is no less persuasive than the purchaser who believes he is purchasing more land than his deed described.

In the final analysis, however, we believe the requirement of "privity" is no more than judicial recognition of the need for some reasonable connection between successive occupants of real property so as to raise their claim of right above the status of the wrongdoer or the trespasser. We think such reasonable connection exists in this case.

Where, as here, several successive purchasers received record title to tract A under the mistaken belief that they were acquiring tract B, immediately contiguous thereto, and where possession of tract B is transferred and occupied in a continuous manner for more than 10 years by successive occupants, we hold there is sufficient privity of estate to permit tacking and thus establish adverse possession as a matter of law.

We see no reason in law or in equity for differentiating this case from *Faubion v. Elder*, 49 Wash.2d 300, 301 P.2d 153 (1956) where the appellants were

---

6. The English common law does not require privity as a prerequisite for tacking. *See* F. Clark, *Law of Surveying and Boundaries*, § 561 (3d ed. 1959) at 568.

claiming more land than their deed described and where successive periods of occupation were allowed to be united to each other to make up the time of adverse holding. To the same effect see *Naher v. Farmer*, 60 Wash. 600, 111 P. 768 (1910), and cases cited therein; *Buchanan v. Cassell*, 53 Wash.2d 611, 335 P.2d 600 (1959) and cases cited therein; *El Cerrito, Inc. v. Ryndak*, 60 Wash.2d 847, 376 P.2d 528 (1962); *See* 17 A.L.R.2d 1128 (1951). This application of the privity requirement should particularly pertain where the holder of record title to tract B acquired the same with knowledge of the discrepancy.

Judgment is reversed with directions to dismiss plaintiffs' action and to enter a decree quieting defendants' title to the disputed tract of land in accordance with the prayer of their cross-complaint.

NOTES

1. *Summer Occupancy.* The Kuntos only occupied the house during the summer. The court held that summer occupancy satisfies the requirement that the adverse possession be continuous for the statutory period, reasoning that the continuity requirement is satisfied if the adverse possessor acts as a typical owner of that type of property. For a summer home in an area where summer use is typical, summer occupancy satisfies the requirement. Note that this standard—use of the property in the same way that a typical owner would use the property—is essentially the same standard as that used for the open and notorious element. Indeed, summer occupancy could have been discussed as an open and notorious issue rather than a continuity issue.

2. *Tacking.* The Kuntos themselves had not lived on the property long enough to meet the statutory period for adverse possession. The Kuntos nonetheless won, because they were permitted to tack (i.e., add) the prior possessors' time of possession onto theirs to meet the statutory period. Tacking generally is permitted if the prior possessors (here, the Millers) and the adverse possessor (here, the Kuntos) are in privity with each other. Privity is a slippery concept that we will encounter a few times during this course. For now, we can say that parties are in privity of estate with each other if they are on the opposite sides of a consensual real estate transaction. If I convey Blackacre to you, you and I are in privity of estate. The odd facts of *Howard* made the privity issue unusually complex, because the Millers never actually purported to conveyed title to the property being adversely possessed to the Kuntos. Rather, they purportedly conveyed title to the property next door. The appellate court in *Howard* reached the logical conclusion that in this context, the privity requirement could be met by a transfer of possession of the adversely possessed property. Tacking does not apply when the prior possessor and the adverse possessor are not in privity. Here is an example of a fact pattern where the privity requirement would not be met:

EXAMPLE: O is the owner of Blackacre. The jurisdiction where Blackacre is located has a 21-year statute of limitations. A entered Blackacre in 1980 and adversely possessed it for 15 years. A then abandoned Blackacre. A year later, in 1996, B entered and adversely possessed Blackacre. In 2006, O brought an action for ejectment against B. O will win, because B has not satisfied the 21-year statutory period. B alone adversely possessed Blackacre for ten years. A adversely possessed Blackacre for 15 years. Adding the two periods together amounts to 25 years, which is more the statutory period. A and B, however, were not in privity, because A never transferred title or possession of Blackacre to B. Rather, A abandoned Blackacre, and B later entered Blackacre. B therefore cannot tack A's time of possession onto her own, and B fails to satisfy the statutory period.

3. *State of Mind, Again. Howard v. Kunto* has language suggesting that a good faith state of mind is necessary to a claim of adverse possession. The Supreme Court of Washington later clarified its rule on hostility and state of mind in *Chaplin v. Sanders*, 676 P.2d 431 (1984). We think that the court's analysis in *Chaplin* is worth quoting at length:

In order to establish a claim of adverse possession, the possession must be: (1) exclusive, (2) actual and uninterrupted, (3) open and notorious and (4) hostile and under a claim of right made in good faith. *Peeples v. Port of Bellingham*, 93 Wash.2d 766, 613 P.2d 1128 (1980); *Skansi v. Novak*, 84 Wash. 39, 146 P. 160 (1915). The period throughout which these elements must concurrently exist is 10 years. RCW 4.16.020. Hostility, as defined by this court, "does not import enmity or ill-will, but rather imports that the claimant is in possession as owner, in contradistinction to holding in recognition of or subordination to the true owner." *King v. Bassindale*, 127 Wash. 189, 192, 220 P. 777 (1923). We have traditionally treated the hostility and claim of right requirements as one and the same. *Bowden-Gazzam Co. v. Hogan*, 22 Wash.2d 27, 154 P.2d 285 (1944).

Although the definition of hostility has remained fairly constant throughout this last century, the import we have attributed to this definition has varied. For example, in *King v. Bassindale, supra,* we held that, because the claimant believed the land to be his own and treated it as such, his possession was hostile as to the rest of the world. In contrast, in *Bowden-Gazzam Co. v. Hogan, supra,* we held that an adverse user who appropriated land knowing it was not his own, but who used it as his own for over the statutory period, was entitled to title by adverse possession. Our reasoning was that the claimant's subjective belief as to who owned the land was irrelevant so long as he intended to claim the land as his own. Yet, in dicta, we affirmed the age-old requirement that the claimant neither recognize a superior interest nor claim in bad faith. Our interpretation of this definition was further muddied in *Brown v. Hubbard*, 42 Wash.2d 867, 259 P.2d 391 (1953) wherein the claimant had mistakenly included a portion of his neighbor's property when fencing his own land. Although he had openly claimed and used the land as his own for well over the statutory period, we held that he had never formed the requisite hostile intent because he would not have claimed the land as his own had he known it belonged to his neighbor.

Thus, in *Bassindale* we required the claimant to possess a good faith belief that the land possessed was his own, in *Hogan* we deemed the claimant's belief irrelevant and in Hubbard we required the claimant to possess the unrighteous intent to deprive the true owner of his land. Shortly after *Hubbard* we set forth a test for hostility which took much of the emphasis off of the claimant's subjective intent. *O'Brien v. Schultz*, 45 Wash.2d 769, 278 P.2d 322 (1954).

In *O'Brien*, we observed that "[c]ourts have had considerable difficulty in determining 'intention' in adverse possession cases, because intention may be evidenced (1) by the acts of a party, or (2) by his declarations." *O'Brien*, at 780, 278 P.2d 322. We noted that, in Washington,

the acts of the user most frequently control. If his acts clearly evince an intention to claim land as its owner, a general declaration by the user that he did not intend to claim another's land will not prove lack of intention. But a specific declaration by a user that he knew a fence was not the boundary and that he agreed to consider it as a temporary barrier will prove lack of intention. And if his acts are equivocal or do not clearly evince his intention to claim as owner, his declaration that he did not intend to take another's land, though not conclusive proof of lack of intention, may be considered in determining his intention while using the land.

(Citations omitted.) *O'Brien*, at 780, 278 P.2d 322.

O'Brien has not achieved the goal of setting forth a workable definition of hostile intent. Whenever acts are equivocal or declarations arguably specific the courts will be required to inquire into the claimant's subjective intentions, motives and beliefs regarding the land. *See, e.g., Peeples v. Port of Bellingham, supra.* The specific intent, motive and belief required is even less clear. In addition, because *O'Brien* attempted to reconcile, rather than overrule, disparate case law, many post-*O'Brien* cases exhibit a misunderstanding of the applicable rule. *See Fadden v. Purvis*, 77 Wash.2d 23, 459 P.2d 385 (1969); *Roy v. Goerz*, 26 Wash.App. 807, 614 P.2d 1308 (1980); *Hunt v. Matthews*, 8 Wash.App. 233, 505 P.2d 819 (1973). The resulting confusion necessitates our reexamination of this area of the law and mandates a new approach to the requirement of hostility. *See In re Marriage of Johnson*, 96 Wash.2d 255, 264, 634 P.2d 877 (1981).

The doctrine of adverse possession was formulated at law for the purpose of, among others, assuring maximum utilization of land, encouraging the rejection of stale claims and, most importantly, quieting titles. 7 R. Powell, *Real Property* ¶1012[3] (1982); C. Callahan, *Adverse Possession* 91-94 (1961). Because the doctrine was formulated at law and not at equity, it was originally intended to protect both those who knowingly appropriated the land of others and those who honestly entered and held possession in full belief that the land was their own. R. Powell, at ¶1013 [2]; C. Callahan, at 49-50; 3 Am.Jur.2d *Advancements* § 104 (1962). Thus, when the original purpose of the adverse possession doctrine is considered, it becomes apparent that the claimant's motive in possessing the land is irrelevant and no inquiry should be made into his guilt or innocence. *Accord, Springer v. Durette*, 217 Or. 196, 342 P.2d 132 (1959); *Agers v. Reynolds*, 306 S.W.2d 506 (Mo.1957); *Fulton v. Rapp*, 59 Ohio Law Abs. 105, 98 N.E.2d 430 (1950); *see also* Stoebuck, *The Law of Adverse Possession in Washington*, 35 Wash.L.Rev. 53, 76-80 (1960).

Washington is not the only state which looks to the subjective belief and intent of the adverse claimant in determining hostility. *See, e.g., Ellis v. Jansing*, 620 S.W.2d 569 (Tex.1981); *Van Valkenburgh v. Lutz*, 304 N.Y. 95, 106 N.E.2d 28 (1952); *see generally* 3 *American Law of Property* § 15.4 (A.J. Casner ed. 1952). However, the requirement has been regarded as unnecessarily confusing by many legal commentators, see Dockray, *Adverse Possession and Intention—I*, 1981-82 Conv. & Prop.Law. (n.s.) 256; C. Callahan, *supra*; Stoebuck, 35 Wash.L.Rev. at 76-80; and A.J. Casner, *supra*, and has been abandoned by the apparent majority of states. 3 *American Law of Property* § 15.5, at 785.

For these reasons, we are convinced that the dual requirement that the claimant take possession in "good faith" and not recognize another's superior interest does not serve the purpose of the adverse possession doctrine. *See Dunbar v. Heinrich*, 95 Wash.2d 20, 622 P.2d 812 (1980); and *Wickert v. Thompson*, 28 Wash.App. 516, 624 P.2d 747 (1981). The "hostility/claim of right" element of adverse possession requires only that the claimant treat the land as his own as against the world throughout the statutory period. The nature of his possession will be determined solely on the basis of the manner in which he treats the property. His subjective belief regarding his true interest in the land and his intent to dispossess or not dispossess another is irrelevant to this determination. *Cf.* RCW 7.28.070 and 7.28.080.

Under this analysis, permission to occupy the land, given by the true title owner to the claimant or his predecessors in interest, will still operate to negate the element of hostility.

This analysis provides a strong defense of the objective standard for the state of mind element. Consider again the alternatives. Which do you think is best?

Disabilities and the Adverse Possession Clock

In many states, the statute of limitations clock for adverse possession does not run against the owner of the property if the owner is a minor, is mentally incompetent, or is imprisoned. We typically call these categories *disabilities*, because a person falling into any of these categories would be disabled from asserting her legal rights in a timely fashion. The basic concept is fairly intuitive—we do not let the statute of limitations expire in some circumstances where it would be unfair. There are some technical complications, however, that can make it tricky to calculate the time of expiration of the statute of limitations in a disability case.

The exact rules on disabilities in any given jurisdiction will be governed by the text of the statute of limitations in that jurisdiction. Here is a hypothetical statute that contains elements that are common to many jurisdictions:

> An action to recover the title to or possession of real property shall be brought within 21 years after the cause thereof accrued. However, if a person entitled to bring such action, at the time the cause thereof accrues, is within the age of minority [the age of majority in this jurisdiction is 18], of unsound mind, or imprisoned, such person (or anyone claiming from, by, or under such person) may bring such action either (a) within the ordinary 21-year period or (b) within ten years after such disability is removed, whichever is longer.

Our hypothetical statute is a bit clearer than the typical statute and expressly states a number of concepts that are implicit in many state statutes. Here are the key concepts that you need to know to apply the statute:

1. The basic limitations period under this statute is 21 years. If the owner is disabled at the time the cause of action accrues (i.e., when the adverse possessor enters the property), then the owner will have 10 years after the disability is removed to bring an action to eject the adverse possessor. The exact number of years varies by jurisdiction, but our statute follows the typical structure by having a *base period* (here, 21 years) and a *disabilities period* (here, 10 years).
2. The ten-year disabilities period runs from the time the disability is removed. The basic idea is simple—it would be unfair to have the statute run against the owner while the owner is disabled, so we will give the owner extra time to bring a claim after the disability has been removed. The disability of being a minor is removed when the owner reaches the age of majority (here, 18). The disability of mental impairment is removed when the owner recovers mental competency. The disability of imprisonment is removed by release from prison. Further, any disability is removed by the owner's death. The language "or anyone claiming from, by, or under such person" makes it clear that if a disabled owner has died, the owner's executor or the person who

inherits from the owner will get the benefit of the ten-year disabilities period.

3.   The language "whichever is longer" at the end of the statute reminds us to be sure to only use the disabilities period if it benefits the owner. Put another way, be sure to only use the disabilities period if it is longer than the base period. Here is an example that illustrates this point:

> EXAMPLE 1: Adverse Possessor entered the property in 1980. At the time, Owner was 17. Owner reached 18, the age of majority, in 1981. Adding ten years to the time that the disability was lifted would have the disabilities period end in 1991. The base period of 21 years from entry, however, ends in 2001. Clearly, applying the base period is better for the Owner. If Owner brought an action for ejectment in 1999, Owner would win—we would not punish Owner by saying that time had expired when the disabilities period ended in 1991.

4.   Note well the language "at the time the cause thereof accrues." If the owner is disabled when the adverse possessor enters, then the owner will get the benefit of the ten-year disabilities period. If the owner becomes disabled later, then the owner will *not* get the benefit of the disabilities period. Consider these examples:

> EXAMPLE 2: Owner became mentally impaired in 1980, and remained impaired when Adverse Possessor entered in 1981. Because Owner is disabled when Adverse Possessor enters, Owner will get the benefit of the ten-year disabilities period. That is, the statute of limitation will expire ten years after Owner's disability is removed.
>
> EXAMPLE 3: Adverse Possessor entered in 1981. At the time, Owner was not disabled. In 1982, Owner became mentally impaired. Because Owner was not disabled at the time Adverse Possessor entered, Owner will not get the benefit of the ten-year disabilities period. That is, the statute of limitations will expire at the end of the 21-year base period. Owner's disability is irrelevant because it was not in place at the time of Adverse Possessor's entry.

The logic of this distinction, such as it is, is that in Example 3, Owner could have brought an action for ejectment in 1981 when Adverse Possessor entered. In many circumstances, the result will seem unfair. In both of our examples, Owner was disabled for at least 20 years of the statutory period, but in one Owner gets the benefit of the disabilities period while in the other Owner does not. Disabilities statutes, however, are typically applied mechanically. If the owner was not disabled at the time the adverse possessor entered, then the owner will not get the benefit of the disabilities period.

ADVERSE POSSESSION AND FUTURE INTERESTS

We introduced the concept of present and future interests in our section on gifts before *Gruen v. Gruen.* We will cover them in depth in our next chapter. Recall that *Gruen* involved a type of present interest called a life estate. A life estate ends at the holder's death. At that time, present possession of the property will transfer to the holder of a future interest.

What happens if an adverse possessor enters property that is divided between present and future interest holders and later satisfies all of the requirements of adverse possession? For example, imagine that A has a life estate in Blackacre, and B has a remainder. In other words, A has a present interest (the life estate), and B has a future interest (the remainder) that will become possessory on A's death. If Adverse Possessor enters Blackacre and satisfies all of the requirements of adverse possession, then Adverse Possessor will have adversely possessed A's life estate. That is, Adverse Possessor will have a present interest that ends when A dies. B still owns her future interest, however, because *the statute of limitations clock does not run against future interest holders.* In our example, the adverse possession clock will not start running against B until A dies and becomes the owner of a present interest in Blackacre.

This rule only applies if, as in our example, the adverse possessor enters after ownership has been divided into present and future interests. If the adverse possessor enters before the property is divided, then the adverse possession clock runs against both the present and future interest holder. For example, imagine that Blackacre is owned by O. Adverse Possessor enters. Later, O grants a life estate to A and a remainder to B. The clock started running against O when Adverse Possessor entered and continues to run against both A and B after the property is divided into present and future interests. In this sense, the rules on present and future interests resemble the rules on disabilities. Disabilities only matter if they were present when the adverse possessor entered. (See Disability Example 3.) Similarly, future interests only matter if they were in place when the adverse possessor entered.

5. In some circumstances, the owner will be disabled when the adverse possessor enters and then later become subject to a second disability. In these cases, we disregard the second disability that occurs after the adverse possessor has entered. Put another way, the owner cannot tack together two disabilities. Here is an example:

> EXAMPLE 4: Adverse Possessor entered the property in 1980. At the time, Owner was three years old. In 1985, Owner became mentally impaired. Owner died in 2010. We disregard the second disability. Owner reaches the 18, the age of majority, in 1995. The ten-year disability period therefore expires in 2005 (ten years after Owner reached the age of majority), not 2020 (ten years after the mental impairment disability was removed by Owner's death). It is worth noting that the disability period benefits Owner, because the base 21-year period would have expired in 2001.

Combining this point with the prior one, we can see that disabilities that occur after the adverse possessor has entered never count. If the owner has more than one disability at the time the adverse possessor enters, then the owner gets the benefit of whichever disability lasts longer. The key distinction here is between disabilities that are in place when the adverse possessor enters (which count) and disabilities that are not in place when the adverse possessor enters (which do not count).

The same rule applies if the person who inherits from the owner is disabled at the time of inheritance. Because we ignore disabilities that were not in place at the time that the adverse possessor entered, we ignore the fact that the heir is disabled. Consider this example:

> EXAMPLE 5: Owner became mentally impaired in 1980 and remained impaired when Adverse Possessor entered in 1981. Owner died in 1995, leaving all of her property to Granddaughter, who was five years old at the time. The statute of limitations period would expire in Adverse Possessor's favor in 2005. Owner was disabled when Adverse Possessor enters, so Owner gets the benefit of the disability period. The disability period expires in 2005, ten years after the disability was removed by Owner's death. We ignore the fact that Granddaughter was a minor when she became owner of the property, because her disability was not present when Adverse Possessor entered.

We note in conclusion that many of these rules lead to results that might seem unfair or inconsistent. It seems odd, for example, to respect the first disability but to ignore a second disability that occurs after the adverse possessor enters. We think it is best not to think too hard about whether or not these rules make sense. Just learn how to apply them.

The best way to master these rules is to apply them. Some of the questions in the following problem set raise disabilities issues. The remainder raise other adverse possession issues. Explanatory answers to the problem set can be found on page 1031.

Adverse Possession Problems

For the following problems, us the statute of limitations with disabilities provisions that we provided above.

1. O bought Blackacre in 1970. In 1971, O died, leaving Blackacre to B for life, remainder to C. When B died in 1975, C was ten years old. In 1977, A took possession of Blackacre and used it continuously in the typical manner. Presuming that all of the other elements of adverse possession were met, in what year would A satisfy the statutory period and establish adverse possession of Blackacre?

2. O bought Blackacre in Widener in 1970. In 1971, O was imprisoned for assault. In 1972, A took possession of Blackacre and used it continuously in the typical manner. In 1985, O was killed in a prison brawl, leaving Blackacre to B, who at the time was four years old. Presuming that all of the elements of adverse possession were met other than the expiration of the statutory period, who would win if B brings an action for ejectment against A in (a) 1994, (b) 1996, and (c) 2006?

3. O bought Blackacre in 1970. In 1975, A took possession of Blackacre and used it continuously and in the typical manner until his death in 1990. A few months after A's death, B took possession of Blackacre and used it continuously and in the typical manner. In 1997, O brought an action to eject B from Blackacre. Presuming that all elements of adverse possession other than the expiration of the statutory period have been met, who wins and why?

4. O bought Blackacre in 1970. In 1975, A took possession of Blackacre and used it continuously in the typical manner until 1990, when he transferred possession to B, who subsequently used Blackacre continuously and in the typical manner. In 1997, O brought an action to eject B from Blackacre. Presuming that all elements of adverse possession other than the expiration of the statutory period have been met, who wins and why?

5. O bought Blackacre in 1970. In 1975, A bought the adjoining Whiteacre. A immediately took possession of Whiteacre and put up a fence. Although A intended to fence in just Whiteacre, her fence in fact includes an acre of Blackacre. A month later O was severely injured in a car accident and as a result was subsequently mentally incompetent. In 1997, O's guardian discovered that A had fenced off part of Blackacre and brought an action to eject A from Blackacre. Who wins and why?

6. O bought Blackacre in 1970. In 1971, O died, leaving Blackacre to B for life, remainder to C. In 1975, A took possession of Blackacre and used it continuously in the typical manner. In 1979, B died. Presuming that all elements of adverse possession other than the expiration of the statutory period have been met, who would win if C brought an action for ejectment in (a) 1997 and (b) 2002?

ADVERSE POSSESSION SUMMARY

Adverse possession is a product of the statute of limitations. If the limitations period on the owner's claim for trespass has expired, and the other elements have been met, the adverse possessor becomes the owner of the property by operation of law. Adverse possession has four elements:

- *Actual Entry Giving Exclusive Possession.* Entry by the adverse possessor starts the clock on the statute of limitations period. The entry must give the adverse possessor exclusive possession of the land.
- *Open and Notorious.* Generally speaking, an adverse possessor satisfies this element by using the property in the way a typical owner of that type of property would. *Marengo Cave, Mannillo,* and *Howard* all involved open and notorious issues. Watch out in particular for the minor encroachment issue raised by *Mannillo.*
- *Adverse and Under Claim of Right.* This element goes to the adverse possessor's state of mind. We discussed three approaches to this element: the *objective standard* (state of mind is irrelevant), the *good faith* standard (the adverse possessor must have a good faith state of mind—i.e., the adverse possession must have been the result of an honest mistake), and the *bad faith* or *aggressive trespasser* standard (the adverse possessor must have knowingly and intentionally trespassed onto another's property). It is important to remember how a case of mistaken adverse possession plays out under these standards. A mistaken adverse possessor wins under either the objective or good faith standards, but loses under the bad faith standard. This element was discussed in depth in *Mannillo* and in the notes after *Howard.*
- *Continuous for the Statutory Period.* Seemingly straightforward, this element can present some tricky issues. *Howard* presenting the *tacking* issue—if the adverse possessor is in privity with a prior adverse

possessor, she can *tack* on the prior possessor's time of possession onto her own to satisfy the statutory period. The statute of limitations may not run against the owner if the owner is *disabled*.

POSSESSION'S ROLE IN PROPERTY LAW

We began this unit with Lord Mansfield's observation that "Possession is very strong; rather more than nine points of the law." You have now considered a series of legal issues involving possession, you now have a sophisticated understanding of the concept. We close our materials on the subject by suggesting that the idea of possession plays three important, but distinct, roles in property law and theory.[5]

First, possession is central to theories justifying individual ownership of objects that previously had been unowned. We briefly discussed John Locke's theory of property, under which people gain ownership of unowned objects by possessing those objects and mixing labor with them. Initial ownership theories rest on an idea of *first possession*, in which the first possessor becomes the first owner of an object. We saw this kind of thinking in action in *Pierson v. Post* and *Johnson v. M'Intosh*, but first possession has more of a role in property theory than it does in most aspects of property law.

FIRST IN TIME

Second, the idea of *prior possession* lies at the heart of many property law doctrines. Under the rule of prior possession, a prior possessor will generally have a superior claim to an object as compared to a subsequent possessor. If formal ownership cannot be established between two claimants for the same object, the rule of prior possession states that the prior possessor will be given ownership of the object. We saw this rule applied in our materials on bailments and finding.

Third, possession plays an evidentiary role in disputes about ownership. Absent other evidence about ownership, *current possession* may create a presumption of ownership. This evidentiary role of possession is reflected in Lord Mansfield's observation about possession being more than nine points of the law. Despite its evidentiary significance, however, current possession is rarely going to allow a person to win ownership against a prior possessor. If person B has current possession, and person A can demonstrate prior possession, then the rules of property law will generally operate to vindicate A's ownership of the object. Adverse possession is an exception, because an adverse possessor's current possession can defeat the original owner's prior possession. Even here, however, the owner's prior possession will win against the adverse possessor's current possession if the owner brings an action for ejectment before the statute of limitations expires.

---

5. These observations draw on D. Benjamin Barros, *The Biology of Possession*, 20 Widener L.J. 291 (2011).

D. EXCLUSION

As we noted at the beginning of this chapter, there are four classic incidents of property ownership: possession, use, alienation, and exclusion. We have just considered possession in depth and will discuss use and alienation at points throughout this book. In contemporary property law and theory, exclusion is often thought to lie at the heart of property ownership. After all, if you cannot exclude me from your land, it is hard to see how we can call that land your private property. We therefore end our first chapter with a brief discussion of the right to exclude. We begin with an excerpt from an article by Lior Jacob Strahilevitz that gives us an opportunity to think about how we achieve exclusion in practice. We then discuss two classic cases that allow us to consider the full scope of the right to exclude.

LIOR JACOB STRAHILEVITZ, *INFORMATION ASYMMETRIES AND THE RIGHTS TO EXCLUDE*

104 Mich. L. Rev. 1835 (2006)

THE RIGHTS TO EXCLUDE

This Part introduces the four distinct rights to exclude and elaborates on their uses, importance, and relative merits. . . .

A. THE HERMIT'S RIGHT

The traditional account of the property right to exclude emphasizes a solitary, isolated individual who excludes everyone from his land. This is the hermit's property right. Framed so narrowly, it seems to be a right of little value. Few people want to live permanently in total isolation. Rather, the prospect of hosting friends, neighbors, relatives, and service providers on one's property for visits of varying durations is a large part of what makes land ownership valuable. Although the assertion of a hermit's right is rather uncontroversial in the residential context, the law will not let any man truly become an island. Hence the hermit's land may be invaded by another who can raise a necessity defense to trespass, and public agents like firemen or police officers in hot pursuit may be privileged to enter the hermit's land.

The hermit's right, then, is perhaps only useful in a few real-property situations. Surely a true recluse will value his solitude. But beyond that, most uses of the hermit's right will be governmental. The state might establish a protected wilderness area for conservation or wildlife protection reasons, or it may create a minefield as a way to prevent invaders (or anyone else) from traversing a strategic space. Alternatively, the state may embrace paternalistic justifications for a rule that excludes everyone. For example, a government that owns a site where nuclear weapons have been tested may want to prevent anyone from setting foot on the property in question.

Intuitively, profit-making enterprises will have little use for a strict keep-out regime. It is difficult to make a profit off land if its owner will allow neither customers nor employees to set foot on it. We can expect to see firms utilizing their hermit's right only in those rare circumstances when permitting entry onto the land might expose them to substantial legal liability, as with a toxic waste dump that cannot be cleaned up in a cost-effective manner, or when utilizing the hermit's right arises out of a conflict between management and labor (i.e., a lockout).

In light of the very narrow circumstances in which private landowners seek to assert the hermit's right, it is appropriate to deem this right to exclude as practically trivial, except when legitimate, altruistic conservation interests arise. Permanent isolation is usually so unappealing that virtually no one in his right mind aspires to it. The proof for this assertion is in the pudding. It is almost impossible to locate a reported case involving a permanent invocation of the hermit's right with respect to land that has positive economic value but little environmental value. The closest case, *Brown v. Burdett,* involves a testator's wishes that her home be bricked and boarded up "with good long nails" for twenty years following the testator's death, a will provision that the court invalidated on public policy grounds. So although the hermit's right perhaps retains importance in philosophical discussions of real property rights, its practical import is sufficiently minimal so as to warrant little more discussion here.

B. THE BOUNCER'S RIGHT

Once we move away from extreme and economically unproductive exercises of the right to exclude, we arrive quickly at rights that take on enormous economic importance. As soon as an owner wishes to allow potential entrants onto his property at certain times of day, or admit some parties while refusing entry to others, or establish some criteria that will govern entry onto the land, he is exercising the sort of discretion that makes the right to exclude valuable. The greater power to exclude may include the lesser power, but it is the lesser power that takes on greater importance. Moreover, while one cannot exercise the hermit's right and the bouncer's right simultaneously, the latter three rights in the bundle are by no means mutually exclusive. Indeed, the bouncer's right, exclusionary vibes, and exclusionary amenities often will be used conjunctively by a resource owner.

The bouncer's right, then, is the landowner's right to discriminate among various parties, permitting some to enter or use the land while keeping others off the property entirely. Like the bouncer at a nightclub, the owner must exercise discretion as to who can utilize the resource, and the criteria for exclusion need not be transparent to those seeking admission. There are commercial and noncommercial variations on the bouncer's right, but they are analytically similar. A business owner will value the right to admit some customers and vendors but not others, whereas a homeowner will care about his right to invite friends and family into his home while excluding foes and strangers. . . .

C. EXCLUSIONARY VIBES

When I was an undergraduate at a large, state-subsidized university, I got the sense that there was a fair bit of homogeneity within each of the many fraternity and sorority houses on campus and attributed this homogeneity to the rush and pledge processes. But then I moved into cooperative student housing and noticed a similar level of homogeneity within particular houses, which was initially puzzling, since any student could move into a campus cooperative. The co-ops did not exercise the bouncer's right at all (except to exclude non-student residents), and yet each house seemed to have a distinct personality, not unlike the fraternities and sororities that I occasionally visited. Governance and social-ization seemed like incomplete explanations for this homogeneity. If my impres-sions were correct, this homogeneity in the campus cooperatives raised interesting questions about what was substituting for the bouncer's right. . . .

An exclusionary vibes approach involves the landowner's communication to potential entrants about the character of the community's inhabitants. Such communication tells potential entrants that certain people may not feel welcome if they enter the community in question, because they will not share certain affin-ities with existing or future residents. Although the landowner invokes no legal right to exclude anyone from the property in question, an exclusionary vibe may still be effective at excluding a targeted population thanks to two mechanisms. First, a prospective entrant may view the exclusionary vibe as an effective tool for creating a focal point around which people can organize their affairs. A variation on this focal points effect arises if the prospective entrant assumes that the exclu-sionary vibe will create a community population that is likely to embrace bouncer's exclusion at a later date as a means of removing the entrant from the community. Second, the potential entrant may assume, incorrectly, that the exclusionary vibe is backed by a bouncer's right to exclude those who are not made to feel welcome by the exclusionary vibe. I will elaborate on both of these mechanisms in detail, using a hypothetical community.

Suppose that a condo developer sees a market niche for residential commun-ities targeted toward extroverted individuals. To that end, the developer adver-tises his new condominium as "Social Butterfly Place." This advertising should suffice to make the condominium attractive to social butterflies and their fami-lies, and unattractive to more introverted individuals, even if the developer does not invest in any amenities that are designed to appeal to the extroverted.

How come? Here we see the dynamics working together. Extroverted individu-als probably will value proximity to fellow extroverts, so that they can easily find outgoing partners for conversation and joint social activities. Introverts may feel left out or marginalized living in the building, and this marginalization may impose real social and psychological costs on them. Because they may anticipate incurring some of these costs if they move in to Social Butterfly Place, many introverts will opt for a residence in some other building, ceteris paribus. This phenomenon illustrates the possibility for exclusionary vibes to serve as focal points.

Savvier introverted prospective condominium purchasers may be deterred from moving into Social Butterfly Place as well. These potential entrants would understand that the developer could do nothing to stop them from purchasing a home in the building, but would recognize the effectiveness of the focal point strategy at establishing a homogeneous population of residents consisting largely of extroverts. Even if one of these introverts did not care whether he felt left out of his neighbor's social interactions, he would rightly worry about the prospects that his extroverted neighbors might in the future: a) decide to use the bouncer's right to expel introverts if they concluded that there were too many introverts in their midst; or b) adopt, by majority vote, governance rules that made life pleasant for extroverts and unpleasant for introverts, such as manda-tory weekly condominium association meetings, or lax nighttime noise regula-tions for hallway conversations and parties within units.

Finally, some would-be condominium purchasers will see the sign "Social But-terfly Place" and erroneously assume that only extroverts are permitted to reside there. In other words, they may misread the exclusionary vibe as indicative of a developer's intent and authority to exercise a trespass-based right to exclude them. If they were to ask the developer whether introverts may reside in the tower, the developer would say that all are welcome, but many people are embarrassed to ask questions of that sort or ignorant of their legal rights. Hence an exclusionary vibe may act as an effective bluff that prevents some potential entrants who are targeted for exclusion from moving into a community. At some level, then, a fence and a "Beware of Dog" sign are fungible, even if there is no dog.

As these examples indicate, the simple act of naming a new development "Social Butterfly Place" could prove effective at excluding the introverted from residence in the development. Exclusionary vibes can function as a substitute for, or a complement to, the bouncer's right. Thus, what might superficially appear to be a developer's First Amendment commercial speech right actually takes on much greater significance as a property right, and it is appropriate to characterize the exclusionary vibe as a right to exclude. It should be equally clear that every exclusionary message is implicitly inclusionary with respect to those people who would prefer to live in a community that is devoid of those people who are targeted for exclusion.

In the real world, real estate developers sometimes do market their residences as paradise for extroverts. The exclusionary vibes strategy is prevalent where other groups or attributes are targeted for exclusion or inclusion as well. Condominium buildings adopt names like Cotton Hope Plantation and Sholom House. And individual cooperative houses near my old university campus described the character of their communities in great detail on the Internet. Indeed, entire campuses sometimes engage in heated debates over exclusionary vibes, as the recent controversy over the rebranding of "The University of the South" as "Sewanee" makes clear. We need not strain our minds too much in order to see the power of exclusionary vibes. Imagine, for example, the sales center for a mixed-income planned development in a large southern city. The sales center looks identical to any other sales center, with one difference: a large confederate battle flag flies on the flagpole out front. The mere presence of this flag would produce a first generation of homeowners who are overwhelmingly white. [In a passage that has been edited out, Strahilevitz next surveys the legal regulation of exclusionary vibes. We will touch on some of them later in the course, particularly in our discussion of the Fair Housing Act]. . . .

Exclusionary vibes . . . raise a host of new difficulties. For example, exclusionary vibes may be ineffective if too many people whom the landowner would prefer to exclude are oblivious to the signal, are poor at self-assessing, or have contrarian instincts. Alternatively, exclusionary vibes may be too controversial if they are noticed and denounced by third parties who object to the content of the exclusionary message, asserting that such a message implies second-class citizenship for the part of the community that is targeted for exclusion. In such instances, a landowner may seek an exclusion strategy that is both more effective and less in-your-face than an exclusionary vibe. Exclusionary amenity strategies present an attractive alternative.

D. EXCLUSIONARY AMENITIES

An exclusionary amenity is a common amenity that is embedded in a residential community at least in part because willingness to pay for the amenity functions as a proxy for some desired characteristic. An exclusionary amenity is a collective resource that provokes a polarizing response among people who are considering purchasing a home or renting an apartment in a particular community. Prospective purchasers (or renters) whom the developer (or landlord) would like to attract will regard the community as more attractive because of the presence of the amenity, and prospective purchasers whom the developer would not like to attract will regard the community as less attractive because of the amenity's presence. In another paper, I hypothesized that, during the 1990s, golf courses in residential developments functioned as exclusionary amenities because golf participation was a better proxy for race than wealth, income, or virtually any other characteristic. The paper provided circumstantial evidence to indicate that by purchasing homes in mandatory-membership golf communities, some non-golfing homeowners were essentially purchasing Caucasian residential homogeneity. The punch line of that paper was that the exclusionary amenities strategy might permit developers to circumvent laws that prohibit race discrimination in sales (the bouncer's right) and advertising (exclusionary vibes).

The residential golf course is not the only possible manifestation of the exclusionary amenities strategy. On the contrary, real estate developers seeking to create a "Catholic Gated Community" have noticed how placing a new, conservative Catholic school—Ave Maria University—at the center of their planned residential community can help promote the overwhelmingly Catholic character of their new development. Virginia real estate developers interested in minimizing the number of families with school-aged children in their condominium building invested heavily in an attractive bar and billiards room, but consciously avoided putting a playroom anywhere in the structure. And, by the same token, many communities forego investing in public transportation hubs or basketball courts that their residents would very much like to use, because of a fear that such inclusionary amenities might attract the wrong kinds of people to the community.

It is an expensive proposition, of course, to construct a golf course or religious university at the center of a residential development. So why would someone seeking to achieve residential homogeneity go to all that trouble? Precisely because an exclusionary amenities strategy may work better than exclusionary vibes alone. After all, an exclusionary amenity may be as effective in establishing a focal point as an exclusionary vibe, allowing people with similar preferences or attributes to find each other and live as neighbors. And the exclusionary amenity will provide added punch: a tax that falls most heavily on people who lack those similar preferences or attributes. So, let us assume that the Ave Maria Township residents subsidize the adjacent university by picking up the costs of its police protection, utilities, and land acquisition costs. As a result, homeowners in Ave Maria Township will face higher monthly assessments than homeowners in a neighboring homeowners association that is not affiliated with an institution of higher learning. A devout, traditionalist Catholic homeowner might be happy to pay this extra assessment, perhaps because he plans to make use of the theological books in the university's library and values proximity to it, or because he wants to live near the sorts of neighbors who would value proximity to such a library. But a non-Catholic Ave Maria homeowner who did not particularly want to live in an overwhelmingly Catholic neighborhood would get nothing of value in exchange for his higher monthly assessment: He would not use the library himself, and would not particularly care about whether his neighbors used the library or not. If there are otherwise similar neighborhoods surrounding Ave Maria, we should expect to see Ave Maria Township take on an overwhelmingly Catholic character and other neighborhoods take on a relatively non-Catholic character. The result will be religious residential segregation, achieved with no overt discrimination and an advertising campaign that need not include blatant exclusionary vibes. The differential tax on non-Catholic homeowners in Ave Maria will serve the same focal points purpose as the exclusionary vibe and will further exclude prospective entrants who might have been impervious or oblivious to exclusionary vibes. Furthermore, unlike a one-time advertising campaign, the presence of the university will directly affect the purchasing decisions of several generations of owners.

QUESTION

1. What do you think of Professor Strahilevitz's categories? Do exclusionary vibes and exclusionary amenities trouble you? If so, in what contexts? Can you think of ways of addressing the troubling aspects through legal rules?

JACQUE V. STEENBERG HOMES, INC.
Supreme Court of Wisconsin, 1997 563 N.W.2d 154

WILLIAM A. BABLITCH, Justice. Steenberg Homes had a mobile home to deliver. Unfortunately for Harvey and Lois Jacque (the Jacques), the easiest route of delivery was across their land. Despite adamant protests by the Jacques, Steenberg plowed a path through the Jacques' snow-covered field and via that path, delivered the mobile home. Consequently, the Jacques sued Steenberg Homes for intentional trespass. At trial, Steenberg Homes conceded the intentional trespass, but argued that no compensatory damages had been proved, and that punitive damages could not be awarded without compensatory damages. Although the jury awarded the Jacques $1 in nominal damages and $100,000 in punitive damages, the circuit court set aside the jury's award of $100,000. The court of appeals affirmed, reluctantly concluding that it could not reinstate the punitive damages because it was bound by precedent establishing that an award of nominal damages will not sustain a punitive damage award. We conclude that when nominal damages are awarded for an intentional trespass to land, punitive damages may, in the discretion of the jury, be awarded. We further conclude that the $100,000 awarded by the jury is not excessive. Accordingly, we reverse and remand for reinstatement of the punitive damage award.

The relevant facts follow. Plaintiffs, Lois and Harvey Jacques, are an elderly couple, now retired from farming, who own roughly 170 acres near Wilke's Lake in the town of Schleswig. The defendant, Steenberg Homes, Inc. (Steenberg), is in the business of selling mobile homes. In the fall of 1993, a neighbor of the Jacques purchased a mobile home from Steenberg. Delivery of the mobile home was included in the sales price.

Steenberg determined that the easiest route to deliver the mobile home was across the Jacques' land. Steenberg preferred transporting the home across the Jacques' land because the only alternative was a private road which was covered in up to seven feet of snow and contained a sharp curve which would require sets of "rollers" to be used when maneuvering the home around the curve. Steenberg asked the Jacques on several separate occasions whether it could move the home across the Jacques' farm field. The Jacques refused. The Jacques were sensitive about allowing others on their land because they had lost property valued at over $10,000 to other neighbors in an adverse possession action in the mid-1980s. Despite repeated refusals from the Jacques, Steenberg decided to sell the mobile home, which was to be used as a summer cottage, and delivered it on February 15, 1994.

On the morning of delivery, Mr. Jacque observed the mobile home parked on the corner of the town road adjacent to his property. He decided to find out where the movers planned to take the home. The movers, who were Steenberg employees, showed Mr. Jacque the path they planned to take with the mobile home to reach the neighbor's lot. The path cut across the Jacques' land. Mr. Jacque informed the movers that it was the Jacques' land they were planning to cross and that Steenberg did not have permission to cross their land. He told them that Steenberg had been refused permission to cross the Jacques' land.

One of Steenberg's employees called the assistant manager, who then came out to the Jacques' home. In the meantime, the Jacques called and asked some of their neighbors and the town chairman to come over immediately. Once everyone was present, the Jacques showed the assistant manager an aerial map and plat book of the township to prove their ownership of the land, and reiterated their demand that the home not be moved across their land.

At that point, the assistant manager asked Mr. Jacque how much money it would take to get permission. Mr. Jacque responded that it was not a question of money; the Jacques just did not want Steenberg to cross their land. Mr. Jacque testified that he told Steenberg to "[F]ollow the road, that is what the road is for." Steenberg employees left the meeting without permission to cross the land.

At trial, one of Steenberg's employees testified that, upon coming out of the Jacques' home, the assistant manager stated: "I don't give a——what [Mr. Jacque] said, just get the home in there any way you can." The other Steenberg employee confirmed this testimony and further testified that the assistant manager told him to park the company truck in such a way that no one could get down the town road to see the route the employees were taking with the home. The assistant manager denied giving these instructions, and Steenberg argued that the road was blocked for safety reasons.

The employees, after beginning down the private road, ultimately used a "bobcat" to cut a path through the Jacques' snow-covered field and hauled the home across the Jacques' land to the neighbor's lot. One employee testified that upon returning to the office and informing the assistant manager that they had gone across the field, the assistant manager reacted by giggling and laughing. The other employee confirmed this testimony. The assistant manager disputed this testimony.

When a neighbor informed the Jacques that Steenberg had, in fact, moved the mobile home across the Jacques' land, Mr. Jacque called the Manitowoc County Sheriff's Department. After interviewing the parties and observing the scene, an officer from the sheriff's department issued a $30 citation to Steenberg's assistant manager.

The Jacques commenced an intentional tort action in Manitowoc County Circuit Court, Judge Allan J. Deehr presiding, seeking compensatory and punitive damages from Steenberg. The case was tried before a jury on December 1, 1994.

At the completion of the Jacques' case, Steenberg moved for a directed verdict under Wis. Stat. §805.14(3)(1993-94). For purposes of the motion, Steenberg admitted to an intentional trespass to land, but asked the circuit court to find that the Jacques were not entitled to compensatory damages or punitive damages based on insufficiency of the evidence. The circuit court denied Steenberg's motion and the questions of punitive and compensatory damages were submitted to the jury. The jury awarded the Jacques $1 nominal damages and $100,000 punitive damages. . . .

Steenberg argues that, as a matter of law, punitive damages could not be awarded by the jury because punitive damages must be supported by an award of compensatory damages and here the jury awarded only nominal and punitive damages. The Jacques contend that the rationale supporting the compensatory damage award requirement is inapposite when the wrongful act is an intentional trespass to land. We agree with the Jacques. . . .

We turn first to the individual landowner's interest in protecting his or her land from trespass. The United States Supreme Court has recognized that the private landowner's right to exclude others from his or her land is "one of the most essential sticks in the bundle of rights that are commonly characterized as property." *Dolan v. City of Tigard*, 512 U.S. 374, 384, 114 S.Ct. 2309, 2316, 129 L.Ed.2d 304 (1994); (quoting *Kaiser Aetna v. United States*, 444 U.S. 164, 176, 100 S.Ct. 383, 391, 62 L.Ed.2d 332 (1979)). *Accord Nollan v. California Coastal Comm'n*, 483 U.S. 825, 831, 107 S.Ct. 3141, 3145, 97 L.Ed.2d 677 (1987) (quoting *Loretto v. Teleprompter Manhattan CATV Corp.*, 458 U.S. 419, 433, 102 S.Ct. 3164, 3175, 73 L.Ed.2d 868 (1982)). This court has long recognized "[e]very person ['s] constitutional right to the exclusive enjoyment of his own property for any purpose which does not invade the rights of another person." *Diana Shooting Club v. Lamoreux*, 114 Wis. 44, 59, 89 N.W. 880 (1902) (holding that the victim of an intentional trespass should have been allowed to take judgment for nominal damages and costs). Thus, both this court and the Supreme Court recognize the individual's legal right to exclude others from private property.

Yet a right is hollow if the legal system provides insufficient means to protect it. Felix Cohen offers the following analysis summarizing the relationship between the individual and the state regarding property rights:

[T]hat is property to which the following label can be attached:

> To the world:
> Keep off X unless you have my permission, which I may grant or withhold.
> Signed: Private Citizen
> Endorsed: The state

Felix S. Cohen, *Dialogue on Private Property*, IX Rutgers Law Review 357, 374 (1954). Harvey and Lois Jacque have the right to tell Steenberg Homes and any other trespasser, "No, you cannot cross our land." But that right has no practical meaning unless protected by the State. And, as this court recognized as early as 1854, a "halfpenny" award does not constitute state protection. . . .

In sum, the individual has a strong interest in excluding trespassers from his or her land. Although only nominal damages were awarded to the Jacques, Steenberg's intentional trespass caused actual harm. We turn next to society's interest in protecting private property from the intentional trespasser.

Society has an interest in punishing and deterring intentional trespassers beyond that of protecting the interests of the individual landowner. Society has an interest in preserving the integrity of the legal system. Private landowners should feel confident that wrongdoers who trespass upon their land will be appropriately punished. When landowners have confidence in the legal system, they are less likely to resort to "self-help" remedies. In *McWilliams,* the court recognized the importance of "'prevent[ing] the practice of dueling, [by permitting] juries [ ] to *punish* insult by exemplary damages.'" *McWilliams,* 3 Wis. at 428. Although dueling is rarely a modern form of self-help, one can easily imagine a frustrated landowner taking the law into his or her own hands when faced with a brazen trespasser, like Steenberg, who refuses to heed no trespass warnings. . . .

Reversed and remanded with directions.

STATE V. SHACK

Supreme Court of New Jersey, 1971 277 A.2d 369

WEINTRAUB, C.J. Defendants entered upon private property to aid migrant farmworkers employed and housed there. Having refused to depart upon the demand of the owner, defendants were charged with violating N.J.S.A. 2A:170-31 which provides that "(a)ny person who trespasses on any lands . . . after being forbidden so to trespass by the owner . . . is a disorderly person and shall be punished by a fine of not more than $50." Defendants were convicted in the Municipal Court of Deerfield Township and again on appeal in the County Court of Cumberland County on a trial De novo. R. 3:23-8(a). We certified their further appeal before argument in the Appellate Division.

Before us, no one seeks to sustain these convictions. The complaints were prosecuted in the Municipal Court and in the County Court by counsel engaged by the complaining landowner, Tedesco. However Tedesco did not respond to this appeal, and the county prosecutor, while defending abstractly the constitutionality of the trespass statute, expressly disclaimed any position as to whether the statute reached the activity of these defendants.

Complainant, Tedesco, a farmer, employs migrant workers for his seasonal needs. As part of their compensation, these workers are housed at a camp on his property.

Defendant Tejeras is a field worker for the Farm Workers Division of the Southwest Citizens Organization for Poverty Elimination, known by the acronym SCOPE, a nonprofit corporation funded by the Office of Economic Opportunity pursuant to an act of Congress, 42 U.S.C.A. §§ 2861-2864. The role of SCOPE includes providing for the "health services of the migrant farm worker."

Defendant Shack is a staff attorney with the Farm Workers Division of Camden Regional Legal Services, Inc., known as "CRLS," also a nonprofit corporation funded by the Office of Economic Opportunity pursuant to an act of Congress, 42 U.S.C.A. § 2809(a)(3). The mission of CRLS includes legal advice and representation for these workers.

Differences had developed between Tedesco and these defendants prior to the events which led to the trespass charges now before us. Hence when defendant Tejeras wanted to go upon Tedesco's farm to find a migrant worker who needed medical aid for the removal of 28 sutures, he called upon defendant

Shack for his help with respect to the legalities involved. Shack, too, had a mission to perform on Tedesco's farm; he wanted to discuss a legal problem with another migrant worker there employed and housed. Defendants arranged to go to the farm together. Shack carried literature to inform the migrant farmworkers of the assistance available to them under federal statutes, but no mention seems to have been made of that literature when Shack was later confronted by Tedesco.

Defendants entered upon Tedesco's property and as they neared the camp site where the farmworkers were housed, they were confronted by Tedesco who inquired of their purpose. Tejeras and Shack stated their missions. In response, Tedesco offered to find the injured worker, and as to the worker who needed legal advice, Tedesco also offered to locate the man but insisted that the consultation would have to take place in Tedesco's office and in his presence. Defendants declined, saying they had the right to see the men in the privacy of their living quarters and without Tedesco's supervsion. Tedesco thereupon summoned a State Trooper who, however, refused to remove defendants except upon Tedesco's written complaint. Tedesco then executed the formal complaints charging violations of the trespass statute.

The constitutionality of the trespass statute, as applied here, is challenged on several scores. . . . These constitutional claims are not established by any definitive holding. We think it unnecessary to explore their validity. The reason is that we are satisfied that under our State law the ownership of real property does not include the right a bar access to governmental services available to migrant workers and hence there was no trespass within the meaning of the penal statute. The policy considerations which underlie that conclusion may be much the same as those which would be weighed with respect to one or more of the constitutional challenges, but a decision in nonconstitutional terms is more satisfactory, because the interests of migrant workers are more expansively served in that way than they would be if they had no more freedom than these constitutional concepts could be found to mandate if indeed they apply at all.

Property rights serve human values. They are recognized to that end, and are limited by it. Title to real property cannot include dominion over the destiny of persons the owner permits to come upon the premises. Their well-being must remain the paramount concern of a system of law. Indeed the needs of the occupants may be so imperative and their strength so weak, that the law will deny the occupants the power to contract away what is deemed essential to their health, welfare, or dignity.

Here we are concerned with a highly disadvantaged segment of our society. We are told that every year farmworkers and their families numbering more than one million leave their home areas to fill the seasonal demand for farm labor in the United States. . . .

The migrant farmworkers are a community within but apart from the local scene. They are rootless and isolated. Although the need for their labors is evident, they are unorganized and without economic or political power. It is their plight alone that summoned government to their aid. In response, Congress provided under Title III-B of the Economic Opportunity Act of 1964 (42 U.S.C.A. § 2701 et seq.) for "assistance for migrant and other seasonally employed farmworkers and their families." Section 2861 states "the purpose of this part is to assist migrant and seasonal farmworkers and their families to improve their living conditions and develop skills necessary for a productive and self-sufficient life in an increasingly complex and technological society." Section 2862(b)(1) provides for funding of programs "to meet the immediate needs of migrant and seasonal farmworkers and their families, such as day care for children, education, health services, improved housing and sanitation (including the provision and maintenance of emergency and temporary housing and sanitation facilities), legal advice and representation, and consumer training and couseling.' As we have said, SCOPE is engaged in a program funded under this section, and CRLS also pursues the objectives of this section although, we gather, it is funded under § 2809(a)(3), which is not limited in its concern to the migrant and other seasonally employed farmworkers and seeks "to further the cause of justice among persons living in poverty by mobilizing the assistance of lawyers and legal institutions and by providing legal advice, legal representation, counseling, education, and other appropriate services."

These ends would not be gained if the intended beneficiaries could be insulated from efforts to reach them. It is in this framework that we must decide whether the camp operator's rights in his lands may stand between the migrant workers and those who would aid them. The key to that aid is communication. Since the migrant workers are outside the mainstream of the communities in which they are housed and are unaware of their rights and opportunities and of the services available to them, they can be reached only by positive efforts tailored to that end. The Report of the Governor's Task Force on Migrant Farm Labor (1968) noted that "One of the major problems related to seasonal farm labor is the lack of adequate direct information with regard to the availability of public services," and that "there is a dire need to provide the workers with basic educational and informational material in a language and style that can be readily understood by the migrant" (pp. 101-102). The report stressed the problem of access and deplored the notion that property rights may stand as a barrier, saying "In our judgment, 'no trespass' signs represent the last dying remnants of paternalistic behavior" (p. 63).

A man's right in his real property of course is not absolute. It was a maxim of the common law that one should so use his property as not to injure the rights of others. Broom, *Legal Maxims* (10th ed. Kersley 1939), p. 238; 39 *Words and Phrases*, "Sic Utere Tuo ut Alienum Non Laedas," p. 335. Although hardly a precise solvent of actual controversies, the maxim does express the inevitable proposition that rights are relative and there must be an accommodation when they meet. Hence it has long been true that necessity, private or public, may justify entry upon the lands of another. For a catalogue of such situations, see Prosser, *Torts* (3d ed. 1964), § 24, pp. 127-129; 6A *American Law of Property* (A. J. Casner ed. 1954) § 28.10, p. 31; 52 Am.Jur., "Trespass," §§ 40-41, pp. 867-869. *See also* Restatement, Second, Torts (1965) §§ 197-211; *Krauth v. Geller*, 31 N.J. 270, 272-273, 157 A.2d 129 (1960).

The subject is not static. As pointed out in 5 Powell, *Real Property* (Rohan 1970) § 745, pp. 493-494, while society will protect the owner in his permissible interests in land, yet

". . . (s)uch an owner must expect to find the absoluteness of his property rights curtailed by the organs of society, for the promotion of the best interests of others for whom these organs also operate as protective agencies. The necessity for such curtailments is greater in a modern industrialized and urbanized society than it was in the relatively simple American society of fifty, 100, or 200 years ago. The current balance between individualism and dominance of the social interest depends not only upon political and social ideologies, but also upon the physical and social facts of the time and place under discussion."

Professor Powell added in § 746, pp. 494-496:

"As one looks back along the historic road traversed by the law of land in England and in America, one sees a change from the viewpoint that he who owns may do as he pleases with what he owns, to a position which hesitatingly embodies an ingredient of stewardship; which grudgingly, but steadily, broadens the recognized scope of social interests in the utilization of things. . . .

To one seeing history through the glasses of religion, these changes may seem to evidence increasing embodiments of the golden rule. To one thinking in terms of political and economic ideologies, they are likely to be labeled evidences of 'social enlightenment,' or of 'creeping socialism' or even of 'communistic infiltration,' according to the individual's assumed definitions and retained or acquired prejudices. With slight attention to words or labels, time marches on toward new adjustments between individualism and the social interests."

The process involves not only the accommodation between the right of the owner and the interests of the general public in his use of this property, but involves also an accommodation between the right of the owner and the right of individuals who are parties with him in consensual transactions relating to the use of the property. Accordingly substantial alterations have been made as between a landlord and his tenant. See Reste Realty Corp. v. Cooper, 53 N.J. 444, 451-453, 251 A.2d 268 (1969); Marini v. Ireland, 56 N.J. 130, 141-143, 265 A.2d 526 (1970). . . .

We see no profit in trying to decide upon a conventional category and then forcing the present subject into it. That approach would be artificial and distorting. The quest is for a fair adjustment of the competing needs of the parties, in the light of the realities of the relationship between the migrant worker and the operator of the housing facility.

Thus approaching the case, we find it unthinkable that the farmer-employer can assert a right to isolate the migrant worker in any respect significant for the worker's well-being. The farmer, of course, is entitled to pursue his farming activities without interference, and this defendants readily concede. But we see no legitimate need for a right in the farmer to deny the worker the opportunity for aid available from federal, State, or local services, or from recognized charitable groups seeking to assist him. Hence representatives of these agencies and organizations may enter upon the premises to seek out the worker at his living quarters. So, too, the migrant worker must be allowed to receive visitors there of his own choice, so long as there is no behavior hurtful to others, and members of the press may not be denied reasonable access to workers who do not object to seeing them.

It is not our purpose to open the employer's premises to the general public if in fact the employer himself has not done so. We do not say, for example, that solicitors or peddlers of all kinds may enter on their own; we may assume or the present that the employer may regulate their entry or bar them, at least if the employer's purpose is not to gain a commercial advantage for himself or if the regulation does not deprive the migrant worker of practical access to things he needs.

And we are mindful of the employer's interest in his own and in his employees' security. Hence he may reasonably require a visitor to identify himself, and also to state his general purpose if the migrant worker has not already informed him that the visitor is expected. But the employer may not deny the worker his privacy or interfere with his opportunity to live with dignity and to enjoy associations customary among our citizens. These rights are too fundamental to be denied on the basis of an interest in real property and too fragile to be left to the unequal bargaining strength of the parties. *See Henningsen v. Bloomfield Motors, Inc.*, 32 N.J. 358, 403-404, 161 A.2d 69 (1960); *Ellsworth Dobbs, Inc. v. Johnson*, 50 N.J. 528, 555, 236 A.2d 843 (1967).

It follows that defendants here invaded no possessory right of the farmer-employer. Their conduct was therefore beyond the reach of the trespass statute. The judgments are accordingly reversed and the matters remanded to the County Court with directions to enter judgments of acquittal.

NOTES AND QUESTIONS

1. *Jacque v. Steenberg Homes* suggests that the right to exclude is a critically important aspect of our property system. *State v. Shack* suggests that the right to exclude is subject to significant limitations. There is nothing inconsistent with these two positions—just because something is important does not mean that it is immune from limitation. Looking at the facts of the two cases, what do you think led to the different emphasis in the courts' opinions?

2. William Blackstone famously wrote that property is "that sole and despotic dominion which one man claims and exercises over the external things of the world, in total exclusion of the right of any other individual in the universe." As *Shack* illustrates, there are some limits to this dominion. What limits would you place on a property owner's right to exclude?

3. Imagine that you are walking down a beach. You come across a sign stating that part of the beach is closed to the public because it is part of a private nature preserve. A bit later, you come across a sign stating that part of the beach is private property and that access is reserved to beachfront homeowners. Are these signs trying to achieve the same thing? Is the right to exclude a good thing or a bad thing?

FREEDOM-BASED THEORIES OF PRIVATE PROPERTY

Private property is often justified because it protects and promotes individual freedom. Proponents of freedom-based theories make three distinct types of arguments about the relationship between property and freedom. First, property creates zones of individual autonomy and privacy. As Charles Reich put it, property "draw[s] a boundary between public and private power . . . maintaining independence, dignity and pluralism in society by creating zones within which the majority has to yield to the owner." Charles A. Reich, *The New Property*, 73 Yale L.J. 733, 771-772 (1964). Second, private property disperses power that otherwise would be held exclusively by the government. The economist Milton Friedman wrote that private-property-based capitalism "promotes personal freedom because it separates economic power from political power and in this way enables the one to offset the other." Milton Friedman, *Capitalism and Freedom,* 9 (1962). Third, private property gives people access to the resources that they need to make basic life decisions for themselves. As Reich observed, "[p]olitical rights presuppose that individuals and private groups have the will and the means to act independently." Reich, *supra.* People cannot have the will and the means to act independently if they are beholden to others for resources that they need to live their lives. Of course, one person's freedom can conflict with another person's freedom. If I am able to exclude you from my property, I gain a zone of individual autonomy and privacy at the expense of your freedom to access my property. The private property system therefore "is a distribution of freedom *and* unfreedom." G.A. Cohen, *Illusions About Private Property and Freedom,* in 4 *Issues in Marxist Philosophy* 226, 226-227 (1981). Do not make the mistake of associating freedom-based arguments for private property with any particular part of the political spectrum. Comparing Friedman and Reich is instructive. Friedman's arguments about property and freedom were made in the context of defending the institution of free market capitalism. Reich's arguments were made in the context of making an argument for the recognition of a property right to receive welfare payments and other types of government largess.

CHAPTER
3

Intellectual Property/Property
in the Person

A. A BRIEF INTRODUCTION TO INTELLECTUAL PROPERTY

Every year, intellectual property becomes an increasingly important part of our economy. In this section, we provide a very brief overview of the law of intellectual property and of some of the fundamental theoretical issues that underlie our intellectual property rules. Most law schools offer several upper-level classes on intellectual property, and we encourage you to explore them as your legal education progresses.

Our legal system has three major types of intellectual property: copyrights, patents, and trademarks. Article I, Section 8 of the Constitution expressly gives Congress the power to enact laws "[t]o promote the progress of science and useful arts, by securing for limited times to authors and investors the exclusive right to their respective writings and discoveries." The common law gave some protection to intellectual property, and common-law rights can still be important in some contexts. For the most part, however, our modern law of copyright, trademark, and patent is governed by federal statute.

Perhaps the most important policy issue in intellectual property law involves striking a balance between the creation and consumption of intellection property. As we will see, each type of intellectual property gives certain rights to the creators of intellectual property. These rights incentivize the production of intellectual property. While we want to promote the creation of intellectual property, we also want the public to be able to consume the intellectual property. If we give creators too little protection, they may not produce new intellectual property. If we give creators too much protection, then the public consumption of intellectual property will be overly constrained. A related policy issue involves striking the balance between the interests of present and future creators of intellectual property. As we will see, new intellectual property tends to build on older intellectual property. We therefore need to make sure that we do not unduly stifle future creators by giving present creators too much protection.

Each type of intellectual property strikes the balance between creation and consumption in different ways. *Patents* give protection to the inventors of new products and processes. To qualify for protection, the invention must be useful, novel, and non-obvious. Patents incentivize production of intellectual property by giving the patent holder an effective monopoly on the use of the invention for the duration of the patent term. Patents typically last for 20 years from the time that the original application was submitted to the Patent Office. The relatively short duration of patents incentivizes consumption. For example, once a drug patent expires, that drug typically is available to consumers at greatly reduced cost from generic drug manufacturers.

Copyrights protect the expression of ideas. Books, songs, and videos, for example, are copyrightable. Ideas themselves are not copyrightable. Compared to other intellectual property rights, copyrights last for a relatively long time. The duration of copyrights has changed over the years, but today the typical copyright will last for the life of the creator plus 70 years. The interests of consumers and subsequent creators are served by the fair use doctrine, which allows for the limited use of copyrighted work without permission from or payment to the copyright holder. Subsequent creators are protected by a subcategory of fair use called transformative use. As its name suggests, transformative use protects a new creator who uses previously copyrighted material in a completely new or unexpected way. Parodies are good examples of transformative use.

A *trademark* is a "word, name, symbol, or device, or any combination thereof" used by a person "to identify and distinguish his or her goods, including a unique product, from those manufactured or sold by others. . . . " 15 U.S.C.A. § 1127. The interests of creators and consumers are balanced in a slightly different way in the trademark context than in the patent and copyright context. Consumers do not actually consume trademarks. Rather, they consume goods identified and distinguished by trademarks. Trademarks incentivize production by rewarding trademark holders who create brands and products that consumers value. Trademarks help consumers who want a specific product identify that product. Trademark law protection is typically limited by the degree to which a consumer might be confused by an allegedly infringing product. This is why, for example, you will see generic products on store shelves that have a somewhat similar look and feel to a trademarked product. A generic product typically will not infringe on the trademark so long as it is unlikely that a consumer will be confused between the genuine trademarked product and a generic imitation.

We provide excerpts from only two of the hundreds of fascinating cases in the intellectual property cannon. The first case, *International News Service v. Associated Press* is a classic early case involving the collection and dissemination of news. Often referred to by the abbreviation *INS v. AP*, the case gives us an opportunity to think about issues that continue to be relevant in the Internet age. Say that you run a website devoted to covering news on a particular topic. I run a competing website devoted to the same topic. I read news on your website and then post reports on those topics on my website. Can you bring a claim against me for appropriating the news that you gathered?

INTERNATIONAL NEWS SERVICE V. ASSOCIATED PRESS

Supreme Court of the United States, 1918 248 U.S. 215

Mr. Justice PITNEY delivered the opinion of the Court.

The parties are competitors in the gathering and distribution of news and its publication for profit in newspapers throughout the United States. The

Associated Press, which was complainant in the District Court, is a co-operative organization, incorporated under the Membership Corporations Law of the state of New York, its members being individuals who are either proprietors or representatives of about 950 daily newspapers published in all parts of the United States. . . . Complainant gathers in all parts of the world, by means of various instrumentalities of its own, by exchange with its members, and by other appropriate means, news and intelligence of current and recent events of interest to newspaper readers and distributes it daily to its members for publication in their newspapers. The cost of the service, amounting approximately to $3,500,000 per annum, is assessed upon the members and becomes a part of their costs of operation, to be recouped, presumably with profit, through the publication of their several newspapers. Under complainant's by-laws each member agrees upon assuming membership that news received through complainant's service is received exclusively for publication in a particular newspaper, language, and place specified in the certificate of membership, that no other use of it shall be permitted, and that no member shall furnish or permit any one in his employ or connected with his newspaper to furnish any of complainant's news in advance of publication to any person not a member. And each member is required to gather the local news of his district and supply it to the Associated Press and to no one else.

Defendant is a corporation organized under the laws of the state of New Jersey, whose business is the gathering and selling of news to its customers and clients, consisting of newspapers published throughout the United States, under contracts by which they pay certain amounts at stated times for defendant's service. It has widespread news-gathering agencies; the cost of its operations amounts, it is said, to more than $2,000,000 per annum; and it serves about 400 newspapers located in the various cities of the United States and abroad, a few of which are represented, also, in the membership of the Associated Press.

The parties are in the keenest competition between themselves in the distribution of news throughout the United States; and so, as a rule, are the newspapers that they serve, in their several districts.

Complainant in its bill, defendant in its answer, have set forth in almost identical terms the rather obvious circumstances and conditions under which their business is conducted. The value of the service, and of the news furnished, depends upon the promptness of transmission, as well as upon the accuracy and impartiality of the news; it being essential that the news be transmitted to members or subscribers as early or earlier than similar information can be furnished to competing newspapers by other news services, and that the news furnished by each agency shall not be furnished to newspapers which do not contribute to the expense of gathering it. And further, to quote from the answer:

> "Prompt knowledge and publication of worldwide news is essential to the conduct of a modern newspaper, and by reason of the enormous expense incident to the gathering and distribution of such news, the only practical way in which a proprietor of a newspaper can obtain the same is, either through co-operation with a considerable number of other newspaper proprietors in the work of collecting and distributing such news, and the equitable division with them of the expenses thereof, or by the purchase of such news from some existing agency engaged in that business."

The bill was filed to restrain the pirating of complainant's news by defendant in three ways: First, by bribing employees of newspapers published by complainant's members to furnish Associated Press news to defendant before publication, for transmission by telegraph and telephone to defendant's clients for publication by them; second, by inducing Associated Press members to violate its by-laws and permit defendant to obtain news before publication; and, third, by copying news from bulletin boards and from early editions of complainant's newspapers and selling this, either bodily or after rewriting it, to defendant's customers.

The District Court, upon consideration of the bill and answer, with voluminous affidavits on both sides, granted a preliminary injunction under the first and second heads, but refused at that stage to restrain the systematic practice admittedly pursued by defendant, of taking news bodily from the bulletin boards and early editions of complainant's newspapers and selling it as its own. The court expressed itself as satisfied that this practice amounted to unfair trade, but as the legal question was one of first impression it considered that the allowance of an injunction should await the outcome of an appeal. 240 Fed. 983, 996. Both parties having appealed, the Circuit Court of Appeals sustained the injunction order so far as it went, and upon complainant's appeal modified it and remanded the cause, with directions to issue an injunction also against any bodily taking of the words or substance of complainant's news until its commercial value as news had passed away. 245 Fed. 244, 253, 157 C. C. A. 436. The present writ of certiorari was then allowed. 245 U. S. 644, 38 Sup. Ct. 10, 62 L. Ed. 528.

The only matter that has been argued before us is whether defendant may lawfully be restrained from appropriating news taken from bulletins issued by complainant or any of its members, or from newspapers published by them, for the purpose of selling it to defendant's clients. Complainant asserts that defendant's admitted course of conduct in this regard both violates complainant's property right in the news and constitutes unfair competition in business. And notwithstanding the case has proceeded only to the stage of a preliminary injunction, we have deemed it proper to consider the underlying questions, since they go to the very merits of the action and are presented upon facts that are not in dispute. As presented in argument, these questions are: (1) Whether there is any property in news; (2) Whether, if there be property in news collected for the purpose of being published, it survives the instant of its publication in the first newspaper to which it is communicated by the news-gatherer; and (3) whether defendant's admitted course of conduct in appropriating for commercial use matter taken from bulletins or early editions of Associated Press publications constitutes unfair competition in trade. . . .

Complainant's news matter is not copyrighted. It is said that it could not, in practice, be copyrighted, because of the large number of dispatches that are sent daily; and, according to complainant's contention, news is not within the operation of the copyright act. Defendant, while apparently conceding this, nevertheless invokes the analogies of the law of literary property and copyright, insisting as its principal contention that, assuming complainant has a right of property in its news, it can be maintained (unless the copyright act by complied with) only by being kept secret and confidential, and that upon the publication with complainant's consent of uncopyrighted news of any of complainant's members in a newspaper or upon a bulletin board, the right of property is lost, and the subsequent use of the news by the public or by defendant for any purpose whatever becomes lawful. . . .

No doubt news articles often possess a literary quality, and are the subject of literary property at the common law; nor do we question that such an article, as a literary production, is the subject of copyright by the terms of the act as it now stands. In an early case at the circuit Mr. Justice Thompson held in effect that a newspaper was not within the protection of the copyright acts of 1790 (1 Stat. 124) and 1802 (2 Stat. 171). *Clayton v. Stone*, 2 Paine, 382, Fed. Cas. No. 2,872. But the present act is broader; it provides that the works for which copyright may be secured shall include "all the writings of an author," and specifically mentions "periodicals, including newspapers." Act of March 4, 1909, c. 320, §§ 4 and 5, 35 Stat. 1075, 1076 (Comp. St. 1916, §§ 9520, 9521). Evidently this admits to copyright a contribution to a newspaper, notwithstanding it also may convey news; and such is the practice of the copyright office, as the newspapers of the day bear witness. *See* Copyright Office Bulletin No. 15 (1917) pp. 7, 14, 16, 17.

But the news element—the information respecting current events contained in the literary production—is not the creation of the writer, but is a report of matters that ordinarily are publici juris; it is the history of the day. It is not to be supposed that the framers of the Constitution, when they empowered Congress "to promote the progress of science and useful arts, by securing for limited times to authors and inventors the exclusive right to their respective writings and discoveries" (Const. art. 1, § 8, par. 8), intended to confer upon one who might happen to be the first to report a historic event the exclusive right for any period to spread the knowledge of it.

We need spend no time, however, upon the general question of property in news matter at common law, or the application of the copyright act, since it seems to us the case must turn upon the question of unfair competition in business. And, in our opinion, this does not depend upon any general right of property analogous to the common-law right of the proprietor of an unpublished work to prevent its publication without his consent; nor is it foreclosed by showing that the benefits of the copyright act have been waived. We are dealing here not with restrictions upon publication but with the very facilities and processes of publication. The peculiar value of news is in the spreading of it while it is fresh; and it is evident that a valuable property interest in the news, as news, cannot be maintained by keeping it secret. Besides, except for matters improperly disclosed, or published in breach of trust or confidence, or in violation of law, none of which is involved in this branch of the case, the news of current events may be regarded as common property. What we are concerned with is the business of making it known to the world, in which both parties to the present suit are engaged. That business consists in maintaining a prompt, sure, steady, and reliable service designed to place the daily events of the world at the breakfast table of the millions at a price that, while of trifling moment to each reader, is sufficient in the aggregate to afford compensation for the cost of gathering and distributing it, with the added profit so necessary as an incentive to effective action in the commercial world. The service thus performed for newspaper readers is not only innocent but extremely useful in itself, and indubitably constitutes a legitimate business. The parties are competitors in this field; and, on fundamental principles, applicable here as elsewhere, when the rights or privileges of the one are liable to conflict with those of the other, each party is under a duty so to conduct its own business as not unnecessarily or unfairly to injure that of the other. *Hitchman Coal & Coke Co. v. Mitchell*, 245 U. S. 229, 254, 38 Sup. Ct. 65, 62 L. Ed. 260, L. R. A. 1918C, 497, Ann. Cas. 1918B, 461.

Obviously, the question of what is unfair competition in business must be determined with particular reference to the character and circumstances of the business. The question here is not so much the rights of either party as against the public but their rights as between themselves. *See Morison v. Moat*, 9 Hare, 241, 258. And, although we may and do assume that neither party has any remaining property interest as against the public in uncopyrighted news matter after the moment of its first publication, it by no means follows that there is no remaining property interest in it as between themselves. For, to both of them alike, news matter, however little susceptible of ownership or dominion in the absolute sense, is stock in trade, to be gathered at the cost of enterprise, organization, skill, labor, and money, and to be distributed and sold to those who will pay money for it, as for any other merchandise. Regarding the news, therefore, as but the material out of which both parties are seeking to make profits at the same time and in the same field, we hardly can fail to recognize that for this purpose, and as between them, it must be regarded as quasi property, irrespective of the rights of either as against the public.

In order to sustain the jurisdiction of equity over the controversy, we need not affirm any general and absolute property in the news as such. The rule that a court of equity concerns itself only in the protection of property rights treats any civil right of a pecuniary nature as a property right (*In re Sawyer*, 124 U. S. 200, 210, 8 Sup. Ct. 482, 31 L. Ed. 402; *In re Debs*, 158 U. S. 564, 593, 15 Sup. Ct. 900, 39 L. Ed. 1092); and the right to acquire property by honest labor or the conduct of a lawful business is as much entitled to protection as the right to guard property already acquired (*Truax v. Raich*, 239 U. S. 33, 37-38, 36 Sup. Ct. 7, 60 L. Ed. 131, L. R. A. 1916D, 545, Ann. Cas. 1917B, 283; *Brennan v. United Hatters*, 73 N. J. Law, 729, 742, 65 Atl. 165, 9 L. R. A. [N. S.] 254, 118 Am. St. Rep. 727, 9 Ann. Cas. 698; *Barr v. Essex Trades Council*, 53 N. J. Eq. 101, 30 Atl. 881). It is this right that furnishes the basis of the jurisdiction in the ordinary case of unfair competition.

The question, whether one who has gathered general information or news at pains and expense for the purpose of subsequent publication through the press has such an interest in its publication as may be protected from interference, has been raised many times, although never, perhaps, in the precise form in which it is now presented.

Board of Trade v. Christie Grain & Stock Co., 198 U. S. 236, 250, 25 Sup. Ct. 637, 49 L. Ed. 1031, related to the distribution of quotations of prices on dealings upon a board of trade, which were collected by plaintiff and communicated on confidential terms to numerous persons under a contract not to make them public. This court held that, apart from certain special objections that were overruled, plaintiff's collection of quotations was entitled to the protection of the law; that, like a trade secret, plaintiff might keep to itself the work done at its expense, and did not lose its right by communicating the result to persons, even if many, in confidential relations to itself, under a contract not to make it public; and that strangers should be restrained from getting at the knowledge by inducing a breach of trust.

In *National Tel. News Co. v. Western Union Tel. Co.*, 119 Fed. 294, 56 C. C. A. 198, 60 L. R. A. 805, the Circuit Court of Appeals for the Seventh Circuit dealt with news matter gathered and transmitted by a telegraph company, and consisting merely of a notation of current events having but a transient value due to quick transmission and distribution; and, while declaring that this was not copyrightable although printed on a tape by tickers in the offices of the recipients, and that it was a commercial not a literary product, nevertheless held that the business of gathering and communicating the news—the service of purveying it—was a legitimate business, meeting a distinctive commercial want and adding to the facilities of the business world, and partaking of the nature of property in a sense that entitled it to the protection of a court of equity against piracy.

Other cases are cited, but none that we deem it necessary to mention.

Not only do the acquisition and transmission of news require elaborate organization and a large expenditure of money, skill, and effort; not only has it an exchange value to the gatherer, dependent chiefly upon its novelty and freshness, the regularity of the service, its reputed reliability and thoroughness, and its adaptability to the public needs; but also, as is evident, the news has an exchange value to one who can misappropriate it.

The peculiar features of the case arise from the fact that, while novelty and freshness form so important an element in the success of the business, the very processes of distribution and publication necessarily occupy a good deal of time. Complainant's service, as well as defendant's, is a daily service to daily newspapers; most of the foreign news reaches this country at the Atlantic seaboard, principally at the city of New York, and because of this, and of time differentials due to the earth's rotation, the distribution of news matter throughout the country is principally from east to west; and, since in speed the telegraph and telephone easily outstrip the rotation of the earth, it is a simple matter for defendant to take complainant's news from bulletins or early editions of complainant's members in the eastern cities and at the mere cost of telegraphic transmission cause it to be published in western papers issued at least as early as those served by complainant. Besides this, and irrespective of time differentials, irregularities in telegraphic transmission on different lines, and the normal consumption of time in printing and distributing the newspaper, result in permitting pirated news to be placed in the hands of defendant's readers sometimes simultaneously with the service of competing Associated Press papers, occasionally even earlier.

Defendant insists that when, with the sanction and approval of complainant, and as the result of the use of its news for the very purpose for which it is distributed, a portion of complainant's members communicate it to the general public by posting it upon bulletin boards so that all may read, or by issuing it to newspapers and distributing it indiscriminately, complainant no longer has the right to control the use to be made of it; that when it thus reaches the light of day it becomes the common possession of all to whom it is accessible; and that any purchaser of a newspaper has the right to communicate the intelligence which it contains to anybody and for any purpose, even for the purpose of selling it for profit to newspapers published for profit in competition with complainant's members.

The fault in the reasoning lies in applying as a test the right of the complainant as against the public, instead of considering the rights of complainant and defendant, competitors in business, as between themselves. The right of the purchaser of a single newspaper to spread knowledge of its contents gratuitously, for any legitimate purpose not unreasonably interfering with complainant's right to make merchandise of it, may be admitted; but to transmit that news for commercial use, in competition with complainant—which is what defendant has done and seeks to justify—is a very different matter. In doing this defendant, by its very act, admits that it is taking material that has been acquired by complainant as the result of organization and the expenditure of labor, skill, and money, and which is salable by complainant for money, and that defendant in appropriating it and selling it as its own is endeavoring to reap where it has not sown, and by disposing of it to newspapers that are competitors of complainant's members is appropriating to itself the harvest of those who have sown. Stripped of all disguises, the process amounts to an unauthorized interference with the normal operation of complainant's legitimate business precisely at the point where the profit is to be reaped, in order to divert a material portion of the profit from those who have earned it to those who have not; with special advantage to defendant in the competition because of the fact that it is not burdened with any part of the expense of gathering the news. The transaction speaks for itself and a court of equity ought not to hesitate long in characterizing it as unfair competition in business.

The underlying principle is much the same as that which lies at the base of the equitable theory of consideration in the law of trusts—that he who has fairly paid the price should have the beneficial use of the property. Pom. Eq. Jur. §981. It is no answer to say that complainant spends its money for that which is too fugitive or evanescent to be the subject of property. That might, and for the purposes of the discussion we are assuming that it would furnish an answer in a common-law controversy. But in a court of equity, where the question is one of unfair competition, if that which complainant has acquired fairly at substantial cost may be sold fairly at substantial profit, a competitor who is misappropriating it for the purpose of disposing of it to his own profit and to the disadvantage of complainant cannot be heard to say that it is too fugitive or evanescent to be regarded as property. It has all the attributes of property necessary for determining that a misappropriation of it by a competitor is unfair competition because contrary to good conscience.

The contention that the news is abandoned to the public for all purposes when published in the first newspaper is untenable. Abandonment is a question of intent, and the entire organization of the Associated Press negatives such a purpose. The cost of the service would be prohibited if the reward were to be so limited. No single newspaper, no small group of newspapers, could sustain the expenditure. Indeed, it is one of the most obvious results of defendant's theory that, by permitting indiscriminate publication by anybody and everybody for purposes of profit in competition with the news-gatherer, it would render publication profitless, or so little profitable as in effect to cut off the service by rendering the cost prohibitive in comparison with the return. The practical needs and requirements of the business are reflected in complainant's by-laws which have been referred to. Their effect is that publication by each member must be deemed not by any means an abandonment of the news to the world for any and all purposes, but a publication for limited purposes; for the benefit of the readers of the bulletin or the newspaper as such; not for the purpose of making merchandise of it as news, with the result of depriving complainant's other members of their reasonable opportunity to obtain just returns for their expenditures.

It is to be observed that the view we adopt does not result in giving to complainant the right to monopolize either the gathering or the distribution of the news, or, without complying with the copyright act, to prevent the reproduction of its news articles, but only postpones participation by complainant's competitor in the processes of distribution and reproduction of news that it has not gathered, and only to the extent necessary to prevent that competitor from reaping the fruits of complainant's efforts and expenditure, to the partial exclusion of complainant. and in violation of the principle that underlies the maxim "sic utere tuo," etc.

It is said that the elements of unfair competition are lacking because there is no attempt by defendant to palm off its goods as those of the complainant, characteristic of the most familiar, if not the most typical, cases of unfair competition. *Howe Scale Co. v. Wyckoff, Seamans & Benedict,* 198 U. S. 118, 140, 25 Sup. Ct. 609, 49 L. Ed. 972. But we cannot concede that the right to equitable relief is confined to that class of cases. In the present case the fraud upon complainant's rights is more direct and obvious. Regarding news matter as the mere material from which these two competing parties are endeavoring to make money, and treating it, therefore, as quasi property for the purposes of their business because they are both selling it as such, defendant's conduct differs from the ordinary case of unfair competition in trade principally in this that, instead of selling its own goods as those of complainant, it substitutes misappropriation in the place of misrepresentation, and sells complainant's goods as its own.

Besides the misappropriation, there are elements of imitation, of false pretense, in defendant's practices. The device of rewriting complainant's news articles, frequently resorted to, carries its own comment. The habitual failure to give credit to complainant for that which is taken is significant. Indeed, the entire system of appropriating complainant's news and transmitting it as a commercial product to defendant's clients and patrons amounts to a false representation to them and to their newspaper readers that the news transmitted is the result of defendant's own investigation in the field. But these elements, although accentuating the wrong, are not the essence of it. It is something more than the advantage of celebrity of which complainant is being deprived. . . .

In the case before us, in the present state of the pleadings and proofs, we need go no further than to hold, as we do, that the admitted pursuit by complainant of the practice of taking news items published by defendant's subscribers as tips to be investigated, and, if verified, the result of the investigation to be sold—the practice having been followed by defendant also, and by news agencies generally—is not shown to be such as to constitute an unconscientious or inequitable attitude towards its adversary so as to fix upon complainant the taint of unclean hands, and debar it on this ground from the relief to which it is otherwise entitled.

There is some criticism of the injunction that was directed by the District Court upon the going down of the mandate from the Circuit Court of Appeals. In brief, it restrains any taking or gainfully using of the complainant's news, either bodily or in substance from bulletins issued by the complainant or any of its members, or from editions of their newspapers, *"until its commercial value as news to the complainant and all of its members has passed away."* The part complained of is the clause we have italicized; but if this be indefinite, it is no more so than the criticism. Perhaps it would be better that the terms of the injunction be made specific, and so framed as to confine the restraint to an extent consistent with the reasonable protection of complainant's newspapers, each in its own area and for a specified time after its publication, against the competitive use of pirated news by defendant's customers. But the case presents practical difficulties; and we have not the materials, either in the way of a definite suggestion of

LAW AND
EQUITY

amendment, or in the way of proofs, upon which to frame a specific injunction; hence, while not expressing approval of the form adopted by the District Court, we decline to modify it at this preliminary stage of the case, and will leave that court to deal with the matter upon appropriate application made to it for the purpose.

The decree of the Circuit court of Appeals will be

Affirmed.

[The concurring opinion of Justice Holmes and the dissenting opinion of Justice Brandeis are omitted.]

Notes and Questions

1. *Misappropriation of News.* Copyright law has changed since *INS v. AP* was decided, but the basic legal landscape remains the same in some important respects. It is possible to copyright a news story, but it is not possible to copyright the underlying facts in the report. If I copy articles verbatim from your website and post them on my website, you will likely have a copyright claim against me. If I write my own stories based on the facts on your website, you will likely not have a copyright claim against me. The misappropriation of news theory from *INS v. AP* has been raised in some recent Internet-era copying cases. *See* Elaine Stoll, *Hot News Misappropriation: More Than Nine Decades After* INS v. AP, *Still and Important Remedy for News Piracy,* 79 U. Cin. L. Rev. 1239 (2011). Do you think that the Supreme Court reached the right result in *INS v. AP?* Recall that one of the fundamental policy issues in intellectual property law is the balance between incentivizing production and incentivizing consumption. Does the case strike the right balance? When thinking about incentivizing production, recall Justice Livingston's dissent in *Pierson v. Post.* Who would bother getting out of bed in the morning to hunt foxes, he asked, if someone could just come in at the end of the chase and grab the fox? A possible answer to Justice Livingston's objection is that requiring people to obtain physical control of the fox would incentivize them to try harder and invest in better hunting resources and technology. Can a similar argument be made in the news context? That is, if we allow copying of news, would we incentivize companies like AP to improve their product to remain profitable?

2. *Is Imitation the Highest Form of Flattery?* When a high-end designer comes out with a new product, imitators often come out with knockoffs shortly thereafter. Exact copies will typically violate trademark or copyright laws. Companies that make the copies, however, are good at making imitations that resemble the original product but that are different enough to skirt the edge of violating the original designer's intellectual property. Are knockoffs a good thing or a bad thing? Put another way, should intellectual property laws be strengthened to do more to prevent knockoffs?

Our next case involves the *right of publicity.* This right allows a person to control the commercial use of her name, image, likeness, voice, and other aspects of personal identity. The right of publicity has common-law origins but has been codified by statute in some states. The opinion, our second from Judge Kozinski, criticizes an extension of the right of publicity in a highly questionable context. Judge Kozinski's opinion also contains an impassioned defense of the importance of the public domain to the creative process.

Before we get to Judge Kozinski's opinion, we should explain the unusual procedural posture in which it arose. Appellate courts often hear cases in three-judge panels. The losing party may make a motion to have the dispute heard by a larger group of judges. This larger group is often composed of all of the judges on that particular court. For courts with especially large numbers of judges, the larger group might be only a subset of the entire group. In any event, when the larger group hears a case, it is said to be sitting *en banc,* and the losing party's motion to have the case heard by the larger group is typically called a motion or a petition for a rehearing *en banc.* In this case, a losing party petitioned for rehearing *en banc.* The petition was rejected by the judges of the Ninth Circuit. Judge Kozinski's opinion is his dissent, joined by two other judges, from the decision not to grant the petition for a rehearing *en banc.* This type of dissent is very unusual and only occurs when a judge has a strong desire to publish an opinion on the topic at issue.

This case involved a suit by Vanna White against Samsung Electronics. Vanna White's claim to fame was turning the letters on the game show Wheel of Fortune. Samsung ran a series of ads that were intended to show that its products would be used in the future. One of these ads showed a robot standing in front of a game board similar to that used on Wheel of Fortune. The robot and the set were clearly intended to evoke Vanna White and the Wheel of Fortune set. The ad, however, did not actually use Vanna White's name or likeness. The trial court granted summary judgment for Samsung. A panel of the Ninth Circuit reversed in part, holding that disputed issues of material fact precluded a grant of summary judgment. The Ninth Circuit as a whole rejected Samsung's petition for rehearing *en banc.* Judge Kozinski's opinion is his dissent from that decision.

WHITE V. SAMSUNG ELECTRONICS AMERICA

United States Court of Appeals for the Ninth Circuit, 1993 989 F.2d 1512

KOZINSKI, Circuit Judge, with whom Circuit Judges O'SCANNLAIN and KLEINFELD join, dissenting from the order rejecting the suggestion for rehearing en banc.

Saddam Hussein wants to keep advertisers from using his picture in unflattering contexts. Clint Eastwood doesn't want tabloids to write about him. Rudolf Valentino's heirs want to control his film biography. The Girl Scouts don't want their image soiled by association with certain activities. George Lucas wants to keep Strategic Defense Initiative fans from calling it "Star Wars." Pepsico doesn't want singers to use the word "Pepsi" in their songs. Guy Lombardo wants an exclusive property right to ads that show big bands playing on New Year's Eve. Uri Geller thinks he should be paid for ads showing psychics bending metal through telekinesis. Paul Prudhomme, that household name, thinks the same about ads featuring corpulent bearded chefs. And scads of copyright holders see purple when their creations are made fun of.

Trademarks are often reflected in the mirror of our popular culture. *See* Truman Capote, *Breakfast at Tiffany's* (1958); Kurt Vonnegut, Jr., *Breakfast of Champions* (1973); Tom Wolfe, *The Electric Kool-Aid Acid Test* (1968) (which, incidentally, includes a chapter on the Hell's Angels); Larry Niven, *Man of Steel, Woman of Kleenex,* in *All the Myriad Ways* (1971); *Looking for Mr. Goodbar* (1977); *The Coca-Cola Kid* (1985) (using Coca-Cola as a metaphor for American commercialism); *The Kentucky Fried Movie* (1977); *Harley Davidson and the Marlboro Man* (1991); *The Wonder Years* (ABC 1988-present) ("Wonder Years" was a slogan of

Wonder Bread); Tim Rice & Andrew Lloyd Webber, *Joseph and the Amazing Technicolor Dream Coat* (musical).

Hear Janis Joplin, *Mercedes Benz,* on *Pearl* (CBS 1971); Paul Simon, *Kodachrome,* on *There Goes Rhymin' Simon* (Warner 1973); Leonard Cohen, *Chelsea Hotel,* on *The Best of Leonard Cohen* (CBS 1975); Bruce Springsteen, *Cadillac Ranch,* on *The River* (CBS 1980); Prince, *Little Red Corvette, on 1999* (Warner 1982); dada, *Dizz Knee Land,* on *Puzzle* (IRS 1992) ("I just robbed a grocery store—I'm going to Disneyland / I just flipped off President George—I'm going to Disneyland"); Monty Python, *Spam,* on *The Final Rip Off* (Virgin 1988); Roy Clark, *Thank God and Greyhound [You're Gone],* on *Roy Clark's Greatest Hits Volume I* (MCA 1979); Mel Tillis, *Coca-Cola Cowboy,* on *The Very Best of* (MCA 1981) ("You're just a Coca-Cola cowboy / You've got an Eastwood smile and Robert Redford hair . . . ").

Dance to Talking Heads, *Popular Favorites 1976-92: Sand in the Vaseline* (Sire 1992); Talking Heads, *Popsicle,* on *id. Admire* Andy Warhol, *Campbell's Soup Can. Cf.* REO Speedwagon, 38 Special, and Jello Biafra of the Dead Kennedys.

The creators of some of these works might have gotten permission from the trademark owners, though it's unlikely Kool-Aid relished being connected with LSD, Hershey with homicidal maniacs, Disney with armed robbers, or Coca-Cola with cultural imperialism. Certainly no free society can *demand* that artists get such permission.

Something very dangerous is going on here. Private property, including intellectual property, is essential to our way of life. It provides an incentive for investment and innovation; it stimulates the flourishing of our culture; it protects the moral entitlements of people to the fruits of their labors. But reducing too much to private property can be bad medicine. Private land, for instance, is far more useful if separated from other private land by public streets, roads and highways. Public parks, utility rights-of-way and sewers reduce the amount of land in private hands, but vastly enhance the value of the property that remains.

So too it is with intellectual property. Overprotecting intellectual property is as harmful as underprotecting it. Creativity is impossible without a rich public domain. Nothing today, likely nothing since we tamed fire, is genuinely new: Culture, like science and technology, grows by accretion, each new creator building on the works of those who came before. Overprotection stifles the very creative forces it's supposed to nurture.

The panel's opinion is a classic case of overprotection. Concerned about what it sees as a wrong done to Vanna White, the panel majority erects a property right of remarkable and dangerous breadth: Under the majority's opinion, it's now a tort for advertisers to *remind* the public of a celebrity. Not to use a celebrity's name, voice, signature or likeness; not to imply the celebrity endorses a product; but simply to evoke the celebrity's image in the public's mind. This Orwellian notion withdraws far more from the public domain than prudence and common sense allow. It conflicts with the Copyright Act and the Copyright Clause. It raises serious First Amendment problems. It's bad law, and it deserves a long, hard second look.

Samsung ran an ad campaign promoting its consumer electronics. Each ad depicted a Samsung product and a humorous prediction: One showed a raw steak with the caption "Revealed to be health food. 2010 A.D." Another showed Morton Downey, Jr. in front of an American flag with the caption "Presidential candidate. 2008 A.D."[12] The ads were meant to convey—humorously—that Samsung products would still be in use twenty years from now.

The ad that spawned this litigation starred a robot dressed in a wig, gown and jewelry reminiscent of Vanna White's hair and dress; the robot was posed next to a Wheel-of-Fortune-like game board. *See* Appendix [D. Benjamin Barros and Anna P. Hemingway, Property Law, (2015)]. The caption read "Longest-running game show. 2012 A.D." The gag here, I take it, was that Samsung would still be around when White had been replaced by a robot.

Perhaps failing to see the humor, White sued, alleging Samsung infringed her right of publicity by "appropriating" her "identity." Under California law, White has the exclusive right to use her name, likeness, signature and voice for commercial purposes. Cal.Civ.Code § 3344(a); *Eastwood v. Superior Court,* 149 Cal.App.3d 409, 417, 198 Cal.Rptr. 342, 347 (1983). But Samsung didn't use her name, voice or signature, and it certainly didn't use her likeness. The ad just wouldn't have been funny had it depicted White or someone who resembled her—the whole joke was that the game show host(ess) was a robot, not a real person. No one seeing the ad could have thought this was supposed to be White in 2012.

The district judge quite reasonably held that, because Samsung didn't use White's name, likeness, voice or signature, it didn't violate her right of publicity. 971 F.2d at 1396-97. Not so, says the panel majority: The California right of publicity can't possibly be limited to name and likeness. If it were, the majority reasons, a "clever advertising strategist" could avoid using White's name or likeness but nevertheless remind people of her with impunity, "effectively eviscerat[ing]" her rights. To prevent this "evisceration," the panel majority holds that the right of publicity must extend beyond name and likeness, to any "appropriation" of White's "identity"—anything that "evoke[s]" her personality. *Id.* at 1398-99.

But what does "evisceration" mean in intellectual property law? Intellectual property rights aren't like some constitutional rights, absolute guarantees protected against all kinds of interference, subtle as well as blatant. They cast no penumbras, emit no emanations: The very point of intellectual property laws is that they protect only against certain specific kinds of appropriation. I can't publish unauthorized copies of, say, *Presumed Innocent;* I can't make a movie out of it. But I'm perfectly free to write a book about an idealistic young prosecutor on trial for a crime he didn't commit. So what if I got the idea from *Presumed Innocent?* So what if it reminds readers of the original? Have I "eviscerated" Scott Turow's intellectual property rights? Certainly not. All creators draw in part on the work of those who came before, referring to it, building on it, poking fun at it; we call this creativity, not piracy.

The majority isn't, in fact, preventing the "evisceration" of Vanna White's existing rights; it's creating a new and much broader property right, a right unknown in California law. It's replacing the existing balance between the interests of the celebrity and those of the public by a different balance, one substantially more favorable to the celebrity. Instead of having an exclusive right in her name, likeness, signature or voice, every famous person now has an exclusive right to *anything that reminds the viewer of her.* After all, that's all Samsung did: It used an inanimate object to remind people of White, to "evoke [her identity]." 971 F.2d at 1399.

---

12. I had never heard of Morton Downey, Jr., but I'm told he's sort of like Rush Limbaugh, but not as shy.

Consider how sweeping this new right is. What is it about the ad that makes people think of White? It's not the robot's wig, clothes or jewelry; there must be ten million blond women (many of them quasi-famous) who wear dresses and jewelry like White's. It's that the robot is posed near the "Wheel of Fortune" game board. Remove the game board from the ad, and no one would think of Vanna White. *See* Appendix [D. Benjamin Barros and Anna P. Hemingway, Property Law, (2015)]. But once you include the game board, anybody standing beside it—a brunette woman, a man wearing women's clothes, a monkey in a wig and gown—would evoke White's image, precisely the way the robot did. It's the "Wheel of Fortune" set, not the robot's face or dress or jewelry that evokes White's image. The panel is giving White an exclusive right not in what she looks like or who she is, but in what she does for a living.

Once the right of publicity is extended beyond specific physical characteristics, this will become a recurring problem: Outside name, likeness and voice, the things that most reliably remind the public of celebrities are the actions or roles they're famous for. A commercial with an astronaut setting foot on the moon would evoke the image of Neil Armstrong. Any masked man on horseback would remind people (over a certain age) of Clayton Moore. And any number of songs—"My Way," "Yellow Submarine," "Like a Virgin," "Beat It," "Michael, Row the Boat Ashore," to name only a few—instantly evoke an image of the person or group who made them famous, regardless of who is singing. *See also* Carlos V. Lozano, *West Loses Lawsuit over Batman TV Commercial*, L.A. Times, Jan. 18, 1990, at B3 (Adam West sues over Batman-like character in commercial); *Nurmi v. Peterson*, 10 U.S.P.Q.2d 1775, 1989 WL 407484 (C.D.Cal.1989) (1950s TV movie hostess "Vampira" sues 1980s TV hostess "Elvira"); text accompanying notes 7-8 (lawsuits brought by Guy Lombardo, claiming big bands playing at New Year's Eve parties remind people of him, and by Uri Geller, claiming psychics who can bend metal remind people of him). *Cf. Motschenbacher,* where the claim was that viewers would think plaintiff was actually in the commercial, and not merely that the commercial reminded people of him.

This is entirely the wrong place to strike the balance. Intellectual property rights aren't free: They're imposed at the expense of future creators and of the public at large. Where would we be if Charles Lindbergh had an exclusive right in the concept of a heroic solo aviator? If Arthur Conan Doyle had gotten a copyright in the idea of the detective story, or Albert Einstein had patented the theory of relativity? If every author and celebrity had been given the right to keep people from mocking them or their work? Surely this would have made the world poorer, not richer, culturally as well as economically.

This is why intellectual property law is full of careful balances between what's set aside for the owner and what's left in the public domain for the rest of us: The relatively short life of patents; the longer, but finite, life of copyrights; copyright's idea-expression dichotomy; the fair use doctrine; the prohibition on copyrighting facts; the compulsory license of television broadcasts and musical compositions; federal preemption of overbroad state intellectual property laws; the nominative use doctrine in trademark law; the right to make soundalike recordings. All of these diminish an intellectual property owner's rights. All let the public use something created by someone else. But all are necessary to maintain a free environment in which creative genius can flourish.

The intellectual property right created by the panel here has none of these essential limitations: No fair use exception; no right to parody; no idea-expression dichotomy. It impoverishes the public domain, to the detriment of future creators and the public at large. Instead of well-defined, limited characteristics such as name, likeness or voice, advertisers will now have to cope with vague claims of "appropriation of identity," claims often made by people with a wholly exaggerated sense of their own fame and significance. *See* pp. 1512-13 & notes 1-10 *supra*. Future Vanna Whites might not get the chance to create their personae, because their employers may fear some celebrity will claim the persona is too similar to her own. The public will be robbed of parodies of celebrities, and our culture will be deprived of the valuable safety valve that parody and mockery create.

Moreover, consider the moral dimension, about which the panel majority seems to have gotten so exercised. Saying Samsung "appropriated" something of White's begs the question: *Should* White have the exclusive right to something as broad and amorphous as her "identity"? Samsung's ad didn't simply copy White's schtick—like all parody, it created something new. True, Samsung did it to make money, but White does whatever she does to make money, too; the majority talks of "the difference between fun and profit," 971 F.2d at 1401, but in the entertainment industry fun *is* profit. Why is Vanna White's right to exclusive for-profit use of her persona—a persona that might not even be her own creation, but that of a writer, director or producer—superior to Samsung's right to profit by creating its own inventions? Why should she have such absolute rights to control the conduct of others, unlimited by the idea-expression dichotomy or by the fair use doctrine?

To paraphrase only slightly *Feist Publications, Inc. v. Rural Telephone Service Co.*, 499 U.S. 340, _-_, 111 S.Ct. 1282, 1289-90, 113 L.Ed.2d 358 (1991), it may seem unfair that much of the fruit of a creator's labor may be used by others without compensation. But this is not some unforeseen byproduct of our intellectual property system; it is the system's very essence. Intellectual property law assures authors the right to their original expression, but encourages others to build freely on the ideas that underlie it. This result is neither unfair nor unfortunate: It is the means by which intellectual property law advances the progress of science and art. We give authors certain exclusive rights, but in exchange we get a richer public domain. The majority ignores this wise teaching, and all of us are the poorer for it. . . .

For better or worse, we *are* the Court of Appeals for the Hollywood Circuit. Millions of people toil in the shadow of the law we make, and much of their livelihood is made possible by the existence of intellectual property rights. But much of their livelihood—and much of the vibrancy of our culture—also depends on the existence of other intangible rights: The right to draw ideas from a rich and varied public domain, and the right to mock, for profit as well as fun, the cultural icons of our time.

In the name of avoiding the "evisceration" of a celebrity's rights in her image, the majority diminishes the rights of copyright holders and the public at large. In the name of fostering creativity, the majority suppresses it. Vanna White and those like her have been given something they never had before, and they've been given it at our expense. I cannot agree.

NOTES AND QUESTIONS

1. *The Right Plaintiff?* Was Vanna White the right plaintiff to bring this suit? Or should it have been brought by the creators of Wheel of Fortune? Put another way, whose rights were really infringed (if at all) here?

2. *The Public Domain.* Judge Kozinski's opinion in *White v. Samsung* justifiably is famous for its defense of the importance of the public domain. Creators are influenced and inspired by what has come before. If we give too much protection to current creators of intellectual property, we might stifle the efforts of future creators. We don't, however, want to give current creators too little protection. The issue is where to strike the balance. Where do you think the balance should have been struck in *White v. Samsung?*

B. BODY PARTS

1. *Are Body Parts Property?*

MOORE V. REGENTS OF THE UNIVERSITY OF CALIFORNIA
793 P.2d 479 (Cal. 1990)

EDWARD A. PANELLI, Justice.

The plaintiff is John Moore (Moore), who underwent treatment for hairy-cell leukemia at the Medical Center of the University of California at Los Angeles (UCLA Medical Center). The five defendants are: (1) Dr. David W. Golde (Golde), a physician who attended Moore at UCLA Medical Center; (2) the Regents of the University of California (Regents), who own and operate the university; (3) Shirley G. Quan [(Quan)], a researcher employed by the Regents; (4) Genetics Institute, Inc. (Genetics Institute); and (5) Sandoz Pharmaceuticals Corporation and related entities (collectively Sandoz).

Moore first visited UCLA Medical Center on October 5, 1976, shortly after he learned that he had hairy-cell leukemia. After hospitalizing Moore and "withdraw[ing] extensive amounts of blood, bone marrow aspirate, and other bodily substances," Golde confirmed that diagnosis. At this time all defendants, including Golde, were aware that "certain blood products and blood components were of great value in a number of commercial and scientific efforts" and that access to a patient whose blood contained these substances would provide "competitive, commercial, and scientific advantages."

On October 8, 1976, Golde recommended that Moore's spleen be removed. Golde informed Moore "that he had reason to fear for his life, and that the proposed splenectomy operation . . . was necessary to slow down the progress of his disease." Based upon Golde's representations, Moore signed a written consent form authorizing the splenectomy.

Before the operation, Golde and Quan "formed the intent and made arrangements to obtain portions of [Moore's] spleen following its removal" and to take them to a separate research unit. Golde gave written instructions to this effect on October 18 and 19, 1976. These research activities "were not intended to have . . . any relation to [Moore's] medical . . . care." However, neither Golde nor Quan informed Moore of their plans to conduct this research or requested his permission. Surgeons at UCLA Medical Center, whom the complaint does not name as defendants, removed Moore's spleen on October 20, 1976.

Moore returned to the UCLA Medical Center several times between November 1976 and September 1983. He did so at Golde's direction and based upon representations "that such visits were necessary and required for his health and well-being, and based upon the trust inherent in and by virtue of the physician-patient relationship. . . . " On each of these visits Golde withdrew additional samples of "blood, blood serum, skin, bone marrow aspirate, and sperm." On each occasion Moore travelled to the UCLA Medical Center from his home in Seattle because he had been told that the procedures were to be performed only there and only under Golde's direction.

[The court then quoted plaintiff's complaint:] "In fact, [however,] throughout the period of time that [Moore] was under [Golde's] care and treatment, . . . the defendants were actively involved in a number of activities which they concealed from [Moore]. . . . " Specifically, defendants were conducting research on Moore's cells and planned to "benefit financially and competitively . . . [by exploiting the cells] and [their] exclusive access to [the cells] by virtue of [Golde's] on-going physician-patient relationship. . . . "

Sometime before August 1979, Golde established a cell line from Moore's T-lymphocytes. On January 30, 1981, the Regents applied for a patent on the cell line, listing Golde and Quan as inventors. "[B]y virtue of an established policy . . . , [the] Regents, Golde, and Quan would share in any royalties or profits . . . arising out of [the] patent." The patent issued on March 20, 1984, naming Golde and Quan as the inventors of the cell line and the Regents as the assignee of the patent. (U.S. Patent No. 4,438,032 (Mar. 20, 1984).)

The Regents' patent also covers various methods for using the cell line to produce lymphokines. Moore admits in his complaint that "the true clinical potential of each of the lymphokines . . . [is] difficult to predict, [but] . . . competing commercial firms in these relevant fields have published reports in biotechnology industry periodicals predicting a potential market of approximately 3.01 Billion Dollars by the year 1990 for a whole range of [such lymphokines]. . . . "

With the Regents' assistance, Golde negotiated agreements for commercial development of the cell line and products to be derived from it. Under an agreement with Genetics Institute, Golde "became a paid consultant" and "acquired the rights to 75,000 shares of common stock." Genetics Institute also agreed to pay Golde and the Regents "at least $330,000 over three years, including a pro-rata share of [Golde's] salary and fringe benefits, in exchange for . . . exclusive access to the materials and research performed" on the cell line and products derived from it. On June 4, 1982, Sandoz "was added to the agreement," and compensation payable to Golde and the Regents was increased by $110,000. "[T]hroughout this period, . . . Quan spent as much as 70 [percent] of her time working for [the] Regents on research" related to the cell line.

III. DISCUSSION

A. BREACH OF FIDUCIARY DUTY AND LACK OF INFORMED CONSENT

Moore repeatedly alleges that Golde failed to disclose the extent of his research and economic interests in Moore's cells before obtaining consent to the medical procedures by which the cells were extracted. These allegations, in our view, state a cause of action against Golde for invading a legally protected interest of his patient. This cause of action can properly be characterized either as the breach of a fiduciary duty to disclose facts material to the patient's consent or, alternatively, as the performance of medical procedures without first having obtained the patient's informed consent.

B. CONVERSION

Moore also attempts to characterize the invasion of his rights as a conversion—a tort that protects against interference with possessory and ownership interests in personal property. He theorizes that he continued to own his cells following their removal from his body, at least for the purpose of directing their use, and that he never consented to their use in potentially lucrative medical research. Thus, to complete Moore's argument, defendants' unauthorized use of his cells constitutes a conversion. As a result of the alleged conversion, Moore claims a proprietary interest in each of the products that any of the defendants might ever create from his cells or the patented cell line.

1. *Moore's Claim Under Existing Law*

Since Moore clearly did not expect to retain possession of his cells following their removal, to sue for their conversion he must have retained an ownership interest in them.

Moore relies, as did the Court of Appeal, primarily on decisions addressing privacy rights. One line of cases involves unwanted publicity. These opinions hold that every person has a proprietary interest in his own likeness and that unauthorized, business use of a likeness is redressible as a tort.

Moore . . . argues that "[i]f the courts have found a sufficient proprietary interest in one's persona, how could one not have a right in one's own genetic material, something far more profoundly the essence of one's human uniqueness than a name or a face?" However, . . . the goal and result of defendants' efforts has been to manufacture lymphokines. Lymphokines, unlike a name or a face, have the same molecular structure in every human being and the same, important functions in every human being's immune system. Moreover, the particular genetic material which is responsible for the natural production of lymphokines, and which defendants use to manufacture lymphokines in the laboratory, is also the same in every person; it is no more unique to Moore than the number of vertebrae in the spine or the chemical formula of hemoglobin.

[Moore also appeals to privacy cases holding that patients have the right to refuse medical treatment because each person has a right to determine what shall be done with his or her own body. However, we can protect privacy and personal dignity by requiring disclosure under fiduciary duty and informed consent doctrines, rather than] accepting the extremely problematic conclusion that interference with those interests amounts to a conversion of personal property.

The next consideration that makes Moore's claim of ownership problematic is California statutory law, which drastically limits a patient's control over excised cells [by regulating disposal of human tissues to protect public health and safety. *Cal. Health & Safety Code* §§ 7001, 7054.4]. By restricting how excised cells may be used and requiring their eventual destruction, the statute eliminates so many of the rights ordinarily attached to property that one cannot simply assume that what is left amounts to "property" or "ownership" for purposes of conversion law.

Finally, the subject matter of the Regents' patent—the patented cell line and the products derived from it—cannot be Moore's property. This is because the patented cell line is both factually and legally distinct from the cells taken from Moore's body. Federal law permits the patenting of organisms that represent the product of "human ingenuity," but not naturally occurring organisms. *Diamond v. Chakrabarty*, 447 U.S. 303, 309-310 (1980). Human cell lines are patentable because "[l]ong-term adaptation and growth of human tissues and cells in culture is difficult—often considered an art . . . ," and the probability of success is low. It is this inventive effort that patent law rewards, not the discovery of naturally occurring raw materials. Thus, Moore's allegations that he owns the cell line and the products derived from it are inconsistent with the patent, which constitutes an authoritative determination that the cell line is the product of invention.

2. *Should Conversion Liability Be Extended?*

Of the relevant policy considerations, two are of overriding importance. The first is protection of a competent patient's right to make autonomous medical decisions. . . . This policy weighs in favor of providing a remedy to patients when physicians act with undisclosed motives that may affect their professional judgment. The second important policy consideration is that we not threaten with disabling civil liability innocent parties who are engaged in socially useful activities, such as researchers who have no reason to believe that their use of a particular cell sample is, or may be, against a donor's wishes.

Research on human cells plays a critical role in medical research. This is so because researchers are increasingly able to isolate naturally occurring, medically useful biological substances and to produce useful quantities of such substances through genetic engineering. These efforts are beginning to bear fruit. Products developed through biotechnology that have already been approved for marketing in this country include treatments and tests for leukemia, cancer, diabetes, dwarfism, hepatitis-B, kidney transplant rejection, emphysema, osteoporosis, ulcers, anemia, infertility, and gynecological tumors, to name but a few.

The extension of conversion law into this area will hinder research by restricting access to the necessary raw materials. Thousands of human cell lines already exist in tissue repositories, such as the American Type Culture Collection and those operated by the National Institutes of Health and the American Cancer Society. These repositories respond to tens of thousands of requests for samples annually. Since the patent office requires the holders of patents on cell lines to make samples available to anyone, many patent holders place their cell lines in repositories to avoid the administrative burden of responding to requests. At present, human cell lines are routinely copied and distributed to other researchers for experimental purposes, usually free of charge. This exchange of scientific materials, which still is relatively free and efficient, will surely be compromised if each cell sample becomes the potential subject matter of a lawsuit.

To expand liability by extending conversion law into this area would have a broad impact. The House Committee on Science and Technology of the United States Congress found that "49 percent of the researchers at medical institutions surveyed used human tissues or cells in their research." Many receive grants from the National Institutes of Health for this work. In addition, "there are nearly 350 commercial biotechnology firms in the United States actively engaged in biotechnology research and commercial product development and approximately

25 to 30 percent appear to be engaged in research to develop a human therapeutic or diagnostic reagent. . . . Most, but not all, of the human therapeutic products are derived from human tissues and cells, or human cell lines or cloned genes."

If the scientific users of human cells are to be held liable for failing to investigate the consensual pedigree of their raw materials, we believe the Legislature should make that decision. Complex policy choices affecting all society are involved, and "[l]egislatures, in making such policy decisions, have the ability to gather empirical evidence, solicit the advice of experts, and hold hearings at which all interested parties present evidence and express their views. . . . " *Foley v. Interactive Data Corp.*, 765 P.2d 373, 397 n.31 (Cal. 1988).

For these reasons, we hold that the allegations of Moore's third amended complaint state a cause of action for breach of fiduciary duty or lack of informed consent, but not conversion.

ARMAND ARABIAN, Justice, concurring.

Plaintiff has asked us to recognize and enforce a right to sell one's own body tissue for profit. He entreats us to regard the human vessel—the single most venerated and protected subject in any civilized society—as equal with the basest commercial commodity. He urges us to commingle the sacred with the profane. He asks much.

I share Justice Mosk's sense of outrage [at defendants' conduct], but I cannot follow its path. His eloquent paean to the human spirit illuminates the problem, not the solution. Does it uplift or degrade the "unique human persona" to treat human tissue as a fungible article of commerce? Would it advance or impede the human condition, spiritually or scientifically, by delivering the majestic force of the law behind plaintiff's claim? I do not know the answers to these troubling questions, nor am I willing—like Justice Mosk—to treat them simply as issues of "tort" law, susceptible of judicial resolution.

Where then shall a complete resolution be found? Clearly the Legislature, as the majority opinion suggests, is the proper deliberative forum.

ALLEN BROUSSARD, Justice, concurring and dissenting.

If defendants had informed plaintiff, prior to removal, of the possible uses to which his body part could be put and plaintiff had authorized one particular use, it is clear . . . that defendants would be liable for conversion if they disregarded plaintiff's decision and used the body part in an unauthorized manner for their own economic benefit. Although in this case defendants did not disregard a specific directive from plaintiff with regard to the future use of his body part, the complaint alleges that, before the body part was removed, defendants intentionally withheld material information that they were under an obligation to disclose to plaintiff and that was necessary for his exercise of control over the body part; the complaint also alleges that defendants withheld such information in order to appropriate the control over the future use of such body part for their own economic benefit. If these allegations are true, defendants clearly improperly interfered with plaintiff's right in his body part at a time when he had the authority to determine the future use of such part, thereby misappropriating plaintiff's right of control for their own advantage. Under these circumstances, the complaint fully satisfies the established requirements of a conversion cause of action.

[T]he majority's fear that the availability of a conversion remedy will restrict access to existing cell lines is unrealistic. In the vast majority of instances the tissues and cells in existing repositories will not represent a potential source of liability because they will have come from patients who consented to their organ's use for scientific purposes under circumstances in which such consent was not tainted by a failure to disclose the known valuable nature of the cells.

Furthermore, even in the rare instance—like the present case—in which a conversion action might be successfully pursued, the potential liability is not likely "to destroy the economic incentive to conduct important medical research," as the majority asserts. If, as the majority suggests, the great bulk of the value of a cell line patent and derivative products is attributable to the efforts of medical researchers and drug companies, rather than to the "raw materials" taken from a patient, the patient's damages will be correspondingly limited, and innocent medical researchers and drug manufacturers will retain the considerable economic benefits resulting from their own work.

Justice Arabian's concurring opinion suggests that the majority's conclusion is informed by the precept that it is immoral to sell human body parts for profit. But the majority's rejection of plaintiff's conversion cause of action does not mean that body parts may not be bought or sold for research or commercial purposes or that no private individual or entity may benefit economically from the fortuitous value of plaintiff's diseased cells. Far from elevating these biological materials above the marketplace, the majority's holding simply bars plaintiff, the source of the cells, from obtaining the benefit of the cells' value, but permits defendants, who allegedly obtained the cells from plaintiff by improper means, to retain and exploit the full economic value of their ill-gotten gains free of their ordinary common law liability for conversion.

STANLEY MOSK, Justice, dissenting.

[T]he concept of property is often said to refer to a "bundle of rights" that may be exercised with respect to that object—principally the rights to possess the property, to use the property, to exclude others from the property, and to dispose of the property by sale or by gift. . . . But the same bundle of rights does not attach to all forms of property. For a variety of policy reasons, the law limits or even forbids the exercise of certain rights over certain forms of property. For example, both law and contract may limit the right of an owner of real property to use his parcel as he sees fit. Owners of various forms of personal property may likewise be subject to restrictions on the time, place, and manner of their use. Limitations on the disposition of real property, while less common, may also be imposed. Finally, some types of personal property may be sold but not given away,[3] while others may be given away but not sold,[4] and still others may neither be given away nor sold.[5]

In each of the foregoing instances, the limitation or prohibition diminishes the bundle of rights that would otherwise attach to the property, yet what

---

3. A person contemplating bankruptcy may sell his property at its "reasonably equivalent value," but he may not make a gift of the same property. (*See* 11 U.S.C. § 548(a).)

4. A sportsman may give away wild fish or game that he has caught or killed pursuant to his license, but he may not sell it. (*Fish & Game Code*, §§ 3039, 7121.) The transfer of human organs and blood is a special case that I discuss below.

5. *E.g.*, a license to practice a profession, or a prescription drug in the hands of the person for whom it is prescribed.

remains is still deemed in law to be a protectible property interest. [Moore] at least had the right to do with his own tissue whatever the defendants did with it: *i.e.*, he could have contracted with researchers and pharmaceutical companies to develop and exploit the vast commercial potential of his tissue and its products. Defendants certainly believe that their right to do the foregoing is not barred by section 7054.4 and is a significant property right. . . . The Court of Appeal summed up the point by observing that "Defendants' position that plaintiff cannot own his tissue, but that they can, is fraught with irony." It is also legally untenable.

[Nor does the patent on the cell line preclude plaintiff's property claim.] To be sure, the patent granted defendants the exclusive right to make, use, or sell the invention for a period of 17 years. But Moore does not assert any such right for himself. Rather, he seeks to show that he is entitled, in fairness and equity, to some share in the profits that defendants have made and will make from their commercial exploitation of the Mo cell line. I do not question that the cell line is primarily the product of defendants' inventive effort. Yet likewise no one can question Moore's crucial contribution to the invention—an invention named, ironically, after him: but for the cells of Moore's body taken by defendants, there would have been no Mo cell line.

[E]very individual has a legally protectible property interest in his own body and its products. First, our society acknowledges a profound ethical imperative to respect the human body as the physical and temporal expression of the unique human persona. One manifestation of that respect is our prohibition against direct abuse of the body by torture or other forms of cruel or unusual punishment. Another is our prohibition against indirect abuse of the body by its economic exploitation for the sole benefit of another person. The most abhorrent form of such exploitation, of course, was the institution of slavery. Lesser forms, such as indentured servitude or even debtor's prison, have also disappeared. Yet their specter haunts the laboratories and boardrooms of today's biotechnological research-industrial complex. It arises wherever scientists or industrialists claim, as defendants claim here, the right to appropriate and exploit a patient's tissue for their sole economic benefit—the right, in other words, to freely mine or harvest valuable physical properties of the patient's body: " . . . Such research tends to treat the human body as a commodity—a means to a profitable end. The dignity and sanctity with which we regard the human whole, body as well as mind and soul, are absent when we allow researchers to further their own interests without the patient's participation by using a patient's cells as the basis for a marketable product." Danforth, *Cells, Sales, & Royalties: The Patient's Right to a Portion of the Profits*, 6 Yale L. & Pol'y Rev. 179, 190 (1988).

A second policy consideration adds notions of equity to those of ethics. Our society values fundamental fairness in dealings between its members, and condemns the unjust enrichment of any member at the expense of another. This is particularly true when, as here, the parties are not in equal bargaining positions. We are repeatedly told that the commercial products of the biotechnological revolution "hold the promise of tremendous profit." In the case at bar, for example, the complaint alleges that the market for the kinds of proteins produced by the Mo cell line was predicted to exceed $3 billion by 1990. These profits are currently shared exclusively between the biotechnology industry and the universities that support that industry.

There is, however, a third party to the biotechnology enterprise—the patient who is the source of the blood or tissue from which all these profits are derived. While he may be a silent partner, his contribution to the venture is absolutely crucial: . . . but for the cells of Moore's body taken by defendants there would have been no Mo cell line at all. Yet defendants deny that Moore is entitled to any share whatever in the proceeds of this cell line. This is both inequitable and immoral.

NOTES AND QUESTIONS

1. Relatives as owners of deceased family-members' bodies and body parts. In *Brotherton v. Cleveland*, 923 F.2d 477 (6th Cir. 1991), plaintiff Deborah Brotherton alleged that defendants, in the course of performing an autopsy, removed her deceased husband's corneas for use as anatomical gifts without her consent. The court noted that "Ohio Rev. Code § 2108.02(B), as part of the *Uniform Anatomical Gift Act* governing gifts of organs and tissues for research or transplants, granted her the right to control the disposal of Steven Brotherton's body." It held that "the aggregate of rights granted by the state of Ohio to Deborah Brotherton rises to the level of a 'legitimate claim of entitlement' in Steven Brotherton's body, including his corneas," and that this was sufficient to establish a property interest protected by the fourteenth amendment's prohibition on deprivations of property without due process of law. *See also Whaley v. County of Tuscola*, 58 F.3d 1111 (6th Cir. 1991) (recognizing a property interest in body parts and refusing to dismiss lawsuits by relatives of deceased persons whose eyeballs and corneas had been removed without permission by a pathology assistant at a county hospital). Suppose these events had occurred in California. Would the California Supreme Court reach the same result as the Sixth Circuit? *Cf. Perryman v. County of Los Angeles*, 153 Cal. App. 4th 1189 (2007) (relying on *Moore* and holding that the relatives of a murder victim did not have a property interest in the victim's body for the purposes of a claim that the county coroner mishandled the remains), *vacated and remanded for reconsideration by* 208 P.3d 622 (Cal. 2009). *But see Newman v. Sathyavaglswaran*, 287 F.3d 786 (9th Cir. 2002) (assessing California law and holding that parents had a constitutionally protected property interest in deceased children's corneas removed by county workers without their consent).

2. Cell lines and the rights of descendants. In 1951, Henrietta Lacks died of cervical cancer. Doctors removed some cells from her tumors and used them to start a number of cell lines. In the decades since her death, those cell lines have been used around the world in tens of thousands of studies. Lacks's surviving family members were not told about the use of her cells, and did not even discover that the cells were in widespread use until two decades later. Lacks's entire genetic code was even sequenced and published without the knowledge or approval of surviving family members. In 2013, the family entered into an agreement with the National Institutes of Health that would give family members a greater say over how Lacks's cells are used. *See* Carl Zimmer, *A Family Consents to a Medical Gift, 62 Years Later*, N.Y. Times, Aug. 7, 2013. For more on the story of Lacks's case, *see* Rebecca Skloot's 2010 book, *The Immortal Life of Henrietta Lacks*. Should surviving family members be entitled to a share of any profits earned from Lacks's cell lines?

3. Informed consent. Suppose that before Moore's operation Golde had informed Moore of his intent to use Moore's cells to create a cell line. Would the case have come out the same way? If Golde and Moore had signed a contract in which Golde agreed to pay Moore a percentage of the earnings from the cell line, would such a contract be enforceable under the majority's analysis in *Moore*? If Golde did not commit the tort of conversion (an unprivileged appropriation of Moore's property), is Moore free to treat his body parts or cells as property that he can sell for the use of another?

Problem

A man who is sick with cancer deposits his sperm in a sperm bank for the purpose of impregnating his fiancée through in vitro fertilization. He dies before they are married and before the procedure can be completed, having left a will bequeathing all his "personal property" to his two adult children. The children claim the sperm are their property and want them to be destroyed, while the fiancée wants to try to have a child using the sperm. What should the court do? *See Hecht v. Superior Court*, 59 Cal. Rptr. 2d 222, 226 (Ct. App. 1996) (wrestling with the question of whether sperm should be treated as "property" and deciding in the negative).

2.   *Markets in Body Parts*

The *National Organ Transplant Act*, 42 U.S.C. § 274e, makes it a federal crime "to knowingly acquire, receive, or otherwise transfer any human organ for valuable consideration for use in human transplantation if the transfer affects interstate commerce." It defines organs as "the human (including fetal) kidney, liver, heart, lung, pancreas, bone marrow, cornea, eye, bone, and skin or any subpart thereof and any other human organ (or any subpart thereof, including that derived from a fetus) specified by the Secretary of Health and Human Services by regulation." *Id.* Thus, blood is not an "organ" and so can be donated in exchange for valuable consideration. It is common for blood donors to receive cash and other incentives in exchange for their donation. Is it reasonable for the law to treat blood differently than other organs? Consider the following case.

FLYNN V. HOLDER
684 F.3d 852 (9th Cir. 2012)

ANDREW KLEINFELD, Senior Circuit Judge:

I.   FACTS

The complaint challenges the constitutionality of the ban on compensation for human organs in the National Organ Transplant Act, as applied to bone marrow transplants.

Some plaintiffs are parents of sick children who have diseases such as leukemia and a rare type of anemia, which can be fatal without bone marrow transplants.

Another plaintiff is a physician and medical school professor, and an expert in bone marrow transplantation. He says that at least one out of five of his patients dies because no matching bone marrow donor can be found, and many others have complications when scarcity of matching donors compels him to use imperfectly matched donors. One plaintiff is a parent of mixed race children, for whom sufficiently matched donors are especially scarce, because mixed race persons typically have the rarest marrow cell types. One plaintiff is an African-American man suffering from leukemia who received a bone marrow transplant from his sister. She was an imperfect match and, though the transplant saved his life, he continues to suffer from life-threatening and disabling complications on account of the slight genetic mismatch.

Another plaintiff is a California nonprofit corporation that seeks to operate a program incentivizing bone marrow donations. The corporation proposes to offer $3,000 awards in the form of scholarships, housing allowances, or gifts to charities selected by donors, initially to minority and mixed race donors of bone marrow cells, who are likely to have the rarest marrow cell type. The corporation, MoreMarrowDonors.org, alleges that it cannot launch this program because the National Organ Transplant Act criminalizes payment of compensation for organs, and classifies bone marrow as an organ.

We generally use the word "marrow" to refer to the soft, fatty material in the central cavities of big bones, what some people suck out of beef bones. Bone marrow is the body's blood manufacturing factory. Bone marrow transplants enable sick patients, whose own blood cells need to be killed to save their lives, to produce new blood cells. For example, patients with leukemia, which is cancer of the blood or bone marrow, may need chemotherapy or radiation to kill the cancer cells in their blood. The treatments kill the white blood cells essential to their immune systems. The patients will die if the killed cells are not quickly replaced with healthy cells. And they cannot be replaced without the stem cells, which we describe below, that can mature into white blood cells. These stem cells can only be obtained through bone marrow transplants.

Until about twenty years ago, bone marrow was extracted from donors' bones by "aspiration." Long needles, thick enough to suck out the soft, fatty marrow, were inserted into the cavities of the anesthetized donor's hip bones. These are large bones with big central cavities full of marrow. Aspiration is a painful, unpleasant procedure for the donor. It requires hospitalization and general or local anesthesia, and involves commensurate risks.

Most blood stem cells stay in the bone marrow cavity and grow into mature blood cells there, before passing into the blood vessels. But some blood stem cells flow into and circulate in the bloodstream before they mature. These are called "peripheral" blood stem cells, "peripheral" meaning outside the central area of the body. [A] new bone marrow donation technique, developed during the past twenty years, is called "peripheral blood stem cell apheresis." "Apheresis" means the removal or separation of something. [W]ith no need for sedatives or anesthesia, a needle is inserted into the donor's vein. Blood is withdrawn from the vein and filtered through an apheresis machine to extract the blood stem cells. The remaining components of the blood are returned to the donor's vein. The blood stem cells extracted in the apheresis method are replaced by the donor's bone marrow in three to six weeks. Complications for the donor are exceedingly rare.

The main difference between an ordinary blood donation and apheresis is that instead of just filling up a plastic bag with whole blood, the donor sits for some hours in a recliner while the blood passes through the apheresis machine. When used to separate out and collect hematopoietic stem cells from the donor's bloodstream, apheresis is called "peripheral blood stem cell apheresis" or a "bone marrow donation."

All donations from another person, except for one's identical twin, produce at least some graft-versus-host disease in the recipient, but the closer the genetic match, the less disease. Matching is easy in ordinary blood transfusions, because there are only four basic blood types. But there are millions of marrow cell types, so good matches are hard to find. The more diverse the patient's genetic heritage, the rarer the match. For example, African-Americans have especially great difficulty finding a compatible unrelated donor, as they tend to have a mix of African, Caucasian, and Native-American genes, and fewer potential donors are registered in the national civilian registry.

The establishment of this registry, the National Marrow Donor Program, which is funded by the federal government to assist in finding matches, was an important aspect of the statute at issue here. But even with this registry, good matches often cannot be found. And even when a good match is found in the registry, tracking down the potential donor from what may be an outdated address may be impossible to accomplish in time to save the patient's life—assuming the potential donor is willing to go through with the process when found.

The plaintiff nonprofit proposes to mitigate this matching problem by using a financial incentive. The idea is that the financial incentive will induce more potential donors to sign up, stay in touch so that they can be located when necessary, and go through with the donations. The nonprofit plans to focus its attention initially on minority and mixed race donors, because their marrow cell types are rarer. The financial incentives would be $3,000 in scholarships, housing allowances, or gifts to charities of the donor's choice, which the nonprofit acknowledges would be "valuable consideration" under the statutory prohibition.

Plaintiffs argue that the National Organ Transplant Act, as applied to MoreMarrowDonors.org's planned pilot program, violates the Equal Protection Clause.

II. ANALYSIS

The core of plaintiffs' argument is that there is no rational basis for allowing compensation for blood, sperm, and egg donations, while disallowing compensation for bone marrow donations, because bone marrow donations can now be accomplished through apheresis without removing marrow, and the donor's body quickly regenerates the donated stem cells. Since the distinction, they argue, is without a rational basis, it violates the Equal Protection Clause, despite highly deferential "rational basis" review.

The Attorney General responds that the statute plainly classifies "bone marrow" as an organ for which compensation is prohibited, and that the congressional determination is indeed rational. The statute makes it a felony "to knowingly acquire, receive, or otherwise transfer any human organ for valuable consideration for use in human transplantation." And it defines the term "human organ" to include "bone marrow." Ergo, the statute expressly prohibits compensating bone marrow donors. According to the government's brief, Congress took the view that "human body parts should not be viewed as commodities," and had several policy reasons for disallowing compensation to donors, which suffice to serve as a rational basis for the prohibition.

Plaintiffs address their arguments largely to the peripheral blood stem cell apheresis method of extracting hematopoietic stem cells, but their complaint appears to challenge the prohibition on bone marrow transplants regardless of method. They do not, in their complaint or their brief, confine their challenge to transplants by means of apheresis. They apparently propose to give compensated donors the choice between aspiration and apheresis. To the extent that plaintiffs challenge the constitutionality of the compensation ban on bone marrow donation by the old aspiration method—where a long needle is inserted into the cavity of the hip bone to extract the soft, fatty marrow—the challenge must fail.

The statute says that the term "human organ" includes "bone marrow." It is irrelevant that the legislative history indicates that Congress viewed certain types of regenerable tissue, such as blood, as falling outside the statutory definition of "human organ." [T]he statute does not say that compensation is permitted for organs or body parts that regenerate and prohibited for those that do not. Nor is the statute consistent with such a construction. The statute defines the liver "or any subpart thereof" as an organ for which compensation is prohibited. The drafters doubtless knew that a partial resection of a liver can yield a donation that will save the recipient's life, and that the donor's liver will grow back. So the statute does expressly prohibit compensation for at least one explicitly denoted "human organ" that will regenerate.

As for whether the distinction between the organs or other body substances for which compensation is permitted and those for which it is prohibited has a rational basis, there are two classes of rational basis here: policy concerns and philosophical concerns. The policy concerns are obvious. Congress may have been concerned that if donors could be paid, rich patients or the medical industry might induce poor people to sell their organs, even when the transplant would create excessive medical risk, pain, or disability for the donor. Or, looking from the other end, Congress might have been concerned that every last cent could be extracted from sick patients needful of transplants, by well-matched potential donors making "your money or your life" offers. The existing commerce in organs extracted by force or fraud by organ thieves might be stimulated by paying for donations. Compensation to donors might also degrade the quality of the organ supply, by inducing potential donors to lie about their medical histories in order to make their organs marketable. Plaintiffs argue that a $3,000 housing subsidy, scholarship, or charitable donation is too small an amount to create a risk of any of these evils, but for a lot of people that could amount to three to six months' rent.

Congress may have had philosophical as well as policy reasons for prohibiting compensation. People tend to have an instinctive revulsion at denial of bodily integrity, particularly removal of flesh from a human being for use by another, and most particularly "commodification" of such conduct, that is, the sale of one's bodily tissue. While there is reportedly a large international market for the buying and selling of human organs, in the United States, such a market is criminal and the commerce is generally seen as revolting. Leon Kass examines the philosophical issue of commodification with his observation that nonprofit hospitals, donor registries, and physicians are permitted to make a lot of money from organ transplants, and the only people who get nothing are those whose organs are donated:

> [A]lthough we allow no commerce in organs, transplant surgeons and hospitals are making handsome profits from the organ-trading business, and even the not-for-profit transplant registries and procurement agencies glean for their employees a middleman's livelihood. Why . . . should everyone be making money from this business except the person whose organ makes it possible? Could it be that [the] real uneasiness [lies] with organ donation or with transplantation itself, for if not, what would be objectionable about its turning a profit?

Leon R. Kass, *Life, Liberty and the Defense of Dignity: The Challenge for Bioethics* 177 (2002). Kass suggests that the revulsion for commodification of human flesh is reflected in our language, *see id.* at 195: we call donors who are paid for their organs "donors" rather than "sellers" or "vendors." To account for why most of us are revolted by the notion of a poor person selling a kidney to feed his family, Kass cites the taboos we have against cannibalism, defilement of corpses, and necrophilia. *Id.* at 183. Kass points to the idea of "psychophysical unity, a position that regards a human being as largely, if not wholly, self-identical with his enlivened body," so that, as Kant put it, to " 'dispose of oneself as a mere means to some end of one's own liking is to degrade the humanity in one's person.' " *Id.* at 181-82, 185. In this view, "organ transplantation . . . is—once we strip away the trappings of the sterile operating rooms and their astonishing technologies—simply a noble form of cannibalism." *Id.* at 185.

These reasons are in some respects vague, in some speculative, and in some arguably misplaced. There are strong arguments for contrary views. But these policy and philosophical choices are for Congress to make, not us. The distinctions made by Congress must have a rational basis, but do not need to fit perfectly with that rational basis, and the basis need merely be rational, not persuasive to all. Here, Congress made a distinction between body material that is compensable and body material that is not. The distinction has a rational basis, so the prohibition on compensation for bone marrow donations by the aspiration method does not violate the Equal Protection Clause.

C. BONE MARROW TRANSPLANTS BY APHERESIS

The focus, though, of plaintiffs' arguments is compensation for "bone marrow donations" by the peripheral blood stem cell apheresis method. For this, we need not answer any constitutional question, because the statute contains no prohibition. Such donations of cells drawn from blood flowing through the veins may sometimes anachronistically be called "bone marrow donations," but none of the soft, fatty marrow is donated, just cells found outside the marrow, outside the bones, flowing through the veins.

Congress could not have had an intent to address the apheresis method when it passed the statute, because the method did not exist at that time. We must construe the words of the statute to see what they imply about extraction of hematopoietic stem cells by this method. This issue has not been addressed by any of our sister circuits.

Since payment for blood donations has long been common, the silence in the National Organ Transplant Act on compensating blood donors is loud. The statute says "human organ" is defined as a human "kidney, liver, heart, lung, pancreas, bone marrow, cornea, eye, bone, and skin or any subpart thereof and any other human organ . . . specified by the Secretary of Health and Human Services by regulation." 42 U.S.C. § 274e(c)(1). The government concedes that the common practice of compensating blood donors is not prohibited by the statute.

The government argues that hematopoietic stem cells in the veins should be treated as "bone marrow" because "bone marrow" is a statutory organ, and the statute prohibits compensation not only for donation of an organ, but also "any subpart thereof." We reject this argument, because it proves too much, and because it construes words to mean something different from ordinary usage. If the government's argument that what comes from the marrow is a subpart of the marrow were correct, then the statute would prohibit compensating blood donors. The red and white blood cells that flow through the veins come from the bone marrow, just like hematopoietic stem cells. But the government implicitly concedes that these red and white blood cells are not "subparts" of bone marrow under the statute, because it explicitly concedes that the statute does not prohibit compensation for blood donations.

As for ordinary usage, the bloodstream consists of plasma containing red cells, white cells, platelets, stem cells that will mature into one of these, and other material. We call this liquid as a whole "blood." No one calls it "bone marrow," even though these cells come from the marrow. There is no reason to think that Congress intended "bone marrow" to mean something so different from ordinary usage.

Likewise, every blood draw includes some hematopoietic stem cells. The word "subpart" refers to the organ from which the material is taken, not the organ in which it was created. Taking part of the liver for a liver donation would violate the statute because of the "subpart thereof" language. But taking something from the blood that is created in the marrow takes only a subpart of the blood.

III. CONCLUSION

It may be that "bone marrow transplant" is an anachronism that will soon fade away, as peripheral blood stem cell apheresis replaces aspiration as the transplant technique, much as "dial the phone" is fading away now that telephones do not have dials. Or it may live on, as "brief" does, even though "briefs" are now lengthy arguments rather than, as they used to be, brief summaries of authorities. Either way, when the "peripheral blood stem cell apheresis" method of "bone marrow transplantation" is used, it is not a transfer of a "human organ" or a "subpart thereof" as defined by the statute and regulation, so the statute does not criminalize compensating the donor.

NOTES AND QUESTIONS

1. Markets in organs. Consider the following argument in favor of allowing sales of at least some organs by Virginia Postrel:

Outlawing payments to donors is ostensibly a way to keep the system fair, giving rich and poor an equally lousy chance of getting a kidney. But wealthier people can already more easily register at distant centers with short lists. They're also more likely to have friends and relatives who can afford the nonmedical expenses that living donation often entails, including time off from work, child care, hotel rooms, or cross-country travel. (It is legal for recipients or third parties to pay such expenses, but, unlike medical costs, they are not covered by insurance.)

Patients with enough money and the right networks have yet another option. They can go abroad, to countries where the authorities sanction or ignore payments to living donors.

Such "transplant tourism" is growing. Laparoscopic surgery is a First World luxury, as are desk jobs to which donors can safely return soon after surgery. With few protections beyond the surgeon's need to maintain a good reputation among potential donors, kidney vendors may not receive the full payments they're promised. In China[,] organs may come not only from paid living vendors but also from executed prisoners. Transplant tourism is, in short, an ethical morass.

It is also a completely predictable byproduct of the current system, willed into being by policy makers who ignore the plight of kidney patients and by doctors who see above-board payments—and the protections of contract and malpractice law that would go with them—as pollution. Living donation is a low-risk procedure for the donor that offers life-changing rewards for the recipient. Yet the donor is the only person involved in the process who receives no compensation. To people who like to celebrate living donors as heroes, payment seems terribly crass. But the vicarious thrill of someone else's altruism comes at a terrible cost.

Virginia Postrel, *With Functioning Kidneys for All*, The Atlantic, July 9, 2009. Who do you think has the stronger argument concerning organ sales? How are the considerations the same as those at issue with surrogacy and preembryos? How are they different?

2. The impact of markets. In defending the rationality of Congress's distinction between blood and organs, the court in *Flynn* notes that "[c]ompensation to donors might also degrade the quality of the organ supply, by inducing potential donors to lie about their medical histories in order to make their organs marketable." The court may have had in mind a famous argument by Richard Titmuss that, because blood donation is altruistic behavior, offering to pay for it discourages those motivated by altruism from donating, leading to a degradation in both quantity and quality of blood donated. *See* Richard Titmuss, *The Gift Relationship* (1970).

Economists find this claim puzzling, because, in their view, offering a financial incentive should attract those who would not donate absent the incentive without changing the cost-benefit calculus of those who are willing to donate without the incentive. But social scientists have found that monetary incentives can sometimes change the social meaning of a civic or charitable act into a commercial one. This deprives altruists of the benefit of acting for the sake of duty and may cause the incentive to backfire. *See, e.g.,* Uri Gneezy & Aldo Rustichini, *A Fine Is a Price*, 29 J. Legal Stud. 1 (2000) (finding that the introduction of a fine for late pick-ups at an Israeli daycare increased late pickups); Bruno S. Frey & Felix Oberholzer-Gee, *The Cost of Price Incentives: An Empirical Investigation of Motivation Crowding Out*, 87 Am. Econ. Rev. 746, 749-750 (1997). The economist Fred Hirsch calls this transformation of social meaning the "commercialization effect." Michael Sandel, *What Money Can't Buy* 120 (2012) (citing Fred Hirsch, *The Social Limits to Growth* (1976)).

For decades, the World Health Organization has affirmed Titmuss's views about the superior safety of donated blood, arguing that all blood donation should be uncompensated. *See* World Health Organization, *Towards 100% Voluntary Blood Donation* (2010) (*available at http://www.who.int/bloodsafety/publications/9789241599696_eng.pdf*). But recent empirical studies have tended to contradict Titmuss. According to a recent summary of the research in the journal *Science*, the availability of incentives for blood donation increases both the overall quantity and quality of donated blood. *See* Nicola Lacetera et al., *Economic Rewards to Motivate Blood Donations*, 340 Science 927 (May 24, 2013); *see also* Lorenz Goette & Alois Stutzer, *Blood Donations and Incentives*, IZA Working Paper 3580, July 2008 (*available for download at http://papers.ssrn.com/sol3/papers.cfm?abstract_id=1158977*). Others have found differences in how men and women respond to incentives, with women displaying a greater "crowding out" effect. *See* Carl Mellstrom & Magnus Johannesson, *Crowding Out in Blood Donation*, 6 J. Eur. Econ. Assn. 845 (2010). Does this argument about crowding out relate to the distinction between blood and organs? If Titmuss was wrong, might there still be reasons to oppose the sale of organs?

CONTEXT

Since the first paired donation in 2000, the number has steadily grown, reaching 443 in 2012. *See* Virginia Postrel, *An Economics Nobel for Saving Lives*, Bloomberg.com (Oct. 16, 2012), http://www.bloomberg.com/news/2012-10-16/an-economics-nobel-for-saving-lives.html.

---

3. Paired donations. Under the *National Organ Transplant Act*, 42 U.S.C. § 274e, it is legal to make a gift of an organ to a specific individual. It is also legal to engage in a "paired donation." In a **paired donation**, the first donor is incompatible with the person to whom she wants to donate her organ but is compatible with another person who has a willing donor who is compatible with the first donor's recipient. The statute exempts from its coverage an agreement between the two donor/recipient pairs to swap organs (giving the second donor's organ to the first recipient and the first donor's organ to the second recipient). The law also allows for several pairs of donors and recipients to link together in a daisy chain of "paired donations" in order to move organs from donors to compatible recipients. Although paired donations began in 2000, Congress amended the law in 2007 to make it clear that they are legal. Do you see why the express exemption for paired donations was necessary?

CHAPTER

4

Estates and Future Interests

In this chapter, we will learn about the system of present and future interests that form the backbone of our system of property ownership. This system applies to both real and personal property, but we will focus on the ownership of land. Our system of ownership has its origins in feudal England, and some feudal concepts still crop up from time to time in this area of law. We will focus on the modern system of ownership and will note important historical events and concepts in places along the way.

To this point, we have generally focused on ownership of objects by one person. Our ownership system, however, includes various ways to divide ownership of the same object among multiple people. Division of ownership will be a theme that comes up in many contexts throughout the course.

DIVISION OF OWNERSHIP

The type of division of ownership allowed by the estates and future interests system is *division of ownership by time.* When we divide ownership in this way, one person might have the present right to possession of piece of land, and another person might have a future right of possession of that land. You are probably already intuitively familiar with this kind of division if you have ever rented an apartment. During the term of your lease, you have the right to possess the apartment. The landlord maintains the right to possess the apartment once the lease expires. We therefore have two people with rights to possession of the apartment—you (the tenant), with a present right of possession, and the landlord, with a future right of possession.

To divide ownership over time, our system of ownership distinguishes between present and future interests in property. *Present interests* give the owner a present right of possession (or in some cases use) of the land. *Future interests* give the owner a future right of possession (or use) of the land. Note that present and future interests are defined in terms of possession, not ownership. This is because *a future interest exists at the time it is created.* If I have a future interest in Blackacre, that means that I own that future interest now. It is my right of possession, not my ownership, that is delayed to the future. It is therefore misleading to speak of a future interest giving its holder future ownership of the land at issue. The future interest holder has present ownership of an interest that gives a future right of possession. We have already seen the importance of this point in *Gruen v. Gruen.* Victor's gift to Michael was valid because it was a present gift of a future interest, rather than a promise of a later gift at death.

In the text that follows, we will introduce the present and future interests. Pay very close attention to the terminology. It is often said that learning the present and future interests is like learning a foreign language. This subject is not actually that difficult, but you will need to keep the names and characteristics of the different interests straight in your mind. In this area of law, labels matter.

A. PRESENT INTERESTS: THE SYSTEM OF PRESENT ESTATES IN LAND

In our system of ownership, present interests in land are typically called *estates in land.* Consistent with our theme of dividing ownership over time, we begin with three types of interests that are defined, at least in part, by their duration: the fee simple absolute, the life estate, and the leasehold estates. These three types of estates form the core of our present interests system. We then examine some specialized estates that are defined by characteristics other than time.

1. *The Fee Simple Absolute*

The *fee simple absolute* is unlimited in duration and is the closest thing that the U.S. legal system has to absolute ownership of land. Ownership of land in fee simple absolute is ownership forever. Because the fee simple absolute is of unlimited duration, it is not accompanied by a future interest. In this sense, the fee simple absolute is unique. All other estates in land are of at least potentially limited duration and so are accompanied by a future interest.

Lawyers often leave off the "absolute," and refer to this estate simply as a "fee simple." In later chapters in this book, we will do the same thing. The word "absolute" is needed to distinguish this estate from some relatively uncommon estates that are discussed further below. "Fee simple," standing alone, is generally presumed to mean "fee simple absolute."

Ownership in fee simple absolute is common in the United States. If you buy a house, you will typically purchase the house in fee simple absolute. Note the phrasing we just used—we first described what was owned (the house), then said that you owned the house "in" fee simple absolute. We will often use the word "in" in this way to describe an owner's interest in property.

LANGUAGE OF CONVEYANCE

A critical point here is that interests in property are created by the use of specific words. We are looking for specific *language of conveyance*—this will be a recurring theme in our course. When we read a document that conveys property (typically a deed or a will), we look at the granting language to determine the interest in property created by the document. Perhaps the most important thing to learn at this stage is what language creates what interest.

In our examples of language of conveyance, we follow common convention and denote the grantor with the letter O, signifying that this person was the owner of the land before the conveyance. Grantees are typically denoted with letters A, B, C, and so on.

The language of conveyance required to create a fee simple absolute has changed over time. At traditional common law, a fee simple absolute was created by the language "to A and her heirs." The "to A" part of this phrase historically was called *words of purchase*—those words identified the recipient of the interest. The "and her heirs" part was called *words of limitation*—those words identified the interest being created. The "to A and her heirs" language still creates a fee simple absolute at modern law, but today we no longer need the words "and her heirs." Today, all states by statute or court decision recognize that a grant of property "to A" creates a fee simple absolute.

> EXAMPLE 1: O grants Blackacre "to A and her heirs." Under both modern and common law, A owns Blackacre in fee simple absolute.
> EXAMPLE 2: O grants Blackacre "to A." Under modern law, A owns Blackacre in fee simple absolute.

The use of "and her heirs" in the traditional common-law language of conveyance can be confusing. This language was required to make it clear that the conveyance was of an interest of unlimited duration. Under the old (and now obsolete) common-law rule, a grant of "to A" would create a life estate—a different interest that we discuss next. The *only* significance of the language "and her heirs" is to signify that the grant is in of fee simple absolute. *A's heirs get absolutely nothing in the conveyance.* (For more on "heirs," see the sidebar.)

> EXAMPLE 3: O grants Blackacre "to A and her heirs." A sells Blackacre to B. A few years later, A dies. A's heirs have no interest whatsoever in Blackacre.

Most of the conveyances in this chapter will transfer an interest in land to one person. Sometimes conveyances transfer interests in land to more than one person. Here are two examples:

> EXAMPLE 4: O grants Blackacre "to A and B." A and B own Blackacre in fee simple absolute in common.
> EXAMPLE 5: O grants Blackacre "to A's children who are now living." A has two children, B and C. B and C own Blackacre in common.

The phrase "in common" indicates that the holders have a concurrent interest in the land—that is, they both own the land at the same time. We will look at concurrent interests in depth in the next chapter.

As we noted at the outset, the system of present and future interests applies to both real and personal property. The personal property equivalent for the fee simple absolute is called *absolute ownership*. For all of the other interests we will study in this chapter, the name is the same for both real and personal property.

COMMON INHERITANCE TERMS AND RULES

Property conveyances often include terms that have specific legal meaning. Here are some of the most common terms:

Children are fairly self-explanatory. Under modern law, adopted children count as children in conveyances.

Issue are lineal descendants—children, grandchildren, great grandchildren, and so on.

Ancestors are parents, grandparents, and so on. In inheritance situations, it is rare for ancestors other than parents to be relevant.

Collaterals are blood relatives who are not descendants or ancestors— brothers, sisters, cousins, aunts, uncles, nephews, nieces.

Devisees are people who inherit from a person who dies testate. *Testate* means with a will. If a person dies testate, then the provisions of the person's will control the distribution of the person's property.

Heirs are people who inherit from a person who dies intestate. *Intestate* means without a will. Each state has rules of intestate succession. These rules define who qualifies as an heir and set priorities between categories of potential heirs. State law varies, but a fairly common approach is for surviving spouses and children to be in the first category of heirs. (The rules for surviving spouses can be complex and are discussed in Chapter 5). If a person dies without a surviving spouse or children, then issue inherit next. If there are no issue, then preference typically goes in order to parents then collaterals. Collaterals with a more direct relationship to the decedent typically inherit before collaterals with a more remote relationship—for example, siblings typically inherit before cousins.

Escheat: If a person dies intestate and without heirs (generally this means that they die without a will and without a surviving spouse or surviving blood relatives), then the person's property goes to the state. The legal term for this process is that the property *escheats* to the state.

Note that *a living person has no heirs or devisees*. A living person will have potential heirs or devisees, but actual heirs and devisees are determined at death. This point may help you understand the reason why the "and her heirs" language in a fee simple absolute conveyance does not give anything to the heirs. If O grants Blackacre "to A and her heirs" and A is a living person, A has no heirs at the time of conveyance.

Executor: The person appointed to administer a deceased person's estate. In some jurisdictions, the person fulfilling this role is known as a *personal representative*.

Note that you will often see the suffix –trix used to denote that the person being described is female, especially in older decisions. A testatrix is a female testator. An executrix is a female executor. The use of the –trix suffix is gradually falling out of favor, with the same term (testator, executor, etc.) being used for both men and women.

Per stirpes and *per capita by generation*: These terms refer to different approaches to the division of inherited property across generations. The underlying problem, and the difference between the two approaches, are best illustrated with an example:

Parent:		A	
Children:	~~B~~	C	~~D~~
Grandchildren:	B1 B2		D1

This diagram shows three generations of a family—A, the parent, had three children, B,C, and D. B had two children, B1 and B2. D had one child, D1. As indicated by the strikethroughs, B and D predeceased A.

The problem that we have is how to divide A's estate. To be clear on the facts, when A dies, A is survived by one child, C, and three grandchildren,

B1, B2, and D1. A *per stirpes* distribution gives equal shares of A's estate to each branch of the family. In this example, there are three branches, one for each of A's three children. Each of these branches would get one-third of the estate. B's one-third would go in equal shares to B1 and B2, so each of these two children would get one-sixth of the estate. C would get one-third. D's one-third would go to D1. The end result is that under the *per stirpes* approach, B1 would get one-sixth, B2 would get one-sixth, C would get one-third, and D1 would get one-third:

Parent: A

Children: B̶   C (1/3)   D̶

Grandchildren: B1 (1/6)   B2 (1/6)   D1 (1/3)

A per capita by generation distribution gives equal shares to each person at each generational level. C, as the only living child of A's three children, would get a one-third share. The three grandchildren, B1, B2, and D1 would share the remaining two-thirds equally among themselves. So B1, B2, and D1 would each get two-ninths of the estate.

Parent: A

Children: B̶   C (1/3)   D̶

Grandchildren: B1 (2/9)   B2 (2/9)   D1 (2/9)

As you can see, the difference between the two approaches is reflected in the amounts inherited by the grandchildren. Under the *per stirpes* approach, where each branch of the family gets an equal share, B1 and B2 would share their branch's one-third, and would each get one-sixth—half as much as D1, who as an only child does not have to share D's branch's one-third. Under the per capita by generation approach, all three grandchildren get equal shares.

These two rules are often applied in intestacy situations. They are also often selected by a grantor in a conveyance—for example, "then to my issue *per stirpes*." In the United States, the *per stirpes* approach is more common, both as a default rule and as selected by grantors. The per capita by generation approach also has its adherents and is used in provisions of the Uniform Probate Code that have been adopted in 12 states.

2.   The Life Estate

A *life estate* is an interest that has a duration measured by a human life. It is created by the language "to A for life." Here are two examples:

EXAMPLE 6: O grants Blackacre "to A for life."
EXAMPLE 7: O grants Blackacre "to A for life, then to B."

In both of these examples, A owns a life estate in Blackacre. The owner of a life estate is commonly called a "life tenant." A's life estate will end at her death, and a life estate is of obviously limited duration. A life estate is always accompanied by a future interest. If the future interest is created in the grantor, it will be a reversion. In Example 6, O has a reversion. If the future interest is created in someone other than the grantor, it typically will be a remainder. In Example 7, B has a remainder. We will learn more about these future interests below.

Like other property interests, life estates can be sold. For example, A could sell her life estate to C. The life estate, however, would be continued to be measured by A's life. The traditional legal term for a life estate measured by another person's life is a life estate *pur autre vie*. By its nature, the life estate that C has bought from A will end when A dies.

As suggested by our initial definition, a life estate must be measured by a human life. A life estate cannot be measured by the life of a non-human animal or a non-human entity such as a corporation. Although we will generally use "to A for life," language that clearly creates an estate measured by a human life will suffice create a life estate. For example, grants "to A until A's death" or "to A for the duration of her life" will create a life estate.

3.   The Tenancies

Our legal system recognizes three basic types of tenancies: the term of years, the periodic tenancy, and the tenancy at will. At traditional common law, these property interests were leasehold estates. The fee simple absolute and life estate, in contrast, were freehold estates. Traditionally, freehold estates were superior to leasehold estates (see the sidebar). Today, the freehold-leasehold distinction no longer has any significant legal impact.

SEISIN, THE FREEHOLD-LEASEHOLD DISTINCTION, AND FOUR IMPORTANT PROPERTY STATUTES

In feudal England, the crucial distinction between freehold and leasehold estates was that the owner of a freehold estate had *seisin* while the owner of a leasehold estate did not. Seisin gave the owner of a freehold estate certain privileges and obligations in the feudal system. It also had a number of important legal consequences. Here are two things that are useful to know about seisin. First, feudal law would not accept breaks in seisin of land— someone had to have seisin at all times. Second, in feudal England, a freehold estate could only be transferred by a ceremony called *feoffment with livery of seisin*. In this ceremony, the grantor and grantee met on the land with witnesses. The grantor made a physical indication of transferring possession of the land to the grantee, for example by handing the grantee a handful of soil, and said words to the effect that the grantor was transferring the land to the grantee. In Chapter 2, we discussed the possession of real property at some length. However antiquated it might be, the ritual of transfer of seisin is an example of a method of achieving a physical manifestation of a transfer of possession of real property.

The requirement of the ritual of transfer of seisin was eroded by the 1536 Statute of Uses, which allowed an alternative form of conveyance called a bargain and sale. It was eliminated by the 1677 Statute of Frauds. The original Statute of Frauds, and the successor versions that are still in force today, require that real property be transferred by a written document—today we typically use a written instrument called a deed to transfer title. We will study the Statute of Frauds in some depth in Chapter 5 [D. Benjamin Barros and Anna P. Hemingway, Property Law, (2015)]. For now, it is useful to briefly note the Statute of Uses and the Statute of Frauds are two of four statutes that had particularly significant impacts on property law:

> *Statute* Quia Emptores (1290). This statute made important changes to the feudal rules on land ownership. For our purpose, *Quia Emptores* is important because it made the fee simple absolute freely alienable.
>
> *Statute of Uses* (1536). The Statute of Uses undercut the requirement of the ritual transfer of seisin to convey a freehold interest in property. It also permitted executory interests, a type of future interest that we will study later in this chapter.
>
> *Statute of Wills* (1540). This statute allowed the transfer of real property by will. It also created rules for the transfer of property at death. As we already saw in our material on gifts of personal property, courts are often hostile to attempts to circumvent the requirements of the Statute of Wills. We will see this hostility again when we study real estate transactions in Chapter 5 [D. Benjamin Barros and Anna P. Hemingway, Property Law, (2015)].
>
> *Statute of Frauds* (1677). This statute was intended to prevent fraud by requiring certain types of agreements and transactions to be made in writing. As we will see later in the course, documents that actually transfer title must be in writing. Contracts for the sale of real property must be in writing, or at least evidenced by a written memorandum that satisfies the Statute.

The *term of years* is created by language that establishes the duration of the tenancy by reference to a fixed period of time or to calendar dates for its beginning or ending time.

EXAMPLE 8: O grants Blackacre "to A for one year."

A owns a term of years in Blackacre. It is possible to convey a term of years with a duration of much more than one year—terms of 25 or 50 years are not unusual for commercial properties, and terms of 999 years are not unheard of. When a tenancy is created, O and A most often are referred to as the landlord and tenant, respectively. All of the tenancies are of limited duration and are accompanied by a future interest. In Example 8, O retains a reversion in fee simple absolute in Blackacre.

The *periodic tenancy* is created by language that is measured by a fixed period of time and automatically continues for successive periods of time until either the landlord or tenant gives notice of termination.

EXAMPLE 9: O grants Blackacre "to A from year to year."

A owns a periodic tenancy in Blackacre. O has a reversion in fee simple absolute.

The *tenancy at will* is created by language that sets no fixed period for the duration of the tenancy.

EXAMPLE 10: O grants Blackacre "to A so long we mutually agree to continue the tenancy."

A owns a tenancy at will in Blackacre. A tenancy at will terminates at the latest on the death of the landlord or tenant and therefore is of limited duration. O has a reversion in fee simple absolute.

We will return to the tenancies below in Chapter 4 [D. Benjamin Barros and Anna P. Hemingway, Property Law, (2015)], when we cover the law of landlord-tenant in depth.

4. The (Largely Extinct) Fee Tail

The fee tail was a traditional common-law estate intended to keep land in a particular family. The estate was designed to pass to the grantee's lineal descendants generation after generation. If the grantee's line ever died out, the land would revert back to the grantor or the grantor's successors in interest. The fee tail therefore was of potentially limited duration. It was created by language in the form of "to A and the heirs of her body."

EXAMPLE 11: O grants Blackacre "to A and the heirs of her body." At traditional common law, A would own Blackacre in fee tail. Because A's line could eventually die out, O would have a reversion in fee simple absolute.

The fee tail has been abolished in most U.S. jurisdictions and is of largely historical interest. It only survives, in a modified form, in Delaware, Maine, Massachusetts, and Rhode Island. In a majority of states, the "to A and the heirs of her body" language today creates a fee simple absolute. Prior to 1290, the "to A and the heirs of her body" language created a similar estate called a *fee simple conditional*. Due to a historical quirk, a few U.S. states recognized the fee simple conditional, rather than the fee tail. Today, the fee simple conditional appears to survive in South Carolina and Iowa. For more on these subjects, see *Powell on Real Property* §§ 14.04-14.06.

5. Defeasible Interests

Defeasible interests are interests that will terminate on the happening of an uncertain event. Here is an example:

EXAMPLE 12: O grants Blackacre "to the School Board, so long as the land is used for school purposes."

The idea of the conveyance is clear from the language. The School Board will own the land as long it is used for school purposes. If the land is no longer used for school purposes, the School Board's interest will terminate. The happening of this event—the land no longer being used for school purposes—is uncertain. The School Board might use the land for school purposes forever. Or, it might stop using it for school purposes tomorrow. The School Board's interest is one that will terminate on the happening of an uncertain event, and under our definition this interest is defeasible.

Traditionally, only fee simple interests could be defeasible. The modern approach is to allow any interest—fee simple, life estate, or tenancy—to be defeasible. For simplicity, however, we will focus largely on defeasible fee simple interests.

There are three types of defeasible fee simple interests. Each is created by a conveyance that includes a condition that, if broken, will lead to the termination of the present possessory estate. All of them are of potentially unlimited duration—if the termination event never occurs, then the interest will never end. Because they can terminate, they are accompanied by a future interest.

The first type is called a *fee simple determinable*. A fee simple determinable is created if the conditional language is phrased in terms of duration, such as "so long as" or "until." The School Board's interest in Example 12 is a fee simple determinable because it used the words "so long as." The future interest that accompanies a fee simple determinable is called a *possibility of reverter*. The possibility of reverter does not arise in any other context—it only exists as the future interest that accompanies a determinable interest. In Example 12, O has a possibility of reverter in fee simple absolute.

The second type is called a *fee simple subject to condition subsequent*. This interest is created if the conditional language is phrased in terms of condition, such as "but if," "on the condition that," or "provided that." Here are two examples:

> EXAMPLE 13: O grants Blackacre "to the School Board, *but if* the property is not used for school purposes, then grantor may re-enter and retake the property."
>
> EXAMPLE 14: O grants Blackacre "to the School Board *on the condition that* the property is used for school purposes, and if it is not, then grantor may re-enter and retake the property."

In each of these two examples, the School Board owns Blackacre in fee simple subject to condition subsequent. The future interest that accompanies a fee simple subject to condition subsequent is called a *right of entry*. This future interest goes by various other names, including *power of termination*. In Examples 13 and 14, O retains a right of entry in fee simple absolute.

The most important distinction between the fee simple determinable and fee simple subject to condition subsequent is in the way they terminate if the condition is broken. A fee simple determinable terminates automatically by operation of law once the termination event occurs. A fee simple subject to condition subsequent, in contrast, terminates only when the holder of the right of entry exercises her right to terminate the fee simple interest. This disparate treatment follows the language that creates the two interests. In Example 12, the School Board received the land "so long as" it was used for school purposes. By its terms, this interest should terminate automatically as soon as the land is no longer used for school purposes. In Example 13, conveyance granted the land "to the School Board, but if the property is not used for school purposes, then grantor may re-enter and retake the property." By its terms, this interest terminates only when the holder of the right of entry exercises her right to terminate the fee simple interest. Another way of putting this distinction is that a possibility of reverter operates automatically, while a right of entry must be affirmatively exercised by the future interest holder.

The difference in how these interests terminate can impact the rules for when the statute of limitations starts running on the future interest holder. Because the fee simple determinable terminates automatically, a case can be made that the fee simple determinable holder becomes an adverse possessor immediately upon the happening of the termination event and that the statute of limitations should start to run immediately against the holder of the possibility of reverter on the happening of that event. In contrast, the statute of limitations would not run immediately against the holder of a right of entry because the fee simple subject to condition subsequent did not terminate automatically. Until termination, the holder of the fee simple subject to condition subsequent has rightful possession of the land, and the holder arguably cannot be adverse to the right of entry holder. Some jurisdictions follow this distinction for the statute of limitations. Others by statute or judicial decision have made the statute of limitations start to run immediately for both the fee simple determinable and the fee simple subject to condition subsequent.

With both the fee simple determinable and fee simple subject to condition subsequent, the accompanying future interest is created in the grantor of the land. Our third type of defeasible fee simple, the *fee simple subject to executory limitation*, is created when the accompanying future interest is created in someone other than the original grantor.

> EXAMPLE 15: O grants Blackacre "to the School Board so long as it is used for school purposes, then to the State College."
> EXAMPLE 16: O grants Blackacre "to the School Board, but if the property is not used for school purposes, then the State College may enter and take the property."

These conveyances are identical to those in Examples 12 and 13, except that in each the future interest is held by a third party—the State College. This type of future interest, called an *executory interest*, is discussed further below. In Examples 15 and 16, the School Board has a fee simple subject to executory limitation. Note that in placing a label on the School Board's interest, no distinction is made between durational language ("so long as") and conditional language ("but if") if the future interest is created in someone other than the grantor. In both examples, the State College has an executory interest in fee simple absolute.

As we noted above, life estates and tenancies may be defeasible. One type of defeasible life estate warrants special mention. At one time it was not unusual for a man to leave to his widow a life estate that was defeasible if she remarried. The idea behind this kind of conveyance was that the widow would hold the life estate to support her so long as she remained unmarried, but that if she remarried her new husband would support her so she would no longer need the life estate in the devised property. Social and legal changes have made life estates defeasible on remarriage increasingly rare. In case you ever come across this kind of conveyances, you should be aware that the condition in a grant requiring defeasance on remarriage may be invalid as violating the common-law rule against restraints on marriage. Generally speaking, if the purpose of the condition was to inhibit remarriage courts would invalidate the provision, but if the purpose of the condition was to provide support until remarriage, courts would allow it.

SUMMARY TABLE: PRESENT INTERESTS

Interest	Duration	Created By	Accompanying Future Interest
Fee Simple Absolute	Unlimited	"to A""to A and A's heirs"	None
Life Estate	Limited	Conveyance indicating creation of interest measured by a human life."to A for life	Remainder or reversion
The Tenacies			
Term of Years	Limited	Conveyance indicating creation of an interest measured by a fixed period of time or fixed calendar dates."to A for one year""to A from January 1, 2014 to June 30, 2015""to A for 999 years"	Remainder or reversion
Periodic Tenancy	Limited	Conveyance indicating creation of an interest measured by successive periods of time."to A from year to year""to A from month to month"	Remainder or reversion
Tenancy at Will	Limited	Conveyance indicating creation of an interest that sets no fixed time."to A for as long as we both desire"	Remainder or reversion
DEFEASIBLE INTERESTS			
Fee Tail (largely extinct)	Potentially Unlimited	"to A and the heirs of A's body"	Typically a reversion
Fee Simple Determinable	Potentially Unlimited	Conveyance indicating potential defeasance condition expressed in terms of duration."to A, so long as . . .""to A, until . . ."	Possibility of Reverter

Interest	Duration	Created By	Accompanying Future Interest
Fee Simple Subject to Condition Subsequent	Potentially Unlimited	Conveyance indicating potential defeasance condition expressed in terms of condition."to A, but if . . .""to A, on the condition that . . .""to A, provided that"	Right of Entry, a.k.a., Power of Termination
Fee Simple Subject to Executory Limitation	Potentially Unlimited	Conveyance that would create a fee simple determinable or fee simple subject to condition subsequent, but the future interest is held by a third person, rather than the grantor.	Executory Interest

B.   FUTURE INTERESTS

The system of future interests is illustrated in the following chart:

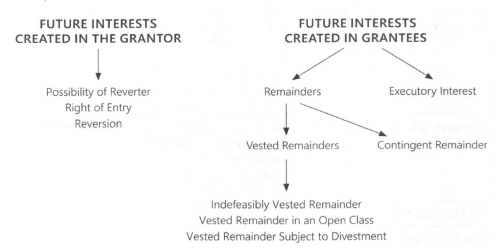

We will follow the structure of the chart, first covering the future interests created in the grantor and then moving on to future interests created in the grantee.

Before we get to the details of the future interests we should note three important points.

First, as we noted above, a future interest exists at the time it is created. It is the right of possession, not the existence of the interest itself, that is delayed to the future.

Second, under modern law future interests are transferrable. They can be sold or given away by their owner during her life. They can also pass by will or intestacy after their holder's death. Under traditional common law, some contingent interests were not transferrable. In the text and examples that follow, we follow the modern approach and presume that any future interest is freely transferrable during life and at death.

Third, future interests get their basic characteristics when they are created. As we will see, future interests created in grantors are categorized separately from future interests created in grantees. The words "created in" are important. A future interest created in a grantor that is later transferred to a grantee does not change into a future interest created in a grantee. Rather, it is a future interest created in a grantor that is not owned by a grantee. For example, if a reversion (an interest only created in grantors) is transferred to a grantee, it is still an interest created in a grantor and is still called a reversion. Similarly, if a remainder (an interest only created in a grantee) is transferred to a grantor, it is still an interest created in a grantee, and is still called a remainder.

1. Future Interests Created in the Grantor

**FUTURE INTERESTS
CREATED IN THE GRANTOR**

Possibility of Reverter
Right of Entry
Reversion

a. The Possibility of Reverter and the Right of Entry

As we have already seen, the *possibility of reverter* is the future interest that accompanies a fee simple determinable. In Example 12, O held a possibility of reverter. The *right of entry* is the future interest that accompanies a fee simple subject to condition subsequent. In Examples 13 and 14, O held a right of entry.

b. The Reversion

The *reversion* is any future interest created in the grantor that is not a possibility of reverter or a right of entry. A reversion can be understood as the portion of the grantor's interest that the grantor retains after transferring an interest that is of limited or potentially limited duration. In Example 6, above, O transferred Blackacre to "A for life." O's reversion can be understood to be the portion of O's fee simple absolute that remained after O transferred the life estate to A. Sometimes, as in Example 6, O's reversion is certain to become possessory— when A dies, the land will revert back to O.

What, you might ask, happens if O has died before A dies? O's reversion will have passed to some other person at some point. O might have sold it during life, or it might have transferred by will or intestacy after O's death. The new owners of the reversion might have transferred the interest themselves. This is an illustration of the point we made above about future interests being transferrable. When A dies, someone will own the reversion. If O has died intestate without heirs, then the reversion will have escheated to the state. Even here, the reversion survives, and whoever owns the reversion at A's death will get present possession of Blackacre.

Sometimes a reversion will not be certain to be possessory. Here is an example:

> EXAMPLE 17: O grants Blackacre "to A for life, then to B if B survives A." A is still alive.

After this transfer, A has a life estate. B has a contingent remainder in fee simple absolute. We will explore contingent remainders below. For now, the important point is that B's interest might or might not become possessory. If A dies before B, then B will have possession of Blackacre on A's death. If B dies before A, however, B's contingent remainder fails. In this case, possession of Blackacre will revert back to O. Because of the contingency in B's future interest, O has a reversion in the conveyance in Example 17. Note that even though O's reversion is not certain to become possessory, we simply call it a reversion, not a contingent reversion. We will never use the term "contingent reversion."

As these two examples show, any time a grantor fails to transfer all of her interest *with certainty*, the grantor will have a reversion. If the grantor gives away all of her interest with certainty, then there will be no reversion. We will see many examples of each type of case as we discuss future interests created in grantees.

2. *Future Interests Created in Grantees*

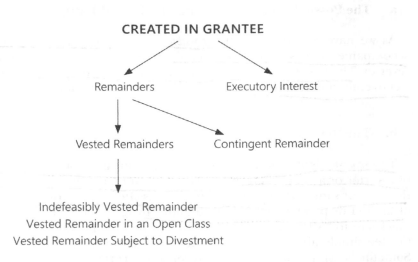

Following our chart, future interests created in grantees are divided into two categories: remainders and executory interests. The conceptual difference between the two is clear:

A *remainder* is a future interest created in a grantee that will become possessory, if at all, on the *natural end* of the preceding interest. Remainders are *polite*—they patiently wait around for the prior interest to end. We have already seen some remainders, including the one in Example 7. That conveyance was "to A for life, then to B." B has a remainder. This remainder will wait patiently until the end of A's life estate and will then become possessory.

An *executory interest* is a future interest created in a grantee that will *cut short or divest* the preceding interest. Executory interests are *rude*—they jump in and end the preceding interest. Executory interests can cut short a preceding present interest, giving the executory interest holder present possession of the land. We saw some executory interests like this in Examples 15 and 16, where they were laying in wait to rudely end the fee simple subject to executory limitation on the occurrence of a defeasance condition. Executory interests can also divest (i.e., take away) a future interest. We will see some examples of this kind of executory interest shortly.

a.   The Remainders

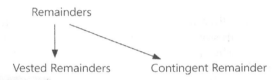

Our next key distinction is between contingent and vested remainders. A remainder is *vested* if it is *both* in an ascertained person *and* not subject to a condition precedent other than the natural end of the preceding estate. An interest is in an *ascertained person* if it is possible to point to a living person who holds the interest. In our examples, people denoted by letters (A, B, C, etc.) are ascertained people. Conversely, a remainder is *contingent* if it is *either* in an unascertained person *or* subject to a condition precedent other than the natural end of the preceding estate.

We have already seen an example of a vested remainder in Example 7, where O conveyed "to A for life, then to B." B's remainder is in an ascertained person, B, and is not subject to a condition precedent.

Here are two examples of contingent remainders:

EXAMPLE 18: O conveys Blackacre "to A for life, then to A's first child." A does not yet have any children.
EXAMPLE 19: O conveys Blackacre "to A for life, then to B if B reaches the age of 21." B is not yet 21.

The remainder in Example 18 is contingent because it is in an unascertained person—A has no children, so there is no living person who can be identified as A's first child. The remainder in Example 19 is in an ascertained person, B, but is contingent because it is subject to a condition precedent—B must reach the age of 21. In Examples 18 and 19, O also has a reversion that will become possessory if the contingent remainder fails.

We have already seen the classic example of a vested remainder in Example 7, where O granted "to A for life, then to B." B is an ascertained person, and there is no condition precedent, so B has a vested remainder. (As a reminder from our definition above, the natural end of the preceding estate—here, A's life estate—is not a condition precedent.) Here are two other examples of vested remainders:

> EXAMPLE 20: O conveys Blackacre "to A for life, then to A's first child." A has one child, C.
>
> EXAMPLE 21: O conveys Blackacre "to A for life, then to B if B reaches the age of 21." B is now 22.

These are the same conveyances as in Examples 18 and 19, but we have now changed some relevant facts. In Example 20, A has a child, C. C is A's first child, and so we now have an ascertained person holding the remainder in "A's first child." Because the remainder is in an ascertained person and is not subject to a condition precedent, C's remainder is vested. In Example 21, B is now 22 and has satisfied the condition of living to age 21. Because the condition is satisfied, B's interest is no longer subject to a condition precedent, and B's remainder is now vested. Because the remainders are vested, O's reversion disappears in both examples.

This set of examples illustrates an important characteristic of present and future interests—they can sometimes change over time as contingencies resolve themselves. We noted earlier in this section that future interests take their name when they are created and keep their basic name into the future. This is true—a remainder, for example, will never become a reversion. Contingent remainders, however, can become vested over time. Similarly, defeasible present interests can sometimes become non-defeasible if it becomes impossible for the uncertain defeasance event to occur. For example, in the conveyance "to A, but if A dies before reaching the age of 21, then B may enter and take the land," A will have a fee simple subject to executory limitation until A reaches the age of 21. If and when A lives to reach the age of 21, then it is impossible for the uncertain defeasance event to occur. A will own Blackacre in fee simple absolute, and B's executory interest will disappear. We will see more examples below.

i.   The Vested Remainders

Vested Remainders

↓

Indefeasibly Vested Remainder
Vested Remainder in an Open Class
Vested Remainder Subject to Divestment

As we can see on our chart, there are three types of vested remainders: indefeasibly vested, vested in an open class, and vested subject to divestment. We will look at each in turn.

An *indefeasibly vested remainder* is one that is certain to become possessory in the future. Our prototypical vested remainder from Example 7 is an indefeasibly vested remainder. In that example, O granted "to A for life, then to B." B's remainder is an indefeasibly vested remainder in fee simple absolute. It is certain to become possessory upon A's death. (Remember that if B dies before A, B's vested remainder will have passed on to someone else and will still become possessory.)

A *vested remainder in an open class* is one that is held by an open class of people. Here is an example:

> EXAMPLE 22: O grants Blackacre "to A for life, then to my [O's] children." A and O are alive, and O has one child, B.

The remainder in this grant was made to a class of people—here, O's children—rather than an individual. Because O is alive, the class of O's children is open—that is, additional people can come into the class. In this and other contexts involving present and future interests, *we presume that any living person can have children.* We will discuss this presumption further below. For now it is sufficient for our purposes to know that the class of O's children is still open. Therefore in our example B has a vested remainder in an open class in fee simple absolute. If O later has another child, C, then B and C will both have vested remainders in an open class. If O then dies, the class will close and B and C will have indefeasibly vested remainders in fee simple absolute in common. If A then dies, then B and C would own Blackacre in fee simple absolute in common.

The vested remainder in an open class also is often called a *vested remainder subject to open* or a *vested remainder subject to partial divestment.* The subject to partial divestment label is descriptive of what happened to B in our example when C was born. When C joined the class of A's children, C took away part of B's interest. Prior to C's birth, B had a vested remainder in an unshared interest in Blackacre; after C's birth, B had a vested remainder in an interest in Blackacre in common with C. We prefer the name vested remainder in an open class because it is more descriptive of the nature of the interest.

A *vested remainder subject to divestment* is a vested remainder that may be divested by an executory interest before it becomes possessory. Here is an example:

> EXAMPLE 23: O grants Blackacre "to A for life, then to B, but if B ever becomes a lawyer, then to C."

Here, B has a vested remainder subject to divestment in fee simple absolute, and C has an executory interest in fee simple absolute. B's remainder is vested, but may be divested by C's executory interest if B violates the condition and becomes a lawyer. If A dies and B still has not become a lawyer, then B will have a possessory fee simple subject to executory limitation; C will still have an executory interest in fee simple absolute.

A vested remainder can be both in an open class and subject to divestment. Here is an example:

> EXAMPLE 23A: O grants Blackacre "to A for life, then to B's children, but if B ever becomes a lawyer, then to C. A and B are alive, and B has one child, D."

D has a vested remainder in an open class subject to divestment. D's remainder is in an open class because B could have more children. It is subject to divestment because it will be divested by C's executory interest if B ever becomes a lawyer.

ii. The Contingent Remainder

Our next category of future interests is the contingent remainder. As we discussed above, a remainder is contingent if it is *either* in an unascertained person *or* subject to a condition precedent. Example 18 involved a remainder that was contingent because it was in an unascertained person. The grant conveyed Blackacre "to A for life, then to A's first child," and at the time of conveyance A did not have any children. Because there was no living person who qualified as A's first child, the remainder was in an unascertained person and therefore was contingent. If A dies without children, the interest will fail. Example 19 involved a remainder that was contingent because it was subject to a condition precedent. The grant conveyed Blackacre "to A for life, then to B if B reaches the age of 21," and B was not yet 21. Because B was still subject to the condition precedent, B's remainder was contingent. Generally speaking, when a conveyance ends with a contingent remainder in fee simple absolute, O will have a reversion in fee simple absolute that will become possessory if the contingent remainder fails. Sometimes conveyances create contingent remainders in open classes of people. Here is an example:

> EXAMPLE 24: O grants Blackacre "to A for life, then to A's children who survive A." A is alive and has one child, B.

In this conveyance, A has a life estate. B has a contingent remainder in fee simple absolute because of the condition precedent requiring the children to survive A. This contingent remainder also is in an open class—A could have more children who end up surviving A. We do not, however, use the term "contingent remainder in an open class." By convention, B's interest is simply called a contingent remainder. The conditionality created by the open class is captured by this label. Some conveyances create what are called *alternative contingent remainders*. Here is an example:

COMMON MISTAKES

Here are some common mistakes in future-interests terminology that you should be sure to avoid:

- Possibility of reversion. There is no such thing. There is a possibility of reverter and a reversion. Be sure not to confuse "reverter" and "reversion."
- Contingent remainder in an open class. It is true that contingent remainders can be in an open class. By convention, however, we leave off the words "in an open class" to describe a contingent remainder.

- Contingent reversion. Not all reversions are certain to become possessory. By convention, however, we never use the term "contingent" when we are talking about a reversion.
- Fee simple defeasible. This term could be used to accurately describe the set of the fee simple determinable, the fee simple subject to condition subsequent, and the fee simple subject to executory limitation. If, however, you are talking about the specific estate of fee simple determinable, be sure to use "determinable," not "defeasible."

EXAMPLE 25: O grants Blackacre "to A for life, then to B if B survives A, and if B does not survive A, then to C." A, B, and C are alive.

The key thing to note here is that we have two contingent remainders and that they revolve around the same contingency—whether B survives A or not. If B survives A, then B's contingent remainder will become possessory. If B does not survive A, then C's contingent remainder will become possessory. You can think of these contingencies as flip sides of the same coin. Heads, A dies before B, and B's interest becomes possessory. Tails, B dies before A, and C's interest becomes possessory. Although both remainders are contingent, O has transferred her entire fee simple interest with certainty—right now, we are not sure whether B's or C's remainder will become possessory, but we are sure one will. For this reason, when there are alternative contingent remainders in fee simple absolute, as in Example 25, O does not have a reversion. This is an exception to our general rule that if the conveyance ends with a contingent remainder in fee simple absolute, then O has a reversion in fee simple absolute. Note that this only occurs if the remainders are truly alternative and together account for all possible scenarios because they both revolve around the same contingency. Consider this variant on Example 25:

EXAMPLE 25A: O grants Blackacre "to A for life, then to B if B survives A, and to C if B does not survive A and if C lives to the age of 21." A, B, and C are alive, and C is 18 years old.

This conveyance adds an extra contingency to C's interest. For C's interest to become possessory, (i) B must die before A, and (ii) C must live to age 21. The extra contingency creates the possibility that both contingent remainders will fail. Because O has not given away her entire interest with certainty, O has a reversion. Consider, for example, what happens if B and C die tomorrow. A is still alive. B's contingent remainder fails because B did not survive A. C's contingent remainder fails because C did not live to age 21. Because both remainders fail, Blackacre reverts back to O.

Here is another example of alternative contingent remainders:

EXAMPLE 26: O grants Blackacre "to A and B for the life of the first of them to die, then to the survivor."

The life estate portion of the conveyance might look strange at first, but on reflection you will see that A and B have a life estate in common measured by the life of whichever of them dies first. A and B also have alternative contingent remainders in fee simple absolute. If A dies before B, B will get Blackacre in fee simple absolute. If B dies before A, then A will get Blackacre in fee simple absolute.

You might ask what would happen in Examples 25 and 26 if A and B die at the same time. For the answer to this question, see the sidebar on simultaneous death.

SIMULTANEOUS DEATH

At one time, the simultaneous death of two or more people who might take property under a conveyance was a highly unusual event. The increase in automobile and airplane travel in the twentieth century made simultaneous deaths less unusual. Faced with an increasing number of court cases involving simultaneous death, the Uniform Law Commission developed the Uniform Simultaneous Death Act. There have been two major version of this Act, and most U.S. jurisdictions have adopted at least one of them. For our purposes, the Act does two things.

First, when an interest is contingent on the holder surviving the death of another person, in a simultaneous death situation the holder will be treated as having predeceased the other person and the condition will fail. In Example 25, B's interest was contingent on B surviving A. If A and B died at the same time, B would be deemed to have predeceased A, and B's contingent remainder would fail. As a result, on A and B's simultaneous death, C would take Blackacre in fee simple absolute.

Second, if each of the people who died simultaneously would have been entitled to a property interest if they had survived the other, the Act divides the interest into equal portions shared between the people who died simultaneously. Example 26 raises the possibility of this scenario. There, A and B had a life estate in common measured by the life of whichever of them died first, and A and B each had alternative contingent remainders in fee simple absolute that turned on which of the two survived the other. If A and B died simultaneously, the Act first would presume that A predeceased B and then presume that B predeceased A. The result is an equal division of the interest—each of their estates would take an equal portion in common of Blackacre.

The original 1940 version of the Uniform Simultaneous Death Act (which is still in force in many U.S. jurisdictions) applies only if there is insufficient evidence to prove which person died first. Disputes would sometimes arise where litigants would try to prove that one person died before the other, often offering gruesome medical evidence in support of their position. The more recent 1993 version of the Act avoids this problem by treating people as having died simultaneously unless there is clear evidence that one has survived the other by 120 hours.

Distinguishing between conveyances that create two (often alternative) contingent remainders and conveyances that create a vested remainder subject to divestment and an executory interest can be challenging. Consider this example:

> EXAMPLE 27: O grants Blackacre "to A for life, then to B, but if B does not survive A, then to C." A, B, and C are alive.

This conveyance appears to try to do the same thing as the conveyance in Example 25—give Blackacre to B if B survives A, but give Blackacre to C if B dies before A. This conveyance, however, creates a vested remainder subject to divestment followed by an executory interest, where the conveyance in Example 25 created two contingent remainders. We will explain how to correctly identify the interests in each conveyance below.

b.   Executory Interests

As we noted above, executory interests are future interests in grantees that may cut short or divest the preceding interest. Unlike the polite remainders, which patiently wait around for the end of the preceding estate, executory interests are rude—they can cut short or take away another interest. If an interest created in a grantee is not a remainder, by definition it is an executory interest.

We have already seen examples of executory interests. Examples 15 and 16 involved fee simples subject to executory limitation accompanied by executory interests. On the occurrence of the uncertain defeasance condition, the executory interest would operate to cut short the fee simple subject to executory limitation, giving ownership and possession of Blackacre in fee simple absolute to the holder of the executory interest. Example 23 involved a vested remainder subject to divestment accompanied by an executory interest. On the occurrence of the uncertain event, the executory interest would operate to divest, or take away, the vested remainder and give it to the holder of the executory interest.

We have followed convention and used the term "subject to executory limitation" to describe a present interest that is subject to an executory interest and the term "subject to divestment" to describe a future interest that is subject to an executory interest. As a matter of substance, the two terms are equivalent—both mean that the described interest is subject to being taken away by an executory interest.

Executory interests are often divided further into two categories: springing and shifting. A *springing executory interest* divests the grantor. A *shifting executory interest* divests a grantee. All of the examples of executory interests we have seen so far are shifting executory interests—each would divest an interest held by a grantee. Here is an example of a springing executory interest:

> EXAMPLE 28: O grants Blackacre: "to A on the occasion of her marriage." A is alive and presently unmarried. O owns Blackacre in fee simple subject to executory limitation. A has an executory interest in fee simple absolute that will become possessory if and when A gets married.

Beyond noting it here, we do not use the springing/shifting terminology in this book. There is no legal difference between shifting and springing executory interests in modern law, and the distinction has not mattered at least since the Statute of Uses was enacted in 1536.

C. CLASSIFYING PRESENT AND FUTURE INTERESTS

Our next step is to put our basic understanding of the present and future interests to work in interpreting the interests created by conveyances of land. This process is called *classification*—going through a conveyance interest by interest and identifying each in turn. The conveyances in this section will be clear, and there will be only one correct classification for each conveyance. We will address the problem of ambiguous conveyances later in this chapter.

Here are some easy examples to start with:

O grants Blackacre "to A."

A owns Blackacre in fee simple absolute.

O grants Blackacre "to A for life, then to B."

A has a life estate.
B has an indefeasibly vested remainder in fee simple absolute.

More complicated conveyances can be harder to classify. There are a few basic rules and tips that will help us.

Rule 1: Classify interests comma by comma. At each comma, stop. If the words you have so far create an interest, stop and classify the interest. If not, move on to the next comma and try to classify the interest. Then move on through the conveyance.

Moving comma to comma helps with the difficult classification task that we mentioned above—distinguishing between contingent remainders and executory interests. Let's look first at the conveyance from Example 25:

O grants Blackacre "to A for life, then to B if B survives A, and if B does not survive A, then to C." A, B, and C are alive. ~~*Contingent*~~

Moving comma to comma, we have:

"to A for life"—A has a life estate.
"then to B if B survives A"—B has a contingent remainder in fee simple absolute.
"and if B does not survive A, then to C"—C has a contingent remainder in fee simple absolute. Because B's and C's contingent remainders revolve around the only two possible outcomes of the same contingency (whether B survives A or not), the two contingent remainders are alternative. Because they are alternative, O does not have a reversion.

Let's now look at the conveyance in Example 27:

O grants Blackacre "to A for life, then to B, but if B does not survive A, then to C." A, B, and C are alive.

Moving comma to comma, we have:

"to A for life"—A has a life estate.
"then to B"—B has a vested remainder in fee simple absolute. We will find out more about this vested remainder as we proceed through the conveyance.
"but if B does not survive A, then to C"—this is an executory interest that will divest B's vested remainder if B dies before A. So C has an executory interest in fee simple absolute, and we now know that B has a vested remainder subject to divestment in fee simple absolute.

If we had not moved comma to comma, it would be easy to become confused and label B's interest a contingent remainder—looking at the conveyance as a whole, it is obvious that B's interest is subject to some contingency. When the conveyance is properly classified, this contingency is reflected in the fact that B's vested remainder is subject to divestment.

This outcome leads us to our next rule:

> **Rule 2:** If the first future interest in fee simple absolute is a vested remainder, then the next future interest (if any) in fee simple absolute will be an executory interest. If the first future interest in fee simple absolute is a contingent remainder, then the next future interest (if any) in fee simple absolute will be a contingent remainder.

The two conveyances that we just classified are examples. You will never have a vested remainder in fee simple absolute followed by a contingent remainder in fee simple absolute, and you will never have a contingent remainder in fee simple absolute followed by an executory interest.

Our next rule and our first tip both have to do with reversions. We have already seen this rule in our discussion of future interests.

> **Rule 3:** O will have a reversion any time O does not give away her entire interest with certainty.
>
> **Corollary 3.1:** A reversion occurs any time a conveyance ends with a contingent remainder (except for alternative contingent remainders). This is a corollary of Rule 3 because a conveyance that ends with a nonalternative contingent remainder does not give away all of the grantor's interest *with certainty*.
>
> **Tip:** Watch out for reversions! They can be tricky because they typically arise by implication, rather than the express language of the conveyance.

Here are classifications of two conveyances that include reversions:

O grants Blackacre "to A for life."

    A has a life estate.
    O has a reversion in fee simple absolute.

O grants Blackacre "to A for life, then to B if B reaches the age of 21." B is alive and is 18 years old.

A has a life estate.

B has a contingent remainder in fee simple absolute.

O has a reversion in fee simple absolute. This is an example of Corollary 3.1 in action.

As we have seen before, interests can change over time as circumstances change. We will formalize this as a rule:

Rule 4: Classification of interests can change over time as circumstances change. This most often occurs when (a) a future interest becomes possessory, (b) an interest transfers to another person, (c) a class closes, or (d) a contingency resolves itself. Remember, though, that an interest created in a grantor will never become an interest created in a grantee, and vice versa.

Let's look at a conveyance that can illustrate all four types of changes:

O grants Blackacre "to A for life, then to B's children." A and B are alive, and B has no children.

A has a life estate.

B's children have a contingent remainder in fee simple absolute, because this interest is in an unascertained person—there is no living person we could point to as being one of B's children.

O has a reversion in fee simple absolute (Corollary 3.1).

Tip: Watch out for interests in unascertained persons!

Moving forward in time, A and B are alive, and B now has two children, C and D.

A has a life estate.

C and D have vested remainders in an open class in fee simple absolute. These remainders are no longer contingent because the interests are now in ascertained persons, and there is no condition precedent (*Contingency resolving itself*). Note that as a result, O's reversion disappears.

Moving further forward, A, B, and C are still alive, but D has died, leaving all of his property to his spouse E.

A has a life estate.

C and E have vested remainders in an open class in fee simple absolute. D's will has simply transferred D's interest to E. The same thing would have happened if D had sold his interest to someone else (*Interest being transferred to another person*).

Moving further forward again, A, C, and E are alive, but B has just died.

A has a life estate.

C and E have indefeasibly vested remainders in fee simple absolute in common, because B's death has closed the class of B's children (*Class closing*).

Finally, A has just died; C and E are alive.

C and E own Blackacre in fee simple absolute in common (*Future interest becoming possessory*).

Next, here is another example of a contingent interest that changes over time, using the conveyance from Example 19:

> O grants Blackacre "to A for life, then to B if B reaches the age of 21." A is alive. B is alive and is age five.

> A has a life estate.
> B has a contingent remainder in fee simple absolute.
> O has a reversion in fee simple absolute (Corollary 3.1 again!).

Moving forward in time, A is still alive and B is now 22.

> A has a life estate.
> B has an indefeasibly vested remainder in fee simple absolute.

Let's stay with this conveyance but move back in time and change our facts:

> O grants Blackacre "to A for life, then to B if B reaches the age of 21." B is alive and is age five. A now dies.

The problem in classifying this interest should be clear—A's life estate has ended, but the contingency in B's interest has not resolved itself one way or the other. Under traditional common law, the *rule of destructibility of contingent remainders* would destroy B's contingent remainder. O's reversion would become possessory, and O would own Blackacre in fee simple absolute. We will discuss the historical rule of destructibility of contingent remainders further below.

The modern approach does not destroy B's future interest. Rather, it converts it into an executory interest that can divest O. So under the modern approach, this conveyance is classified as follows:

> O has a fee simple subject to executory limitation.
> B has an executory interest in fee simple absolute.

If B dies before reaching 21, B's executory interest will fail, and O will own Blackacre in fee simple absolute. If B survives to 21, B's executory interest will take away O's interest, and B will own Blackacre in fee simple absolute.

Estates and Future Interests Problem Set

All of the topics we have covered so far come together in the following problem set. The set is divided into two parts. Part 1 involves relatively straightforward conveyances. Part 2 involves some harder conveyances. We recommend that you complete Part 1 and review the answers before you move on to Part 2.

Part 1

For each of the following conveyances, classify the estates and future interests created by the grant. Unless the question states otherwise, presume that all people named in the conveyance are alive. Answers to this part of the problem set are on page 1032.

1. O grants Blackacre "to A for life."
2. O grants Blackacre "to the School Board so long as used for school purposes."
3. O grants Blackacre "to A for life, then to B." A year later, B conveys her interest to O.
4. O grants Blackacre "to A for 20 years."
5. O grants Blackacre "to A for life, then to B if B survives A."
6. O grants Blackacre "to A and A's heirs."
7. O grants Blackacre "to A and the heirs of A's body."
8. O grants Blackacre "to the School Board so long as used for school purposes, then to the State University."
9. O grants Blackacre "to A for life, then to A's children." A is alive and has no children.
10. Same conveyance as 9, but now A has one child, B.
11. O grants Blackacre "to A for life, then to B, but if B ever is convicted of drunk driving, then to C."
12. O grants Blackacre "to the School Board, but if the property is no longer used for school purposes, then O may re-enter and retake the property."
13. O grants Blackacre "to A for life, then to B if B survives A, and if B does not survive A, then to C."
14. O grants Blackacre "to A for life, then to B for life, then to A's children." A and B are alive, and A has no children.
15. Same conveyance as in 14, but now A has one child, C.

Part 2

For each of the following conveyances, classify the estates and future interests created by the grant. Unless the question states otherwise, presume that all people named in the conveyance are alive. Answers to this part of the problem set are on page 1033.

16. O grants Blackacre "to A for life, then to the School Board so long as used for school purposes."
17. Same conveyance as 16, but now A has died.
18. Same conveyance as 16, but now A has died and the School Board has stopped using the property for school purposes.
19. O grants Blackacre "to A for life, then to A's children who survive A and their heirs, but if A dies without being survived by children, then to B's children and their heirs." A and B are alive, and B has one child, C.
20. Same conveyance as 19, but now A has a child, D.
21. Same conveyance as 19, but now A dies, survived by B, C, and D.
22. O grants Blackacre "to A for life, then to B for life, then to C so long as C survives both A and B."
23. Same conveyance as 22, but B has died. A and C are both still alive.
24. Same conveyance as 22, but B has died and C has died. A is alive.
25. O conveys Blackacre "to A for life, then to A's children and their heirs who reach the age of 21, but if any of A's children are arrested for drug possession prior to the age of 21, then Blackacre shall go to B and her heirs." A's only child C, is 17 and is a fine, upstanding young man.

26. O conveys Blackacre "to A for life, then to A's children, but if C passes the Bar Exam, then to C." A is alive and has one child, B.
27. Same conveyance as 26, but now A has had another child, D, and A has just died. B and C are alive. C has not yet attended law school.
28. Same conveyance as 26, and same facts as 27, but C has just died never having attended law school.
29. O conveys Blackacre "to A for life, then to B for life if B survives A."
30. Same conveyance as 29, but now A has sold her life estate to C. A and B are alive.
31. O conveys Blackacre "to A for life so long as A is a member of the First Baptist Church, then at A's death to B."
32. O conveys Blackacre "to A for life, then to A's children and their heirs, but if A dies without surviving children, then to C." A is alive and has one child, B.
33. Same conveyance as 32, but now B has died, leaving all of his property to D. A is alive, but has no other children.
34. O conveys Blackacre "to A for life, then to A's children who survive A, and if A has no surviving children, then to C." A is alive and has one child, B.
35. O conveys Blackacre "to A for life, then to A's children who survive A, but if A dies without surviving issue, then to C." A is alive and has one child, B.

Now that you have a good handle on future interests, go back and review *Gruen v. Gruen a*nd our discussion of the rule that the adverse possession clock does not run against future interest holders. Both should be more intuitive now than they were the first time you encountered them.

D. RULES AGAINST RESTRAINTS ON ALIENABILITY

Recall that alienation is one of the four classic incidents of property ownership. Courts tend to be hostile to restraints on the alienation of property. Whether they will allow them or not depends in significant part on three factors. The *first factor* is the *type of interest* being restricted: is it a fee simple, life estate, tenancy, or other kind of property interest?

The *second factor* is which of three categories the restraint falls into:

Category 1: *disabling restraints*. A disabling restraint denies the grantee of the property the power to alienate the property:

EXAMPLE 29: O conveys Blackacre "to A, but A does not have the power to transfer the property to any other person."

EXAMPLE 30: O conveys Blackacre "to A, but any transfer of the property to any other person shall be null and void."

Category 2: *promissory restraints*. In a promissory restraint, the grantee promises not to alienate the property:

RULES OF CONSTRUCTION

EXAMPLE 31: O conveys Blackacre "to A." In return, A promises "not to convey or otherwise transfer Blackacre to any other person."

Category 3: *forfeiture restraints.* In a forfeiture restraint, the grantee will forfeit the property if the grantee attempts to alienate the property:

EXAMPLE 32: O conveys Blackacre "to A, but if A attempts to transfer the property to another person, then the property shall return to the grantor."

The *third factor* is whether the restraint is *total,* on the one hand, or *partial* or *temporary* on the other. All of the examples we have used so far are total—they prevent the alienation of the property to any person at any time. Here are some examples of *partial* restraints on alienation:

EXAMPLE 33: O conveys Blackacre "to A, but any transfer by A to any member of his mother's family will be null and void."

EXAMPLE 34: O conveys Blackacre "to A, but A agrees not to transfer the property to B."

These restraints are partial because they do not completely prevent the alienation of property. Rather, they prevent alienation to a specific person or class of people. Restraints may also be *temporary:*

EXAMPLE 35: O conveys Blackacre "to A, but A agrees not to transfer the property for two years."

Restating these factors as questions, we have three things to consider when we are considering the validity of a restraint on alienation:

1. What type of interest is involved? Fee simple, life estate, tenancy, or something else?
2. What type of restraint is it? Disabling, promissory, or forfeiture?
3. Is the restraint total, or is it partial or temporary?

Courts historically have been especially hostile to restraints on the alienation of fee simple interests. As we noted above, the Statute *Quia Emptores,* enacted in 1290, made the fee simple absolute freely alienable. In part because of *Quia Emptores,* courts often say that restraints on alienation are contrary to the very nature of the fee simple interest. Total restraints on the alienability of fee simple interests are void and unenforceable, whether disabling, promissory, or forfeiture. Courts are also hostile to partial or temporary restraints on the alienability of fee simple interests, but these are sometimes held to be valid if a court finds them to be reasonable. The partial and temporary restraints on fee simple interest that are upheld tend to be modest in scope and duration.

You may have noticed that the conveyance in Example 32 created what appears to be a fee simple subject to condition subsequent. Because the total forfeiture restraint would be void, this language in fact conveys an unencumbered fee simple absolute. Many of the conveyances that we have seen, however, seem to create practical restraints on alienability. A conveyance "to the School Board so long as it is used for school purposes," for example, greatly restrains the ability of the School Board to sell the property. As long as the condition is framed in terms of a restriction on use, rather than on restraints on alienability, courts tend to allow the condition.

Courts are more tolerant of restraints on the alienation of life estates. Even in the context of life estates, total disabling restraints on alienation are void. Forfeiture and promissory restraints on life estates, however, typically are valid. A minority of courts will treat promissory and forfeiture restraints on life estates as void, as they would with total restraints on fee simple interests. Partial and temporary restraints on the alienability of a life estate are also more likely to be allowed than they would be if applied to a fee simple interest.

We will discuss restraints on the alienability of tenancies in Chapter 4 [D. Benjamin Barros and Anna P. Hemingway, Property Law, (2015)], and the general topic will come up from time to time in some other contexts throughout the book. Generally speaking, the farther we move from a fee simple interest, the more likely courts will be to allow a reasonable restraint on alienation. Remember, however, that courts will still police these restraints on reasonableness grounds and that courts are generally suspicious of restraints on alienation of property.

You may have noticed that we used a lot of words and phrases like "generally," "tend to," and "more likely" in the preceding paragraphs. We also used the word "reasonable," which can be hard to pin down. The truth is that once we move away from the clear rule against total restraints on the alienation of a fee simple, the details of rules on restraints on alienation can be very fact dependent and become a bit blurry across jurisdictions. For more on these topics, see *Thomson on Real Property* (Thomas ed.) § 29; Restatement (Second) of Property, Donative Transfers Ch. 4.

E.   AMBIGUOUS CONVEYANCES AND NUMERUS CLAUSUS

You might not have believed it as you were going through the prior sections, but the conveyances we have seen so far have been clear. There are conveyances that are ambiguous even if you know the rules cold. Here is an example:

> EXAMPLE 36: O grants Blackacre "to the State College for so long as it is used for college purposes, but if the land is no longer used for college purposes, then O may re-enter and retake the land."

Does the State College have a fee simple determinable or a fee simple subject to condition subsequent? It is hard to tell. We learned that a fee simple determinable is created by language of duration, such as "so long as" or "until." We also learned that a fee simple subject to condition subsequent is created by language of condition, such as "but if." The problem with this conveyance is that it uses both kinds of language. Looking at the conveyance alone, it is not clear what interest was created.

We have some tools to deal with problems like this. The first thing we need to know is that we have to fit every interest created by a conveyance into one of our established categories of present and future interests. This follows from the *numerus clausus* principle. Under this principle, we have a fixed number of property interests—numerus clausus literally means "closed number." A grantor cannot intentionally or inadvertently create a new property interest by using creative language. When a conveyance is ambiguous, we need to fit the interests into our existing categories. If the best fit involves cramming a round peg into a square hole, we just need to hit the hammer harder and get it in there.

The law frequently deals with ambiguity in language by looking to *rules of construction*. These rules give us principles to use to help interpret ambiguous language. We will see these rules often throughout this course. Rules of construction are used in contexts other than grants of land: statutes and contracts, for example, often contain ambiguities that can be addressed by rules of construction. Here are some rules of construction that are commonly applied to interpret ambiguous property conveyances:

1. *Conveyances should be interpreted to best achieve the intent of the grantor.* This rule is straightforward in principle, but can be difficult to apply in practice. The grantor's intent often is not clear from the language of the conveyance. Even if the intent is clear, the grantor's intent might run contrary to an important policy reflected in another rule of construction.

RULES OF
CONSTRUCTION

2. *Conveyances should be interpreted to favor a fee simple absolute.* This rule helps explain why the conveyance "to A" creates a fee simple absolute in all states. Because we have a rule of construction that that presumes that a grant, absent clear language to the contrary, creates a fee simple absolute, we do not need additional language to create the interest. This modern rule reverses the traditional common-law rule of construction that presumed ambiguous language conveyed a life estate.

3. *Conveyances in wills should be interpreted to avoid partial intestacy.* If a person dies with a will, then conveyances in the will should be interpreted to avoid partial intestacy—that is, a situation where the will gives away some, but not all, of the testator's assets. This rule can be seen as a corollary of the rule requiring an interpretation that honors the grantor's intent. If someone went through the trouble of leaving a will, it is reasonable to presume that the person intended the will to give away all of her assets.

4. *Conveyances should be interpreted to favor the free alienability of property.* As we saw in the prior section, the law disfavors restraints on alienability. Sometimes a court will void language in a conveyance restricting alienability and disregard this language entirely. Other times, a court will apply a more flexible rule interpreting an ambiguous conveyance in a way that best favors the free alienability of property.

5. *Conveyances should be interpreted to favor a fee simple subject to condition subsequent over a fee simple determinable.* This rule would help us resolve the problem presented in Example 36 and would favor an interpretation of that conveyance as creating a fee simple subject to condition subsequent. The justification for this rule is that the law generally disfavors the forfeiture of property. Because the right of entry that accompanies a fee simple subject to condition subsequent must be affirmatively exercised, it makes forfeiture of the present interest less likely than the self-actuating possibility of reverter that accompanies a fee simple determinable.

6. *Conveyances should be interpreted to favor vested interests and disfavor contingent interests.* Like the other rules of construction, this one can be overcome by clear language. It is possible to create contingent interests, but the grantor needs to use clear language to do so. Any ambiguity should be resolved in favor of vesting.

7. *Documents should be read as a whole. Provisions in a document should be read, if possible, to be consistent with one another, and one provision in a document should not be read in a way that renders another section of a document inoperative or a nullity.* These broadly applicable rules of construction are based on the reasonable idea that the authors of a document intended to be consistent throughout the document.

Ambiguous provisions should therefore be read, if possible, in a way that is consistent with the rest of the document.

It is important to recognize that rules of construction do not turn the interpretation of ambiguous language into a science. They are designed to create presumptions and can be overcome by the language of the grant, or, in some circumstances, other evidence. Beyond this inherent limitation in scope, rules of construction sometimes conflict with each other. It is not unusual to see a majority opinion cite one rule of construction and a dissent cite another one. Other times, there is room for disagreement about how a given rule applies to a particular conveyance. Rules of construction therefore are useful, but imperfect, tools.

The following case is a classic and illustrates how hard the interpretation of some conveyances can be.

WHITE V. BROWN
Supreme Court of Tennessee, 1977 559 S.W.2d 938

BROCK, Justice.

This is a suit for the construction of a will. The Chancellor held that the will passed a life estate, but not the remainder, in certain realty, leaving the remainder to pass by inheritance to the testatrix's heirs at law. The Court of Appeals affirmed.

Mrs. Jessie Lide died on February 15, 1973, leaving a holographic [i.e., handwritten] will which, in its entirety, reads as follows:

April 19, 1972

I, Jessie Lide, being in sound mind declare this to be my last will and testament. I appoint my niece Sandra White Perry to be the executrix of my estate. I wish Evelyn White to have my home to live in and *not* to be *sold*.

I also leave my personal property to Sandra White Perry. My house is not to be sold.

Jessie Lide
(Italics by testatrix).

Mrs. Lide was a widow and had no children. Although she had nine brothers and sisters, only two sisters residing in Ohio survived her. These two sisters quitclaimed any interest they might have in the residence to Mrs. White. The nieces and nephews of the testatrix, her heirs at law, are defendants in this action.

Mrs. White, her husband, who was the testatrix's brother, and her daughter, Sandra White Perry, lived with Mrs. Lide as a family for some twenty-five years. After Sandra married in 1969 and Mrs. White's husband died in 1971, Evelyn White continued to live with Mrs. Lide until Mrs. Lide's death in 1973 at age 88.

Mrs. White, joined by her daughter as executrix, filed this action to obtain construction of the will, alleging that she is vested with a fee simple title to the home. The defendants contend that the will conveyed only a life estate to Mrs. White, leaving the remainder to go to them under our laws of intestate succession. The Chancellor held that the will unambiguously conveyed only a life interest in the home to Mrs. White and refused to consider extrinsic evidence concerning Mrs.

Lide's relationship with her surviving relatives. Due to the debilitated condition
of the property and in accordance with the desire of all parties, the Chancellor
ordered the property sold with the proceeds distributed in designated shares
among the beneficiaries.

I.

Our cases have repeatedly acknowledged that the intention of the testator is to
be ascertained from the language of the entire instrument when read in the light
of surrounding circumstances. *See, e.g., Harris v. Bittikofer,* 541 S.W.2d 372, 384
(Tenn.1976); *Martin v. Taylor,* 521 S.W.2d 581, 584 (Tenn.1975); *Hoggatt v. Clop-
ton,* 142 Tenn. 184, 192, 217 S.W. 657, 659 (1919). But, the practical difficulty in
this case, as in so many other cases involving wills drafted by lay persons, is that
the words chosen by the testatrix are not specific enough to clearly state her
intent. Thus, in our opinion, it is not clear whether Mrs. Lide intended to convey
a life estate in the home to Mrs. White, leaving the remainder interest to descend
by operation of law, or a fee interest with a restraint on alienation. Moreover, the
will might even be read as conveying a fee interest subject to a condition subsequent (Mrs. White's failure to live in the home).

In such ambiguous cases it is obvious that rules of construction, always yielding
to the cardinal rule of the testator's intent, must be employed as auxiliary aids in
the courts' endeavor to ascertain the testator's intent.

In 1851 our General Assembly enacted two such statutes of construction,
thereby creating a statutory presumption against partial intestacy.

Chapter 33 of the Public Acts of 1851 (now codified as T.C.A. §§ 64-101 and
64-501) reversed the common law presumption that a life estate was intended
unless the intent to pass a fee simple was clearly expressed in the instrument.
T.C.A. § 64-501 provides:

> Every grant or devise of real estate, or any interest therein, shall pass all the estate
> or interest of the grantor or devisor, unless the intent to pass a less estate or interest
> shall appear by express terms, or be necessarily implied in the terms of the
> instrument.

Chapter 180, Section 2 of the Public Acts of 1851 (now codified as T.C.A. § 32-
301) was specifically directed to the operation of a devise. In relevant part,
T.C.A. § 32-301 provides:

> A will . . . shall convey all the real estate belonging to (the testator) or in which he
> had any interest at his decease, unless a contrary intention appear by its words and
> context.

Thus, under our law, unless the "words and context" of Mrs. Lide's will clearly
evidence her intention to convey only a life estate to Mrs. White, the will should
be construed as passing the home to Mrs. White in fee. "'If the expression in the
will is doubtful, the doubt is resolved against the limitation and in favor of the
absolute estate.'" *Meacham v. Graham,* 98 Tenn. 190, 206, 39 S.W. 12, 15 (1897)
(quoting *Washbon v. Cope,* 144 N.Y. 287, 39 N.E. 388); *Weiss v. Broadway Nat'l Bank,*
204 Tenn. 563, 322 S.W.2d 427 (1959); *Cannon v. Cannon,* 182 Tenn. 1, 184
S.W.2d 35 (1945).

Several of our cases demonstrate the effect of these statutory presumptions against intestacy by construing language which might seem to convey an estate for life, without provision for a gift over after the termination of such life estate, as passing a fee simple instead. In *Green v. Young*, 163 Tenn. 16, 40 S.W.2d 793 (1931), the testatrix's disposition of all of her property to her husband "to be used by him for his support and comfort during his life" was held to pass a fee estate. Similarly, in *Williams v. Williams*, 167 Tenn. 26, 65 S.W.2d 561 (1933), the testator's devise of real property to his children "for and during their natural lives" without provision for a gift over was held to convey a fee. And, in *Webb v. Webb*, 53 Tenn.App. 609, 385 S.W.2d 295 (1964), a devise of personal property to the testator's wife "for her maintenance, support and comfort, for the full period of her natural life" with complete powers of alienation but without provision for the remainder passed absolute title to the widow.

II.

Thus, if the sole question for our determination were whether the will's conveyance of the home to Mrs. White "to live in" gave her a life interest or a fee in the home, a conclusion favoring the absolute estate would be clearly required. The question, however, is complicated somewhat by the caveat contained in the will that the home is "not to be sold" a restriction conflicting with the free alienation of property, one of the most significant incidents of fee ownership. We must determine, therefore, whether Mrs. Lide's will, when taken as a whole, clearly evidences her intent to convey only a life estate in her home to Mrs. White.

Under ordinary circumstances a person makes a will to dispose of his or her entire estate. If, therefore, a will is susceptible of two constructions, by one of which the testator disposes of the whole of his estate and by the other of which he disposes of only a part of his estate, dying intestate as to the remainder, this Court has always preferred that construction which disposes of the whole of the testator's estate if that construction is reasonable and consistent with the general scope and provisions of the will. *See Ledbetter v. Ledbetter*, 188 Tenn. 44, 216 S.W.2d 718 (1949); *Cannon v. Cannon, supra; Williams v. Williams, supra; Jarnagin v. Conway*, 21 Tenn. 50 (1840); 4 Page, *Wills* § 30.14 (3d ed. 1961). A construction which results in partial intestacy will not be adopted unless such intention clearly appears. *Bedford v. Bedford*, 38 Tenn.App. 370, 274 S.W.2d 528 (1954); *Martin v. Hale*, 167 Tenn. 438, 71 S.W.2d 211 (1934). It has been said that the courts will prefer any reasonable construction or any construction which does not do violence to a testator's language, to a construction which results in partial intestacy. *Ledbetter, supra.*

RULES OF CONSTRUCTION

The intent to create a fee simple or other absolute interest and, at the same time to impose a restraint upon its alienation can be clearly expressed. If the testator specifically declares that he devises land to A "in fee simple" or to A "and his heirs" but that A shall not have the power to alienate the land, there is but one tenable construction, viz., the testator's intent is to impose a restraint upon a fee simple. To construe such language to create a life estate would conflict with the express specification of a fee simple as well as with the presumption of intent to make a complete testamentary disposition of all of a testator's property. By extension, as noted by Professor Casner in his treatise on the law of real property:

Since it is now generally presumed that a conveyor intends to transfer his whole interest in the property, it may be reasonable to adopt the same construction, (conveyance of a fee simple) even in the absence of words of inheritance, if there is no language that can be construed to create a remainder. 6 *American Law of Property* § 26.58 (A. J. Casner ed. 1952).

In our opinion, testatrix's apparent testamentary restraint on the alienation of the home devised to Mrs. White does not evidence such a clear intent to pass only a life estate as is sufficient to overcome the law's strong presumption that a fee simple interest was conveyed.

Accordingly, we conclude that Mrs. Lide's will passed a fee simple absolute in the home to Mrs. White. Her attempted restraint on alienation must be declared void as inconsistent with the incidents and nature of the estate devised and contrary to public policy. *Nashville C & S.L. Ry. v. Bell,* 162 Tenn. 661, 39 S.W.2d 1026 (1931).

The decrees of the Court of Appeals and the trial court are reversed and the cause is remanded to the chancery court for such further proceedings as may be necessary, consistent with this opinion. Costs are taxed against appellees.

HARBISON, J., dissenting. With deference to the views of the majority, and recognizing the principles of law contained in the majority opinion, I am unable to agree that the language of the will of Mrs. Lide did or was intended to convey a fee simple interest in her residence to her sister-in-law, Mrs. Evelyn White.

The testatrix expressed the wish that Mrs. White was "to have my home to live in and *not* to be *sold.*" The emphasis is that of the testatrix, and her desire that Mrs. White was not to have an unlimited estate in the property was reiterated in the last sentence of the will, to wit: "My house is not to be sold."

The testatrix appointed her niece, Mrs. Perry, executrix and made an outright bequest to her of all personal property.

The will does not seem to me to be particularly ambiguous, and like the Chancellor and the Court of Appeals, I am of the opinion that the testatrix gave Mrs. White a life estate only, and that upon the death of Mrs. White the remainder will pass to the heirs at law of the testatrix.

The cases cited by petitioners in support of their contention that a fee simple was conveyed are not persuasive, in my opinion. Possibly the strongest case cited by the appellants is *Green v. Young,* 163 Tenn. 16, 40 S.W.2d 793 (1931), in which the testatrix bequeathed all of her real and personal property to her husband "to be used by him for his support and comfort during his life." The will expressly stated that it included all of the property, real and personal, which the testatrix owned at the time of her death. There was no limitation whatever upon the power of the husband to use, consume, or dispose of the property, and the Court concluded that a fee simple was intended.

In the case of *Williams v. Williams,* 167 Tenn. 26, 65 S.W.2d 561 (1933), a father devised property to his children "for and during their natural lives" but the will contained other provisions not mentioned in the majority opinion which seem to me to distinguish the case. Unlike the provisions of the present will, other clauses in the Williams will contained provisions that these same children were to have "all the residue of my estate personal or mixed of which I shall die possessed or seized, or to which I shall be entitled at the time of my decease, to have and to hold the same to them and their executors and administrators and assigns forever."

Further, following some specific gifts to grandchildren, there was another bequest of the remainder of the testator's money to these same three children. The language used by the testator in that case was held to convey the fee simple interest in real estate to the children, but its provisions hardly seem analogous to the language employed by the testatrix in the instant case.

In the case of *Webb v. Webb*, 53 Tenn.App. 609, 385 S.W.2d 295 (1964), the testator gave his wife all the residue of his property with a clear, unqualified and unrestricted power of use, sale or disposition. Thereafter he attempted to limit her interest to a life estate, with a gift over to his heirs of any unconsumed property. Again, under settled rules of construction and interpretation, the wife was found to have a fee simple estate, but, unlike the present case, there was no limitation whatever upon the power of use or disposition of the property by the beneficiary.

On the other hand, in the case of *Magevney v. Karsch*, 167 Tenn. 32, 65 S.W.2d 562 (1933), a gift of the residue of the large estate of the testator to his daughter, with power "at her demise (to) dispose of it as she pleases . . . . " was held to create only a life estate with a power of appointment, and not an absolute gift of the residue. In other portions of the will the testator had given another beneficiary a power to use and dispose of property, and the Court concluded that he appreciated the distinction between a life estate and an absolute estate, recognizing that a life tenant could not dispose of property and use the proceeds as she pleased. 167 Tenn. at 57, 65 S.W.2d at 569.

In the present case the testatrix knew how to make an outright gift, if desired. She left all of her personal property to her niece without restraint or limitation. As to her sister-in-law, however, she merely wished the latter have her house "to live in," and expressly withheld from her any power of sale.

The majority opinion holds that the testatrix violated a rule of law by attempting to restrict the power of the donee to dispose of the real estate. Only by thus striking a portion of the will, and holding it inoperative, is the conclusion reached that an unlimited estate resulted.

In my opinion, this interpretation conflicts more greatly with the apparent intention of the testatrix than did the conclusion of the courts below, limiting the gift to Mrs. White to a life estate. I have serious doubt that the testatrix intended to create any illegal restraint on alienation or to violate any other rules of law. It seems to me that she rather emphatically intended to provide that her sister-in-law was not to be able to sell the house during the lifetime of the latter a result which is both legal and consistent with the creation of a life estate.

In my opinion the judgment of the courts below was correct and I would affirm.

NOTES AND QUESTIONS

1. *What Did She Intend?* Look back at the language from Jessie Lide's will. Leaving all presumptions and rules of construction aside, what do you think she was trying to achieve?

2. *Rules of Construction.* What rules of construction were used by the court in this case? Did the majority and dissent disagree on the rules to use or on their application?

3. *Restraints on Alienability.* How did the majority and dissent use the concept that restraints on alienability are repugnant to a fee simple interest?

F. FUTURE INTERESTS AND ALIENABILITY

Imagine that you want to buy Blackacre from me, and that I own Blackacre in fee simple absolute. This would be a simple transaction—you and I agree on the terms of the deal, and then I convey my fee simple absolute interest to you.

Now imagine that you want to buy Blackacre, but now the ownership is a little more complicated. A has a life estate in Blackacre, and B has an indefeasible vested remainder in fee simple absolute. If you want to buy Blackacre in fee simple absolute, you have to negotiate with both A and B. If you are able to buy all of the existing present and future interests in Blackacre, these interests will merge into a fee simple absolute (see the sidebar on merger). Negotiating with two people is obviously more complicated than negotiating with one. Problems might arise, for example, in valuing the present and future interests (see the sidebar on valuation).

MERGER OF INTERESTS

In our simple example, A has a life estate in Blackacre, and B has an indefeasibly vested remainder in fee simple absolute. If A transfers the life estate to B, then B will own both the life estate and the vested remainder. These two interests added together constitute a fee simple absolute. Once they are owned by one person (here, B), the life estate and vested remainder will *merge* into a fee simple absolute. B would therefore own Blackacre in fee simple absolute. B could convey a fee simple absolute to you, and there would be no need for B to separately convey to you the life estate and the vested remainder. The same thing would happen anytime all of the outstanding interests in an asset, that together would constitute a fee simple absolute, come into ownership by one person.

VALUATION OF FUTURE INTERESTS

In our example, A has a life estate in Blackacre and B has an indefeasibly vested remainder in fee simple absolute. Let's assume that Blackacre is worth $100,000. If Blackacre is sold, how would this be divided between A and B? In some contexts, A and B might be able to come to an agreement on how to divide the purchase price. In other contexts, however, we might need to come up with a valuation of the life estate and the remainder.

In this particular context, valuing the two interests is relatively straightforward. The first step is to look at actuarial life expectancy tables to determine the expected duration of the life estate. The Internal Revenue Service publishes life expectancy tables that are often used for this purpose, although they are relatively crude—they do not distinguish, for example, between the life expectancies of men and women. In any event, according to these tables, if a life tenant is 10 years old, the expected duration of her life, and therefore the life estate, is another 72.8 years. If the life tenant is 55, the expected duration is 29.6 years. If the life tenant is 90, the expected duration is 5.5 years. And so on.

If you know how to discount to present value, then you can fairly easily place values on the life estate and the remainder. We will not go through the discounting calculations here. It is sufficient for our purposes to know that at a 7 percent discount rate, if the life tenant is 10 years old, the life estate is worth $97,405 and the remainder is worth $2,595. Another way of putting this is that the right to own a $100,000 parcel of property 72.8 years from now (recall that the tables tell us that a 10-year old is expected to live another 72.8 years) is worth $2,595. If the life tenant is 90, the life estate is worth $24,253 and the remainder is worth $75,748.

The valuation process becomes more complex as the number and complexity of interests increases. Contingent interests are especially hard to value because of the lack of certainty about whether they will ever become possessory. In some circumstances, the likelihood of the contingent interest becoming possessory might be so remote that the interest will be considered valueless. *See Right of Owner of Contingent or Defeasible Future Interest to Maintain Action for Relief in Respect of Property,* 144 A.L.R. 769.

Despite these potential problems, negotiation with A and B might be manageable. To make it more complicated, now imagine that Blackacre was conveyed as follows:

EXAMPLE 37: O granted Blackacre "to C for life, then to C's children for life, then to C's grandchildren who are alive at C's death." C is alive, and has two children, D and E, and two grandchildren, F and G.

First, let's classify the present and future interests:

C has a life estate.
D and E have vested remainders in an open class in life estate. The class is open because C is still alive.
F and G have contingent remainders in fee simple absolute. The remainders are contingent because there is a condition precedent—the grandchildren have to be alive at the time of C's death. For our purposes, it also is useful to note that the class of C's grandchildren is also open.
O has a reversion in fee simple absolute.

You are faced with a number of difficulties if you want to purchase a fee simple absolute interest in Blackacre. First, there are five living people with interests in Blackacre, and you would have to negotiate with each one. Second, there are interests held by open classes of people. How do you negotiate with the potential future members of the open class of people? Third, there is a contingent remainder, and the contingency will not resolve itself until A dies. That makes it impossible to know who will hold the future interest on A's death. It could be an individual grandchild, a combination of grandchildren, or O if none of A's grandchildren survive A. Even if you could identify the holders of the contingent interests, placing a value on them would be difficult, and it is hard to negotiate a selling price for hard-to-value assets.

The major point being made here is that future interests can substantially impair the alienability of property. The alienability problems associated with future interests increase when (a) the number of future interest holders increases, (b) some future interests are held in open classes, and (c) some future interests are contingent. As the conveyance in Example 37 shows, open classes and contingent interests can create particularly acute alienability problems.

In the remainder of this section, we cover two topics. First, we look at how the trust can cure the alienability problems created by future interests. Second, we look at a number of rules intended to further the alienability of property by destroying certain future interests.

1. How Trusts Solve Alienability Problems

LAW AND
EQUITY
The trust is one of the great inventions of the Anglo-American legal system. It arose in part due to a historical quirk in the English court system. There were two sets of courts in England. The first were the law courts. The second were the equity courts. The sidebar summarizes some of the relevant history and the key differences between law and equity. The distinction between law and equity plays an important role in property law and will be a recurring theme in this course.

LAW AND EQUITY

The distinction between law and equity in the U.S. legal system is the product of the history of the English courts. The judgments of early English law courts could be appealed to the King, who could overturn or alter the courts' judgments as an exercise of mercy or conscience. This review function was often delegated to the Chancellor, a senior government official. Over time, the Chancellor's office developed into the Court of Chancery. As a result, the English legal system had two parallel court systems applying different rules. The law courts applied legal rules, and the Court of Chancery applied equitable rules.

It can be difficult to pin down the precise differences between law and equity. Generally speaking, law courts were concerned with the strict application of legal rules that had developed over time. Equity courts were more flexible and concerned with notions of fairness and justice. The equity courts were particularly concerned with the good faith of the parties and with preventing overreaching by parties exercising their legal rights.

In both England and a majority of U.S. jurisdictions, the law and equity courts have been merged. One court system applies both sets of rules. Some states still have separate courts of law and equity. Today, equitable rules resemble legal rules in some respects: you will research them in the same way and typically look to court precedent for authority. It is important to remember, however, that the sets of rules can operate differently in some important respects. A person, for example, can often act in bad faith and still enforce her legal rights, where bad faith is often a bar to the enforcement of equitable rights.

The distinction between law and equity remains especially important in our rules on remedies. Remedies are the redress that a court can award a party that wins a legal claim. The most common legal remedy is money damages. Equitable remedies include injunctions and specific performance. An injunction is a court order requiring a person to do or refrain from doing a particular act. Specific performance is a court order requiring a person to fulfill an obligation, typically one incurred by contract.

Trusts became possible because the law/equity division allowed the English legal system to separate legal and equitable ownership. In a trust, the *trustee* is the legal owner of the assets held in trust. The *beneficiaries* are the equitable owners of the assets. Equity is superior to law, so the beneficiaries' interest is superior to the trustee's interest. The trustee holds legal ownership for the benefit of the beneficiaries and owes fiduciary duties to them (see the sidebar).

FIDUCIARY DUTIES

Fiduciary relationships, and the fiduciary duties that accompany them, arise when one person acts for another in a relationship of special trust and confidence. Trustees are fiduciaries of the beneficiaries of a trust. Executors are fiduciaries of the devisees of a will or the heirs of a person who dies intestate. Lawyers are fiduciaries of their clients. Agents are fiduciaries of their principals.

You will study fiduciary duties in depth in courses in business organizations, wills, and trusts. For now, it is sufficient to know that there are two basic fiduciary duties, the *duty of loyalty* and the *duty of care.* In a trust, for example, duty of loyalty makes the interests of the beneficiary paramount. The trustee must place the beneficiary's interests above her own. The duty of loyalty prevents, among other things, self-dealing—the trustee, for example, cannot have the trust purchase an asset that she owns. The duty of care requires the trustee to act in a careful and professionally prudent manner. These duties are strictly enforced, and courts take breaches of fiduciary duties very seriously.

The person who creates a trust is called a *settlor.* We will identify the settlor as S and the trustee as T. Trusts often convey to beneficiaries successive interests in the income generated by the trust assets, with the assets being distributed to a different set of beneficiaries in the future. Here is an example:

EXAMPLE 38: S conveys $100,000 "to T in trust, to pay the income to A for life, then to pay the income to B for life, then to pay the principal to B's issue then living *per stirpes,* and if B dies without living issue, then to pay the principal to the American Cancer Society." Note first that the trust assets are conveyed to T, as trustee. T is the legal owner of the assets. All of the other interests created by the conveyance are equitable. A has an equitable life estate in the income generated by the trust assets. B has an indefeasibly vested remainder in life estate in the income of the trust. B's issue have an alternative contingent remainder in the principal (i.e., the assets) of the trust. The American Cancer Society has an alternative contingent remainder in the principal of the trust.

During A's life, T will pay the trust income to A. After A dies, T will pay the income to B, if B is still alive. When B dies, T will pay the trust principal to B's issue then living *per stirpes*. If B has no living issue, T will pay the trust principal to the American Cancer Society. Once the principal is paid out, the trust will terminate. If T is an individual and dies or resigns at any time during this process, T will be replaced with another trustee. Banks and other institutions may be trustees, and the settlors of trusts of long expected durations often choose institutional trustees.

Note the terminology used in Example 38. The present and future interests created in this example are *equitable* interests. The conveyance in Example 38 creates an equitable life estate in A. The future interests likewise are equitable. In contrast, the interests in the other examples that we have seen are *legal* interests. In the conveyance "to A for life, then to B," for example, A has a legal life estate, and B has a legal indefeasibly vested remainder in fee simple absolute.

In Example 38, the trust asset was a sum of money. Trusts can be created with any sort of property. Most often, the trustee has the power to sell trust assets and reinvest the proceeds in other assets. Because of this power to alienate trust assets, conveyances that create equitable future interests in trust avoid many of the alienability problems that are created by conveyances that create legal future interests. If Blackacre is conveyed in trust to T, for the benefit of a set of equitable present and future interest holders, then T in most circumstances can sell Blackacre and reinvest the proceeds in another asset. If you wanted to purchase Blackacre, you only need to negotiate with T, rather than a host of present and future interest holders.

Because of alienability and other issues, *you should almost never advise clients to convey property in a way that creates legal future interests.* When future interests are involved, creating a trust should be your default rule, and you should deviate from this default rule only if you have a good reason to do so.

2. *Rules Favoring Alienability*

As we saw above, future interests in open class and contingent interests can present substantial alienability problems. In this section, we consider four traditional rules that were designed to further the alienability of property by in some circumstances destroying these interests. The first three rules are largely archaic, and our consideration of them will be very brief. The fourth, the Rule Against Perpetuities, is still important in many U.S. jurisdictions, and we will cover it in some depth.

a. The Doctrine of Worthier Title

The operation of the Doctrine of Worthier Title is best illustrated through an example:

EXAMPLE 39: O conveys Blackacre "to A for life, then to O's heirs."

Classifying this conveyance, A has a life estate, O's heirs have a contingent remainder in fee simple absolute, and O has a reversion in fee simple absolute.

Heirs are not identified until a person's death, so the remainder is contingent because it is in an unascertained person. The Doctrine of Worthier Title destroyed the contingent remainder in O's heirs, leaving O with a more straight-forward reversion in fee simple absolute. The operation of the doctrine therefore rewrites the conveyance to read "to A for life." By destroying the contingent remainder, the Doctrine of Worthier Title promoted the alienability of property—if you want to buy Blackacre, you only need to negotiate with A and O, and don't have to wait around until A's death to identify O's heirs.

The Doctrine of Worthier Title originally applied to both transfers at death and transfers during life. The branch that applied to transfers at death is now defunct. Section 2-710 of the Uniform Probate Code (which, to be clear, has not been adopted by all states) abolishes the doctrine. The branch applying to transfers during life is out of favor and has been abolished in many jurisdictions. To the extent it survives, today it is more of a rule of construction than a rule of law—that is, it is used as an aid in interpreting the language of a conveyance, rather than a hard-and-fast rule that is always binding. The Doctrine gained its second life as a rule of construction in Judge Cardozo's opinion in *Doctor v. Hughes*, 122 N.E. 221 (N.Y. 1919). Whatever the abstract merits of Judge Cardozo's position, the use of the Doctrine as a rule of construction has been something of a fiasco in practice. One court remarked that the rule of construction approach has led "to a shower of strained decisions difficult to reconcile with one another and [has been] generative of considerable confusion in the law." *Hatch v. Riggs National Bank*, 361 F.2d 559, 563 (D.C. App. 1966). The Doctrine was abolished in England in 1833 and is sliding into oblivion here. It may, however, still have some life in some jurisdictions.

b.   The Rule in Shelley's Case

The Rule in Shelley's Case, like the Doctrine of Worthier Title, promotes alienability by destroying a contingent remainder created in a person's heirs. The Rule applies to the following scenario:

EXAMPLE 40: O conveys Blackacre "to A for life, then to A's heirs."

Note that the contingent remainder in this example is in A's heirs, rather than O's heirs as was the case with the Doctrine of Worthier Title. The Rule operates to merge the remainder and the life estate, creating a fee simple absolute in A. As with the Doctrine of Worthier Title, the destruction of the contingent remainder in A's heirs by the Rule encourages the alienability of property. If you want to buy Blackacre, you do not have to worry about who might qualify as A's heirs at A's death.

The Rule in Shelley's Case has been abolished in most U.S. jurisdictions—it appears to thrive only in Arkansas and Delaware. The Rule was abolished in England in 1925.

c.   Destructibility of Contingent Remainders

In our materials on contingent remainders, we looked at the conveyance "to A for life, then to B if B reaches the age of 21." What happens if A dies and B is 18 years old? Under the common-law rule of destructibility, B's interest was destroyed. The result under the traditional rule is that Blackacre would revert back to O in fee simple absolute. The destruction of the contingent remainder aids alienability by reducing the number of interests and eliminating the need to worry about the resolution of the contingency.

The destructibility rule has been widely abolished and appears to thrive only in Florida. In jurisdictions that have abolished the rule, on A's death O would have a fee simple subject to executory limitation and B would have an executory interest in fee simple absolute that would take away O's interest if and when B reaches the age of 21.

d.   The Rule Against Perpetuities

The Rule Against Perpetuities is our most important rule favoring alienability. It is more broadly applicable than the other three rules and still survives in some form in most U.S. jurisdictions. It is also incredibly hard to apply. The California Supreme Court famously dismissed a malpractice action against an attorney who botched the Rule because of the Rule's complexity. *See Lucas v. Hamm,* 364 P.2d 685 (Cal. 1961).

Despite its complexity, we think that it is possible for everyone to achieve a good basic understanding of the Rule and its operation. We will take the Rule in a series of steps and will focus on examples of Rule in action. We will also explain how an attorney with even an imperfect understanding of the Rule can competently advise clients. We do not want you to find yourself in a position of having to rely on *Lucas v. Hamm.*

Before we go any further, you should be sure you have completed the present and future interest problem sets and know the classification of future interests cold. The application of the Rule turns on the identity of future interests, and if you are still confused about how to identify interests, you will be even more confused with this material.

The Rule applies to only a limited set of types of interests. It applies to:

> Contingent remainders
> Executory Interests
> Vested Remainders in an Open Class
> Option and similar contracts

It does *not* apply to:

Future interests created in the grantor:

> Reversions
> Possibilities of Reverter
> Rights of Entry

Vested interests not in an open class created in the grantee:

Indefeasibly Vested Remainders
Vested Remainders Subject to Divestment

We will focus on the Rule's application to future interests and will cover options and similar contracts towards the end of our discussion.

John Chipman Gray gave us the classic statement of the Rule, to which we have added two small insertions: "No interest [subject to the Rule] is good unless it must vest [in a closed class], if at all, no later than 21 years after some life in being at the creation of the interest." Let's take each part of this statement in turn:

"No interest [subject to the Rule] is good . . . " As we noted above, three types of future interests are subject to the Rule: contingent remainders, executory interests, and vested remainders in an open class. *If they do not satisfy the Rule, they are void from the time of creation—it is as if they never existed.* If an interest violates the Rule, we simply cross it out of the conveyance. We added the modification "[subject to the Rule]" to remind us that the Rule does not apply to all future interests.

"unless it must vest [in a closed class], if at all . . . " To satisfy the Rule, the interest in question must vest, or fail, within a certain period.

For contingent remainders and executory interests, this means that the contingencies reflected in the interest must resolve themselves one way or the other within the period stated by the Rule. Note well that the Rule *does not* require the interests to vest within this period. Rather, it requires that they either vest *or* fail during the period. We just want to know how things turn out, one way or the other. Note also that we are concerned here about when the interests vest or fail, not about when they might become possessory.

For vested remainders in an open class, this means that the *class must close* within the period set by the Rule. We added "[in a closed class]" to highlight the application of the Rule to vested remainders in an open class. For these interests, we care about the class closing, not vesting.

"no later than 21 years after some life in being at the creation of the interest." This part of the rule sets the period within which the interests subject to the Rule must vest in a closed class or fail. This period—which we will call the "perpetuities period"—is defined as 21 years after a life in being at the time of creation of the interest. We will need to be more precise in our definition of a "life in being," but for now, we can understand it as a person who was alive when the interest was created. The perpetuities period ends 21 years after the death of the last life in being. Interests subject to the Rule that do not vest in a closed class or fail within this time period are void.

Before we get further into the operation of the Rule, we should pause to see how it accomplishes its policy goals. As we have already noted, one goal of the Rule is to further the alienability of property. We have seen how contingent remainders, executory interests, and vested remainders in an open class can impede the alienability of property. The Rule aids alienability by limiting the amount of time for the contingencies in contingent remainders and executory interests to resolve themselves, and for the open classes in vested remainders in an open class to become closed. It also aids alienability by destroying interests that do not comply with the Rule.

The Rule has other policy justifications. One of these justifications is limiting the period of dead hand control of property. The dead hand issue is just what it sounds like—problems might arise when a person tries to control land or other assets after their death. Circumstances change, and what might have seemed like a good idea when the grantor made a decision might not seem like a good idea now. Because the grantor is dead, she cannot change her mind based on new circumstances. By limiting the time for future interests to vest or fail, the Rule places some limits on the practical duration of dead hand control. Another justification for the Rule is inhibiting the creation of permanent concentrations of wealth. By forcing land and other assets into certain ownership by the end of the perpetuities period, the Rule makes it easier for concentrations of wealth to be broken up or dissipate.

To apply the Rule, we first classify the future interests created by the grant without regard to their validity under the Rule. We then see if any of these interests are subject to the Rule. Next, we test those interests to see if they vest or fail in a closed class within the perpetuities period. If they do, they are valid. If they do not, they are void. Finally, if any of the interests are invalid under the Rule, we reclassify the valid interests created by the grant. Of these steps, the third—identifying lives in being—is by far the hardest.

There are two major ways to test whether an interest satisfies the Rule. The first is the *common-law approach*. The common-law approach looks forward from the time an interest is created and asks whether the interest is certain to vest or fail in a closed class within the perpetuities period. The common-law approach is often described as making the Rule a matter of mathematical or logical proof. We need to be able to prove, with certainty, that the interest will vest or fail in a closed class within 21 years of a life in being. An advantage of the common-law approach is that it allows us to know right away whether an interest is valid under the Rule. A disadvantage is that, as we will see, the common-law approach often voids interests because of the possibility of extremely unlikely events.

The second is the *wait-and-see approach*. Rather than looking forward from the date of creation of the interest, this approach waits to see how facts actually develop. It looks backward at the end of the perpetuities period and asks whether the interests in question have vested or failed in a closed class. Any interest that satisfies the common-law approach will also satisfy the wait-and-see approach: if we have proved with certainty that the interest will vest or fail in a closed class during the perpetuities period, we don't have to wait and see how things actually turn out. The wait-and-see approach will validate some interests that would be invalid under the common-law approach. This approach has the advantage of avoiding the often silly results that follow from the common-law approach. It has the disadvantage of leading to uncertainty about whether an interest is valid while the perpetuities period plays itself out.

As we apply the Rule to various conveyances, we will analyze each interest under both the common-law and wait-and-see approaches. Before we get to our first examples, we need establish two more important points:

> First, when we apply the common-law approach, we evaluate the interests at the time the conveyance is made. Transfers made by will occur *when the testator dies*, not when the will is written. Wills can be changed at any time up to the testator's death.

We should note that conveyances made in trust are evaluated when they become irrevocable. We will not present examples involving revocable trusts and note this rule simply to be thorough.

Second, not everyone alive at the time of conveyance qualifies as a life in being. Rather, only *people who in some way affect the vesting* (or class closing) of the interest count. Often potential lives in being are obvious from the language of the convey-ance. Other times, potential lives in being are more subtle, as we will see from our examples below.

Let's look at some examples to see the Rule in operation.

EXAMPLE 41: O grants Blackacre "to A for life, then to B if B reaches the age of 50." At the time of the conveyance, B is alive and is two years old.
Classifying without the RAP. A has a life estate, B has a contingent remainder in fee simple absolute, and O has a reversion in fee simple absolute. B's contingent remainder is subject to the Rule.
Common-law approach: B's contingent remainder will vest or fail during B's life — either B will live to 50, or will not. B therefore provides the life in being for this interest, and it is valid under the common-law approach.
Wait-and-see approach: Any interest that is valid under the common-law approach will also be valid under the wait-and-see approach. We could wait around to see if B lives to age 50 or not, but we don't need to do so — we know that this contingency will resolve itself one way or the other during B's life.
EXAMPLE 42: O grants Blackacre "to A for life, then to A's children." At the time of conveyance, A has one child, B.
Classifying without the RAP. A has a life estate and B has a vested remainder in an open class. B's vested remainder in an open class is subject to the Rule.
Common-law approach: B's vested remainder will vest *in a closed class* on A's death. A is alive, and so provides the life in being to validate B's vested remainder in an open class.
Wait-and-see approach: Because B's vested remainder in an open class is valid under the common-law approach, it also is valid under the wait-and-see approach. We do not need to wait around for the class to actually close to determine whether B's interest is valid under the Rule.
EXAMPLE 43: O grants Blackacre "to A for life, then to A's first child to reach the age of 25." A is alive, and has one child, B, who is 22 years old.
Classifying without the RAP. A has a life estate. B has a contingent remainder in fee simple absolute. O has a reversion in fee simple absolute.
Common-law approach: The contingent remainder in fee simple absolute is void under the common-law approach. You might think that it is valid because B is alive and B will reach the age of 25, or not, during B's lifetime. Plus, B is only three years away from reaching the age of 25! There are scenarios, however, where the contin-gent remainder might vest or fail outside of the perpetuities period. Here is an example:

> 2000: Grant is made. A is alive, and has one child B, who is 22 years old.
> 2001: A has a second child, C.
> 2002: A and B die.
> 2026: C reaches the age of 25 more than 21 years after a life in being at the time of the creation of the grant.

Because of this possibility, the contingent remainder is void. Under the common-law approach, we would reclassify the interests in the grant: A has a life estate. O has a reversion in fee simple absolute. B has nothing whatsoever. Note that this is true even if B has reached the age of 25 by the time the dispute is adjudicated. *An interest that violates the Rule is void from the time of the grant*—we treat it as if it never existed in the first place.

In this example, C is an *afterborn child*—that is a child born after the grant was made. The possibility of afterborn children is a frequent source of problems under the Rule Against Perpetuities.

Wait-and-see approach: The contingent remainder in fee simple absolute might be void or it might be valid—we have to wait and see. If B or another of A's children reaches the age of 25 during the perpetuities period, the contingent remainder will vest and be valid. If an afterborn child scenario like the one set forth above occurs, then the contingent remainder will be void. Note that there is also a possibility that the contingent remainder will simply fail on its own terms—for example, if A and B die in 2001 and A has no other children.

---

watch out for afterborn children!

EXAMPLE 44: O grants Blackacre "to A for life, then to A's first child to reach the age of 21." A is alive, and has one child, B.

Classifying without the RAP. A has a life estate. B has a contingent remainder in fee simple absolute. O has a reversion in fee simple absolute.

Common-law approach: The contingent remainder in fee simple absolute is valid. Even in an afterborn child scenario, the contingent remainder will vest or fail within the perpetuities period because any child of A will reach 21, or not, within 21 years of A's death. Here is an example:

> 2000: Grant is made. A is alive, and has one child B.
> 2001: B dies.
> 2022: A has another child, C.
> 2023: A dies.
> 2041: C reaches the age of 21.

Because the contingent remainder must vest or fail within 21 years of A's death, it is valid under the common-law approach.

Wait-and-see approach: Because the contingent remainder is valid under the common-law approach, it is valid under the wait-and-see approach.

You might think from the last two examples that conveyances that create contingencies requiring people to reach an age of greater than 21 are problematic under the Rule Against Perpetuities. This is an overgeneralization. An age restriction of more than 21 years should raise a red flag, but many such restrictions are valid. For instance, the conveyance in Example 41, created this contingent remainder: "then to B if B reaches the age of 50." Conveyances turning on the age of a specific named person will be valid because the contingency will resolve itself one way or the other during that person's lifetime. Note in this context the difference between "then to B if B reaches the age of 50" and "then to A's first child to reach the age of 50." The first is to a specific living person. The second is not.

Interests created in unspecified people with age restrictions of more than 21 years may also be valid in other context. Our next example introduces a new character to our cast: T. T stands for Testator. When we say that T granted Blackacre "to A," we mean that T died and left Blackacre to A in her will. The key thing to understand is that the conveyance is made at T's death. One important ramification of this fact is that T is dead and so cannot have any more children. Another is that some interests in the text of the conveyance might not become possessory because facts might have changed between the time the testator wrote her will and the time the testator died. Here are some examples of how T's death at the time of conveyance can affect the validity of conveyances under the Rule Against Perpetuities.

EXAMPLE 45: T grants Blackacre "to A for life, then to my first child to reach the age of 25." A is alive and T has one child, B, age one.
Classifying without the RAP. A has a life estate. B has a contingent remainder in fee simple absolute. T's estate has a reversion in fee simple absolute. This conveyance is similar to that in Example 43, but the contingent remainder is in T's first child to reach 25, not A's first child to reach 25.
Common-law approach: B's contingent remainder is valid under the common-law approach. This is because T is dead and therefore cannot have any more children. The afterborn child problem that was present in Example 43 therefore is absent here. B was alive at the time of conveyance and provides her own measuring life to validate her interest.
Wait-and-see approach: Because B's interest is valid under the common-law approach, it is valid under the wait-and-see approach.

EXAMPLE 46: T grants Blackacre "to A for life, then to A's first child to reach the age of 25." At the time of the conveyance (T's death), A has died and has one child, B, age 23.
Classifying without the RAP. Because A is dead at the time of conveyance, A's life estate never becomes possessory—it effectively disappears. Under the modern approach that does not follow the rule of destructibility of contingent remainders, B's contingent remainder is converted into an executory interest. To classify the grant, T's estate has a fee simple subject to executory limitation, and B has an executory interest in fee simple absolute. This executory interest is subject to the Rule.
Common-law approach: B's executory interest is valid under the Rule. B was alive at the time of conveyance, and provides the measuring life that validates her executory interest—B obviously will reach 25 or not within her own lifetime.
Note three things about this conveyance. First, we care about the facts at the time of conveyance. With testamentary conveyances, this is the time of death. The facts at the time the will was drafted are irrelevant. Second, because A was dead at the time of conveyance, there was no afterborn child problem. Third, the result is that the exact same language that was a problem in Example 43 was not a problem here.

Wait-and-see approach: Because B's interest is valid under the common-law approach, it is valid under the wait-and-see approach.

The differences between conveyances made during life and those made at death are further illustrated by the following examples involving class gifts.

EXAMPLE 47: O grants Blackacre "to my children for life, then to my grandchildren." O is 80 years old, and has one child, A, and one grandchild, B.

Classifying without the RAP. A has a life estate that may have to be shared if additional children are born. B has a vested remainder in an open class in fee simple absolute.

Common-law approach: B's vested remainder in an open class is void under the common-law approach because of the potential for afterborn children. Classifying the interests applying the common-law Rule, A has a life estate that may have to be shared if additional children are born; O has a reversion in fee simple absolute.

Here is an example of a scenario that would cause the remainder to vest in a closed class outside of the perpetuities period:

> 2000: Conveyance is made. O, A, and B are alive.
> 2001: O has another *child*, C.
> 2002: O, A, and B die.
> 2030: C has a child, D.
> 2080: C dies, closing the class of O's *grandchildren*.

As this scenario shows, the class of O's grandchildren could close well past the perpetuities period. You might intuitively rebel against the idea of O having another child after the age of 80. Remember, however, in this area *the law will act as if any living person can have additional children* (see the sidebar).

PRESUMPTIONS OF FERTILITY AND CHILDREN BORN AFTER DEATH

As this problem shows, the legal presumption that any living person can have a child can sometimes lead to absurd results. The presumption applies to people of any age, whether they are 2 years old or 80 years old. At least where older people are concerned, recent medical developments and the possibility of adoption both make this presumption possibility less unrealistic than it may once have been.

Advances in reproductive technology present another potential problem. Because human reproductive cells can be frozen (whether fertilized or not), there is now a very real possibility that a person might have a child many years after her death. The possibility that a child might be born after a parent's death has always existed—a father might conceive a child and die before the child was born. Children born in this particular circumstance are typically treated as being alive at the time of their parent's death for property law purposes. But what do we do with a child born 15 years after a parent's death? Do they, for example, fall into the class of a conveyance made to the parent's children? The answer is blurry. *See* Benjamin C. Carpenter, *A Chip Off the Old Iceblock: How Cryopreservation Has Changed Estate Law, Why Attempts to Address the Issue Have Fallen Short, and How to Fix It*, 21 Cornell J.L. & Pub. Pol'y 347 (2011). As to our topic at hand, the possibility of this type of children should not be relevant to the operation of the Rule Against Perpetuities, at least unless the grantor clearly contemplated including such children in the conveyance at issue. *See* Sharona Hoffman & Andrew P. Morriss, *Birth After Death: Perpetuities and the New Reproductive Technologies*, 38 Ga. L. Rev. 575 (2004).

There are three important lessons to take from this scenario. First, remember that for the Rule Against Perpetuities, any living person can have children. Second, conveyances in this general pattern are often called *fertile octogenarian problems*, for the obvious reason that they turn on the idea that an 80-year old can have children. Third, conveyances to *a living person's grandchildren* are often problematic under the common-law approach to the Rule Against Perpetuities.

Wait-and-see approach: B's vested remainder in an open class may or may not be valid. If O dies without having any further children, then the vested remainder in the open class of O's grandchildren will be valid—all of O's *children* are lives in being, and when the last child dies, the class of O's *grandchildren* will vest in a closed class. If O does have an afterborn child, the vested remainder might vest too late and be void under the Rule.
EXAMPLE 48: T grants Blackacre "to my children for life, then to my grandchildren." At her death, T is survived by one child, A, and one grandchild, B.

Classifying without the RAP: A has a life estate that may have to be shared if additional children are born. B has a vested remainder in an open class in fee simple absolute.

Common-law approach: B's vested remainder in an open class is valid. The key difference from Example 47 is that at the time of conveyance, T was dead. Because T has died, T cannot have afterborn children. The class of T's *children* is closed at the time of conveyance. T's children provide the measuring lives for the class of T's *grandchildren*, because the class of grandchildren will close on the death of the last child.

Wait-and-see approach: Because B's interest is valid under the common-law approach, it is valid under the wait-and-see approach.
The last two examples show us that a conveyance to a living person's grandchildren raises problems under the common-law Rule Against Perpetuities, but that a conveyance to a dead person's grandchildren avoids these problems. This is not to say that all conveyances to a dead person's grandchildren will be valid—a conveyance to "any of T's grandchildren to reach the age of 25" will raise problems. At this point, you should be able to work out why this conveyance is problematic for yourself. If you need some help, it is included in the exercises with explanatory answers below.

The fertile octogenarian is one of three classic Rule Against Perpetuities problems that you should be familiar with. Here are the other two:

EXAMPLE 49: O conveys Blackacre "to A for life, then to A's widow for life, then to A's children then living." A is alive and is married to B. A has one child, C.
Classifying without the RAP: A has a life estate. A's widow has a contingent remainder in life estate. Why is this remainder contingent? Because it is in an unascertained person—we do not know the identity of A's widow until A dies. C has a contingent remainder in fee simple absolute, and O has a reversion in fee simple absolute.
Common-law approach: Both of the contingent remainders are subject to the Rule. A's widow's contingent remainder is valid under the Rule, because it will vest or fail on A's death, and A is a life in being. C's contingent remainder, however, is void under the Rule. We therefore need to reclassify the interests as follows: A has a life estate, A's widow has a contingent remainder in life estate, and O has a reversion in fee simple absolute.
Here is a scenario that illustrates the invalidity of the contingent remainder in O's children who survive A and A's widow:

> 2000: Conveyance is made. A, B, and C are alive.
> 2001: D is born. D is unrelated to A, B, or C.
> 2002: B and C die.
> 2025: A marries D.
> 2026: A and D have a child, E.
> 2027: A dies. D is now A's widow.
> 2075: D dies. C's contingent remainder, if valid, would become possessory.

In this scenario, the contingent remainder in A's children vests or fails far outside of the perpetuities period. The problem is created because *both* (a) A's widow might be born after the conveyance, *and* (b) the contingent remainder will not vest or fail until A's widow's death. Unsurprisingly, the name of this problem is *the unborn widow.*

Do not make the mistake in thinking that all conveyances that create remainder in life estate in a widow raise perpetuities problems. For example, if the remainder at the end of this conveyance is rewritten to be "then to A's children," the remainder would be valid, because it would vest in a closed class on A's death.

Wait-and-see approach: The contingent remainder in A's children who survive A's widow may or may not be valid. So long as the person who becomes A's widow was alive at the time of conveyance, the remainder will vest or fail during the perpetuities period (at the end of the widow's life) and will be valid.

EXAMPLE 50: O conveys Blackacre "to A for life, then to B when A's will is probated."

Classifying without the RAP: A has a life estate. O has a reversion in fee simple subject to executory limitation. B has an executory interest. Why isn't B's interest a remainder? Because it will not become possessory, if at all, on the natural end of the preceding estate. When A dies, some period of time will pass before A's will is probated—probate is a legal process that takes some time.

Common-law approach: B's executory interest is void under the common-law approach. Reclassifying the interests taking the application of the Rule into account, A has a life estate and O has a reversion in fee simple absolute. Here is a scenario that illustrates why the executory interest is void.

> 2000: Conveyance is made. A and B are alive.
> 2001: A dies.
> 2002: B dies. If it was valid, the executory interest would now be held by B's devisees or heirs.
> 2025: A's will is finally probated. The contingency in the executory interest has resolved itself more than 21 years after the death of A and B, who are the only people in the conveyance who affect the vesting and could possibly be lives in being.

The name of this problem is *the slothful executor.* Most wills are probated within a short time of the testator's death. There remains a possibility, however remote, that the executor will not successfully probate the will for more than 21 years after lives in being. As a result, the executory interest is void under the common-law approach.

Like the slothful executor, our next few examples involve executory interests.

> Three classic problems: the fertile octogenarian (Example 47), the unborn widow (Example 49), and the slothful executor (Example 50).

EXAMPLE 51: O conveys Blackacre "to the School Board so long as it is used for school purposes."

Classifying without the RAP. The School Board has a fee simple determinable. O has a possibility of reverter in fee simple absolute. All interests created in the grantor (reversions, possibilities of reverter, and rights of entry) are exempt from the Rule Against Perpetuities, so the Rule does not apply here at all.

EXAMPLE 52: O conveys Blackacre "to the School Board so long as it is used for school purposes, then to A."

Classifying without the RAP. The School Board has a fee simple subject to executory limitation. A has an executory interest in fee simple absolute.

Common-law approach: The exectory interest violates the Rule Against Perpetuities. This one should be fairly intuitive—the School Board could stop using Blackacre 500 years from now. Therefore it is possibility for the executory interest to vest or fail well outside of the perpetuities period.

Reclassifying the interest to take the application of the Rule into account, the School Board has a fee simple determinable and O has a possibility of reverter in fee simple absolute.

Wait-and-see approach: The executory interest may or may not be valid. If the School Board stops using Blackacre for school purposes within the perpetuities period, then the executory interest will be valid. If not, it will be void.

EXAMPLE 53: O conveys Blackacre "to the School Board, but if the property is no longer used for school purposes then A may enter and take the property."

Classifying without the RAP. The School Board has a fee simple subject to executory limitation. A has an executory interest in fee simple absolute.

Common-law approach: The executory interest violates the Rule Against Perpetuities. The reason is the same as in the last example—the School Board could stop using Blackacre for school purposes 500 years from now.

Remember that if an interest violates the Rule, we simply cross it out of the conveyance. Note what happens when you cross the language creating the executory interest out of this conveyance—you are left with "to the School Board." The School Board owns Blackacre in fee simple absolute. It is best not to try to think of a good reason for the difference in result between this example and Example 52, where the elimination of the executory interest resulted in a fee simple determinable. The Rule Against Perpetuities is a mechanical rule, so apply it mechanically.

Wait-and-see approach: As in the previous example, the executory interest may or may not be valid. If the School Board stops using Blackacre for school purposes within the perpetuities period, then the executory interest will be valid. If not, it will be void.

EXAMPLE 54: O conveys Blackacre "to the School Board for so long as the property is used for school purposes, then to the State University."

Classifying without the RAP. The School Board has a fee simple subject to executory limitation. The State University has an executory interest in fee simple absolute.

Common-law approach. The State University's executory interest is valid under the Rule Against Perpetuities. This is due to the *charity-to-charity exception.* This exception states that if both interests—the interest subject to executory limitation or divestment, and the executory interest that might take it away—are held by charities, then the executory interest is exempt from the Rule Against Perpetuities.

Wait-and-see approach. Because the State University's executory interest is valid under the common-law approach, it is valid under the wait-and-see approach.

Finally, as we noted at the outset, the Rule Against Perpetuities has been held to apply to options and similar contracts. We will distinguish between two types of contracts—*options* and *rights of first refusal.* A purchase option gives the holder the right to purchase the property in question in accordance with the terms of the option agreement. A right of first refusal gives the holder the right to purchase the property in accordance with the terms of the agreement, but only if the owner offers to sell the property to someone else first. The crucial difference is that the holder of an option has the power to compel the sale of the subject property, where the holder of a right of first refusal does not have the power to compel the sale if the owner has not offered to sell to someone else. Before we get to the application of the Rule Against Perpetuities to these contracts, let's take a look at an example of each.

> EXAMPLE 55: O grants A an option to purchase Blackacre "for $100,000 within one year of the date of this option agreement." O has an option to purchase Blackacre for $100,000 within one year. If O refuses to sell Blackacre to A, A can compel the sale.
> EXAMPLE 56: O grants A a right of first refusal to purchase Blackacre "within one year of the date of this agreement." A has a one-year right of first refusal in Blackacre. If O offers to sell Blackacre to anyone else during the one-year period, A has the right to step in and purchase the property. If O does not offer to sell to anyone else, however, A cannot compel O to sell Blackacre.

The majority common-law view is that options are subject to the Rule Against Perpetuities. A less strong majority of jurisdictions also hold that rights of first refusal are subject to the Rule. In our examples that follow, we will follow this majority rule. We should note that the majority common-law rule applying the Rule to options has been altered in many states by statute. The Uniform Statutory Rule Against Perpetuities (USRAP), adopted in about half of U.S. jurisdictions and discussed further below, abolishes the application of the Rule to options and rights of first refusal.

An option satisfies the common-law Rule Against Perpetuities if it must be exercised, if at all, within the perpetuities period. The option in Example 55 easily satisfies the Rule—it must be exercised within one year of its creation. The following two options raise perpetuities problems:

> EXAMPLE 57: O grants A an option to purchase Blackacre "for $100,000 at any time prior to 30 years from the date of this agreement."

Classifying without the RAP: O owns Blackacre in fee simple absolute. A has an option to purchase Blackacre.

Common-law approach: A's option is void. O and A could die tomorrow, and A's estate could try to exercise the option in 30 years—more than 21 years after the deaths of O and A, who are our potential lives in being.

Wait-and-see approach: A's option may or may not be valid. So long as either O or A survives for nine years, the option period will fall within the perpetuities period of lives in being plus 21 years, and the interest will be valid. Even if O and A die soon after the option was executed, the option will be valid if A exercises the option during the perpetuities period.
EXAMPLE 58: ABC Inc. grants XYZ LLC an option to purchase Blackacre "for $100,000 at any time prior to 30 years from the date of this agreement."

Classifying without the RAP: ABC Inc. owns Blackacre in fee simple absolute. XYZ LLC has an option to purchase Blackacre.

Common-law approach: XYZ LLC's option is void. This is the same basic conveyance as the previous example. Here, however, both the grantor and the grantee are legal entities, not natural people. As a result, neither can provide lives in being. The perpetuities period therefore ends up being 21 years. Because the option by its terms has a 30-year period, it is possible that the option will be exercised outside of the perpetuities period.

Wait-and-see approach: XYZ LLC's option may or may not be valid. Because both the grantor and the grantee are entities, the perpetuities period will be 21 years. If XYZ LLC exercises the option within 21 years, it will be valid. If not, it will be void.

G.   RULE AGAINST PERPETUITIES PROBLEM SET

For each of the following conveyances, classify the interests (a) without application of the Rule Against Perpetuities, (b) with application of the common-law approach to the Rule Against Perpetuities, and (c) with application of the wait-and-see approach to the Rule Against Perpetuities. Explanatory answers to this set of exercises are provided on page 1034.

1. O grants Blackacre "to A for life, then to A's oldest child then living for life, then to A's grandchildren then living and their heirs."
2. T devises Blackacre "to A for life, then to B for life, then to B's children."
3. O grants Blackacre "to A for life, then to A's children, but if any of A's issue are ever convicted of a felony, then the interest in A's children will be divested and shall go to the Widener City School Board."
4. T devises Blackacre "to A for life, then to A's children for life, then to A's grandchildren for life, then to A's great-grandchildren and their heirs." At the time of T's death, A is alive and has two children, B and C, each of which have two children, B1 and B2, and C1 and C2.

5. Same as (4), but 25 years later, A, B, and C have died without having more children. B1 has had a child, B3. C2 has had two children, C3 and C4.
6. T devises "to my widow for life, then to my issue then living."
7. O sells A an option to purchase Blackacre "for $100,000 at any time prior to the date 30 years from the date of execution of this agreement."
8. T's will gives Blackacre "to A for life, then to A's children for their lives, then to B's children." When T dies, A is alive and has two children, A1 and A2. B has died and is survived by three children, B1, B2, and B3.
9. O gives Blackacre "to my children for life, then to my first grandchild to reach the age of 25."
10. O conveys Blackacre "to my children for life, then to my grandchildren who reach the age of 21."
11. T grants Blackacre to "to my children for life, then to their children for life, then to my surviving issue." T is survived by two children, A and B.
12. T dies, leaving a will that states in part: "my estate in North Widener City shall be sold and the proceeds divided equally amongst my surviving issue."
13. T grants Blackacre "to my child, A, for life, then to A's children, but if any of A's children fail to graduate from college by age 30, then that child's share shall go to A's other children." A is alive and has two children, B and C. B received her B.A. in 1999; C is a junior in high school.
14. T conveys Blackacre "to my children for life, then to my grandchildren who reach the age of 25." At T's death, T is survived by her children A and B, and one grandchild, C, who is 18 years old.
15. O conveys Blackacre "to A for life, then to A's children for life, then to A's issue born during the lifetime of any of the issue of President John F. Kennedy alive at the time of this conveyance."
16. T devises Blackacre "to A and her heirs, but if A dies childless, then to B's children then living."
17. T conveys Blackacre "to my sister, Maura, for life, then to Maura's husband Max for his life should he still be married to Maura at her death, then to Maura and Max's children then living."
18. O conveys Blackacre "to A until my first grandchild reaches the age of 21, then to that grandchild."
19. T grants Blackacre "to my son, David, for life, then to his children for their lives, then to his grandchildren and their heirs." At T's death, David is alive and has two children, Katie and Laura.
20. Same as 19, but now 15 years later, David has died, survived by Katie and Laura. Neither Katie nor Laura have children.

1. Perpetuities Reform

As we discussed above, the Rule Against Perpetuities serves several important policy goals. It promotes the alienability of property, limits dead hand control, and places some limits on the development of concentrations of wealth across generations. As we have seen, however, the Rule imperfectly promotes these goals. It does not eliminate all problematic future interests, and it is possible to have a conveyance that satisfies the common-law rule that creates uncertain interests that might last for more than 100 years. It is very difficult to apply, even for people with a solid understanding of the Rule. The Rule therefore has presented a ripe target for reform.

The pure common-law rule only survives in a handful of jurisdictions. We will highlight four broad categories of reforms to the Rule:

1. *The Wait-and-See Approach.* As we have seen, the wait-and-see approach judges the validity of interests under the Rule based on facts as they actually occur, rather than speculating on what might happen. It has the advantage of validating some interests that would have been voided under the common-law approach because of the possible occurrence of highly unlikely events. It has the downside of leaving the validity of some interests uncertain while we wait and see how facts will develop. It also has the downside of being just as technically difficult to apply as the common-law Rule.

2. *USRAP.* The Uniform Statutory Rule Against Perpetuities (USRAP) was promulgated in 1986. It has been adopted, often with some modification, by about half of U.S. jurisdictions. Under USRAP, an interest is valid if it either (a) satisfies the common-law Rule or (b) vests or fails within 90 years. The 90-year provision is a modification of the wait-and-see approach—rather than wait and see whether the interest vests or fails within the traditional perpetuities period of lives in being plus 21 years, we wait and see whether it vests or fails within a flat 90 years. USRAP makes a number of other modifications to the common-law Rule. For example, as noted above, it abolishes the application of the Rule to options.

3. *Elimination of Application to Trusts.* A number of states have abolished the application of the Rule to property held in trust. Some states limit this exclusion to personal property held in trust; others apply it to both real and personal property held in trust. As we discussed above, many of the alienability problems created by contingent future interests disappear when the property is held in trust. These reforms to the Rule allow what are often called *dynasty trusts*—trusts that have the potential to last forever.

4. *Outright Abolition of the Rule.* An increasing number of states have abolished the Rule Against Perpetuities outright. These states include Alaska, Idaho, Kentucky, New Jersey, Pennsylvania, Rhode Island, and South Dakota.

In thinking about reform to the Rule Against Perpetuities, we should keep in mind that there are other potential ways to achieve the policy goals of the Rule. As we have already seen, alienability concerns can be addressed with the use of trusts. Concerns about accumulations of wealth over time can be addressed through tax policy. Courts also have the authority of doctrine of cy pres ("as near as is possible") to alter the language of the conveyance to achieve the presumed intent of the grantor. Combining these and other tools may allow us to achieve our policy goals without resort to the complex and unwieldy Rule Against Perpetuities.

2.   *Avoiding Perpetuities Problems in Practice*

At the outset of our discussion of the Rule Against Perpetuities, we noted that there are ways to avoid perpetuities problems even if you have an imperfect understanding of the technical operation of the Rule. Here are five tips for avoiding perpetuities problems in practice:

1. *Know the Rule in your jurisdiction.* This is an obvious lawyering basic, but the Rule Against Perpetuities has been substantially modified in most U.S. jurisdictions. You need to know the current state of the Rule in the jurisdiction where you are practicing.

2. *Use trusts whenever future interests are being created.* This is more of a general practice point than a perpetuities-specific point. As discussed above, trusts are incredibly useful devices, and they avoid many of the problems created by legal

future interests. In some jurisdictions, use of a trust will protect future interests from the application of the Rule Against Perpetuities.

3. *Watch out for conveyances to grandchildren and age contingencies of more than 21 years.* As we saw in our examples, the potential for afterborn children can cause perpetuities problems with conveyances to grandchildren. Age contingencies of more than 21 years can also cause problems. Each can be valid in some circumstances, but be careful with them. Concerns about both are likely to be reduced in wait-and-see jurisdictions.

4. *Watch out for options and rights of first refusal.* Unless you are certain of its validity in your jurisdiction, you should not create an option or right of first refusal that can last more than 21 years.

5. *Use savings clauses.* A perpetuities savings clause is a clause in an instrument that prevents a Rule Against Perpetuities violation. These clauses can take various forms, but the most common approach is to have the clause terminate all interests created by the document at the end of the perpetuities period. Here is an example of a perpetuities savings clause from a trust:

> Notwithstanding any other provision of this instrument, any interest created by this instrument shall terminate, if it has not already terminated, 21 years after the death of the last surviving beneficiary who was alive at the time of the creation of this trust. Any remaining trust assets will be disbursed on that date in equal shares to the beneficiaries then living, and if none are then living, to the American Cancer Society.

This provision terminates all interests created by the trust, if they have not already terminated, on the last day of the perpetuities period. Because these interests have terminated within the perpetuities period, they cannot violate the Rule Against Perpetuities.

H. RELATIONS BETWEEN PRESENT AND FUTURE INTEREST HOLDERS—THE LAW OF WASTE

It is easy to see how conflicts could arise between present and future interest holders. Imagine that I hold the life estate in Blackacre and you have an indefeasible vested remainder in fee simple absolute. If I fail to maintain the house located on Blackacre, I have harmed not only my interest but yours as well. Similarly, I might harm your interest if I cut timber or extract mineral from the property.

As the present interest holder, I can generally use Blackacre as I see fit. As the future interest holder, you have no present right of possession or use, so you cannot tell me what to do with Blackacre. My ability to freely use Blackacre, however, is limited by an obligation not to harm your interest. I have an obligation to ensure that you receive the land in the same basic condition that it was in when I first took possession.

The obligation of the present interest holder to leave the land in an essentially unchanged condition is the subject of the law of waste. If a present interest holder breaches this obligation, the future interest holder may bring a claim for waste against the present interest holder. There are two basic categories of waste:

1. *Affirmative Waste.* Affirmative waste involves a voluntary act by the present interest holder that damages the property. The classic example of affirmative

waste is the intentional destruction or alteration of a building or other valuable improvement to the land. Cutting timber or mining minerals could also be considered affirmative waste, although here the law is more flexible. Under what is often called the *good husbandry doctrine,* the present interest holder may harvest timber to the extent that it is consistent with good management of the forest, but excessive timber harvesting is prohibited. Under the *open mines doctrine,* the present interest holder may continue to extract mineral resources if extraction was already being done when the present estate began. The present interest holder may not, however, begin new mineral extraction.

2. *Permissive Waste.* Permissive waste involves the failure of the present interest holder to exercise reasonable care to protect and maintain the property. It is a matter of negligence, rather than an affirmative intentional act. The classic examples of permissive waste are the failure to maintain a building and the failure to pay taxes. Failure to eject an adverse possessor may also constitute permissive waste.

There is a third, more controversial, category of waste:

3. *Ameliorative Waste.* Ameliorative waste involves a voluntary act by the present interest holder that *increases* the value of the property. Remember that the present interest holder is obligated to leave the property in a substantially unchanged condition. A valuable improvement would violate this obligation. A claim for ameliorative waste would probably be rejected in a majority of U.S. jurisdictions. A leading case rejecting a claim for ameliorative waste is *Melms v. Pabst Brewing Co.,* 79 N.W. 738 (Wis. 1899).

Litigated waste claims often arise in the context of life estates, but the theory of waste applies to other contexts where ownership is shared. For example, it applies to landlord-tenant contexts, where the tenant is obligated not to commit waste. It also applies in the mortgage context, where the borrower is obligated not to commit waste. Lease and mortgage documents, however, typically set out in detail the obligations of the party in possession to maintain the property. Disputes in these other contexts are therefore less likely to turn on the common law of waste. The instruments creating life estates often do not cover these issues, leaving their resolution to the law of waste. If an instrument does address these issues, the instrument will control. A grantor can even absolve the present interest holder from claims of waste in the document creating the interest.

Many U.S. jurisdictions allow claims for waste only by holders of vested future interests. Holders of contingent future interests can in some cases get some protection in equity against waste by the present interest holder. Generally speaking, the more speculative and remote the possibility that the contingent interest will become possessory, the less likely a court will be to step in on the future interest holder's behalf. Similarly, courts tend to give present interest holders more latitude to act when the duration of their interest is likely to be long.

The potential for conflict between present and future interest holders is yet another area where the use of a trust can avoid problems. The trustee is responsible for balancing between the interests of present and future beneficiaries. Striking this balance can be a challenge, but the problem of unilateral action (or inaction) by the present interest holder is less likely when a trust is used.

I. COMMERCIAL FUTURE INTERESTS AND THE RULE AGAINST PERPETUITIES

SYMPHONY SPACE, INC. V. PERGOLA PROPERTIES, INC.
669 N.E.2d 799 (N.Y. 1996)

> Map: 2537 Broadway at 95th Street, New York, New York

JUDITH KAYE, Chief Judge.

This case presents the novel question whether options to purchase commercial property are exempt from the prohibition against remote vesting embodied in New York's Rule against Perpetuities (N.Y. Est. Powers & Trusts §9-1.1[b]). Because an exception for commercial options finds no support in our law, we decline to exempt all commercial option agreements from the statutory Rule against Perpetuities.

Here, we agree with the trial court and Appellate Division that the option defendants seek to enforce violates the statutory prohibition against remote vesting and is therefore unenforceable.

I. FACTS

The subject of this proceeding is a two-story building situated on the Broadway block between 94th and 95th Streets on Manhattan's Upper West Side. In 1978, Broadwest Realty Corporation owned this building, which housed a theater and commercial space. Broadwest had been unable to secure a permanent tenant for the theater—approximately 58% of the total square footage of the building's floor space. Broadwest also owned two adjacent properties, Pomander Walk (a residential complex) and the Healy Building (a commercial building). Broadwest had been operating its properties at a net loss.

Plaintiff Symphony Space, Inc., a not-for-profit entity devoted to the arts, had previously rented the theater for several one-night engagements. In 1978, Symphony and Broadwest engaged in a transaction whereby Broadwest sold the entire building to Symphony for the below-market price of $10,010 and leased back the income-producing commercial property, excluding the theater, for $1 per year. Broadwest maintained liability for the existing $243,000 mortgage on the property as well as certain maintenance obligations. As a condition of the sale, Symphony, for consideration of $10, also granted Broadwest an option to repurchase the entire building. Notably, the transaction did not involve Pomander Walk or the Healy Building.

The purpose of this arrangement was to enable Symphony, as a not-for-profit corporation, to seek a property tax exemption for the entire building—which constituted a single tax parcel—predicated on its use of the theater. The sale-and-leaseback would thereby reduce Broadwest's real estate taxes by $30,000 per year, while permitting Broadwest to retain the rental income from the leased commercial space in the building, which the trial court found produced

$140,000 annually. The arrangement also furthered Broadwest's goal of selling all the properties, by allowing Broadwest to postpone any sale until property values in the area increased and until the commercial leases expired. Symphony, in turn, would have use of the theater at minimal cost, once it received a tax exemption.

Thus, on December 1, 1978, Symphony and Broadwest—both sides represented by counsel—executed a contract for sale of the property from Broadwest to Symphony for the purchase price of $10,010. The contract specified that $10 was to be paid at the closing and $10,000 was to be paid by means of a purchase-money mortgage.

The parties also signed several separate documents, each dated December 31, 1978: (1) a deed for the property from Broadwest to Symphony; (2) a lease from Symphony to Broadwest of the entire building except the theater for rent of $1 per year and for the term January 1, 1979 to May 31, 2003, unless terminated earlier; (3) a 25-year, $10,000 mortgage and mortgage note from Symphony as mortgagor to Broadwest as mortgagee, with full payment due on December 31, 2003; and (4) an option agreement by which Broadwest obtained from Symphony the exclusive right to repurchase all of the property, including the theater.

It is the option agreement that is at the heart of the present dispute. Section 3 of that agreement provides that Broadwest may exercise its option to purchase the property during any of the following "Exercise Periods":

"(a) at any time after July 1, 1979, so long as the Notice of Election specifies that the Closing is to occur during any of the calendar years 1987, 1993, 1998 and 2003;

"(b) at any time following the maturity of the indebtedness evidenced by the Note and secured by the Mortgage, whether by acceleration or otherwise;

"(c) during the ninety days immediately following any termination of the Lease by the lessor thereof other than for nonpayment of rent or any termination of the Lease by the lessee thereof;

"(d) during the ninety days immediately following the thirtieth day after Broadwest shall have sent Symphony a notice specifying a default by Symphony of any of its covenants or obligations under the Mortgage."

Section 1 states that "Broadwest may exercise its option at any time during any Exercise Period."

The following purchase prices of the property, contingent upon the closing date, are set forth in section 4: $15,000 if the closing date is on or before December 31, 1987; $20,000 if on or before December 31, 1993; $24,000 if on or before December 31, 1998; and $28,000 if on or before December 31, 2003.

Importantly, the option agreement specifies in section 5 that "Broadwest's right to exercise the option granted hereby is . . . unconditional and shall not be in any way affected or impaired by Broadwest's performance or nonperformance, actual or asserted, of any obligation to be performed under the Lease or any other agreement or instrument by or between Broadwest and Symphony," other than that Broadwest was required to pay Symphony any unpaid rent on the closing date.

Symphony ultimately obtained a tax exemption for the theater. In the summer of 1981, Broadwest sold and assigned its interest under the lease, option agreement, mortgage and mortgage note, as well as its ownership interest in the contiguous Pomander Walk and Healy Building, to defendants' nominee for $4.8 million. The nominee contemporaneously transferred its rights under these agreements to defendants Pergola Properties, Inc., Bradford N. Swett, Casandium Limited and Darenth Consultants as tenants in common.

Subsequently, defendants initiated a cooperative conversion of Pomander Walk, which was designated a landmark in 1982, and the value of the properties increased substantially. An August 1988 appraisal of the entire blockfront, including the Healy Building and the unused air and other development rights available from Pomander Walk, valued the property at $27 million assuming the enforceability of the option. By contrast, the value of the leasehold interest plus the Healy Building without the option were appraised at $5.5 million.

[In 1985, Swett and Pergola sought to terminate the lease and exercise the option to purchase. After much litigation, both the trial court and the Appellate Division held that the option was void under the rule against perpetuities.]

II. STATUTORY BACKGROUND

The Rule against Perpetuities evolved from judicial efforts during the 17th century to limit control of title to real property by the dead hand of landowners reaching into future generations. Underlying both early and modern rules restricting future dispositions of property is the principle that it is socially undesirable for property to be inalienable for an unreasonable period of time. These rules thus seek "to ensure the productive use and development of property by its current beneficial owners by simplifying ownership, facilitating exchange and freeing property from unknown or embarrassing impediments to alienability" (*Metropolitan Transp. Auth. v. Bruken Realty Corp.*, 492 N.E.2d 379, 381 (N.Y. 1986)).

In New York, the rules regarding suspension of the power of alienation and remoteness in vesting—the Rule against Perpetuities—have been statutory since 1830. Prior to 1958, the perpetuities period was two lives in being plus actual periods of minority. Widely criticized as unduly complex and restrictive, the statutory period was revised in 1958 and 1960, restoring the common-law period of lives in being plus 21 years.

Formerly, the rule against remote vesting in New York was narrower than the common-law rule, encompassing only particular interests. A further 1965 amendment enacted a broad prohibition against remote vesting. This amendment was intended to make clear that the American common-law rule of perpetuities was now fully in force in New York.

New York's current statutory Rule against Perpetuities is found in N.Y. Est. Powers & Trusts § 9-1.1. Subdivision (a) sets forth the suspension of alienation rule and deems void any estate in which the conveying instrument suspends the absolute power of alienation for longer than lives in being at the creation of the estate plus 21 years. The prohibition against remote vesting is contained in subdivision (b), which states that "[n]o estate in property shall be valid unless it must vest, if at all, not later than twenty-one years after one or more lives in being at the creation of the estate and any period of gestation involved." This Court has described subdivision (b) as "a rigid formula that invalidates any interest that may not vest within the prescribed time period" and has "capricious consequences" (*Wildenstein & Co. v. Wallis*, 595 N.E.2d 828, 831-32 (N.Y. 1992)). Indeed, these rules are predicated upon the public policy of the State and constitute non-waivable, legal prohibitions.

In addition to these statutory formulas, New York also retains the more flexible common-law rule against unreasonable restraints on alienation. Unlike the statutory Rule against Perpetuities, which is measured exclusively by the passage of time, the common-law rule evaluates the reasonableness of the restraint based on its duration, purpose and designated method for fixing the purchase price.

III. Validity of the Option Agreement

Defendants proffer three grounds for upholding the option: that the statutory prohibition against remote vesting does not apply to commercial options; that the option here cannot be exercised beyond the statutory period; and that this Court should adopt the "wait and see" approach to the Rule against Perpetuities. We consider each in turn.

A. Applicability of the Rule to Commercial Options

Under the common law, options to purchase land are subject to the rule against remote vesting. Such options are specifically enforceable and give the option holder a contingent, equitable interest in the land. This creates a disincentive for the landowner to develop the property and hinders its alienability, thereby defeating the policy objectives underlying the Rule against Perpetuities.

Typically, however, options to purchase are part of a commercial transaction. For this reason, subjecting them to the Rule against Perpetuities has been deemed "a step of doubtful wisdom" (Leach, *Perpetuities in Perspective: Ending the Rule's Reign of Terror*, 65 Harv. L. Rev. 737). As one vocal critic, Professor W. Barton Leach, has explained,

> "[t]he Rule grew up as a limitation on family dispositions; and the period of lives in being plus twenty-one years is adapted to these gift transactions. The pressures which created the Rule do not exist with reference to arms-length contractual transactions, and neither lives in being nor twenty-one years are periods which are relevant to business men and their affairs" (Leach, *Perpetuities: New Absurdity, Judicial and Statutory Correctives*, 73 Harv. L. Rev. 1318, 1321-1322).

Professor Leach, however, went on to acknowledge that, under common law, "due to an overemphasis on concepts derived from the nineteenth century, we are stuck with the application of the Rule to options to purchase," urging that "this should not be extended to other commercial transactions" (*id.*, at 1322).

It is now settled in New York that, generally, N.Y. Est. Powers & Trusts § 9-1.1(b) applies to options. While defendants offer compelling policy reasons— echoing those voiced by Professor Leach—for refusing to apply the traditional rule against remote vesting to these commercial option contracts, such statutory reformation would require legislative action similar to that undertaken by numerous other State lawmakers.

Our decision in *Metropolitan Transp. Auth. v. Bruken Realty Corp.*, 492 N.E.2d 379, *supra*, is not to the contrary. In *Bruken*, we held that § 9-1.1(b) did not apply to a preemptive right in a "commercial and governmental transaction" that lasted beyond the statutory perpetuities period. In doing so, we explained that, unlike options, preemptive rights (or rights of first refusal) only marginally affect transferability. Enforcement of the preemptive right in the context of the governmental and commercial transaction, moreover, actually encouraged the use and development of the land, outweighing any minor impediment to alienability. *Id.*

Here, the option agreement creates precisely the sort of control over future disposition of the property that we have previously associated with purchase options and that the common-law rule against remote vesting—and thus § 9-1.1(b)—seeks to prevent. As the Appellate Division explained, the option grants its holder absolute power to purchase the property at the holder's whim and at a token price set far below market value. This Sword of Damocles necessarily discourages the property owner from investing in improvements to the property. Furthermore, the option's existence significantly impedes the owner's ability to sell the property to a third party, as a practical matter rendering it inalienable.

That defendants, the holder of this option, are also the lessees of a portion of the premises does not lead to a different conclusion here.

Generally, an option to purchase land that originates in one of the lease provisions, is not exercisable after lease expiration, and is incapable of separation from the lease is valid even though the holder's interest may vest beyond the perpetuities period. Such options—known as options "appendant" or "appurtenant" to leases—encourage the possessory holder to invest in maintaining and developing the property by guaranteeing the option holder the ultimate benefit of any such investment. Options appurtenant thus further the policy objectives underlying the rule against remote vesting and are not contemplated by § 9-1.1(b).

To be sure, the option here arose within a larger transaction that included a lease. Nevertheless, not all of the property subject to the purchase option here is even occupied by defendants. The option encompasses the entire building—both the commercial space and the theater—yet defendants are leasing only the commercial space. With regard to the theater space, a disincentive exists for Symphony to improve the property, since it will eventually be claimed by the option holder at the predetermined purchase price.

Where, as here, the parties to a transaction are corporations and no measuring lives are stated in the instruments, the perpetuities period is simply 21 years. Section 1 of the parties' agreement allows the option holder to exercise the option "at any time during any Exercise Period" set forth in section three. Section 3(a), moreover, expressly provides that the option may be exercised "at any time after July 1, 1979," so long as the closing date is scheduled during 1987, 1993, 1998 or 2003.

Even factoring in the requisite notice, then, the option could potentially be exercised as late as July 2003—more than 24 years after its creation in December 1978. Defendants' contention that section 3(a) does not permit exercise of the option beyond the 21-year period is thus contradicted by the plain language of the instrument. [Each of the other time periods provided for exercising the option could also be exercised until 2003.]

C. "WAIT AND SEE" APPROACH

Defendants next urge that we adopt the "wait and see" approach to the Rule against Perpetuities: an interest is valid if it actually vests during the perpetuities period, irrespective of what might have happened. The option here would survive under the "wait and see" approach since it was exercised by 1987, well within the 21-year limitation.

This Court, however, has long refused to "wait and see" whether a perpetuities violation in fact occurs. As explained in *Matter of Fischer*, 307 N.Y. 149, 157, 120 N.E.2d 688, "[i]t is settled beyond dispute that in determining whether a will has illegally suspended the power of alienation, the courts will look to what might have happened under the terms of the will rather than to what has actually happened since the death of the testator."

IV. REMEDY

As a final matter, defendants argue that, if the option fails, the contract of sale conveying the property from Broadwest to Symphony should be rescinded due to the mutual mistake of the parties. We conclude that rescission is inappropriate and therefore do not pass upon whether Broadwest's claim for rescission was properly assigned to defendant Pergola.

A contract entered into under mutual mistake of fact is generally subject to rescission. CPLR 3005 provides that when relief against mistake is sought, it shall not be denied merely because the mistake is one of law rather than fact. Relying on this provision, defendants maintain that neither Symphony nor Broadwest realized that the option violated the Rule against Perpetuities at the time they entered into the agreement and that both parties intended the option to be enforceable.

The remedy of rescission . . . moreover, lies in equity and is a matter of discretion. Defendants' plea that the unenforceability of the option is contrary to the intent of the original parties ignores that the effect of the Rule against Perpetuities—which is a statutory prohibition, not a rule of construction—is always to defeat the intent of parties who create a remotely vesting interest.

The Rule against Perpetuities reflects the public policy of the State. Granting the relief requested by defendants would thus be contrary to public policy, since it would lead to the same result as enforcing the option and tend to compel performance of contracts violative of the Rule.

Accordingly, the order of the Appellate Division should be affirmed, with costs, and the certified question answered in the affirmative.

CONTEXT

As a result of the decision, Symphony Space acquired a property worth millions for $10,010. Today, Symphony Space remains a unique multimedia performing arts center, hosting over 600 events a year, including dance, music, theater performances, films, dramatic readings (including for the NPR show *Selected Shorts*), and other cultural events.

NOTES AND QUESTIONS

1. Options to purchase.   Options to purchase have traditionally been considered to be executory interests and subject to the rule against perpetuities. *Arundel Corp. v. Marie*, 860 A.2d 886 (Md. 2004); *Bortolotti v. Hayden*, 866 N.E.2d 882 (Mass. 2007). As in *Symphony Space*, this is true even if the right is in the original grantor of the property, because the need to *purchase* the property to reacquire indicates that the option is not simply the reversion of an already vested right in the property, but a new interest cutting off an existing estate. It is easy to see how an option to purchase for a fixed price at a period far in the future might hinder productive use of land. *See, e.g., Central Delaware County Authority v. Greyhound Corp.*, 588 A.2d 485 (Pa. 1991) (plaintiff sued to invalidate option to purchase created in 1941, which would permit the land to be purchased for the original sales price, $5,500, if it ever ceased to be used for public purposes). Is it true that allowing the option in *Symphony Space* would have hindered the productive use of the property?

2. Options to purchase and renew in leases.   Despite the general rule, most courts hold that options to purchase in commercial leases are exempt from the rule against perpetuities. William B. Stoebuck & Dale A. Whitman, *The Law of Property* § 3.18, at 123 (3d ed. 2000). As Chief Justice Ellen Peters explained in *Texaco Refining & Marketing, Inc. v. Samowitz*, 570 A.2d 170 (Conn. 1990), "[a]n option coupled with a long-term commercial lease . . . stimulates improvement of the property and thus renders it more rather than less marketable." *Id.* at 174. Similarly, many courts hold that options to renew leases during the lease term are not subject to the rule against perpetuities. *See Bleecker Street Tenants Corp. v. Bleeker Jones, LLC*, 945 N.E.2d 484 (N.Y. 2011). What if an option in a lease is exercised by a tenant who has become a month-to-month tenant after her initial term of years expires? In *Bleecker Street Tenants Corp.*, the New York Court of Appeals considered this to be still within the lease term and therefore not violative of the rule. Was this the right resolution?

3. *Uniform Statutory Rule Against Perpetuities* and commercial options.   The drafters of the USRAP intended it to supersede the common law rule against perpetuities entirely and so provided in § 9 of the act. Because the USRAP applies only to donative transfers, the USRAP's drafters suggested that states pass separate laws limiting executory interests such as options to purchase to a 30-year period, and some states have done so. Mass. Gen. Laws ch. 184A, § 5; N.C. Gen. Stat. § 41-29. *Cf.* 765 Ill. Comp. Stat. 305/4(a)(7) (40-year limit). Some states adopted the USRAP without imposing any limit on commercial options. *See, e.g., Larson Operating Co. v. Petroleum, Inc.*, 84 P.3d 626 (Kan. Ct. App. 2004) (interpreting Kan. Stat. § 59-340). Some states that adopted the USRAP refused to enact § 9 but did not pass any supplementary legislation concerning nondonative interests. In those states, such interests are probably still governed by the traditional rule against perpetuities. *See Buck v. Banks*, 668 N.E.2d 1259 (Ind. Ct. App. 1996). Some states adopted statutes that explicitly apply the rule against perpetuities as modified by the wait and see test to nondonative transfers. *See* Va. Code § 55-13.3. Even in states that have adopted both the USRAP and a limit on commercial options, moreover, the common law rule against perpetuities may bar options created before their enactment. *Compare Bauermeister v. Waste Management Co. of Nebraska*, 783 N.W.2d 594 (Neb. 2010) (statutory abolition reflected policy regarding nondonative transfers created before enactment), *with New Bar Partnership v. Martin*, 729 S.E.2d 625 (N.C. Ct. App. 2012) (right of first refusal barred by common law rule against perpetuities).

In states that have abolished the rule against perpetuities with respect to nondonative transfers, options to purchase are still regulated by the common law rule against **unreasonable restraints on alienation**. *See* Chapter 8 [Joseph William Singer, Bethany R. Berger, Nestor M. Davidson and Eduardo Moisés Peñalver, Property Law, 6th ed., (2014)], §5.4. Courts may refuse to enforce an option, especially if it is for a fixed price, if the option has no time limit and the option was not exercised within a reasonable period after its creation (unless the option is included in a lease). *Mr. Sign Sign Studios, Inc. v. Miguel*, 877 So. 2d 47 (Fla. Dist. Ct. App. 2004).

   4. Preemptive rights or rights of first refusal.   Some jurisdictions retain the traditional rule that preemptive rights, also called rights of first refusal, are subject to the rule against perpetuities. *See Selig v. State Highway Administration*, 861 A.2d 710 (Md. 2004) (noting that rule still generally applied to preemptive rights, although transportation statute exempted preemptive rights against state); *Hensley-O'Neal v. Metropolitan National Bank*, 297 S.W.3d 610 (Mo. Ct. App. 2009); *New Bar Partnership v. Martin*, 729 S.E.2d 625 (N.C. Ct. App. 2012). Preemptive rights give the holder the right to purchase the property if the owner chooses to sell, either by offering the market price for the property, or by matching the offer made by any bona fide purchaser. Some courts reason that preemptive rights may restrict alienability by deterring other bidders for the land, or leading sellers to accept below-market prices rather than litigate over fair market value. *Selig*, 861 A.2d at 718-719.

As *Symphony Space* discusses, an increasing number of courts hold that preemptive rights are wholly exempt from the rule against perpetuities. *See Bortolotti v. Hayden*, 866 N.E.2d 882 (Mass. 2007); *Old Port Cove Holdings v. Old Port Cove Condominium Association*, 986 So. 2d 1279 (Fla. 2008); *Hartnett v. Jones*, 629 P.2d 1357 (Wyo. 1981). As the Massachusetts Supreme Court argued in *Bortolli*, "[b]ecause the holder of a right of first refusal may only choose to purchase property on the same terms as a bona fide offer, if and when the owner decides to sell, there is no power either to compel an owner to sell the property at an unfavorable price, or to encumber an owner's ability to sell the property for a lengthy period of time. There is no casting of a cloud of uncertainty on the title to the property, and no potential to forestall a sale." 866 N.E.2d, at 889. When preemptive rights are held by owners associations to purchase units in common interest developments, moreover, they may increase the market value of the properties held by association members. *Cambridge Co. v. East Slope Investment Corp.*, 700 P.2d 537 (Colo. 1985). Courts adopting this approach may hold that preemptive rights must be exercised within a reasonable time in order to avoid invalidation as unreasonable restraints on alienation, *see Shiver v. Benton*, 304 S.E.2d 903 (Ga. 1983), or interpret them to be exercisable only during a particular person's lifetime, thereby validating them under the rule. *See Firebaugh v. Whitehead*, 559 S.E.2d 611 (Va. 2002).

5. The *Restatement (Third)*. The *Restatement (Third) of Property (Servitudes)* § 3.3 (2000) provides that the rule against perpetuities "does not apply to servitudes or powers to create servitudes," which it defines to include options and rights of first refusal. The reason for the exemption is explained in Comment b:

> [The] vice [of the rule against perpetuities is] that it operate[s] arbitrarily, applying a time limit totally unsuited to commercial transactions. Lives in being plus 21 years is too long for some servitude arrangements and irrational in others. For example, an option in gross should rarely, if ever be permitted to last as long as the rule would permit. As another example, the power of a property owners association to grant easements in common areas should be limited by the duration of the association, rather than by the lives of the developer's family and friends plus 21 years, or by a fixed period of 21 or 90 years.

Instead, the "purpose of the restriction must be balanced against the harm caused by the nature of the restraint, a process that is best carried out under the rules against restraints on alienation, which permit a contextualized inquiry into the utility of the arrangement." The proposed exemption of options and preemptive rights from the rule against perpetuities applies not only to commercial transactions but to family gifts as well. The Reporter's note to § 3.3 candidly admits that the *Restatement* has chosen a minority position in an attempt to influence the future course of the law. Do you agree with the *Restatement* position?

Problem

Grantor, *O*, conveys property to *A* so long as it is used for residential purposes. *A* opens a law office on the premises, and *O* sues for a declaratory judgment that title has reverted to *O*. Possibilities of reverter are, of course, viewed as "vested" and thus exempt from the rule against perpetuities. *Alby v. Banc One Financial*, 82 P.3d 675 (Wash. Ct. App. 2003) (a possibility of reverter is "immediately vested in the grantor"). *A* responds that the policies underlying the common law rule against perpetuities apply to possibilities of reverter as well as to executory interests, and that it is nonsensical to continue to exempt possibilities of reverter from the rule on the grounds that they are "vested." *A* further argues that this proposed change in the law (applying the rule against perpetuities to possibilities of reverter) should be applied retroactively, on the ground that when the rule was first developed in the *Duke of Norfolk's Case*, 22 Eng. Rep. 931 (1681), it was applied retroactively to the conveyance in that case. What arguments could you make for the plaintiff? For the defendant? What should the court do?

Consider that in *Washington State Grange v. Brandt*, 148 P.3d 1069 (Wash. Ct. App. 2006), a conveyance provided that "the land herein deeded reverts back to original plot in event it is no longer used for Grange purposes." The court interpreted "to original plot" to mean to the "current owner of the retained land at the time the condition is violated"; since this was an executory interest in a third party, the court held that it was void under the rule against perpetuities. However, this left language creating a possibility of reverter ("the land . . . reverts back . . . in the event it is no longer used for Grange purposes"). Since possibilities of reverter are not subject to the rule, the court deemed that interest valid. Does this make sense?

CHAPTER

5

Concurrent Ownership

In our last chapter, we saw how present and future interests can be used to divide ownership among multiple people over time. The conveyance of Blackacre "to A for life, then to B" creates a life estate in A and a vested remainder in fee simple absolute in B. A holds the present possessory interest, and B holds a future interest.

Our topic in this chapter is *concurrent ownership*. More than one person can own a property interest at the same time. Consider, for example, the conveyance of Blackacre "to A and B." A and B together own Blackacre in fee simple absolute. They both own a present interest and share ownership at the same time.

There are three concurrent interests in common use in the United States today: the *tenancy in common,* the *joint tenancy,* and the *tenancy by the entirety.* We will consider each of these in turn. We begin with the most basic interest, the tenancy in common, which gives us an opportunity to consider some of the issues and difficulties that can arise when multiple people own the same property at the same time. We will then move to joint tenancies, tenancies by the entirety, and marital property. Married couples, of course, commonly have concurrent ownership of property. The legal status of marriage adds a number of layers to concurrent ownership problems, and we consider those issues separately at the end of the chapter.

A. THE TENANCY IN COMMON

The tenancy in common is our default concurrent interest. As we will soon see, the joint tenancy and tenancy by the entirety both have certain requirements for creation. Joint tenancies, for example, require special language for creation. The tenancy in common does not require special language. Here are some examples of conveyances and other property transfers that create tenancies in common:

EXAMPLE 1: O grants Blackacre "to A and B." A and B own Blackacre as tenants in common. (More specifically, they own Blackacre in fee simple absolute as tenants in common. In this chapter, we will omit the nature of the present interest if it is a fee simple absolute.)

EXAMPLE 2: O grants Blackacre "to A, B, C, D, E, F, and G." A, B, C, D, E, F, and G own Blackacre as tenants in common. There is no limit to the number of people who can be tenants in common. As we will see, though, there are some complications that can arise as the number of tenants in common increases.

EXAMPLE 3: O grants Blackacre "to A for life, then to my children." A has now died. At the time of A's death, O is survived by three children: B, C, and D. B, C, and D own Blackacre as tenants in common. (Before A died, A's children had a vested remainder in an open class in fee simple absolute in common. As we saw in the last chapter, we often leave off the "in common" when we are talking about future interests. This convention is due in part to the fact that, as we will see, concurrent ownership problems arise most often among present interest holders.)

EXAMPLE 4: T dies, and in her will leaves Blackacre "to my grandchildren living at the time of my death." At the time of her death, T is survived by five grandchildren, A, B, C, D, and E. A, B, C, D, and E own Blackacre as tenants in common.

EXAMPLE 5: T, the owner of Blackacre, dies intestate. Under her state's laws of intestacy, Blackacre goes to her three children, A, B, and C. A, B, and C own Blackacre as tenants in common.

So far, in all of our examples, the tenants in common have equal shares of the property. In Example 1, the two tenants in common each have one-half interests. In Example 2, the seven tenants in common each have one-seventh interests. In Example 5, the three tenants in common each have one-third interests. Tenants in common, however, need not have equal shares. Here are two examples:

EXAMPLE 6: O grants Blackacre "to my son, A, who will take a one-half share, and my grandchildren, B and C, who each will take a one-quarter share." A, B, and C are tenants in common. A has a one-half share. B and C each have one-quarter shares.

EXAMPLE 7: T, the owner of Blackacre, dies intestate. T had three children, A, B, and C. C predeceased T. C was survived by two children, D and E. Under her state's laws of intestacy, on T's death, D and E inherit their deceased parent's share. A and B each have a one-third share. D and E split their parent C's one-third share, so each have a one-sixth share. As a result, on T's death, A, B, D, and E are tenants in common. A and B each have one-third shares, and D and E each have one-sixth shares.

Example 7 gives us an opportunity to preview one of the issues that we will consider in this chapter. Imagine that Blackacre has been in the same family for several generations. Initially, it was owned by a married couple. When the couple died, it first passed to their children. When the children died, it passed to their children, and so on. You can imagine how after just a few generations Blackacre could be owned by tens, or even hundreds, of people, with a range of different shares. Just repeat the scenario in Example 7 for three successive generations and you start to see the scope of the problem. When a parcel of property is owned by many people, each of whom owns a relatively small fraction of the whole, we call the ownership *highly fractionated*. We will look at some of the problems that can arise from highly fractionated ownership shortly.

Co-tenants each have an *undivided* share of the ownership of the whole property. This means that each co-tenant has the right to possess and use the entire property. If you and I are co-tenants, neither of us has the right to exclude the other from the property, and neither of us has the ability to prevent the other from using the property in a particular way. This is true regardless of the number of co-owners or of the proportionality of the shares. Even if you have a 1 percent interest and I have a 99 percent interest, I cannot exclude you from the property. It should be intuitive that the undivided nature of co-tenancy can lead to a host of potential problems. If you and I own a house as tenants in common, and we cannot agree on when each of us can use the house, we will be stuck at an impasse because neither of us can exclude the other. Similarly, if you want to build an office park on what had been our family's farm, I won't have the power to stop you so long as we remain in the co-tenancy relationship.

Although things easily can go wrong in a tenancy in common, the law makes it easy for co-tenants to get out of the relationship. At any time and for any reason, any tenant in common can petition a court for *partition* of the co-owned property. We consider partition in the next section. We will then consider the rights of co-tenants and the obligations that co-tenants owe to each other.

1. Partition

The partition process begins when one or more co-tenants bring an equitable action for partition in a court. Co-tenants have a right to partition, and in almost all circumstances the court will grant the request for partition. At the end of the partition process, the co-tenancy relationship will be terminated, and the property will be divided between the former co-tenants. There are two types of partition. *Partition in kind* involves a physical division of the property between the former co-tenants. *Partition by sale* involves a sale of the property at auction, with the proceeds divided among the co-tenants according to their shares. Here are two examples of each kind of partition:

REMEDIES

LAW AND
EQUITY

> EXAMPLE 8: Imagine that you and I own a ten-acre parcel of land as tenants in common. Each of us has a one-half share. The ten acres are all identical to each other, and no part of the land is more valuable than any other. If the land was partitioned in kind, the land would be physically divided, and we would each receive a five-acre parcel. If the land was partitioned by sale and sold for $100,000, then proceeds of sale would be divided between us, and each of us would receive $50,000.
>
> EXAMPLE 9: Let's take the same ten-acre parcel as in the last example, but now there are three owners, A, B, and C. A has a one-half share. B and C each have one-quarter shares. If the land was partitioned in kind, then A would receive a five-acre parcel (half of the ten acres). B and C would receive two-and-a-half-acre parcels (each one-quarter of the ten acres). If the land was partitioned by sale and sold for $100,000, then A would receive $50,000. B and C would each receive $25,000.

> You may wonder why we start with partition and then move to the rights and obligations of co-tenants. After all, partition involves the end of a co-tenancy relationship, so it would make a degree of sense to end with partition, rather than start with it. We start with partition because the availability of the partition remedy helps explain why the rights and obligations of co-tenants are structured the way they are. When we are thinking about rights and obligations of co-tenants, it is important to understand that co-tenants can get out of the co-tenancy relationship at any time by seeking partition.

ARK LAND CO. V. HARPER

Supreme Court of West Virginia, 2004 599 S.E.2d 754

DAVIS, Justice. This is an appeal by Rhonda Gail Harper, Edward Caudill, Rose M. Thompson, Edith D. Kitchen, Therman R. Caudill, John A. Caudill, Jr., Tammy Willis, and Lucille M. Miller (hereinafter collectively identified as the "Caudill heirs"), appellants/defendants below, from an order of the Circuit Court of Lincoln County. The circuit court's order authorized a partition and sale of real property jointly owned by the Caudill heirs and Ark Land Company (hereinafter referred to as "Ark Land"), appellee/plaintiff below. Here, the Caudill heirs contend that the legal precedents of this Court warrant partitioning the property in kind, not a sale. After a careful review of the briefs and record in this case, we agree with the Caudill heirs and reverse the circuit court.

I. FACTUAL AND PROCEDURAL HISTORY

This is a dispute involving approximately 75 acres of land situate in Lincoln County, West Virginia. The record indicates that "[t]he Caudill family has owned the land for nearly 100 years." The property "consists of a farmhouse, constructed around 1920, several small barns, and a garden[.]" Prior to 2001, the property was owned exclusively by the Caudill family. However, in 2001 Ark Land acquired a 67.5% undivided interest in the land by purchasing the property interests of several Caudill family members. Ark Land attempted to purchase the remaining property interests held by the Caudill heirs, but they refused to sell. Ark Land sought to purchase all of the property for the express purpose of extracting coal by surface mining.

After the Caudill heirs refused to sell their interest in the land, Ark Land filed a complaint in the Circuit Court of Lincoln County in October of 2001. Ark Land filed the complaint seeking to have the land partitioned and sold. The circuit court appointed three commissioners, pursuant to W. Va.Code § 37-4-3 (1957) (Repl. Vol. 1997), to conduct an evidentiary hearing. The commissioners subsequently filed a report on August 19, 2002, wherein they concluded that the property could not be conveniently partitioned in kind.

The Caudill heirs objected to the report filed by the commissioners. The circuit court held a *de novo* review that involved testimony from lay and expert witnesses. On October 30, 2002, the circuit court entered an order directing the partition and sale of the property.... From this ruling the Caudill heirs appealed....

III. DISCUSSION

The dispositive issue is whether the evidence supported the circuit court's conclusion that the property could not be conveniently partitioned in kind, thus warranting a partition by sale. During the proceeding before the circuit court, the Caudill heirs presented expert testimony by Gary F. Acord, a mining engineer. Mr. Acord testified that the property could be partitioned in kind. Specifically, Mr. Acord testified that lands surrounding the family home did not have coal deposits and could therefore be partitioned from the remaining lands. On the other hand, Ark Land presented expert testimony which indicated that such a partition would entail several million dollars in additional costs in order to mine for coal.

We note at the outset that "[p]artition means the division of the land held in cotenancy into the cotenants' respective fractional shares. If the land cannot be fairly divided, then the entire estate may be sold and the proceeds appropriately divided." 7 Powell on Real Property, § 50.07[1] (2004). It has been observed that, "[i]n the United States, partition was established by statute in each of the individual states. Unlike the partition in kind which existed under early common law, the forced judicial sale was an American innovation." Phyliss Craig-Taylor, *Through a Colored Looking Glass: A View of Judicial Partition, Family Land Loss, and Rule Setting*, 78 Wash. U.L.Q. 737, 752 (2000). This Court has recognized that, by virtue of W. Va.Code § 37-4-1 *et seq.*, "[t]he common law right to compel partition has been expanded by [statute] to include partition by sale." Syl. pt. 2, in part, *Consolidated Gas Supply Corp. v. Riley*, 161 W.Va. 782, 247 S.E.2d 712 (1978).[5]

Partition by sale, when it is not voluntary by all parties, can be a harsh result for the cotenant(s) who opposes the sale. This is because "'[a] particular piece of real estate cannot be replaced by any sum of money, however large; and one who wants a particular estate for a specific use, if deprived of his rights, cannot be said to receive an exact equivalent or complete indemnity by the payment of a sum of money.'" *Wight v. Ingram-Day Lumber Co.*, 195 Miss. 823, 17 So.2d 196, 198 (1944) (quoting *Lynch v. Union Inst. for Savings*, 159 Mass. 306, 34 N.E. 364, 364-365 (1893)). Consequently, "[p]artition in kind . . . is the preferred method of partition because it leaves cotenants holding the same estates as before and does not force a sale on unwilling cotenants." Powell, § 50.07[4][a]. The laws in all jurisdictions "appear to reflect this longstanding principle by providing a presumption of severance of common ownership in real property by partition in-kind[.]" Craig-Taylor, 78 Wash. U.L.Q. at 753. "Thus, partitioning sale statutes should be construed narrowly and used sparingly because they interfere with property rights." John G. Casagrande, Jr., *Acquiring Property Through Forced Partitioning Sales: Abuses and Remedies*, 27 Boston C.L. Rev. 755, 775 (1986). *See also* Syllabus, in part, *Smith v. Greene*, 76 W.Va. 276, 85 S.E. 537 (1915) ("The right to a

---

5. All jurisdictions provide for partition in kind or by sale. *See* Ala.Code § 35-6-57 (Law. Co-op. 1991); Alaska Stat. tit. 9, § 09.45.290 (Lexis 2000); Ariz.Rev.Stat. Ann. § 12-1218 (West 2003); Ark. Stat. Ann. § 18-60-420 (Lexis 2003); Cal.Civ.Proc.Code § 872.820 (West 1980); Colo.Rev.Stat. § 38-28-107 (Bradford 2002); Conn. Gen.Stat. Ann. § 52-500 (West 1991); Del.Code Ann. tit. 25, § 729 (Michie 1989); D.C.Code Ann. § 16-2901 (Lexis 2001); Fla. Stat. Ann. § 64.071 (West 1997); Ga.Code Ann. § 44-6-166.1 (Michie 1991); Haw.Rev.Stat. § 668-7 (1993); Idaho Code § 6-512 (Lexis 1998); 735 Ill. Comp. Stat. § 5/17-101 (West 2003); Ind.Code Ann § 32-17-4-12 (Lexis 2002); Iowa Code Ann. Rule 1.1201 (West 2002); Kan. Stat. Ann. § 60-1003 (1994); Ky.Rev.Stat. Ann. § 389A.030 (Lexis 1999); La. Stat. Ann. Civ.Code art. 1336 (West 2000); Me.Rev.Stat. Ann. tit. 18-A, § 3-911 (West 1998); Md. Real Prop.Code Ann. § 14-107 (Lexis 2003); Mass. Gen. Laws Ann. ch. 241, § 31 (West 1988); Mich. Comp. Laws § 600.3332 (West 2000): Minn.Stat. Ann. § 558.14 (West 2000); Miss.Code Ann. § 11-21-27 (West 1999); Mo. Ann. Stat. § 528.340 (Vernon 1953); Mont.Code Ann. § 70-29-202 (West 2003); Neb.Rev.Stat. § 25-2181 (1995); Nev.Rev.Stat. § 39.120 (2003); N.H.Rev.Stat. Ann. § 547-C:25 (Michie 1997); N.J. Stat. Ann. § 2A:56-2 (West 2000); N.M. Stat. Ann. § 42-5-7 (Michie 1978); N.Y. Real Prop. Acts. Proc. Law § 922 (West 1979); N.C. Gen.Stat. § 46-22 (Lexis 2003); N.D. Cent.Code § 32-16-12 (Michie 1996); Ohio Rev.Code Ann. § 5307.09 (Anderson 1989); Okla. Stat. Ann. tit. 12, § 1509 (West 1993); Or.Rev.Stat. § 105.245 (2003); Pa. Cons.Stat. Ann., R. Civ. Pro. Rule 1558 (West 2002); R.I. Gen. laws § 34-15-16 (Michie 1995); S.C.Code Ann. § 15-61-50 (Law. Co-op. 1977); S.D. Codified Laws Ann. § 21-45-28 (Michie 1987); Tenn.Code Ann. § 29-27-201 (Lexis 2000); Tex.Code Ann. Property § 23.001 (West 2000); Utah Code Ann. § 78-39-12 (Lexis 2002); Vt. Stat. Ann. tit. 12, § 5174 (Lexis 2002); Va.Code Ann. § 8.01-83 (Lexis 2000); Wash. Rev.Code Ann. § 7.52.080 (West 1992); Wis. Stat. Ann. § 842.11 (West 1994); Wyo. Stat. § 1-32-109 (Lexis 2003).

partition of real estate in kind, as required at the common law, cannot be denied, where demanded, unless it affirmatively appears upon the record that such partition cannot conveniently be made[.]").

In syllabus point 3 of *Consolidated Gas Supply Corp.*, this Court set out the following standard of proof that must be established to overcome the presumption of partition in kind:

> By virtue of W. Va. Code § 37-4-3, a party desiring to compel partition through sale is required to demonstrate (1) that the property cannot be conveniently partitioned in kind, (2) that the interests of one or more of the parties will be promoted by the sale, and (3) that the interests of the other parties will not be prejudiced by the sale.[6]

(Footnote added). In its lengthy order requiring partition and sale, the circuit court addressed each of the three factors in *Consolidated Gas Supply Corp.* as follows:

> (14) That upon the Court's review and consideration of the entire record, even after the [Caudill heirs'] expert witness testified, the Court has determined that it is clearly evident that the subject property's nature, character, and amount are such that it cannot be conveniently, (that is "practically or justly") partitioned, or divided by allotment among its owners. Moreover, it is just and necessary to conclude that such a proposal as has been made by the [Caudill heirs], that of allotting the manor house and the surrounding "bottom land" unto the [Caudill heirs], cannot be affected without undeniably prejudicing [Ark Land's] interests, in violation of the mandatory provisions of Code § 37-4-3; and,
>
>   (15) That while its uniform topography superficially suggests a division-in-kind, as proposed by Mr. Acord, the access road, the bottom lands and the relatively flat home site is, in fact, integral to establishing the fair market value of the subject property in its entirety, as its highest and best use as mining property, as shown by the uncontroverted testimony of [Ark Land's] experts Mr. Morgan and Mr. Terry; and,
>
>   (16) That from a review of the Commissioners' Report, it indicates that sale of the subject property will promote the interests of [Ark Land], "but may prejudice the best interest of the [Caudill heirs]." Obviously, from the legal principles and the reviewing standards set out above, the "best interests" of either party is not the standard upon which the Court must determine these issues. In that respect, it is undisputed that the remaining heirs, that are [the Caudill heirs] herein, do not wish to sell, or have the Court sell, their interests in the subject property, solely due to their sincere sentiment for it as the family's "home place." Other family members, however, did not feel the same way. Given the equally undisputed testimony of [Ark Land's] experts, it is just and reasonable for the Court to conclude that the interests of all the subject property's owners will not be financially prejudiced, but will be financially promoted, by sale of the subject property and distribution among them of the proceeds, according to their respective interests. The subject

---

6. The relevant part of W. Va.Code § 37-4-3 reads as follows:

When partition cannot be conveniently made, the entire subject may be allotted to any party or parties who will accept it, and pay therefor to the other party or parties such sum of money as his or their interest therein may entitle him or them to; *or in any case in which partition cannot be conveniently made, if the interests of one or more of those who are entitled to the subject, or its proceeds, will be promoted by a sale of the entire subject, or allotment of part and sale of the residue, and the interest of the other person or persons so entitled will not be prejudiced thereby*, the court . . . may order such sale[.]

(Emphasis added). . . .

property's value as coal mining property, its uncontroverted highest and best use, would be substantially impaired by severing the family's "home place" and allotting it to them separately. Again, the evidence is not only a preponderance, but unrebutted, that Mr. Acord's proposal would greatly diminish the value of the subject property. Accordingly, the Court does hereby conclude as a matter of law that the subject property should be sold as a whole in its entirety, and that it cannot be partitioned in kind by allotment of part and a sale of the residue.

We are troubled by the circuit court's conclusion that partition by sale was necessary because the economic value of the property would be less if partitioned in kind. We have long held that the economic value of property *may* be a factor to consider in determining whether to partition in kind or to force a sale.

> "Whether the aggregate value of the several parcels into which the whole premises must be divided will, when distributed among, and held in severalty by, the different parties, be materially less than the value of the same property if owned by one person, is a fair test by which to determine whether the interests of the parties will be promoted by a sale."

Syl. pt. 6, *Croston v. Male*, 56 W.Va. 205, 49 S.E. 136. However, our cases *do not* support the conclusion that economic value of property is the exclusive test for determining whether to partition in kind or to partition by sale. In fact, we explicitly stated in *Hale v. Thacker*, 122 W.Va. 648, 650, 12 S.E.2d 524, 526 (1940), "that many considerations, other than monetary, attach to the ownership of land, and courts should be, and always have been, slow to take away from owners of real estate their common-law right to have the same set aside to them in kind." *See also Wilkins v. Wilkins*, 175 W.Va. 787, 791, 338 S.E.2d 388, 392 (1985) (per curiam) ("Prejudice is not measured solely in monetary terms." (citing *Vincent v. Gustke*, 175 W.Va. 521, 336 S.E.2d 33 (1985); *Harris v. Crowder*, 174 W.Va. 83, 322 S.E.2d 854 (1984); and *Murredu v. Murredu*, 160 W.Va. 610, 236 S.E.2d 452 (1977)) (additional citation omitted)).

Other courts have also found that monetary consideration is not the only factor to contemplate when determining whether to partition property in kind or by sale. In the case of *Eli v. Eli*, 557 N.W.2d 405 (S.D.1997), the South Dakota Supreme Court addressed the issue of the impact of monetary considerations in deciding whether to partition property in kind or by sale. In that case over 100 acres of land were jointly owned by three members of the Eli family. The land had been owned by the Eli family for almost 100 years, and was used solely as farm land. Two of the co-owners sought to have the land partitioned and sold. A trial judge found that the land would be worth less if partitioned in kind, therefore the court ordered the land be sold at public auction. The co-owner who sought a partition in kind appealed the trial court's decision. The South Dakota Supreme Court found that the trial court erroneously relied upon the fact that the property would be worth less if partitioned in kind. In reversing the trial court's decision, the *Eli* court reasoned as follows:

> [M]onetary considerations, while admittedly significant, do not rise to the level of excluding all other appropriate considerations. . . . The sale of property "without [the owner's] consent is an extreme exercise of power warranted only in clear cases." We believe this to be especially so when the land in question has descended from generation to generation. While it is true that the Eli brothers' expert testified

that if partitioned, the separate parcels would sell for $50 to $100 less per acre, this fact alone is not dispositive. One's land possesses more than mere economic utility; it "means the full range of the benefit the parties may be expected to derive from their ownership of their respective shares." Such value must be weighed for its effect upon all parties involved, not just those advocating a sale.

557 N.W.2d at 409-410 (internal citations omitted). *See also Harris v. Harris,* 51 N.C.App. 103, 275 S.E.2d 273, 276 (1981) ("[M]any considerations, other than monetary, attach to the ownership of land."); *Schnell v. Schnell,* 346 N.W.2d 713, 721 (N.D.1984) (finding sentimental attachment to land by co-owner was sufficient to prevent forced sale by other co-owner); *Fike v. Sharer,* 280 Or. 577, 571 P.2d 1252, 1254 (1977) ("[S]entimental reasons, especially an owner's desire to preserve a home, may also be considered [in a partition suit].").

Similarly, in *Delfino v. Vealencis,* 181 Conn. 533, 436 A.2d 27 (1980), two plaintiffs owned a 20.5 acre tract of land with the defendant. The defendant used part of the property for her home and a garbage removal business. The plaintiffs filed an action to force a sale of the property so that they could use it to develop residential properties. The trial court concluded that a partition in kind could not be had without great prejudice to the parties, and that the highest and best use of the property was through development as residential property. The trial court therefore ordered that the property be sold at auction. The defendant appealed. The Connecticut Supreme Court reversed for the following reasons:

> The [trial] court's . . . observations relating to the effect of the defendant's business on the probable fair market value of the proposed residential lots . . . are not dispositive of the issue. *It is the interests of all of the tenants in common that the court must consider; and not merely the economic gain of one tenant, or a group of tenants.* The trial court failed to give due consideration to the fact . . . that the [defendant] has made her home on the property; and that she derives her livelihood from the operation of a business on this portion of the property, as her family before her has for many years. A partition by sale would force the defendant to surrender her home and, perhaps, would jeopardize her livelihood. It is under just such circumstances, which include the demonstrated practicability of a physical division of the property, that the wisdom of the law's preference for partition in kind is evident.

Delfino, 436 A.2d at 32-33 (emphasis added). *See also Leake v. Casati,* 234 Va. 646, 363 S.E.2d 924, 927 (1988) ("Even evidence that the property would be less valuable if divided [has been] held 'insufficient to deprive a co-owner of his 'sacred right' to property.'" (quoting *Sensabaugh v. Sensabaugh,* 232 Va. 250, 349 S.E.2d 141, 146 (1986))).

PERSONAL VS. FUNGIBLE PROPERTY

The court's focus on emotional ties to property brings to mind Margaret Jane Radin's arguments in her classic article *Property and Personhood,* 34 Stan. L. Rev. 957 (1982). Radin observed that people become personally attached to certain types of property. Building on this observation, Radin divided property into two categories—personal and fungible. Personal property cannot be completely replaced by market value compensation;

fungible property in contrast can be replaced by market value compensation.

Radin's classic example of the distinction used a wedding ring. To a jeweler, a wedding ring is fungible—the jeweler would be equally happy with one ring, another similar ring, or the monetary value of the ring. Once wedding rings are exchanged with a spouse, the rings take on personal meaning and cannot be fully replaced with their monetary value. Other examples include personal photographs, heirlooms, and homes. The family homestead at issue in *Ark Land* would qualify as personal in Radin's categories: the Caudill heirs were concerned about their personal connection to the property and would not be satisfied by market value compensation. Radin argued that ownership of personal property should be given more legal protection than ownership of fungible property. *Ark Land* can be seen as an example of this approach, with the court giving special protection to ownership in circumstances where the owner has a personal connection to the property.

In view of the prior decisions of this Court, as well as the decisions from other jurisdictions, we now make clear and hold that, in a partition proceeding in which a party opposes the sale of property, the economic value of the property is not the exclusive test for deciding whether to partition in kind or by sale. Evidence of longstanding ownership, coupled with sentimental or emotional interests in the property, may also be considered in deciding whether the interests of the party opposing the sale will be prejudiced by the property's sale. This latter factor should ordinarily control when it is shown that the property can be partitioned in kind, though it may entail some economic inconvenience to the party seeking a sale.

In the instant case, the Caudill heirs were not concerned with the monetary value of the property. Their exclusive interest was grounded in the longstanding family ownership of the property and their emotional desire to keep their ancestral family home within the family.[7] It is quite clear that this emotional interest would be prejudiced through a sale of the property.

The expert for the Caudill heirs testified that the ancestral family home could be partitioned from the property in such a way as to not deprive Ark Land of any coal. The circuit court summarily and erroneously dismissed this uncontradicted fact because of the increased costs that Ark Land would incur as a result of a partition in kind. In view of our holding, the additional economic burden that would be imposed on Ark Land, as a result of partitioning in kind, is not determinative under the facts of this case.

We have held that "[t]he question of what promotes or prejudices a party's interest when a partition through sale is sought must necessarily turn on the particular facts of each case." *Consolidated Gas Supply Corp.*, 161 W.Va. at 788, 247 S.E.2d at 715. The facts in this case reveal that, prior to 2001, Ark Land had no

---

7. The circuit court's order suggests that, because some family members sold their interest in the property, no real interest in maintaining the family home existed. While it may be true that the family members who sold their interest in the property did not have any emotional attachment to the family home, this fact cannot be dispositively attributed to the Caudill heirs. The interest of the Caudill heirs cannot be nullified or tossed aside, simply because other family members do not share the same sentiments for the family home.

ownership interest in the property. Conversely, for nearly 100 years the Caudill heirs and their ancestors owned the property and used it for residential purposes.[8] In 2001 Ark Land purchased ownership rights in the property from some Caudill family members. When the Caudill heirs refused to sell their ownership rights, Ark Land immediately sought to force a judicial sale of the property. In doing this, Ark Land established that its proposed use of the property, surface coal mining, gave greater value to the property. This showing is self-serving. In most instances, when a commercial entity purchases property because it believes it can make money from a specific use of the property, that property will increase in value based upon the expectations of the commercial entity. This self-created enhancement in the value of property cannot be the determinative factor in forcing a pre-existing co-owner to give up his/her rights in property. To have such a rule would permit commercial entities to always "evict" pre-existing co-owners, because a commercial entity's interest in property will invariably increase its value. *See Butte Creek Island Ranch v. Crim*, 136 Cal.App.3d 360, 368, 186 Cal.Rptr. 252 (1982) ("Plaintiff . . . sought a forced sale of the land in order to acquire defendant's interest which he did not desire to sell. This is nothing short of the private condemnation of private land for private purposes, a result which is abhorrent to the rights of defendant as a freeholder.").

We are very sensitive to the fact that Ark Land will incur greater costs in conducting its business on the property as a result of partitioning in kind. However, Ark Land voluntarily took an economical gamble that it would be able to get all of the Caudill family members to sell their interests in the property. Ark Land's gamble failed. The Caudill heirs refused to sell their interests. The fact that Ark Land miscalculated on its ability to acquire outright all interests in the property cannot form the basis for depriving the Caudill heirs of their emotional interests in maintaining their ancestral family home. The additional cost to Ark Land that will result from a partitioning in kind simply does not impose the type of injurious inconvenience that would justify stripping the Caudill heirs of the emotional interest they have in preserving their ancestral family home. *See* Syl. pt. 4, in part, *Croston v. Male*, 56 W.Va. 205, 49 S.E. 136 ("Inconvenience of partition as one of the circumstances authorizing such sale, . . . is not satisfied by anything short of a real and substantial obstacle of some kind to division in kind, such as would make it injurious to the owners[.]"). . . .

IV. CONCLUSION

In view of the foregoing, we find that the circuit court erred in determining that the property could not be partitioned in kind. We, therefore, reverse the circuit court's order requiring sale of the property. This case is remanded with directions to the circuit court to enter an order requiring the property to be partitioned in kind, consistent with the report and testimony of the Caudill heirs' mining engineer expert, Gary F. Acord.

Reversed and Remanded.

MAYNARD, Chief Justice, concurring, in part, and dissenting, in part. I concur with the new law created by the majority in this case. That is to say, I agree that evidence of longstanding ownership along with sentimental or emotional attachment to property are factors that should be considered and, in some instances,

---

8. No one lives permanently at the family home. However, the family home is used on weekends and for special family events by the Caudill heirs.

control the decision of whether to partition in kind or sale jointly-owned property which is the subject of a partition proceeding.

I dissent in this case, however, because I do not believe that evidence to support the application of those factors was presented here. In that regard, the record shows that none of the appellants have resided at the subject property for years. At most, the property has been used for weekend retreats. While this may have been the family "homeplace," a majority of the family has already sold their interests in the property to the appellee. Only a minority of the family members, the appellants, have refused to do so. I believe that the sporadic use of the property by the appellants in this case does not outweigh the economic inconvenience that the appellee will suffer as a result of this property being partitioned in kind.

I am also troubled by the majority's decision that this property should be partitioned in kind instead of being sold because I don't believe that such would have been the case were this property going to be put to some use other than coal mining. For instance, I think the majority's decision would have been different if this property was going to be used in the construction of a four-lane highway. Under those circumstances, I believe the majority would have concluded that such economic activity takes precedence over any long-term use or sentimental attachment to the property on the part of the appellants. In my opinion, coal mining is an equally important economic activity. This decision destroys the value of this land as coal mining property because the appellee would incur several million dollars in additional costs to continue its mining operations. As a result of the majority's decision in this case, many innocent coal miners will be out of work.

Accordingly, for the reasons set forth above, I respectfully concur, in part, and dissent, in part, to the decision in this case.

NOTES

1. *Presumptions vs. Actual Outcomes.* As *Ark Land* illustrates, there is a strong legal presumption in favor of partition in kind. Although this presumption is widely recognized in U.S. case law, partition by sale is more common than partition in kind. The presumption in one direction and the common outcome in the other are not inconsistent with each other. Partition by sale is more common because there are many circumstances where partition in kind is impossible or impracticable. Consider, for example, the partition of a ten-acre parcel among 50 tenants in common. Or, the partition of a house on a one-acre parcel among five tenants in common. Or, the partition of a five-acre parcel among two tenants in common, where the local zoning regulations require all residential lots to be a minimum of five acres.

2. *Potential Worries About Partition by Sale.* Partition by sale is typically accomplished by the court-ordered auction of the property, with the proceeds divided among the co-tenants according to their share of the property. There are at least two potential worries presented by partition by sale. First, if one co-tenant has more resources than the others, that co-tenant typically will be able to buy the property at auction. For example, there is little doubt that Ark Land could have outbid the Caudill heirs for the property at auction. Second, courts and commentators often assume that a partition by sale process will lead to the sale of the

property for its fair market value. Often, however, the property is sold at auction for a below-market price. Property sold at court-ordered auction typically is not widely marketed or advertized, and it often is harder to get mortgage financing to buy auctioned property than it is to buy property in a typical sale. These and other factors can combine to depress partition by sale auction prices. *See* Thomas W. Mitchell, Stephen Malpezzi & Richard K. Green, *Forced Sale Risk: Class, Race, and the "Double Discount,"* 37 Fla. St. U. L. Rev. 589 (2010).

HEIRS PROPERTY AND THE UNIFORM PARTITION OF HEIRS PROPERTY ACT

As we noted above, property that has been held in one family for generations often ends up being owned by a large number of relatives, each of whom has a relatively small interest. The eight Caudill heirs who objected to the partition by sale in *Ark Land,* for example, together owned 32.5 percent of the property, with the average share for each individual being around 4 percent. It is not unusual for family shares to be even more fractionated, especially when the land has passed by intestacy over several generations. Family property that passes by will, rather than intestacy, can also end up highly fractionated. With a will, however, the testator has to make a conscious choice about whether to divide the property further in the next generation. When property passes through intestacy, the property will typically be divided among members of the following generation or generations. For example, if a person dies intestate with four children, the person's interest in the property typically will be divided in equal shares among the four children. If this happens over several generations, the property will likely end up with highly fractionated ownership.

The term *heirs property* is often used to describe property that has been held in a family for multiple generations. The term is also often used to refer more specifically to property that has passed in African-American communities through multiple generations of intestacy. A number of scholars called attention to the problem of land loss in African-American communities that was the result of partition by sale scenarios similar to that in *Ark Land,* where an outsider bought some family members' shares and then used the partition by sale process to force the sale of the remainder of the property. *See, e.g.,* Phyliss Craig-Taylor, *Through a Colored Looking Glass: A View of Judicial Partition, Family Land Loss, and Rule Setting,* 78 Wash. U. L.Q. 737 (2000); Thomas W. Mitchell, *From Reconstruction to Deconstruction: Undermining Black Landownership, Political Independence, and Community Through Partition Sales of Tenancies in Common,* 95 N.W. U. L. Rev. 505 (2001); Faith Rivers, *Inequity in Equity: The Tragedy of Tenancy in Common for Heirs' Property Owners Facing Partition in Equity,* 17 Temp. Pol. & Civ. Rts. L. Rev. 1 (2007).

In response to the heirs property problem, the National Conference of Commissioners on Uniform State Laws approved the Uniform Partition of Heirs Property Act (UPHPA) in 2010. As of this writing, the UPHPA has been enacted in four states (Alabama, Georgia, Montana, and Nevada), and has been introduced in several others. The UPHPA takes a number of steps to make the partition process more fair and less subject to abuse.

Among the law's more notable provisions, Section 6 of the UPHPA sets up an appraisal process to protect co-tenants from being bought out at a below-market price. Section 7 then sets up a co-tenant buyout process. If a co-tenant petitions for partition by sale, the other co-tenants have the option of buying that co-tenant out at a fair price based on the appraisal required by Section 6:

> **Uniform Partition of Heirs Property Act**
> Section 7. Cotenant Buyout
> (a) If any cotenant requested partition by sale, after the determination of value under section 6 of this act, the court shall send notice to the parties that any cotenant except a cotenant that requested partition by sale may buy all the interests of the cotenants that requested partition by sale.
> (b) Not later than forty-five days after the date on which the notice is sent under subsection (a) of this section, any cotenant except a cotenant that requested partition by sale may give notice to the court that it elects to buy all the interests of the cotenants that requested partition by sale.
> (c) The purchase price for each of the interests of a cotenant that requested partition by sale is the value of the entire parcel determined under section 6 of this act, multiplied by the cotenant's fractional ownership of the entire parcel. . . .

Problem

The Schulenburg family has owned an undeveloped 12-acre parcel of land, called the Schulenburg Farm, for years. The parcel currently is owned by siblings Zach, John, and Cathy Schulenburg as tenants in common. The three have been using the property for recreation since they were children. The zoning in the area where Schulenburg Farm is located limits development of the Farm to residential use and requires a five-acre minimum lot size. That is, the only way to develop the property is by building houses, and each house must be placed on a lot that is at least five acres. John is starting a business and so wants to sell his share of the Farm. After failing to agree on a price to sell his share to his siblings, John has petitioned to partition the property and has requested partition by sale. Zach and Cathy have opposed this request and instead have asked the court to partition the property in kind. How should the court rule? Answer the question first under the common law of partition, then think about how the alternative approach suggested by the Uniform Partition of Heirs Property Act might help solve the problem. An explanatory answer can be found on page 1040.

2.   Rights and Obligations of Co-Tenants

In our next two cases, we will consider the financial obligations of co-tenants to each other. We want to highlight two types of issues at the outset. One type of issue involves co-tenant's liability to one another for the basic costs of ownership of the property. For example, if one co-tenant pays for necessary repairs or pays a tax bill, is she entitled to contribution from the other co-tenants for their share of the costs? Say that you and I are co-tenants in a beach house, with each of us having a one-half share. You spend $10,000 to pay the entire property tax bill.

Am I liable to you for my proportional share of the taxes? The other type of issue involves the liability of a co-tenant who is in sole possession of the property for rent to the other co-tenants. Again, let's say that you and I are co-tenants in a beach house. You live in the beach house year round. I live in London and never go to the beach house. Are you liable to me for my proportional share of the rental value of the beach house?

WASTE

We discussed the law of waste at the end of the previous chapter. The rules of waste apply to concurrent interests, and a co-tenant who commits waste will be liable to the other co-tenants.

We should note at the outset that co-tenants are generally free to resolve these issues by agreement. The cases and the notes that follow discuss the default rules that apply when, as is typically the case, there is no agreement between the parties.

ESTEVES V. ESTEVES

Superior Court of New Jersey, Appellate Division, 2001 775 A.2d 163

LESEMANN, J.A.D. This appeal deals with the proper division of the proceeds from the sale of a one-family house held by a tenancy in common, with plaintiffs, the parents of defendant owning one-half of the house and defendant owning the other half.

The trial court held that plaintiffs, who had occupied the house by themselves for approximately eighteen years before it was sold, and had paid all of the expenses relating to the house during that period, were entitled to reimbursement from defendant for one-half of the sums they had paid, without any offset for the value of their occupancy. The net effect of that ruling amounted to a determination that plaintiffs were permitted to occupy the premises "rent free" for approximately eighteen years, while they paid one-half of the costs attributable to the house and defendant paid the other half. The trial court found that such a result was compelled by applicable law. We disagree, and conclude that when plaintiffs sought reimbursement from defendant for one-half of the costs of occupying and maintaining the premises, plaintiffs were required to allow defendant credit for the reasonable value of their occupancy of the house. Accordingly we reverse.

The case involves an unhappy family schism, but the facts, as found by the trial court and not disputed on appeal, are uncomplicated. In December 1980, plaintiffs Manuel and Flora Esteves, together with their son Joao Esteves, bought a house. They took title as tenants in common, with Manuel and Flora owning a one-half interest and Joao owning the other one-half. The purchase price was $34,500. Manuel and Flora paid $10,000 in cash as did Joao, and the parties took a mortgage loan for the remaining $14,500. They then moved into the house, and Joao undertook a considerable amount of work involving repairs and improvements while he lived there with his parents for somewhere between three months and eighteen months after closing. Joao then moved out and for approximately the next eighteen years, until the house was sold on February 26, 1998, Manuel and Flora lived there by themselves. At no time did they rent out any portion of the house.

Sale of the house produced net proceeds of $114,453.18. With the parties unable to agree on distribution of the proceeds, they agreed to each take $10,000 and deposit the remaining $94,453.18 in escrow. They then proceeded to trial, after which the trial court made the following findings and conclusions.

The court found that Manuel and Flora had paid out $17,336 in mortgage payments, including principal and interest; $14,353 for capital expenses; $21,599 for real estate taxes; $3,971 for sewer charges; and $4,633 for homeowners insurance. Those amounts totaled $61,892, and the court found that Joao was obligated to reimburse his parents for one-half that amount. However, the court also found that Joao had supplied labor with a value of $2,000 more than any labor expended by Manuel and Flora, and thus Joao was entitled to a credit for that amount. On the critical issue of credit for the value of plaintiffs' occupancy of the house, the court said this:

> I conclude there being no ouster of the defendant by the plaintiffs that there is no entitlement to the equivalent rent or rental value of the premises where the plaintiffs lived. The defendant could have continued to live there if he wanted to; he chose not to. And the law is clear that that being the case, he's not—there being no ouster, he's not entitled to anything for the rental value or what the rental could have been to the plaintiffs.

Over the years, there have been varying statements by our courts as to the rights and obligations of tenants in common respecting payment for maintenance of the parties' property and their rights and obligations respecting occupancy thereof. *See, e.g., Baker v. Drabik,* 224 N.J.Super. 603, 541 A.2d 229 (App.-Div.1988); *Asante v. Abban,* 237 N.J.Super. 495, 568 A.2d 146 (Law Div.1989); and the most frequently cited decision, *Mastbaum v. Mastbaum,* 126 N.J. Eq. 366, 9 A.2d 51 (Ch.1939). While those decisions may not always have been consistent, in *Baird v. Moore,* 50 N.J.Super. 156, 141 A.2d 324 (App.Div.1958), this court, in a comprehensive, scholarly opinion by Judge Conford set out what we conceive to be the most appropriate, fair and practical rules to resolve such disputes. Those principles can be summarized as follows.

First, as a general proposition, on a sale of commonly owned property, an owner who has paid less than his pro-rata share of operating and maintenance expenses of the property, must account to co-owner who has contributed more than his pro-rata share, and that is true even if the former had been out of possession and the latter in possession of the property.

Second, the fact that one tenant in common occupies the property and the other does not, imposes no obligation on the former to make any contribution to the latter. All tenants in common have a right to occupy all of the property and if one chooses not to do so, that does not give him the right to impose an "occupancy" charge on the other.

Third, notwithstanding those general rules, when on a final accounting following sale, the tenant who had been in sole possession of the property demands contribution toward operating and maintenance expenses from his co-owner, fairness and equity dictate that the one seeking that contribution allow a corresponding credit for the value of his sole occupancy of the premises. To reject such a credit and nonetheless require a contribution to operating and maintenance expenses from someone who (like the defendant here) had enjoyed none of the benefits of occupancy would be patently unfair.

Finally, this court held in *Baird*, that the party seeking the credit for the other's occupancy of the property has the burden of demonstrating the "actual rental value" of the property enjoyed by the occupying co-tenant (*id.* at 172, 141 A.2d 324).[2]

We believe the principles of *Baird* are sound and should be applied here. They support the trial court's conclusions as to defendant's obligation to contribute one-half of the $61,892 expended by his parents respecting the house they all owned. However, against that obligation, the court should offset a credit for the reasonable value of the occupancy enjoyed by the parents over the approximately eighteen years while they, and not their son, occupied the property. The obligation to present evidence of that value, which would normally be represented by rental value of the property, rests on the defendant. Although no such proof was presented at the prior trial, the uncertainty of the law in this area satisfies us that it would be unreasonable to deprive the defendant of the opportunity to do so now. Accordingly, the matter is reversed and remanded to the trial court for further proceedings at which the defendant shall have an opportunity to present evidence related to the value of the plaintiffs' sole occupancy of the property. We do not retain jurisdiction.

SPILLER V. MACKERETH

Supreme Court of Alabama, 1976 334 So. 2d 859

JONES, Justice. This is an appeal from a suit based upon a complaint by John Robert Spiller seeking sale for division among tenants in common and a counterclaim by Hettie Mackereth and others seeking an accounting for Spiller's alleged "ouster" of his cotenants. By agreement of the parties, the trial Court entered a decree on the complaint ordering the sale of the property. A trial was then held . . . on the counterclaim.

At the conclusion of the trial, the Judge entered a finding that Spiller had ousted Mackereth . . . Based on these findings, the trial Judge awarded Mackereth $2,100 rental . . . Spiller appeals . . . We reverse. . . .

The pertinent facts are undisputed. In February, 1973, Spiller purchased an undivided one-half interest in a lot in downtown Tuscaloosa. Spiller's cotenants were Mackereth and the other appellees. At the time Spiller bought his interest, the lot was being rented by an automobile supply business called Auto-Rite. In May, 1973, Spiller offered to purchase Mackereth's interest in the property. Mackereth refused and made a counteroffer to purchase Spiller's interest which

[handwritten left margin: Disposition ⋆]

---

2. The court in *Baird* also said that in any final accounting between the co-tenants, equitable considerations which would weigh against a simple mathematical balancing should be considered and could have an effect. Thus, *e.g.*, in *Baird*, where the co-tenants were brother and sister and the sister had expended extraordinary efforts to maintain the property for their mother and care for their mother in the property, those efforts were to be recognized in considering what if any occupancy credit should be imposed against the daughter. We *see* no such extraordinary equitable considerations here, but in the hearing which must follow the remand of this case, either party may submit evidence thereof for consideration by the trial court.

Spiller refused. Spiller then filed the complaint seeking sale for division on July 11, 1973.

In October, 1973, Auto-Rite vacated the building which it had been renting for $350 per month and Spiller begun to use the entire building as a warehouse. On November 15, 1973, Mackereth's attorney sent a letter to Spiller demanding that he either vacate one-half of the building or pay rent. Spiller did not respond to the letter, vacate the premises, or pay rent; therefore, Mackereth brought this counterclaim to collect the rental she claimed Spiller owed her.

Since there is no real dispute concerning the essential facts in this case, we will limit our review to the trial Judge's application of the law to the facts. On the question of Spiller's liability for rent, we start with the general rule that in absence of an agreement to pay rent or an ouster of a cotenant, a cotenant in possession is not liable to his cotenants for the value of his use and occupation of the property. *Fundaburk v. Cody,* 261 Ala. 25, 72 So.2d 710, 48 A.L.R.2d 1295 (1954); *Turner v. Johnson,* 246 Ala. 114, 19 So.2d 397 (1944). Since there was no agreement to pay rent, there must be evidence which establishes an ouster before Spiller is required to pay rent to Mackereth. The difficulty in this determination lies in the definition of the word "ouster." Ouster is a conclusory word which is used loosely in cotenancy cases to describe two distinct fact situations. The two fact situations are (1) the beginning of the running of the statute of limitations for adverse possession and (2) the liability of an occupying cotenant for rent to other cotenants. Although the cases do not acknowledge a distinction between the two uses of "ouster," it is clear that the two fact situations require different elements of proof to support a conclusion of ouster.

The Alabama cases involving adverse possession require a finding that the possessing cotenant asserted complete ownership to the land to support a conclusion of ouster. The finding of assertion of ownership may be established in several ways. Some cases find an assertion of complete ownership from a composite of activities such as renting part of the land without accounting, hunting the land, cutting timber, assessing and paying taxes and generally treating the land as if it were owned in fee for the statutory period. *See Howard v. Harrell,* 275 Ala. 454, 156 So.2d 140 (1963). Other cases find the assertion of complete ownership from more overt activities such as a sale of the property under a deed purporting to convey the entire fee. *Elsheimer v. Parker Bank & Trust Co.,* 237 Ala. 24, 185 So. 385 (1938). But whatever factual elements are present, the essence of the finding of an ouster in the adverse possession cases is a claim of absolute ownership and a denial of the cotenancy relationship by the occupying cotenant.

In the Alabama cases which adjudicate the occupying cotenant's liability for rent, a claim of absolute ownership has not been an essential element. The normal fact situation which will render an occupying cotenant liable to out of possession cotenants is one in which the occupying cotenant refuses a demand of the other cotenants to be allowed into use and enjoyment of the land, regardless of a claim of absolute ownership. *Judd v. Dowdell,* 244 Ala. 230, 12 So.2d 858 (1943); *Newbold v. Smart,* 67 Ala. 326 (1880).

The instant case involves a cotenant's liability for rent. Indeed, the adverse possession rule is precluded in this case by Spiller's acknowledgment of the cotenancy relationship as evidenced by filing the bill for partition. We can affirm the trial Court if the record reveals some evidence that Mackereth actually sought to occupy the building but was prevented from moving in by Spiller. To prove ouster, Mackereth's attorney relies upon the letter of November 15, 1973, as a sufficient demand and refusal to establish Spiller's liability for rent. This letter, however, did not demand equal use and enjoyment of the premises; rather, it demanded only that Spiller either vacate half of the building or pay rent. The question of whether a demand to vacate or pay rent is sufficient to establish an occupying cotenant's liability for rent has not been addressed in Alabama; however, it has been addressed by courts in other jurisdictions. In jurisdictions which adhere to the majority and Alabama rule of nonliability for mere occupancy, several cases have held that the occupying cotenant is not liable for rent notwithstanding a demand to vacate or pay rent. *Grieder v. Marsh*, 247 S.W.2d 590 (Tex.Civ.App.1952); *Brown v. Havens*, 17 N.J.Super. 235, 85 A.2d 812 (1952).

There is a minority view which establishes liability for rents on a continued occupancy after a demand to vacate or pay rent. *Re Holt's Estate*, 14 Misc.2d 971, 177 N.Y.S.2d 192 (1958). We believe that the majority view on this question is consistent with Alabama's approach to the law of occupancy by cotenants. As one of the early Alabama cases on the subject explains:

> " . . . Each [co-tenant] has an equal right to occupy; and unless the one in actual possession denies to the other the right to enter, or agrees to pay rent, nothing can be claimed for such occupation." *Newbold v. Smart, supra.*

Thus, before an occupying cotenant can be liable for rent in Alabama, he must have denied his cotenants the right to enter. It is axiomatic that there can be no denial of the right to enter unless there is a demand or an attempt to enter. Simply requesting the occupying cotenant to vacate is not sufficient because the occupying cotenant holds title to the whole and may rightfully occupy the whole unless the other cotenants assert their possessory rights.

Besides the November 15 letter, Mackereth's only attempt to prove ouster is a showing that Spiller put locks on the building. However, there is no evidence that Spiller was attempting to do anything other than protect the merchandise he had stored in the building. Spiller testified that when Auto-Rite moved out they removed the locks from the building. Since Spiller began to store his merchandise in the building thereafter, he had to acquire new locks to secure it. There is no evidence that either Mackereth or any of the other cotenants ever requested keys to the locks or were ever prevented from entering the building because of the locks. There is no evidence that Spiller intended to exclude his cotenants by use of the locks. Again, we emphasize that as long as Spiller did not deny access to his cotenants, any activity of possession and occupancy of the building was consistent with his rights of ownership. Thus, the fact that Spiller placed locks on the building, without evidence that he intended to exclude the other cotenants, is insufficient to establish his liability to pay rent.

After reviewing all of the testimony and evidence presented at trial, we are unable to find any evidence which supports a legal conclusion of ouster. We are, therefore, compelled to reverse the trial Court's judgment awarding Mackereth $2,100 rental. . . .

NOTES

1. *Ouster.* As the court explained in *Spiller*, ouster is a conclusion. Most courts will find ouster only if (a) the co-tenant out of possession has demanded entry or

shared possession of the co-owned property, and (b) the co-tenant in possession has refused. You should be sure that you understand why Spiller did not oust Mackereth even though Spiller put locks on the building. Ouster is important because the rules on the liability of co-tenants to each other for rent and contribution for expenses turn in part on whether there has been an ouster. Ouster is also important because if one co-tenant ousts the other, it starts the adverse possession clock running against the ousted tenant. If the ousted co-tenant does not bring an action to assert her interest within the statutory period, the ousting co-tenant may obtain her interest by adverse possession.

2. *Co-Tenant in Possession Liability for Rental Value. Esteves* and *Spiller* explain the basic rules on the liability of co-tenants to each other for the rental value of the property. Absent ouster, a co-tenant in possession is not liable to other co-tenants for rent. If there has been an ouster, the co-tenant in possession is liable to the others for their shares of the fair rental value of the property. Let's return to our example where you and I own a beach house as tenants in common. You live there full time, and I live in London. Absent ouster, you are not liable to me for rent. (As explained in *Esteves*, though, I might be able to make a claim for the rental value to set off against a claim by you for maintenance costs. It would be unfair to charge me for my share of the maintenance if you have sole possession and are not paying me rent.) If you did oust me, you would be liable to me for my share of the rental value of the property.

3. *Co-Tenant in Possession Liability for Rents and Profits Collected from Third Parties.* Say that in our beach house example you rent the house to a third party for the summer. In considering whether you are liable to me for rent, we need to distinguish between two scenarios. In the first, you only purport to lease your share, and the third party would need to share the house with me if I decided to show up. In this scenario, you would not be liable to me for rent, because I still retain all my rights to share in the possession and use of the house. In the second, you purport to lease the entire property, and the third party would not expect to share the property with me. In this scenario, you would need to account to me for the rent that you collected. If you rented the beach house to a third person for the summer with the understanding that they would have sole possession, and collected $8,000, you would have to account to me (i.e., pay me) $4,000, representing my 50 percent share of the rents that you collected. To add one more layer of complication, if you had ousted me, you would have to account to me for my share of the fair rental value of the property, rather than the amount you actually collected. Let's say that you collected $8,000 in rent from a third party, but that the fair rental value was actually $20,000. Absent ouster, you would need to pay me my share of the $8,000 actually collected, or $4,000. If you had ousted me, however, you would likely need to pay me $10,000, representing my 50 percent share of the fair rental value of $20,000. This rule protects the ousted co-tenant from the possibility that the co-tenant in possession might collude with a third party to rent the property for less than it is worth. The same basic rules typically apply to other payments received by one co-tenant, such as payments for the sale of minerals, timber, and other natural resources. *See generally* W.W. Allen, *Accountability of Cotenants for Rents and Profits or Use and Occupation,* 51 A.L.R.2d 388.

4. *Co-Tenant Right to Contribution for Costs and Improvements.* One co-tenant who bears more than her share of the costs of necessary repairs to the property generally has the right to receive contribution from the other co-tenants. The same rule applies to taxes and mortgage payments—if one co-tenant pays more than

her share, she is entitled to contribution from the other co-tenants. The rule is different for valuable, but non-necessary improvements. If one co-tenant pays for a voluntary improvement to the property, that co-tenant cannot make an independent claim for contribution from her co-tenants. If the property is later sold or partitioned, however, the co-tenant can obtain some credit for the improvement. *Esteves* illustrates many of these rules in action.

5. *Rental Value as Set-Off Against Charges for Maintenance.* In note 2, we discussed the rule that co-tenants out of possession generally are not entitled to rent from a co-tenant in possession absent ouster. *Esteves* illustrates an exception to this rule. If on the sale of the co-owned property the co-tenant in possession seeks an allowance for costs she incurred in maintaining the property (note 4), then the tenant out of possession can claim rental value from the tenant in possession as a set-off against these costs. The idea here is that the co-tenant in possession had the benefit of occupying the co-owned property. It would be unfair for the co-tenant in possession to get both this benefit and to charge the other co-tenants for a share of the costs of maintenance. With this set-off, the co-tenant in posses-

sion should not be liable for the entire fair rental value. Rather, the set-off amount should be the based on the co-tenants' proportional shares of the rental value. After all, the co-tenant in possession did have the right to possess the property to begin with. For example, if the co-tenant in possession had a one-third interest, and the co-tenants out of possession had the remaining two-thirds interest, the set-off should be limited to two-thirds of the fair rental value.

6. *Default Rules vs. Agreement.* As we noted at the beginning of this section, the rules that we are discussing here are all legal default rules. The co-tenants generally can agree on their own arrangements on any of these issues. A grantor creating a co-tenancy can also set rules governing these issues in the conveyance.

7. *Co-Tenants Generally Are Not Fiduciaries.* Recall that we discussed fiduciary duties in the previous chapter when we introduced the trust. Generally speaking, co-tenants do not owe fiduciary duties to each other. Some courts have made exceptions to this general rule and have held co-tenants to be fiduciaries if the co-tenants are siblings or other closely related members of the same family.

Problem

Angela and Maya Wong are sisters. They own a warehouse as tenants in common, with each owning a one-half share. For years, the sisters were partners in a business that used the warehouse. Two years ago, they sold the business but kept ownership of the warehouse. Angela continued to occupy the warehouse. For the past two years, Angela alone made the mortgage payments and paid the cost of upkeep of the warehouse. These costs together amounted to $15,000 per year. For the first year, Angela used the warehouse for a new business that she started. For the second year, Angela vacated the warehouse and rented it to her friend Sidney Sloan for $500 per month. Sidney's understanding was that she was renting the entire warehouse and did not have to share it with Maya. The fair rental value of the warehouse during this time period was $1,000 per month. At the end of the second year, Angela and Maya sold the warehouse. They got in a dispute over the allocation of costs and rents between them, and Maya has now brought an action for an accounting. How should costs and rents be allocated between the parties? How would your answer change if Angela had ousted Maya from the warehouse? An explanatory answer can be found on page 1041.

B.   THE JOINT TENANCY

Our second type of concurrent interest is the joint tenancy. Unlike the tenancy in common, the joint tenancy has a *right of survivorship*. This means that if A and B own Blackacre as joint tenants and A dies, A's share disappears, leaving B the sole owner of Blackacre. Lawyers often speak of A's share passing or transferring to B upon A's death. This way of speaking will rarely lead to practical problems. We think, however, that it is easier to understand the legal issues that come up with joint tenancies if you use the correct terminology. When one joint tenant dies, that joint tenant's interest in the property disappears into thin air. The proportional share of the other joint tenant (or joint tenants) increases, but there is no actual transfer of an interest from one party to another.

Let's look at two examples to see the difference between a tenancy in common and a joint tenancy when one co-owner dies:

Joint tenancies are often used as a way to make a transfer at death that avoids probate. Joint tenancies are also often used as a substitute for a will by lay people. While joint tenancies may have their place in estate planning, lawyers should use them as a compliment to, rather than a substitute for, a will.

EXAMPLE 10:
A and B are co-tenants:

A ———— TIC ———— B

A dies, leaving all of her property in her will to her spouse C. After A's death, B and C are tenants in common:

EXAMPLE 11:
A and B are joint tenants:

A ———— JT ———— B

A dies, leaving all of her property in her will to her spouse C. After A's death, B alone owns Blackacre:

B

The crucial thing to understand about the last example is that C gets *nothing*. The heirs and devisees do not receive anything when a joint tenant dies. A's interest disappeared, and B owns Blackacre.

The existence of the right of survivorship is the only practical difference between a tenancy in common and a joint tenancy. That's it. Joint tenancies are treated just like tenancies in common for the issues that we examined in the prior section. Joint tenancies can be partitioned like a tenancy in common, and the rights and obligations of joint tenants are the same as those of co-tenants.

Joint tenancies present two sets of issues. The first involves their creation. There are certain requirements for the creation of a joint tenancy. If a grantor intends to create a joint tenancy and fails to meet the requirements of creation, then a tenancy in common will result. The second involves the *severance* of the joint tenancy relationship. As we will see, a joint tenant can sever, or end, the joint tenancy relationship, converting it to a tenancy in common and ending the right of survivorship.

1.   *Creation of Joint Tenancies*

Joint tenancies require clear language of conveyance for creation. There is a rule of construction in favor of tenancies in common. As a result, ambiguous language will be read to create a tenancy in common. Unfortunately, the language needed to create a joint tenancy varies from jurisdiction to jurisdiction. Here are some examples of conveyances, some of which are more likely to create joint tenancies than the others:

EXAMPLE 12: O conveys "to A and B as joint tenants." This conveyance will create a joint tenancy in most jurisdictions. A relatively small number of jurisdictions require more specificity. In these jurisdictions, one of the conveyances in the next two examples is likely to work.

EXAMPLE 13: O conveys "to A and B as joint tenants with right of survivorship." This conveyance will create a joint tenancy in most jurisdictions. Some states expressly require this language to create a joint tenancy. In some jurisdictions, the requirement of clear language of survivorship is the result of statutes that abolish the joint tenancy unless the grant creates an express right of survivorship.[1] On the other hand, in a few jurisdictions, this conveyance would be interpreted as creating a joint life estate in A and B, with a contingent remainder in the survivor.[2]

EXAMPLE 14: O conveys "to A and B as joint tenants and not as tenants in common." The intent of the grantor to create a joint tenancy is clear in this conveyance. It should create a joint tenancy in all jurisdictions other than those that require the conveyance in the previous example.

EXAMPLE 15: O conveys "to A and B jointly." This conveyance will be interpreted as creating a joint tenancy in many jurisdictions, but using it is asking for trouble. A court could easily interpret this conveyance as reflecting an intent to create a concurrent interest, but not an intent to create a right of survivorship.

The practical lesson here is that you should be completely clear on the required language in your jurisdiction before you draft a conveyance intended to create a joint tenancy. For further discussion of this issue, see Stoebuck & Whitman, *The Law of Property* § 5.3 (3d ed. 2000).

---

1. *See Hoover v. Smith*, 444 S.E.2d 546 (Va. 1994); *Zomisky v. Zamiska*, 449 A.2d 722 (Pa. 1972).
2. *See Albro v. Allen*, 454 N.W.2d 85 (Mich. 1990); *Sanderson v. Saxon*, 834 S.W.2d 676 (Ky. 1992).

Joint tenancies also require certain "unities" for the creation of a joint tenancy. The common law required four. Modern courts tend to be more lenient. The original four common-law unities are as follows:

Time. The joint tenants must acquire their interests at the same time.
EXAMPLE 16: A and B receive their interests in the property at the same time on the same day. The unity of time is met.

> The modern rule of construction in favor of tenancies in common is the opposite of the old common-law rule, which preferred joint tenancies to avoid the division of land that can result from tenancies in common.

EXAMPLE 17: A receives her interest on Monday, while B receives his interest on Tuesday. The unity of time is not met.
Title. The joint tenants must acquire title from the same instrument.
EXAMPLE 18: A and B receive their interest in the same deed (or will). The unity of title is met.
EXAMPLE 19: A receives her interest in one deed, while B receives her interest in a different deed. The unity of title is not met.
Interest. The joint tenants must have equal shares in the property.
EXAMPLE 20: A and B each receive one-half shares of the property. The unity of interest is met.
EXAMPLE 21: A receives a two-thirds share of the property, while B receives a one-third share of the property. The unity of interest is not met.
Possession. The joint tenants must have equal rights of possession and use.
EXAMPLE 22: The conveyance imposes no restrictions on the possession or use of the property by either A or B. The unity of possession is met.
EXAMPLE 23: The conveyance does not restrict A's use or possession, but allows B to use the property only six months out of the year. The unity of possession is not met.
   Here is a common scenario that creates unities problems:
A owns Blackacre. A wants to create a joint tenancy in Blackacre between herself and her daughter, B.
A grants Blackacre "to A and B as joint tenants with right of survivorship."

A may have created a tenancy in common between A and B, rather than a joint tenancy, because the unities of time and title have not been met. A already had her interest in Blackacre before the conveyance. Therefore A and B did not receive their interest in Blackacre at the same time from the same instrument. In many jurisdictions, the conveyance would not have created a joint tenancy. In those jurisdictions, how does A create a joint tenancy between herself and B?

   The answer is to use a *straw person.* A straw person is a person—for example, a paralegal in A's lawyer's office—who holds title temporarily as a convenience to another party. Here is how a straw person can be used to solve our conveyance problem:

A owns Blackacre. A wants to create a joint tenancy in Blackacre between herself and her daughter, B.
A conveys Blackacre to Straw Person.

Straw Person conveys Blackacre "to A and B as joint tenants with right of survivorship."

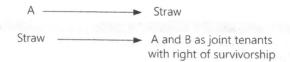

Now the conveyance meets the unities of time and title, because A and B both receive their interests in Blackacre at the same time from the same instrument. If it strikes you that this process is an artifice, you are correct. It would make more sense to allow A to create a joint tenancy with B without the use of a straw person, and some jurisdictions allow A to create a joint tenancy simply by conveying to herself and B. This approach makes sense, but many jurisdictions still require the use of a straw person to create a joint tenancy in these circumstances.

Many jurisdictions still follow the traditional common-law approach that a conveyance that does not meet the four unities creates a tenancy in common. Other jurisdictions have relaxed the unities requirements by statute or by judicial decision. The jurisdictions that allow the creation of a joint tenancy in our last scenario (A granting "to A and B as joint tenants with right of survivorship") without the use of a straw person, for example, have relaxed the requirement that the conveyance meet the unities of time and title. Jurisdictions that relax some or all of the unities requirements tend to focus their analysis on the grantor's intent and tend to find a joint tenancy if the grantor clearly intended to create a joint tenancy.

2.   Severance of Joint Tenancies

If a joint tenancy is severed, the joint tenancy relationship is terminated. Joint tenancies are easy to sever. Any joint tenant can unilaterally sever the joint tenancy by conveying her interest to a third party. Here is an example:

EXAMPLE 24:
A and B own Blackacre as joint tenants:

A ———— JT ———— B

B conveys her interest to C. This conveyance severs the joint tenancy and creates a tenancy in common between A and C:

A ———— ✗ ———— B
   TIC   │ Conveys
                    ↓
         C

The conveyance from B to C severs the joint tenancy because it destroys the unities of time and title. A and C did not receive their interests in Blackacre at the same time or from the same instrument.

If there are more than two joint tenants, the transfer by one joint tenant of her interest will sever the joint tenancy relationship between her and the other joint tenants, but the other joint tenants will still be joint tenants with each other. For example:

EXAMPLE 25:
A, B, and C own Blackacre as joint tenants:

C conveys her interest to D. This conveyance severs the joint tenancy for C's interest. A and B are tenants in common with D, but remain joint tenants with each other:

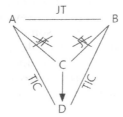

If A later dies, B and D would be tenants in common, with B owning a two-thirds share and D owning a one-third share:

$$B \xrightarrow{\text{TIC}} D$$

2/3   1/3

The severance of a joint tenancy is a big deal because it destroys the right of survivorship. Disputes about the severance of a joint tenancy tend to arise after one joint tenant dies, and the surviving joint tenant is arguing about ownership with the deceased joint tenant's heirs or devisees. As we just explained, a joint tenancy is clearly severed when one joint tenant conveys title to a third party. There are a few circumstances, however, where severance of a joint tenancy can be ambiguous.

> Interests in tenancies in common are freely transferrable during life and devisable at death. Interests in joint tenancies are freely transferrable during life. Of course, interests in joint tenancies are not devisable at death, because of the right of survivorship.

The first circumstance where severance can be ambiguous involves a unilateral conveyance between a joint tenant and herself. Here is an example:

EXAMPLE 26:
A and B own Blackacre as joint tenants:

A ———— JT ———— B

B then conveys her interest "to B." In other words, she conveys her interest to herself:

A ———— JT ———— B
                │
                ▼
                B

The issue is whether this conveyance severs the joint tenancy. Under the traditional common-law approach, this conveyance would not sever the joint tenancy. This is because the traditional common law would view a conveyance from one person to herself as not being an actual conveyance. If you think about it, you can see why a conveyance from B "to B" is something of a nullity. The traditional common-law approach is still the majority rule in the United States. Under the modern/minority rule, the unilateral conveyance from B to herself would sever the joint tenancy. The modern/minority approach is informed by the fact that B could unilaterally sever the joint tenancy even in a traditional/majority jurisdiction by using a straw person:

EXAMPLE 27:
A and B own Blackacre as joint tenants:

A ———— JT ———— B

B then conveys her interest to Straw Person. Straw Person then conveys the interest back "to B":

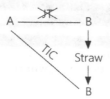

This approach will sever a joint tenancy in all jurisdictions. The modern/minority approach recognizes the fact that a transfer of an interest by a person to herself has its oddities, but takes the position that it would be silly to force a person to go through the trouble of using a straw person to sever a joint tenancy. *Riddle v. Harmon*, 162 Cal. Rptr. 530 (1980) is a case that applied the modern/

minority approach. Francis and Jack Riddle, a married couple, owned property as joint tenants. Francis and Jack were estranged, and Francis did not want Jack to get her share of the property through the right of survivorship. Shortly before her death Francis conveyed her interest to herself in an attempt to sever the joint tenancy. The court held that her unilateral conveyance to herself severed the joint tenancy, and the opinion includes a well-reasoned defense of the modern/minority approach.

The second circumstance in which a severance can be ambiguous is if one joint tenant conveys something less than a fee simple interest to a third party. One common scenario that can raise this ambiguity involves on joint tenant leasing her share to a third person. Another common scenario involves one joint tenant mortgaging her share to a third person. We will cover mortgages in depth later. For now, you need to know that a mortgage is a security interest in property that a borrower gives a lender to secure an obligation. The mortgage is the property interest that allows the lender to foreclose if the borrower defaults on the obligation. The key point for our purposes is that if one joint tenant mortgages her share, she grants a property interest to the lender.

There are majority and minority rules for both the lease scenario and the mortgage scenario. A majority of jurisdictions hold that the conveyance of a lease by one joint tenant does not sever the joint tenancy. The split on mortgages is more even. We will take a closer look at the different approaches to the mortgage issue in our next case. Before we get there, let's take a look at an example that illustrates the consequences of severance in the mortgage context. The example would work just as well in the lease context.

EXAMPLE 28:
A and B own Blackacre as joint tenants:

$$A \underline{\quad\quad JT \quad\quad} B$$

B then grants a mortgage on her interest to Lender. On the left we have an illustration of the relationships between the parties if the mortgage severs the joint tenancy. On the right we have an illustration of the relationships if the mortgage does not sever the joint tenancy.

Mortgage Severs: Mortgage Does Not Sever:

$$A \underline{\overset{\times\!\!\!\times}{\quad TIC \quad}} B \qquad\qquad A \underline{\quad JT \quad} B$$

with B's Mortgage arrow down to Lender on each side.

Now B has died, leaving all of her property to C. On the left, the mortgage survives because the joint tenancy has been severed, ending the right of survivorship. C owns what had been B's share, as a tenant in common with A. C's share is still encumbered by the mortgage. On the right, however, B's interest has vanished into thin air on B's death. The mortgage therefore also disappears.

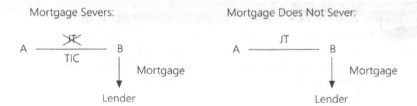

As this example shows, it is in Lender's interest for the mortgage to sever the joint tenancy if the mortgaging joint tenant (B in our example) dies. This is one context in which it is useful to have a good conceptual understanding of what happens to a joint tenant's interest at death. It disappears. The mortgage (or lease) on that interest therefore also disappears.

Let's look at another example, identical to the last one up to the stage where B grants the mortgage to Lender. In this example, A, rather than B, will die.

EXAMPLE 29:

As before, A and B owned Blackacre as joint tenants, and B granted a mortgage on her interest to Lender. On the left we have an illustration of the relationships between the parties if the mortgage severs the joint tenancy. On the right we have an illustration of the relationships if the mortgage does not sever the joint tenancy.

Now A has died, leaving all of her property to D. The illustration on the left is similar to the prior example. B owns Blackacre in a tenancy in common with D. Lender's mortgage on B's share survives. The illustration on the right is very different. B now owns Blackacre alone. D gets nothing because of the right of survivorship. Lender's mortgage survives. Rather than being only on B's half share, the mortgage is now on the entire interest in Blackacre.

In this example, the Lender benefits when the joint tenancy is not severed because the mortgage is on the whole interest, not just the portion that was initially mortgaged. Even so, no commercial lender would take the risk of having the mortgage wiped out if the mortgaging joint tenant dies. This fact pattern tends to occur when an individual is the lender, or when a commercial lender makes a mistake.

Our next case involves a mortgage of one joint tenant's share. As you will see, the outcome turns in part on the jurisdiction's approach to mortgages. Some jurisdictions follow the *title theory* of mortgages, where the granting of a mortgage is viewed as a conveyance of title to the lender. Other jurisdictions follow the *lien theory* of mortgages, where the granting of a mortgage is viewed as the granting of a lien (i.e., a security interest) to the lender. Unsurprisingly, title theory states are more likely to view the granting of a mortgage by one joint tenant as severing the joint tenancy, because the title theory views a mortgage as a conveyance of the property, rather than the granting of a mere lien in the property.

HARMS V. SPRAGUE

Supreme Court of Illinois, 1984 473 N.E.2d 930

Thomas J. MORAN, Justice. Plaintiff, William H. Harms, filed a complaint to quiet title and for declaratory judgment in the circuit court of Greene County. Plaintiff had taken title to certain real estate with his brother John R. Harms, as a joint tenant, with full right of survivorship. The plaintiff named, as a defendant, Charles D. Sprague, the executor of the estate of John Harms and the devisee of all the real and personal property of John Harms. Also named as defendants were Carl T. and Mary E. Simmons, alleged mortgagees of the property in question. Defendant Sprague filed a counterclaim against plaintiff, challenging plaintiff's claim of ownership of the entire tract of property and asking the court to recognize his (Sprague's) interest as a tenant in common, subject to a mortgage lien. At issue was the effect the granting of a mortgage by John Harms had on the joint tenancy. Also at issue was whether the mortgage survived the death of John Harms as a lien against the property.

John later died, leaving all his property to Charles Sprague. Whether Charles is entitled to John's share, and whether the mortgage survives, depends on whether the mortgage severed the joint tenancy:

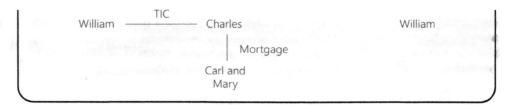

The trial court held that the mortgage given by John Harms to defendants Carl and Mary Simmons severed the joint tenancy. Further, the court found that the mortgage survived the death of John Harms as a lien against the undivided one-half interest in the property which passed to Sprague by and through the will of the deceased. The appellate court reversed, finding that the mortgage given by one joint tenant of his interest in the property does not sever the joint tenancy. Accordingly, the appellate court held that plaintiff, as the surviving joint tenant, owned the property in its entirety, unencumbered by the mortgage lien. (119 Ill.App.3d 503, 75 Ill.Dec. 155, 456 N.E.2d 976.) Defendant Sprague filed a petition for leave to appeal in this court. (87 Ill.2d R. 315.) . . . .

Two issues are raised on appeal: (1) Is a joint tenancy severed when less than all of the joint tenants mortgage their interest in the property? and (2) Does such a mortgage survive the death of the mortgagor as a lien on the property?

A review of the stipulation of facts reveals the following. Plaintiff, William Harms, and his brother John Harms, took title to real estate located in Roodhouse, on June 26, 1973, as joint tenants. The warranty deed memorializing this transaction was recorded on June 29, 1973, in the office of the Greene County recorder of deeds.

Carl and Mary Simmons owned a lot and home in Roodhouse. Charles Sprague entered into an agreement with the Simmons whereby Sprague was to purchase their property for $25,000. Sprague tendered $18,000 in cash and signed a promissory note for the balance of $7,000. Because Sprague had no security for the $7,000, he asked his friend, John Harms, to co-sign the note and give a mortgage on his interest in the joint tenancy property. Harms agreed, and on June 12, 1981, John Harms and Charles Sprague, jointly and severally, executed a promissory note for $7,000 payable to Carl and Mary Simmons. The note states that the principal sum of $7,000 was to be paid from the proceeds of the sale of John Harms' interest in the joint tenancy property, but in any event no later than six months from the date the note was signed. The note reflects that five monthly interest payments had been made, with the last payment recorded November 6, 1981. In addition, John Harms executed a mortgage, in favor of the Simmonses, on his undivided one-half interest in the joint tenancy property, to secure payment of the note. William Harms was unaware of the mortgage given by his brother.

John Harms moved from his joint tenancy property to the Simmons property which had been purchased by Charles Sprague. On December 10, 1981, John Harms died. By the terms of John Harms' will, Charles Sprague was the devisee of his entire estate. The mortgage given by John Harms to the Simmonses was recorded on December 29, 1981.

Prior to the appellate court decision in the instant case (119 Ill.App.3d 503, 75 Ill.Dec. 155, 456 N.E.2d 976) no court of this State had directly addressed the principal question we are confronted with herein—the effect of a mortgage, executed by less than all of the joint tenants, on the joint tenancy. Nevertheless, there are numerous cases which have considered the severance issue in relation to other circumstances surrounding a joint tenancy. All have necessarily focused on the four unities which are fundamental to both the creation and the perpetuation of the joint tenancy. These are the unities of interest, title, time, and possession. (*Jackson v. O'Connell* (1961), 23 Ill.2d 52, 55, 177 N.E.2d 194; *Tindall v. Yeats* (1946), 392 Ill. 502, 507, 64 N.E.2d 903.) The voluntary or involuntary destruction of any of the unities by one of the joint tenants will sever the joint tenancy. *Van Antwerp v. Horan* (1945), 390 Ill. 449, 451, 61 N.E.2d 358.

In a series of cases, this court has considered the effect that judgment liens upon the interest of one joint tenant have on the stability of the joint tenancy. In *Peoples Trust & Savings Bank v. Haas* (1927), 328 Ill. 468, 160 N.E. 85, the court found that a judgment lien secured against one joint tenant did not serve to extinguish the joint tenancy. As such, the surviving joint tenant "succeeded to the title in fee to the whole of the land by operation of law." 328 Ill. 468, 471, 160 N.E. 85. . . .

Clearly, this court adheres to the rule that a lien on a joint tenant's interest in property will not effectuate a severance of the joint tenancy, absent the conveyance by a deed following the expiration of a redemption period. (*See Johnson v. Muntz* (1936), 364 Ill. 482, 4 N.E.2d 826.) It follows, therefore, that if Illinois perceives a mortgage as merely a lien on the mortgagor's interest in property rather than a conveyance of title from mortgagor to mortgagee, the execution of a mortgage by a joint tenant, on his interest in the property, would not destroy the unity of title and sever the joint tenancy.

Early cases in Illinois, however, followed the title theory of mortgages. In 1900, this court recognized the common-law precept that a mortgage was a conveyance of a legal estate vesting title to the property in the mortgagee. (*Lightcap v. Bradley* (1900), 186 Ill. 510, 519, 58 N.E.2d 221.) Consistent with this title theory of mortgages, therefore, there are many cases which state, in *dicta*, that a joint tenancy is severed by one of the joint tenants mortgaging his interest to a stranger. (*Lawler v. Byrne* (1911), 252 Ill. 194, 196, 96 N.E. 892; *Hardin v. Wolf* (1925), 318 Ill. 48, 59, 148 N.E. 868; *Partridge v. Berliner* (1927), 325 Ill. 253, 258-59, 156 N.E. 352; *Van Antwerp v. Horan* (1945), 390 Ill. 449, 453, 61 N.E.2d 358; *Tindall v. Yeats* (1946), 392 Ill. 502, 511, 64 N.E.2d 903; *Illinois Public Aid Com. v. Stille* (1958), 14 Ill.2d 344, 353, 153 N.E.2d 59 (personal property).) Yet even the early case of *Lightcap v. Bradley,* cited above, recognized that the title held by the mortgagee was for the limited purpose of protecting his interests. The court went on to say that "the mortgagor is the owner for every other purpose and against every other person. The title of the mortgagee is anomalous, and exists only between him and the mortgagor . . . ." *Lightcap v. Bradley* (1900), 186 Ill. 510, 522-23, 58 N.E. 221.

Because our cases had early recognized the unique and narrow character of the title that passed to a mortgagee under the common-law title theory, it was not a drastic departure when this court expressly characterized the execution of a mortgage as a mere lien in *Kling v. Ghilarducci* (1954), 3 Ill.2d 455, 121 N.E.2d 752. In *Kling*, the court was confronted with the question of when a separation of title, necessary to create an easement by implication, had occurred. The court found that title to the property was not separated with the execution of a trust deed but rather only upon execution and delivery of a master's deed. The court stated:

"In some jurisdictions the execution of a mortgage is a severance, in others, the execution of a mortgage is not a severance. In Illinois the giving of a mortgage is not a separation of title, for the holder of the mortgage takes only a lien thereunder. After foreclosure of a mortgage and until delivery of the master's deed under the foreclosure sale, purchaser acquires no title to the land either legal or equitable. Title to land sold under mortgage foreclosure remains in the mortgagor or his grantee until the expiration of the redemption period and conveyance by the master's deed." 3 Ill.2d 455, 460, 121 N.E.2d 752.

Kling and later cases rejecting the title theory (*Department of Transportation v. New Century Engineering & Development Corp.* (1983), 97 Ill.2d 343, 73 Ill.Dec. 538, 454 N.E.2d 635; *Kerrigan v. Unity Savings Association* (1974), 58 Ill.2d 20, 317 N.E.2d 39; *Mutual Life Insurance Co. of New York v. Chambers* (1980), 88 Ill.App.3d 952, 43 Ill.Dec. 829, 410 N.E.2d 962; *Commercial Mortgage & Finance Co. v. Woodcock Construction Co.* (1964), 51 Ill.App.2d 61, 200 N.E.2d 923) do not involve the severance of joint tenancies. As such, they have not expressly disavowed the *dicta* of joint tenancy cases which have stated that the act of mortgaging by one joint tenant results in the severance of the joint tenancy. We find, however, that implicit in *Kling* and our more recent cases which follow the lien theory of mortgages is the conclusion that a joint tenancy is not severed when one joint tenant executes a mortgage on his interest in the property, since the unity of title has been preserved. As the appellate court in the instant case correctly observed: "If giving a mortgage creates only a lien, then a mortgage should have the same effect on a joint tenancy as a lien created in other ways." (119 Ill.App.3d 503, 507, 75 Ill.Dec. 155, 456 N.E.2d 976.) Other jurisdictions following the lien theory of mortgages have reached the same result. *People v. Nogarr* (1958), 164 Cal.App.2d 591, 330 P.2d 858; *D.A.D., Inc. v. Moring* (Fla.App.1969), 218 So.2d 451; *American National Bank & Trust Co. v. McGinnis* (Okla.1977), 571 P.2d 1198; *Brant v. Hargrove* (Ariz.Ct.App.1981), 129 Ariz. 475, 632 P.2d 978.

A joint tenancy has been defined as "a present estate in all the joint tenants, each being seized of the whole . . . . " (*Partridge v. Berliner* (1927), 325 Ill. 253, 257, 156 N.E. 352.) An inherent feature of the estate of joint tenancy is the right of survivorship, which is the right of the last survivor to take the whole of the estate. (*In re Estate of Alpert* (1983), 95 Ill.2d 377, 381, 69 Ill.Dec. 361, 447 N.E.2d 796; *Bonczkowski v. Kucharski* (1958), 13 Ill.2d 443, 451, 150 N.E.2d 443.) Because we find that a mortgage given by one joint tenant of his interest in the property does not sever the joint tenancy, we hold that the plaintiff's right of survivorship became operative upon the death of his brother. As such plaintiff is now the sole owner of the estate, in its entirety.

Further, we find that the mortgage executed by John Harms does not survive as a lien on plaintiff's property. A surviving joint tenant succeeds to the share of the deceased joint tenant by virtue of the conveyance which created the joint tenancy, not as the successor of the deceased. (*In re Estate of Alpert* (1983), 95 Ill.2d 377, 381, 69 Ill.Dec. 361, 447 N.E.2d 796.) The property right of the mortgaging joint tenant is extinguished at the moment of his death. While John Harms was alive, the mortgage existed as a lien on his interest in the joint tenancy. Upon his death, his interest ceased to exist and along with it the lien of the mortgage. (*Merchants National Bank v. Olson* (1975), 27 Ill.App.3d 432, 434, 325 N.E.2d 633.) . . . .

For the reasons stated herein, the judgment of the appellate court is affirmed.

NOTE

More on Title Theory and Lien Theory. As explained in *Harms*, the mortgage by one joint tenant of her share of the property will sever the joint tenancy in a title theory state. The law in lien theory states is less uniform. Some lien theory jurisdictions follow the approach used in *Harms* and hold that the mortgage does not sever the joint tenancy. Other lien theory jurisdictions, typically motivated by the desire to protect the creditor's interest in the property, hold that the mortgage does sever the joint tenancy. Note well that these rules focus only on the effect of the joint tenant's grant of the mortgage to a third party. An actual sale of the joint tenant's interest in a foreclosure sale would be a conveyance of the property and would sever the joint tenancy in all jurisdictions.

Problem

Toby Sinclair had three children, Cathy, John, and Louise. When he died, he left his vacation beach house to his three children "to hold as joint tenants with right of survivorship." In 1985, Louise sold her interest in the beach house to her cousin Ralph. A few years later, Cathy mortgaged her share of the beach house to her acquaintance, Bill.

Cathy died last April, leaving her property to her second husband, Jeremy. Bill just got a letter from Ralph and John stating that his mortgage on the Widener beach property was no longer valid. Ralph and John, in turn, are in a bit of a dispute. They agree that they want to partition the property, but John doesn't want the property to be sold in the partition process. Ralph and John also disagree on the respective shares they should get: Ralph claims he is entitled to one-half, while John claims that Ralph is entitled to one-third. Now Jeremy has shown up and said that he should get one-third of the property.

Explain the current state of ownership of the beach house. An explanatory answer can be found on page 1042.

C.   THE TENANCY BY THE ENTIRETY AND MARITAL PROPERTY

In this section, we examine the tenancy by the entirety and marital property. The tenancy by the entirety is our third type of co-ownership. We place it in the section on marital property because a tenancy by the entirety can only be created between married couples.

1.   *Tenancy by the entirety*

The tenancy by the entirety is a concurrent interest between spouses that in most respects resembles a joint tenancy. It typically will require the same unities as a joint tenancy, plus the additional requirement that the couple be married when they receive the interest. This interest is best created with a conveyance "to

Spouse 1 and Spouse 2 as tenants by the entirety." There is a presumption in favor of a tenancy by the entirety, however, so a conveyance to a married couple that meets the unities requirement is likely to create a tenancy by the entirety even if the words "as tenants by the entirety" are omitted from the conveyance.

For a tenancy by the entirety to be created, the couple must be married at the time of conveyance. Problems will arise if a conveyance to an engaged, but not married, couple purports to convey a tenancy by the entirety. For example, O conveys "to A and B as tenants by the entirety," where A and B are not married. This conveyance will not create a tenancy by the entirety, because A and B are not married. In some jurisdictions, this conveyance will create a tenancy in common. In others, it will create a joint tenancy.

Like a joint tenancy, the tenancy by the entirety has a right of survivorship. Unlike a joint tenancy, the spouses cannot unilaterally convey their interests. An attempted conveyance by one spouse alone of a tenancy by the entirety interest will be ineffective. Consider this example:

EXAMPLE 30:
Spouse 1 and Spouse 2 are tenants by the entirety. Spouse 2 unilaterally conveys her interest to A:

$$\text{Spouse 1} \overset{\text{TBE}}{\rule{3cm}{0.4pt}} \text{Spouse 2}$$

Purports to convey

A

The purported conveyance from Spouse 2 to A will be ineffective. Spouse 1 and Spouse 2 still own the property as tenants by the entirety.

$$\text{Spouse 1} \overset{\text{TBE}}{\rule{3cm}{0.4pt}} \text{Spouse 2}$$

A tenancy by the entirety therefore cannot be severed unilaterally by one tenant in the way that a joint tenancy can be unilaterally severed. There are three basic ways that a tenancy by the entirety can end. First, the spouses may together transfer the property to another person. Second, one spouse may die, with the right of survivorship operating to give sole ownership to the surviving spouse. Third, the spouses may obtain a decree of divorce, which will sever the tenancy by the entirety by ending the marriage.

Fewer than half of U.S. jurisdictions recognize the tenancy by the entirety. In those jurisdictions that do recognize the interest, however, it can be very important. Recall that spouses may not unilaterally convey their interest in a tenancy by the entirety. One consequence of the spouses' inability to unilaterally convey is that the creditor of one spouse may not be able to reach property held by the entirety to satisfy the spouse's debt. Our next case provides a good illustration of why this can be a very big deal. It also provides a good explanation of the different approaches taken by U.S. jurisdictions to the ability of a creditor to reach property held by the entirety.

SAWADA V. ENDO

Supreme Court of Hawaii, 1977 561 P.2d 1291

MENOR, Justice.

This is a civil action brought by the plaintiffs-appellants, Masako Sawada and Helen Sawada, in aid of execution of money judgments in their favor, seeking to set aside a conveyance of real property from judgment debtor Kokichi Endo to Samuel H. Endo and Toru Endo, defendants-appellees herein, on the ground that the conveyance as to the Sawadas was fraudulent.

On November 30, 1968, the Sawadas were injured when struck by a motor vehicle operated by Kokichi Endo. On June 17, 1969, Helen Sawada filed her complaint for damages against Kokichi Endo. Masako Sawada filed her suit against him on August 13, 1969. The complaint and summons in each case was served on Kokichi Endo on October 29, 1969.

On the date of the accident, Kokichi Endo was the owner, as a tenant by the entirety with his wife, Ume Endo, of a parcel of real property situate at Wahiawa, Oahu, Hawaii. By deed, dated July 26, 1969, Kokichi Endo and his wife conveyed the property to their sons, Samuel H. Endo and Toru Endo. This document was recorded in the Bureau of Conveyances on December 17, 1969. No consideration was paid by the grantees for the conveyance. Both were aware at the time of the conveyance that their father had been involved in an accident, and that he carried no liability insurance. Kokichi Endo and Ume Endo, while reserving no life interests therein, continued to reside on the premises.

On January 19, 1971, after a consolidated trial on the merits, judgment was entered in favor of Helen Sawada and against Kokichi Endo in the sum of $8,846.46. At the same time, Masako Sawada was awarded judgment on her complaint in the amount of $16,199.28. Ume Endo, wife of Kokichi Endo, died on January 29, 1971. She was survived by her husband, Kokichi. Subsequently, after being frustrated in their attempts to obtain satisfaction of judgment from the personal property of Kokichi Endo, the Sawadas brought suit to set aside the conveyance which is the subject matter of this controversy. The trial court refused to set aside the conveyance, and the Sawadas appeal.

I

The determinative question in this case is, whether the interest of one spouse in real property, held in tenancy by the entireties, is subject to levy and execution by his or her individual creditors. This issue is one of first impression in this jurisdiction.

A brief review of the present state of the tenancy by the entirety might be helpful. Dean Phipps, writing in 1951,[1] pointed out that only nineteen states and the

---

1. Phipps, "Tenancy by Entireties," 25 Temple L.Q. 24 (1951).

District of Columbia continued to recognize it as a valid and subsisting institution in the field of property law. Phipps divided these jurisdictions into four groups. He made no mention of Alaska and Hawaii, both of which were then territories of the United States.

MARRIED WOMEN'S PROPERTY ACTS

At traditional common law, married women had very little right to own property independent of their husband. The Married Women's Property Acts were laws passed in the 1800s that gave married women more rights to their property than they had at common law. The Acts gave married women, like single women, direct control over their property. We discuss the Married Women's Property Acts further below.

In the Group I states (Massachusetts, Michigan, and North Carolina) the estate is essentially the common law tenancy by the entireties, unaffected by the Married Women's Property Acts. [Since *Sawada* was decided, all three of these states altered their rules for tenancy by the entirety by statute. As a result, no U.S. jurisdiction currently follows the Group I approach.—Ed.] As at common law, the possession and profits of the estate are subject to the husband's exclusive dominion and control. *Pineo v. White*, 320 Mass. 487, 70 N.E.2d 294 (1946); *Speier v. Opfer*, 73 Mich. 35, 40 N.W. 909 (1888); *Johnson v. Leavitt*, 188 N.C. 682, 125 S.E. 490 (1924). In all three states, as at common law, the husband may convey the entire estate subject only to the possibility that the wife may become entitled to the whole estate upon surviving him. *Phelps v. Simons*, 159 Mass. 415, 34 N.E. 657 (1893); *Arrand v. Graham*, 297 Mich. 559, 298 N.W. 281 (1911); *Hood v. Mercer*, 150 N.C. 699, 64 S.E. 897 (1909). As at common law, the obverse as to the wife does not hold true. Only in Massachusetts, however, is the estate in its entirety subject to levy by the husband's creditors. *Splaine v. Morrissey*, 282 Mass. 217, 184 N.E. 670 (1933). In both Michigan and North Carolina, the use and income from the estate is not subject to levy during the marriage for the separate debts of either spouse. *Dickey v. Converse*, 117 Mich. 449, 76 N.W. 80 (1898); *Nood v. Mercer, supra.*

In the Group II states (Alaska, Arkansas, New Jersey, New York, and Oregon) the interest of the debtor spouse in the estate may be sold or levied upon for his or her separate debts, subject to the other spouse's contingent right of survivorship. *Pope v. McBride*, 207 Ark. 940, 184 S.W.2d 259 (1945); *King v. Greene*, 30 N.J. 395, 153 A.2d 49 (1959); *Hiles v. Fisher*, 144 N.Y. 306, 39 N.E. 337 (1895); *Brownley v. Lincoln County*, 218 Or. 7, 343 P.2d 529 (1959). Alaska, which has been added to this group, has provided by statute that the interest of a debtor spouse in any type of estate, except a homestead as defined and held in tenancy by the entirety, shall be subject to his or her separate debts. *Pilip v. United States*, 186 F.Supp. 397 (D.Alaska, 1960).

In the Group III jurisdictions (Delaware, District of Columbia, Florida, Indiana, Maryland, Missouri, Pennsylvania, Rhode Island, Vermont, Virginia, and Wyoming) an attempted conveyance by either spouse is wholly void, and the estate may not be subjected to the separate debts of one spouse only. *Citizens*

Savings Bank Inc. v. Astrin, 5 Terry 451, 44 Del. 451, 61 A.2d 419 (1948); *Golden v. Glens Falls Indemnity Co.*, 102 U.S.App.D.C. 106, 250 F.2d 769 (1957); *Hunt v. Covington*, 145 Fla. 706, 200 So. 76 (1941); *Sharp v. Baker*, 51 Ind.App. 547, 96 N.E. 627 (1911); *McCubbin v. Stanford*, 85 Md. 378, 37 A. 214 (1897); *Otto F. Stifel's Union Brewing Co. v. Saxy*, 273 Mo. 159, 201 S.W. 67 (1918); *O'Malley v. O'Malley*, 272 Pa. 528, 116 A. 500 (1922); *Bloomfield v. Brown*, 67 R.I. 452, 25 A.2d 354 (1942); *Citizens' Savings Bank & Trust Co. v. Jenkins*, 91 Vt. 13, 99 A. 250 (1916); *Vasilion v. Vasilion*, 192 Va. 735, 66 S.E.2d 599 (1951); *Ward Terry and Company v. Hensen*, 75 Wyo. 444, 297 P.2d 213 (1956).

In Group IV, the two states of Kentucky and Tennessee hold that the contingent right of survivorship appertaining to either spouse is separately alienable by him and attachable by his creditors during the marriage. *Hoffmann v. Newell*, 249 Ky. 270, 60 S.W.2d 607 (1933); *Covington v. Murray*, 220 Tenn. 265, 416 S.W.2d 761 (1967). The use and profits, however, may neither be alienated nor attached during coverture.

It appears, therefore, that Hawaii is the only jurisdiction still to be heard from on the question. Today we join that group of states and the District of Columbia which hold that under the Married Women's Property Acts the interest of a husband or a wife in an estate by the entireties is not subject to the claims of his or her individual creditors during the joint lives of the spouses. In so doing, we are placing our stamp of approval upon what is apparently the prevailing view of the lower courts of this jurisdiction.

Hawaii has long recognized and continues to recognize the tenancy in common, the joint tenancy, and the tenancy by the entirety, as separate and distinct estates. *See Paahana v. Bila*, 3 Haw. 725 (1876). That the Married Women's Property Act of 1888 was not intended to abolish the tenancy by the entirety was made clear by the language of Act 19 of the Session Laws of Hawaii, 1903 (now HRS § 509-1). *See also* HRS § 509-2. The tenancy by the entirety is predicated upon the legal unity of husband and wife, and the estate is held by them in single ownership. They do not take by moieties, but both and each are seized of the whole estate. *Lang v. Commissioner of Internal Revenue*, 289 U.S. 109, 53 S.Ct. 534, 77 L.Ed. 1066 (1933).

MOIETY VS. ENTIRETY

The word "moiety" means a share or a part. At common law, joint tenants were seized (i.e., owned their interests) *per my et per tout*. This typically is translated as by the moiety (or share) and by the whole. Tenants by the entirety, in contrast, were seized *per tout et non per my*, or by the entirety (or whole) and not by the moiety (or share). We think it is best to avoid this antiquated terminology, but you will see it from time to time in cases.

Neither husband nor wife has a separate divisible interest in the property held by the entirety that can be conveyed or reached by execution. *Fairclaw v. Forrest*, 76 U.S.App.D.C. 197, 130 F.2d 829 (1942). A joint tenancy may be destroyed by voluntary alienation, or by levy and execution, or by compulsory partition, but a tenancy by the entirety may not. The indivisibility of the estate, except by joint action of the spouses, is an indispensable feature of the tenancy by the entirety. *Ashbaugh v. Ashbaugh*, 273 Mo. 353, 201 S.W. 72 (1918). *Newman v. Equitable Life Assur. Soc.*, 119 Fla. 641, 160 So. 745 (1935); *Lang v. Commissioner of Internal Revenue, supra.* . . .

In *Hurd v. Hughes, supra*, the Delaware court, recognizing the peculiar nature of an estate by the entirety, in that the husband and wife are the owners, not merely of equal interests but of the whole estate, stated:

> "The estate (by the entireties) can be acquired or held only by a man and woman while married. Each spouse owns the whole while both live; neither can sell any interest except with the other's consent, and by their joint act; and at the death of either the other continues to own the whole, and does not acquire any new interest from the other. There can be no partition between them. From this is deduced the indivisibility and unseverability of the estate into two interests, and hence that the creditors of either spouse cannot during their joint lives reach by execution any interest which the debtor had in land so held. . . . One may have doubts as to whether the holding of land by entireties is advisable or in harmony with the spirit of the legislation in favor of married women; but when such an estate is created due effect must be given to its peculiar characteristics." 12 Del.Ch. at 190, 109 A. at 419. . . .

We are not persuaded by the argument that it would be unfair to the creditors of either spouse to hold that the estate by the entirety may not, without the consent of both spouses, be levied upon for the separate debts of either spouse. No unfairness to the creditor in involved here. We agree with the court in *Hurd v. Hughes, supra*:

> "But creditors are not entitled to special consideration. If the debt arose prior to the creation of the estate, the property was not a basis of credit, and if the debt arose subsequently the creditor presumably had notice of the characteristics of the estate which limited his right to reach the property." 12 Del.Ch. at 193, 109 A. at 420.

We might also add that there is obviously nothing to prevent the creditor from insisting upon the subjection of property held in tenancy by the entirety as a condition precedent to the extension of credit. Further, the creation of a tenancy by the entirety may not be used as a device to defraud existing creditors. *In re Estate of Wall*, 142 U.S.App.D.C. 187, 440 F.2d 215 (1971).

Were we to view the matter strictly from the standpoint of public policy, we would still be constrained to hold as we have done here today. In *Fairclaw v. Forrest, supra*, the court makes this observation:

> "The interest in family solidarity retains some influence upon the institution (of tenancy by the entirety). It is available only to husband and wife. It is a convenient mode of protecting a surviving spouse from inconvenient administration of the decedent's estate and from the other's improvident debts. It is in that protection the estate finds its peculiar and justifiable function." 130 F.2d at 833.

It is a matter of common knowledge that the demand for single-family residential lots has increased rapidly in recent years, and the magnitude of the problem is emphasized by the concentration of the bulk of fee simple land in the hands of a few. The shortage of single-family residential fee simple property is critical and government has seen fit to attempt to alleviate the problem through legislation. When a family can afford to own real property, it becomes their single most important asset. Encumbered as it usually is by a first mortgage, the fact remains that so long as it remains whole during the joint lives of the spouses, it is always available in its entirety for the benefit and use of the entire family. Loans for education and other emergency expenses, for example, may be obtained on the security of the marital estate. This would not be possible where a third party has become a tenant in common or a joint tenant with one of the spouses, or where the ownership of the contingent right of survivorship of one of the spouses in a third party has cast a cloud upon the title of the marital estate, making it virtually impossible to utilize the estate for these purposes.

If we were to select between a public policy favoring the creditors of one of the spouses and one favoring the interests of the family unit, we would not hesitate to choose the latter. But we need not make this choice for, as we pointed out earlier, by the very nature of the estate by the entirety as we view it, and as other courts of our sister jurisdictions have viewed it, "(a) unilaterally indestructible right of survivorship, an inability of one spouse to alienate his interest, and, importantly for this case, a broad immunity from claims of separate creditors remain among its vital incidents." *In re Estate of Wall, supra*, 440 F.2d at 218.

Having determined that an estate by the entirety is not subject to the claims of the creditors of one of the spouses during their joint lives, we now hold that the conveyance of the marital property by Kokichi Endo and Ume Endo, husband and wife, to their sons, Samuel H. Endo and Toru Endo, was not in fraud of Kokichi Endo's judgment creditors. *Cf. Jordan v. Reynolds, supra.*

Affirmed. [The dissenting opinion of Justice Kidwell is omitted.].

Disposití?

NOTES

1. *The Three Groups.* The *Sawada* court referenced four groups of jurisdictional approaches to the question of whether the creditor of one spouse can access property held by the entirety to satisfy the debt. The groups were established by Dean Phipps in 1951. As we noted in the text of the case, Group I no longer exists, because the three states that followed this approach have since changed their law by statute. This leaves us with three groups. For consistency's sake, we continue to refer to these as Group II, Group III, and Group IV.

When this issue arises, we typically have three people involved—two spouses and the Creditor. We will call the spouse who owes the debt to the Creditor the Debtor Spouse. We will call the other spouse the Innocent Spouse.

In Group II, the Creditor can access the Debtor Spouse's share of the property to satisfy the debt. This means that the Creditor and the Innocent Spouse are now in an odd co-ownership relationship that looks a little bit like a tenancy in common and a little bit like a joint tenancy. The Creditor and the Innocent Spouse have shared ownership of the property. Think back to all the issues that we discussed in the context of the tenancy in common, and consider how strange it would be to be in a co-ownership relationship with a creditor. As a practical matter, these problems might lead the parties to some kind of financial settlement to satisfy the Creditor. If no settlement is reached, however, the problems remain. The right of survivorship is still in place. If the Debtor Spouse dies first, then the Innocent Spouse will have ownership free and clear of the Creditor's interest (because the Creditor has stepped into the Debtor Spouse's shoes). If the Innocent Spouse dies first, then the Creditor will have complete ownership.

In Group III, the Creditor cannot access any part of the property held by the entirety to satisfy the debt. Period. As a result, tenancy by the entirety is a *very big deal* in Group III jurisdictions. The facts of *Sawada* illustrate why.

In Group IV, the Creditor can access the Debtor Spouse's right of survivorship, but cannot gain access to the property during the spouses' lives. This avoids the complications of having the Creditor and the Innocent Spouse sharing ownership during life that is present in Group II. The outcomes with the right of survivorship are the same as they are in Group II. If the Debtor Spouse dies first, the Innocent Spouse owns the property free and clear of the debt. If the Innocent Spouse dies first, then the Creditor owns the property.

2. *Contract Creditors vs. Tort Creditors.* The *Sawada* court made a serious reasoning error in its opinion when it failed to distinguish between two types of creditors. A *contract creditor* is a creditor who is owed a debt that arises from a consensual transaction. An example would be a bank that voluntarily lends money to the debtor. A *tort creditor* is a creditor who is owed a debt because the creditor was the victim of a tort. The Sawadas were tort creditors—they were owed a debt that arose because Kokichi Endo hit them with his car. In deciding to follow the Group III approach, the *Sawada* court claimed that "[n]o unfairness to the creditor" would result because "there is obviously nothing to prevent the creditor from insisting upon the subjection of property held in tenancy by the entirety as a condition precedent to the extension of credit." That clearly is true with a contract creditor, who can refuse to lend money unless both spouses agree that the property held by the entirety is subject to the debt. Mortgage lenders in Group III states, for example, make sure that both spouses execute the mortgage and related documents so that they can reach the property held by the entirety if the borrowers default on the loan. Tort creditors like the Sawadas, however, do not become creditors voluntarily and do not have the opportunity to bargain with the debtor before the tort is committed. The Sawadas could not have stopped Endo from hitting them with his car unless he and his wife agreed to give them access to the property held by the entirety to satisfy the debt. We are not suggesting here that the *Sawada* court reached the wrong result. Reasonable minds can disagree on the right rule, and the court articulated other justifications for the result it reached. Rather, we are suggesting that in part of its opinion, the court made an error by applying reasoning from the contract creditor context, where it works, to the tort creditor context, where it does not.

3. *Criminal Activity.* The fact that married spouses own property as tenants by the entirety may not protect an innocent spouse from forfeiture of that property on the criminal conviction of the other spouse. There is a split in authority in the U.S. Court of Appeals on this issue. In *United States v. Lee,* 232 F.3d 556 (7th Cir. 2000), the husband/defendant pleaded guilty to money laundering, and the U.S. government attempted to execute a forfeiture judgment against him by taking the home he owned as tenants in the entirety with his wife. The court ruled that "[p]roperty owned as a tenancy by the entiret[y] cannot be made available to answer for the judgment debts of one of the tenants individually." In *United States v. Fleet,* 498 F.3d. 1225 (11th Cir. 2007), the Eleventh Circuit disagreed with the *Lee* decision, holding that property held by spouses as tenants by the entirety is reachable by one spouse's creditors when that spouse commits a federal crime.

In *Fleet*, like *Lee*, the defendant was convicted of the federal crime of money laundering. The court, however, allowed the government to reach the property, stating that "there is no innocent spouse defense to criminal forfeiture because the only property being forfeited is the interest that belongs to the defendant. The fact that the innocent spouse, even though she retains her property interest, may be adversely affected by the forfeiture of her guilty mate's interest is no bar to forfeiture of his interest."

Problem

Julia Barzel and Larry Rose were married in August 1995 and bought a house together as tenants by the entirety in 1997. Julia is an entrepreneur and set up a software company in 1998. In 2000, Julia bought $150,000 in computer equipment from Perry Newman on credit, securing the debt by granting Perry a mortgage on her interest in her house (Julia and Larry own the house in equal shares). Julia's company failed last year, and Perry has now brought an action seeking to attach Julia's share in the house to satisfy the debt. Will Perry's action be successful? An explanatory answer can be found on page 1043.

D.   FAMILY PROPERTY

1.   *Marital Property: Historical Background*

a.   Coverture, Dower, and Curtesy

Under the common law of England, a single woman (a *feme sole*) enjoyed the same rights to hold and manage property and to enter enforceable contracts as did a man. Once married, however, the husband retained the sole power to possess and control the profits of all land owned by himself and his wife. The wife was called a *feme covert*, and her status was described by the institution of *coverture*. The husband and wife were treated as one person in the eyes of the law; that person was the husband. He had the power to convey his wife's property without her consent and to control all the profits of the land. In addition, his consent was required in order to sell her land.

In contrast to the rigidity of the law courts, the equity courts created a variety of mechanisms by which some married women could exercise property rights during marriage. First, they could enforce antenuptial agreements by which some husbands voluntarily gave control over property to their wives. Second, a trust could be created for the benefit of the wife, and she could enforce the trust as the beneficiary without her husband's consent. Fathers often took this route to keep property in their daughters' control rather than allowing it to pass to their prospective sons-in-law. William B. Stoebuck & Dale A. Whitman, *The Law of Property* § 2.13, at 65-66 (3d ed. 2000).

The common law did give the wife certain important property interests to take effect at the death of her husband. The common law gave the surviving spouse a life estate in all or some of the land owned by the deceased spouse at the time of his death. The wife's *dower* interest consisted of a life estate in one-third of the freehold lands of which the husband was seised at any time during the marriage and that could be inherited by the couple's children. The wife's dower interest could not be alienated by her husband without her consent; nor could it be used to satisfy the husband's debts. The husband's equivalent *curtesy* interest consisted of a life estate in *all* the lands in which his wife owned a present freehold estate during the marriage and that was inheritable by issue of the couple. However, the husband's curtesy interest sprang into being *only* if the couple had a child capable of inheriting the property. Stoebuck & Whitman, *supra*, at 67-69.

Dower and curtesy remain in only a few states, and where they exist, the rights of husbands and wives have been equalized. The states that retain these institutions generally allow surviving spouses to choose between dower/curtesy and a statutorily defined share of marital assets owned by the decedent at the time of death.

b. Married Women's Property Acts

In the second half of the nineteenth century (starting with Mississippi in 1839), all common law states passed *Married Women's Property Acts*. These statutes abolished coverture and removed the economic disabilities previously imposed on married women. After passage of the statutes, married women had the same rights as single women and married men to contract, to hold and manage property, and to sue and be sued. The wife's earnings were her separate property and could not be controlled or taken by her husband without her consent; nor could her separate property be seized by her husband's creditors. At the same time, these acts failed to achieve the aims of nineteenth-century women's rights advocates who "sought to emancipate wives' labor in the household as well as in the market, and to do so, advocated 'joint property' laws that would recognize wives' claims to marital assets to which husbands otherwise had title." Reva B. Siegel, *Home as Work: The First Woman's Rights Claims Concerning Wives' Household Labor, 1850-1880*, 103 Yale L.J. 1073, 1077 (1994). They argued that wives were "entitled to joint rights in marital property by reason of the labor they contributed to the family economy." *Id.* Many women worked inside the home for no wages; the *Married Women's Property Acts* failed to grant such women any rights in marital property, while family law doctrines preserved their duties to render services inside the home. Other women engaged in labor inside the home for which wages were earned, such as taking in laundry or sewing, keeping boarders, gardening and dairying, and selling the crops or milk products for cash. Although some states gave married women property rights in such earnings, most *Married Women's Property Acts* granted the husband control over such earnings or were interpreted by courts in this fashion on the ground that these acts were not intended to alter family law doctrines requiring women to provide services inside the home. *Id.* at 1181-1188. Since most men worked outside the home and most married women worked inside the home, gender equality in access to property was a long time in coming.

2.   *Community Property and Separate Property*

Different rules define the property rights of spouses during marriage, on divorce or dissolution of the marriage, and on the death of one of the parties. Two basic systems govern marital property rights in the United States: the *separate property system,* in the majority of states, and the *community property system,* in effect in nine states.[5]

a.   Separate Property

During marriage.   In separate property states, spouses own their property separately, except to the extent they choose to share it or mingle it with their spouse's property. This means that each spouse owns whatever property he or she possessed before the marriage—such as a house, a car, stock, or a bank account—and is individually liable for prior debts. Creditors cannot go after a spouse's property to satisfy a debt individually undertaken by the other spouse. Property earned after the marriage, including wages and dividends, is also owned separately. A husband and wife may of course choose to share property with each other either informally, by sharing the costs of the household or giving part of individual earnings to the spouse, or formally, by having a joint bank account to which either spouse has access as a joint tenant.

It is important to note that spouses in separate property states are not perfectly free to keep all their property to themselves. Spouses have a legal duty to support each other, and this duty may require a sharing of property earned during the marriage. A spouse who fails to comply with this obligation may be forced to do so by a court order for maintenance, although this kind of lawsuit rarely happens outside of divorce or separation.

On divorce.   Most legal disputes about marital property involve divorce or the death of a spouse. All states regulate the distribution of property rights between the parties on divorce. Separate property states have statutes that provide for **equitable distribution** of property owned by each of the parties on divorce, subject to a wide range of factors such as economic need (support for necessities, including child support), status (maintaining the lifestyle shared during the marriage), rehabilitation (support sufficient to allow one spouse to attain marketable skills such that support will no longer be needed), contributions of the parties (treating the marriage as a partnership and dividing the assets jointly earned from the enterprise), and, sometimes, fault. 3 *Family Law and Practice* § 37.06. Some states allow marital fault to be considered and some explicitly exclude "marital misconduct" as a factor. *Id.* § 37.06[1][h]. Specific factors that may be taken into account include age, health, occupation, income, vocational skills, contribution as a homemaker, dissipation of property during the marriage, income tax consequences, debts, obligations prior to marriage and contribution of one spouse to the education of the other. This system gives the trial judge

---

5. Arizona, California, Idaho, Louisiana, Nevada, New Mexico, Texas, Washington, and Wisconsin. A tenth state, Alaska, permits parties to opt in to a community property system. Alaska Stat. § 34.77.090.

great discretion in determining how the property should be shared or shifted between the parties. Often at issue are the standards to be used in dividing property, the weight to be given different factors, and the determination of the kinds of intangible resources that constitute "property" subject to equitable distribution on divorce.

Separate property states also have provision for "alimony," or periodic payments from one spouse to support the other. Until recently, alimony was routinely awarded to wives who were thought to be dependent on their husbands for income. However, with the huge recent increase in women in the workforce, as well as the advent of no-fault divorce, alimony has become exceptional and, when awarded, is often temporary. Current policy in most states aims at financial independence for the parties.

On death.   A spouse may dispose of her property by will. Notwithstanding her right to do so, separate property states may limit her ability to determine who gets her property on death. Many states provide for a statutory **forced share** of the decedent's estate, effectively allowing the widow or widower to override the will and receive a stated portion (usually one-third to one-half) of the estate. There is no obligation to leave separately owned property; spouses are generally free to give away their separate property during their lifetime. But the rules in force do protect the interests of a surviving spouse to the extent of defining an indefeasible right to receive a portion of the testator's **estate** (the property owned by the testator at the time of death). When no will is written, a spouse's separate property is inherited according to the state intestacy statute. While some states grant the surviving spouse the decedent's entire property, other states divide the property between the surviving spouse and the children.

b. Community Property

During marriage.   In community property states, as in separate property states, property owned prior to the marriage, as well as property acquired after marriage by gift, devise, bequest, or inheritance, is separate property. The American Law Institute's *Principles of the Law of Family Dissolution,* adopted in 2002, favors the community property approach rather than the separate property approach. *See id.* §§ 4.01-4.12. All other property acquired during the marriage, including earnings, is community property and is owned equally by both spouses. In some community property states, earnings on separate property remain separate property. In several states, however, earnings from separate property, including interest, rents, and profits, become community property. Most states allow spouses to change, or "transmute," their property from separate to community property, and vice versa, by written agreement.

While community property is somewhat similar to joint tenancy since it is a form of common ownership, a better analogy can be drawn between community property and partnership. Since the 1960s, most states have granted spouses equal rights to manage community property; each spouse individually may deal with the community property without the consent of the other spouse. At the same time, managers of community property are fiduciaries; they have the duty to manage the property for the good of the community and to act in good faith to benefit the community. In addition, most states have statutes requiring *both* parties to agree to convey or mortgage interests in real property and in assets in a business in which both spouses participate. Community property states have widely divergent rules on whether community property can be reached by creditors of individual spouses. Some states protect such property from being reached by creditors of individual spouses unless both spouses consented to the transaction; others allow the community property to be used to satisfy debts incurred by one spouse; still others limit the portion of the community property reachable by such creditors.

On divorce.   A few community property states allocate property on divorce relatively mechanically by giving each spouse his or her separate property and half of the community property. Cal. Fam. Code § 2550. Most community property states adopt the "equitable distribution" principle now existing in separate property states. Ariz. Rev. Stat. § 25-318; Tex. Fam. Code § 7.001; Wash. Rev. Code § 26.09.080. The main issue arising in community property states is how to characterize specific items of property as separate or community property.

On death.   In community property states, a spouse may dispose of her separate property and one-half of the community property by will. Statutory forced share statutes do not generally exist in community property states, given the spouse's vested ownership of one-half of the community property.

c.   Premarital Agreements

Spouses may attempt to vary their respective property rights during marriage or at divorce by signing a premarital or antenuptial agreement. Traditionally, such agreements were unenforceable on public policy grounds because they were thought to undermine stable marriages. *See* J. Thomas Oldham, *Would Enactment of the Uniform Premarital and Marital Agreements Act in All Fifty States Change U.S. Law Regarding Premarital Agreements?*, 46 Fam. L.Q. 367, 368 (2012). Today, however, both premarital and marital agreements are generally enforceable if voluntary and not otherwise against public policy, reflecting both respect for freedom of contract and belief that such agreements may encourage marriage and discourage bitter divorce disputes. *See In re Marriage of Traster*, 291 P.3d 494, 501 (Kan. Ct. App. 2012). The *Uniform Premarital Agreement Act* (UPAA) of 1983 made it extremely difficult to challenge premarital agreements, and although adopted in about half the states, about half of those made substantial changes to provide more protection for the parties. In 2012, the Uniform Laws Commission adopted the *Uniform Premarital and Marital Agreements Act* (UPMAA), seeking to provide a level of protection more in line with state statutes and decisions.

Courts differ in the standards applied to determine whether agreements are voluntary. Factors may include whether the agreement was demanded shortly before the wedding, the relative sophistication of the parties, and whether the challenging party had reasonable time and means to access independent counsel. *See Mamot v. Mamot*, 813 N.W.2d 440, 447, 452 (Neb. 2012) (summarizing tests and finding agreement involuntary when demanded a few days before wedding and prospective wife could not reasonably have consulted an attorney);

UMPAA § 9(a)-(c) (2012) (agreement unenforceable if party did not have time or means to access an attorney and did not knowingly waive right to independent counsel); Cal. Fam. Code § 1612(c) (restrictions on spousal support allowed only if the party waiving rights consulted with independent counsel).

Most jurisdictions will not enforce agreements if they are "unconscionable" at the time of the agreement, but standards vary widely. Oldham at 379 (factors include the relative means of the parties, whether all distribution or economic support is waived, and degree of financial disclosure between the parties). Some jurisdictions will go further and consider whether agreements are equitable or fair. *See Ansin v. Craven-Ansin*, 929 N.E.2d 955, 964 (Mass. 2010) (reviewing to determine whether the terms of the agreement are "fair and reasonable"). Many states determine unconscionability or fairness as of the date of execution of the agreement. *See* Va. Code § 20-151; N.J. Stat. § 37:2-38(c); UPAA § 6. A significant minority of states, however, may prohibit enforcement if unconscionable at the time enforcement is sought, particularly if there has been a substantial change in the circumstances of the parties. Oldham, *supra*, at 371, 380-381; *see also* UPMAA § 9(f)(b) (optional provision permitting court to refuse to enforce agreement if it "would result in substantial hardship for a party because of a material change in circumstances arising after the agreement was signed"); Conn. Gen. Stat. § 46b-36g(a)(2) (prohibiting enforcement if "unconscionable when it was executed or when enforcement is sought"); *Ansin*, 929 N.E.2d at 964 (agreement must be "fair and reasonable at the time of execution and at the time of divorce"); American Law Institute, *Principles of the Law of Family Dissolution* § 9.05 (2008) (recommending against enforcement if it "would work a substantial injustice" and the couple has either had a child or there has been another substantial change in circumstances).

d.   Homestead Laws

Almost all states have homestead laws designed to protect the interests of a surviving spouse and children in the family home from the claims of creditors of the deceased spouse. They generally allow the spouse to live in the family home as long as she lives. Some states require the property to be registered as a homestead before the protections attach, while in others probate judges have the power to set aside homestead property as exempt from creditor's claims. Many states limit the value that can be exempted from execution to pay debts; if the property is worth more than this limit, the property (or a divisible portion of the land) may be sold to pay amounts that exceed the limitation. *See* 3 *Thompson on Real Property, Second Thomas Editions* § 21.04. Some states go further and allow owners to devise homestead property free from the reach of creditors even if there is no surviving spouse or minor child. *See McKean v. Warburton*, 919 So. 2d 341, 343-345 (Fla. 2005).

3.   *Divorce: Equitable Distribution of Property*

Distribution of property differs by gender and age, as well as race. Women, on average, earn less than men. In 2011, the median income of men who worked full time was $48,202, while the median income of women who worked full time was only $37,118, or 77 percent of male earnings. Carmen DeNavas-Walt, Berna-dette D. Proctor & Jessica C. Smith, U.S. Census Bureau, Current Population Reports, P60-243, *Income, Poverty, and Health Insurance Coverage in the United States: 2011* (Sept. 2012), *available at* http://www.census.gov/prod/2012pubs/p60-243.pdf. The reasons for the disparities between women and men are complicated. It is clear, however, that a major factor is that women continue to undertake the bulk of the responsibility for raising children. This work not only is unpaid but also interferes with women's ability to work full time. *See* Martha Albertson Fine-man, *The Illusion of Equality: The Rhetoric and Reality of Divorce Reform* (1991); Victor Fuchs, *Women's Quest for Economic Equality* (1988); Joan Williams, *Unbending Gen-der: Why Family and Work Conflict and What to Do About It* (2000); Vicki Schultz, *Life's Work,* 100 Colum. L. Rev. 1881 (2000).

Women also suffer disproportionately from divorce. After divorce, men's standard of living tends to go up by 10 percent, while women's standard of living declines by 27 percent. Richard R. Peterson, *A Re-evaluation of the Economic Conse-quences of Divorce,* 61 Am. Soc. Rev. 528, 534 (1996); Lenore J. Weitzman, *The Eco-nomic Consequences of Divorce Are Still Unequal: Comment on Peterson,* 61 Am. Soc. Rev. 537, 538 (1996).

Children are more likely to be poor than adults, and some children are very likely to be poor. Although 15.0 percent of the population fell below the poverty line in 2011, 21.9 percent of children did so; moreover, 37.4 percent of African American children and 34.1 percent of Hispanic children were living in poverty. Children who live in households without an adult male are extremely likely to be poor. While only 6.2 percent of children in families of married couples were poor in 2011, 31.2 percent of children living in female-headed households were poor. More than half of all children under six living in female-headed house-holds (57.2 percent) were poor. Although 23.8 percent of white, non-Hispanic, female-headed households were poor, 42.5 percent of African American, female-headed households and 44.0 percent of Hispanic, female-headed house-holds were poor. While the median income of married couples was $74,130, the median income of female-headed households was only $33,637, and the median income of male-headed households was $49,567. DeNavas-Walt, Proctor & Smith, *supra.*

Upon divorce, the property obtained during the marriage is typically divided between the parties according to principles of **equitable distribution**. Equitable distribution is governed by statute, but the statutes contain many factors and pro-vide judges with significant discretion. Montana's equitable distribution statute, below, a version of the *Uniform Marriage and Divorce Act* (1973) adopted in eight states, is typical. The statute is followed by *O'Brien v. O'Brien,* 489 N.E.2d 712 (N.Y. 1985), which considers what can be considered property subject to division under New York's equitable distribution statute.

APPENDIX

A

Finding Problems

1. From the two cases, we have five categories of found property: lost, mislaid, abandoned, treasure trove, and embedded. We can eliminate two relatively quickly. Treasure trove is defined as coins or currency that are concealed by the owner. Treasure trove also has an element of antiquity. The backpack was not concealed (it was on the floor by the door), and facts say that the currency is new, so the element of antiquity is not met. The backpack was not attached to the property or embedded to the ground, so the embedded category does not apply here. We mentioned a sixth category, contraband, in the notes after *Benjamin*. There are no facts given here that would allow the government to prove that the property was contraband, so that category likely does not apply.

That leaves lost, mislaid, or abandoned. It is possible to make arguments in support of each of them, but we think that mislaid probably fits this fact pattern best. Mislaid property is intentionally placed by the owner in a particular location and then later forgotten by the owner. Lost property is not intentionally placed—the owner accidentally drops the object or otherwise unintentionally parts with possession. It seems hard (though not impossible) to imagine a scenario where a person unintentionally parts with possession of a backpack, so it seems likely that the property was mislaid and not lost. Our last category, abandoned, turns on the owner's intent. We typically would presume that someone would not intend to abandon money or anything else of value. We might imagine, however, that it was abandoned if we thought the money was stolen or otherwise obtained illegally. See, in this context, the dissent in *Benjamin*. Because mislaid property goes to the owner of the locus, Cindy seems to have the best claim on these facts. Lost and abandoned property goes to the finder. On these facts, Paul might be able to make a decent claim by arguing that the backpack was abandoned.

What if the money was found in an envelope rather than a backpack? It is easier to imagine a person accidentally losing an envelope than a backpack. Perhaps it was in the owner's bag or coat pocket and fell out when the owner reached in to get something else. This strengthens the argument that the money was lost rather than mislaid, giving Paul a stronger claim. If the envelope was found on the counter rather than on the floor, we would be back to having a good argument that it was mislaid—it is easy to imagine someone placing the envelope on the counter, then forgetting it. On the other hand, we could also imagine the envelope falling out of someone's bag or coat pocket onto the counter. The envelope on the counter strikes us and the scenario that best supports arguments for both lost and mislaid.

We should emphasize here that the lines between the categories of lost, mislaid, and abandoned are blurry and that reasonable minds can disagree about how they apply to a particular set of facts. We discussed the vagueness of these rules in the notes after *Benjamin*. When dealing with vague rules, you should focus on making the best arguments that you can because it is often impossible to identify an answer that is exactly correct.

2. This scenario is even blurrier than the last. We think the most plausible categories are embedded or lost. Mislaid doesn't seem to work well here—it is hard to imagine a person intentionally placing a ring in a gully. Even here, though, it is possible to come up with a scenario—imagine a marriage proposal gone wrong when the person making the proposal hides the ring in the park but then forgets exactly where it is. Abandoned also seems unlikely—who would abandon a valuable ring? Treasure trove might be plausible; the ring is old, satisfying the antiquity element, but treasure trove is typically defined in terms of coin or bullion, not jewelry.

The ring was found in a small gully caused by a recent rainstorm. It may have been embedded and exposed when the rain washed away the soil. The ring was very dirty, suggesting that it may have been buried. If it was embedded, Theresa would get the ring as owner of the locus. We can also imagine, however, the ring falling off of someone's finger while they were walking through the park. The age of the ring would be consistent with this story—it is not unusual for a person today to wear an antique ring. So is the fact that the ring was dirty—rings that sit in the dirt for a while get dirty. If it was lost, then Ryan would get it as the finder.

APPENDIX

B

Gift Problems

1. Maurice made a valid *inter vivos* gift to Sally, but it is revocable. Maurice's words indicate that he intended to make a present gift, not a gift that was to occur on his death. He delivered the ring to Sally, and she accepted it. Because the gift was made by Maurice in view of his impending death, it is a gift *causa mortis*, allowing Maurice to revoke the gift after he recovered.

2. Theresa did not make a valid *inter vivos* gift under the traditional common-law rules. She intended to make an *inter vivos* gift, and we can presume acceptance by Holly. The element of delivery, however, was not met under the traditional standard. A court strictly construing the delivery requirement of "if it can be handed over, it must be handed over" would require the car to be physically delivered to Holly's possession. At a minimum, a traditional court would require delivery of the keys. A court taking a more modern approach might find that symbolic delivery was made through the card. Note that *Gruen* does not lend direct support to Holly because unlike *Gruen*, the problem does not involve the gift of a future interest.

3. Nick did not make a valid *inter vivos* gift to Katie. The delivery and acceptance elements are met here—Nick handed the lamp over to Katie, and Katie took it. The problem here is intent. Nick's words indicate that he intended to transfer ownership at death. Because there was no intent to make a present transfer of ownership during life, and instead a transfer of ownership at death, the attempted gift is invalid. Nick owns the lamp.

APPENDIX

C

Adverse Possession Problems

1. 1998. C's minority doesn't matter on this hypothetical. The statute gives the person under a disability the longer of (a) ten years from when the disability is lifted (here, C turned 18 in 1983, so an extra 10 years would be 1993) or (b) the 21-year period (which expires here in 1998). As we pointed out in Example 1, we only apply the disability period if it benefits the owner.

2. (a) B wins in 1994. As of 1993, A has been in possession for 21 years, but the statute has been tolled because of O's imprisonment. O's disability of imprisonment was removed by death in 1985. B, who is "claiming from, by, or under" O, gets the benefit of the ten-year disabilities period. Adding ten years to 1985, we find that the statute will expire in A's favor in 1995. So B will win in 1994. "But wait," you might say—B is a minor, but this disability wasn't in place at the time A entered. True, but B isn't relying here on being a minor here. Rather, B wins based on O's disability alone. (b) A wins. As we just explained, the extra ten years from O's disability expires in 1995. B cannot claim more time based on being a minor because B was not a disabled owner of Blackacre when A entered. This specific fact pattern, which we illustrated in Example 5, involves a disabled heir, but it is illustrative of the larger point illustrated by Example 4—disabilities do not matter unless they were in place at the time the adverse possessor enters. (c) A wins for same reasons as (b).

3. O wins. The 21-year statute of limitations would have run in A's favor in 1996, but A died before the limitations period expired. B had only been on the property for seven years by the time O sued. So for B to win, B would have to *tack* A's 15 years of possession onto her 7 years of possession. But B can't tack because there was no voluntary transfer of possession, and therefore no *privity*, between A and B.

4. B wins with a caveat. Here, there is a voluntary transfer of *possession* between A and B. A and B therefore are in privity, so B can tack A's 15 years onto her 7 years of possession, satisfying the 21-year statute of limitations. The caveat is that if the court applied the rule used by the *trial court* in *Howard v. Kunto*, that privity requires a transfer of an *estate*, and that transfer of possession alone doesn't qualify, then O would win because without privity B can't tack.

5. It depends. O's disability occurred after A took possession and therefore is irrelevant. A has possessed part of Blackacre for the statutory period and in an open and notorious manner (the fence). If the court follows the Maine rule/ bad faith standard, though, A's mistaken possession won't qualify as adverse and

under a claim of right, and O would win. If the court follows the majority rule that mistaken possession qualifies as adverse, A would win.

6. C would win in 1997. A entered after ownership had been split into present and future interests. The statute of limitations doesn't run against a future interest holder until that person's interest becomes possessory. In other words, the clock does not run against C until B dies. When B dies, B's life estate ends, and C's future interest becomes possessory. So A loses in 1997 even though A has possessed Blackacre for more than 21 years. The statute started to run against C in 1979 and expires against C in 2000. So A would win if the action for ejectment was brought in 2002.

APPENDIX

D

A. ESTATES AND FUTURE INTERESTS
PROBLEM SET—PART 1

1. A has a life estate. O has a reversion in fee simple absolute.

2. The School Board has a fee simple determinable. O has a possibility of reverter in fee simple absolute.

3. A has a life estate. O has a vested remainder in fee simple absolute. The conveyance created a vested remainder in fee simple absolute in B. B then conveyed that interest to O. The remainder keeps its name even though it is now held by the grantor.

4. A has a term of years. O has a reversion in fee simple absolute.

5. A has a life estate. B has a contingent remainder in fee simple absolute. O has a reversion in fee simple absolute.

6. A owns Blackacre in fee simple absolute.

7. Under the most common modern approach, A would own Blackacre in fee simple absolute. At traditional common law, A would own Blackacre in fee tail, and O would have a reversion.

8. The School Board has a fee simple subject to executory limitation. The State University has an executory interest in fee simple absolute.

9. A has a life estate. A's children have a contingent remainder in fee simple absolute. O has a reversion in fee simple absolute. The remainder is contingent because it is in an unascertained person.

10. A has a life estate. B has a vested remainder in an open class in fee simple.

11. A has a life estate. B has a vested remainder subject to divestment in fee simple absolute. C has an executory interest that may divest B's vested remainder in fee simple absolute.

12. The School Board has a fee simple subject to condition subsequent. O has a right of entry in fee simple absolute.

13. A has a life estate. B has an alternative contingent remainder in fee simple absolute. C has an alternative contingent remainder in fee simple absolute.

14. A has a life estate. B has a vested remainder in life estate. A's children have a contingent remainder in fee simple absolute. O has a reversion in fee simple absolute. As in problem 9, the remainder is contingent because it is in an unascertained person.

15. A has a life estate. B has a vested remainder in life estate. C has a vested remainder in an open class.

B. ESTATES AND FUTURE INTERESTS
PROBLEM SET—PART 2

16. A has a life estate. The School Board has a vested remainder in fee simple determinable. O has a possibility of reverter in fee simple absolute.

17. The School Board has a fee simple determinable. O has a possibility of reverter in fee simple absolute.

18. O owns Blackacre in fee simple absolute.

19. A has a life estate. A's children have an alternative contingent remainder in fee simple absolute. C has an alternative contingent remainder in fee simple absolute. The remainder in A's children is contingent both because it is in an unascertained person and because it is subject to a condition precedent.

20. Basically the same answer as 19. A has a life estate. D has an alternative contingent remainder in fee simple. C has an alternative contingent remainder in fee simple. Even though we now have an ascertained person for the remainder in A's children, it is still subject to a condition precedent.

21. D owns Blackacre in fee simple absolute.

22. A has a life estate. B has a vested remainder in life estate. C has a contingent remainder in fee simple absolute. O has a reversion in fee simple absolute.

23. A has a life estate. C has a contingent remainder in fee simple absolute. O has a reversion in fee simple absolute. Because B died before A, B's life estate has disappeared.

24. A has a life estate. O has a reversion in fee simple absolute.

25. A has a life estate. C has a contingent remainder in fee simple absolute. B has a contingent remainder in fee simple, though not one that is alternative to C's—the contingencies are different. O has a reversion in fee simple absolute.

26. A has a life estate. B has a vested remainder in an open class subject to divestment in fee simple absolute. C has an executory interest in fee simple absolute.

27. B and D have a fee simple subject to executory limitation in common. C has an executory interest in fee simple absolute.

28. B and D own Blackacre in common in fee simple absolute.

29. A has a life estate. B has a contingent remainder in life estate. O has a reversion in fee simple absolute.

30. C has a life estate measured by A's life (also known as a life estate *per autre vie*). B has a contingent remainder in life estate. O has a reversion in fee simple absolute.

31. A has a defeasible life estate. B has a vested remainder in fee simple absolute. O has a possibility of reverter in life estate. If A leaves the church, then O's possibility of reverter will automatically transfer the life estate back to O; on A's death, the life estate will expire (regardless of whether A still has it or whether it has reverted back to O), and B will own Blackacre in fee simple absolute.

32. A has a life estate. B has a vested remainder in an open class subject to divestment in fee simple absolute. C has an executory interest in fee simple absolute.

33. A has a life estate. D has a vested remainder in an open class subject to divestment in fee simple absolute. C has an executory interest in fee simple absolute. D has just stepped into B's shoes. If A dies without having more children, C's executory interest will divest D's interest. If A has another child and that child survives A, then D's interest will become possessory.

34. A has a life estate. B has an alternative contingent remainder in fee simple absolute. (If you said that B's contingent remainder was also in an open class, you would be conceptually correct, but by convention we do not use "in an open class" to describe a contingent remainder). C has an alternative contingent remainder in fee simple absolute.

35. A has a life estate. B has a contingent remainder in fee simple absolute. C has a contingent remainder in fee simple absolute. O has a reversion in fee simple absolute. Note that the contingent remainders are not alternative—children and issue are different categories. A could die with no surviving children but a surviving grandchild. In this case, the property would revert back to O.

C.   RULE AGAINST PERPETUITIES PROBLEM SET

1. *Without RAP.* A has a life estate, A's oldest child has a contingent remainder in life estate, A's grandchildren have a contingent remainder in fee simple absolute, and O has a reversion in fee simple absolute. The reversion is exempt from the RAP, so we only need to worry about the two contingent remainders.

Common Law. The correct answer is: A has a life estate, A's oldest child has a contingent remainder in life estate, and O has a reversion in fee simple absolute. The first contingent remainder is fine—it will vest (or fail if no child is living) at A's death, and A is a life in being. The second contingent remainder violates the RAP—(a) A could have a child, B, after the conveyance; (b) B could be the oldest living child on A's death, and any children born before the conveyance could die; (c) B could die more than 21 years after A's death, in which case the contingent remainder would vest or fail more than 21 years after lives in being. So, under the common law, you strike out the invalid conveyance.

Wait and See. The correct answer is: A has a life estate, A's oldest child has a contingent remainder in life estate, A's grandchildren have a contingent remainder in fee simple absolute that may become invalid based on actual events, and O has a reversion in fee simple. Under the wait-and-see approach, you don't invalidate the interest until you find out what actually happens. If A doesn't have a child after the conveyance, then the contingent remainder will be valid (it will vest or fail at the death of A's oldest child, who in this scenario is a life in being). If A has an afterborn child, and if the contingent remainder does not vest within 21 years of a life-in-being who affects vesting (A or A's children), then the contingent remainder will be void.

2. *Without RAP.* A has a life estate, B has a vested remainder in life estate, B's children have a contingent remainder in fee simple absolute (contingent because we don't know whether B has any kids, so "B's children" is

unascertained), O has a reversion in fee simple absolute. Our RAP analysis would not change if B had a living child, making the remainder a vested remainder in an open class because the RAP requires vested remainders in an open class to close during the perpetuities period.

Common Law. The contingent remainder does not violate the RAP, so the answer is as stated above. The contingent remainder will vest or fail at B's death (or at A's death if B predeceases A); because it will vest or fail at the death of a life in being, it is fine.

Wait and See. Same as above.

3. *Without RAP.* A has a life estate, A's children have a contingent remainder in fee simple absolute (because we don't know if A has any children), the Widener City School Board has a contingent remainder in fee simple absolute, O has a reversion in fee simple absolute. (Why does O have a reversion? If A dies without having children neither of the contingent remainders would be satisfied. If A had a child, then A's child would have a vested remainder in an open class subject to divestment, WCSB would have an executory interest, O's reversion would disappear).

Common Law. The correct answer is: A has a life estate, A's children have a contingent remainder in fee simple absolute, O has a reversion in fee simple absolute. The children's contingent remainder is fine because it will vest or fail on A's death. The WCSB's contingent remainder is void under the rule against perpetuities—one of A's great-great grandchildren could be convicted of a felony 200 years from now. The charity-charity exception only applies if both the interests are in charities, which is not the case here.

Wait and See. The correct answer is: A has a life estate, A's children have a contingent remainder in fee simple absolute, the WCSB has a contingent remainder in fee simple absolute that will only be valid for lives in being plus 21 years, O has a reversion in fee simple absolute. Under the wait-and-see approach, WCSB could get the property if the contingency (A's issue convicted of a felony) happens within lives in being plus 21 years. The relevant lives in being would be A and any of A's issue alive at the time of the conveyance. Twenty-one years after the last one of these people dies, the contingent remainder disappears if it hasn't done so already (as it would if A dies without having children).

4. *Without RAP.* A has a life estate; B and C have vested remainders in life estate in an open class; B1, B2, C1 and C2 have vested remainders in life estate in an open class; A's great-grandchildren have a contingent remainder in fee simple absolute; T's estate has a reversion in fee simple absolute.

Common Law. The correct answer is: A has a life estate; B and C have vested remainders in life estate in an open class; T's estate has a reversion in fee simple absolute. B and C's vested remainders are fine because the class (A's children) will close at A's death. The grandchildren's vested remainder in an open class fails because A could have an afterborn child who could die more than 21 years after lives in being. See the discussion of Example 47 in the text for a detailed explanation of why a conveyance in a living person's grandchildren is problematic under the RAP. The contingent remainder in A's great-grandchildren is even more remote.

Wait and See. The correct answer is: A has a life estate; B and C have vested remainders in life estate in an open class; B1, B2, C1, and C2 have vested remainders in life estate in an open class that may become invalid on actual events, A's great-grandchildren have a contingent remainder in fee simple absolute that may become invalid on actual events, T's estate has a reversion in fee simple absolute.

5. *Common Law.* The correct answer is: T's estate owns Blackacre in fee simple. This follows from the result above.

Wait and See. The correct answer is: B1, B2, C1, and C2 [the grandchildren] have a life estate in Blackacre as tenants in common; B3, C3, and C4 [the great-grandchildren] have vested remainders in an open class in fee simple absolute. As things have turned out, there haven't been any afterborn children to screw up the grandchildren's interest, and there haven't been any afterborn grandchildren to screw up the great-grandchildren's interest. The grandchildren's vested remainder closed on the death of B and C (who couldn't have any more children). The great-grandchildren's vested remainder in an open class is fine because it will close at the deaths of the grandchildren, B1, B2, C1, and C2, who all were alive at the time of the conveyance.

A

A's children: B and C

A's grandchildren: B1, B2, C1, and C2

A's great-grandchildren: B2, C3, C4

6. *Without RAP.* T's widow has a life estate, T's issue have a contingent remainder in fee simple absolute, T's estate has a reversion absolute.

Common Law. All of the interests are valid, so the answer is the same as above. But what about the unborn widow problem? At T's death, we know who T's widow is. Put another way, T isn't going to be marrying anyone else. So the contingent remainder is fine; it will vest or fail on T's widow's death.

Wait and See. Same as above.

7. *Without RAP.* O owns Blackacre in fee simple absolute; A has an option to purchase Blackacre from O.

Common Law. The correct answer is: O owns Blackacre in fee simple absolute; the option is invalid. O and A could die tomorrow; A's estate could exercise its option more than 21 years after the death of these lives in being.

Wait and See. The correct answer is: O owns Blackacre in fee simple absolute; A has an option to purchase Blackacre that will either 30 years from the date of execution of the option or 21 years after the deaths of O and A, whichever is first.

8. *Without RAP.* A has a life estate; A1 and A2 have vested remainders in an open class in life estate; B1, B2, and B3 have vested remainders in fee simple absolute. The last interest is not in an open class because at the time of the conveyance B has already died.

Common Law. All of the interests are valid, so the answer is the same as above. The only interest subject to the RAP is the vested remainder in an open class, and that vests or fails on A's death.

Wait and See. Same as above.

9. *Without RAP.* O's children have a life estate in common, O's first grandchild has a contingent remainder in fee simple absolute, O has a reversion in fee simple absolute.

Common Law. The correct answer is: O's children have a life estate in common, O has a reversion in fee simple absolute. This one is fairly easy—O's first grand-child to reach 25 could be born after the conveyance and could outlive all lives in being.

Wait and See. The correct answer is: O's children have a life estate in common, O's first grandchild has a continent remainder in fee simple absolute that may become void on actual events, O has a reversion in fee simple absolute. If any of O's grandchildren reach 25 within 21 years of lives in being, the contingent remainder will become vested and will be valid.

10. *Without RAP.* O's children have a life estate in common, O's grandchildren have a contingent remainder in fee simple absolute, O has a reversion in fee sim-ple absolute.

Common Law. The correct answer is: O's children have a life estate in common, O has a reversion in fee simple absolute. O could have an afterborn child, who in turn could have a child (O's grandchild) who reaches 21 more than 21 years after lives in being.

Wait and See. The correct answer is: O's children have a life estate in common, O's grandchildren have a contingent remainder in fee simple absolute that may become void on actual events, O has a reversion in fee simple absolute. If O's grandchildren reach 21 (or die before doing so) within 21 years of lives in being, the grandchildren's interest is good.

11. *Without RAP.* A and B have a life estate in common, T's grandchildren have a contingent remainder in life estate, T's issue have a contingent remainder in fee simple absolute, T's estate has a reversion in fee simple absolute.

Common Law. The correct answer is: A and B have a life estate in common, T's grandchildren have a contingent remainder in life estate, T's estate has a rever-sion in fee simple absolute. T's grandchildren's interest is fine—T's children provide the measuring lives, and because this is a testamentary gift, we know that there won't be any afterborn children. T's issue's contingent remainder is invalid because one of T's children could have an afterborn child [T's grandchild] who could die more than 21 years after lives in being, causing T's issue's contingent remainder to vest or fail outside of the perpetuities period.

Wait and See. The correct answer is: A and B have a life estate in common, T's grandchildren have a contingent remainder in life estate, T's issue have a contin-gent remainder in fee simple absolute that may become invalid on actual events, T's estate has a reversion in fee simple absolute.

12. *Without RAP.* T's estate owns the NWC estate in fee simple, T's issue have an executory interest in the proceeds of sale.

Common Law. The correct answer is: T's estate owns the NWC estate in fee sim-ple. This is the slothful executor problem—it is possible that the estate won't be sold for more than 21 years after the death of T and other lives in being.

Wait and See. The correct answer is: T's estate owns the NWC estate in fee sim-ple absolute, T's issue have an executory interest in the proceeds of sale that may become invalid on actual events. Presuming that the executor of T's estate is vaguely competent, T's issue's interest will be fine. Something to think about: what does "my surviving issue" mean? Surviving at T's death or surviving when the estate is finally sold? We would argue that the Testator's intent was probably surviving at T's death because T probably imagined that the sale would happen quickly. When you are drafting, you should try to avoid this kind of ambiguity.

13. *Without RAP.* A has a life estate, B has a vested remainder in an open class in fee simple absolute, C has a vested remainder in an open class and subject to divestment in fee simple absolute, B has an executory interest in fee simple absolute.

Common Law. The correct answer is: A has a life estate, B and C have vested remainders in an open class in fee simple absolute. The vested remainders in an open class are fine because the class will become closed on A's death. The executory interest fails because A could have an afterborn child who graduates from college (or fails to do so by age 30) more than 21 years after lives in being.

Wait and See. The correct answer is: A has a life estate, B has a vested remainder in an open class in fee simple absolute, C has a vested remainder in an open class and subject to divestment in fee simple absolute, B has an executory interest in fee simple absolute that may become invalid on actual events.

14. *Without RAP.* A and B have a life estate in common. C has a contingent remainder in fee simple absolute. T's estate has a reversion in fee simple absolute.

Common Law. The correct answer is: A and B have a life estate in common. T's estate has a reversion in fee simple absolute. The contingent remainder is void. A could have an afterborn child, D, who would be one of T's grandchildren. If A, B, and C die the next year, then D would reach the age of 25 (or not), more than 21 years after lives in being.

Wait and See. The correct answer is: A and B have a life estate in common; C has a contingent remainder in fee simple absolute that may become invalid on actual events; T's estate has a reversion in fee simple absolute. So long as all of the grandchildren reach the age of 25 within the perpetuities period, the interest in the grandchildren will be valid.

15. *Without RAP.* A has a life estate, A's children have a contingent remainder in life estate, A's issue have a contingent remainder in fee simple absolute, O has a reversion in fee simple absolute.

Common Law. All of the interests are valid, so same as above. The contingent remainder in A's children is fine because it vests at A's death. The contingent remainder in A's issue is fine because it will vest (i.e., the class will close) on the death of the last Kennedy issue alive at the time of the conveyance. This is a fairly common way around the RAP—the Kennedy issue qualify as lives in being because by the terms of the conveyance they both (a) were alive when the conveyance was made and (b) affect the vesting.

Wait and See. Same as above.

16. *Without RAP.* A has a fee simple subject to executory limitation; B's children have an executory interest in fee simple absolute.

Common Law. All of the interests are valid, so same as above. The executory interest will vest or fail in a closed class of people on A's death.

Wait and See. Same as above.

17. *Without RAP.* Maura has a life estate, Max has a contingent remainder in life estate, their children have a contingent remainder in fee simple absolute, T's estate has a reversion in fee simple absolute.

Common Law. All of the interests are valid, so same as above. Max's contingent remainder will vest or fail on Maura's death. The unborn widow(er) problem is avoided by naming a specific person, Max, so the children's contingent remainder is fine—it will vest or fail in a closed class on either Max's or Maura's death.

(It would work even if the "then living" was omitted because the class of their children would be closed on their death.)

Wait and See. Same as above.

18. *Without RAP.* A has a fee simple subject to executory limitation, A's grandchild has an executory interest in fee simple absolute.

Common Law. The correct answer is: A has a fee simple determinable, O has a possibility of reverter in fee simple absolute. The executory interest in the grandchild fails because O could have an afterborn child, who could then have a child who turns out to be the first grandchild to reach 21 more than 21 years after lives in being. Note that the possibility of reverter would expire, and A would have Blackacre in fee simple absolute, if it turns out that none of O's grandchildren reach the age of 21.

Wait and See. The correct answer is: A has a fee simple subject to executory limitation, A's grandchild has an executory interest that will be valid only if the first grandchild reaches 21 within 21 years of lives in being.

19. *Without RAP.* David has a life estate, Katie and Laura have vested remainders in an open class in life estate, David's grandchildren have contingent remainders in fee simple absolute, T's estate has a reversion in fee simple absolute.

Common Law. The correct answer is: David has a life estate, Katie and Laura have vested remainders in an open class in life estate, T's estate has a reversion in fee simple absolute. The grandchildren's interest fails because David could have another child, who in turn could have a child more than 21 years after lives in being.

Wait and See. The correct answer is: David has a life estate, Katie and Laura have vested remainders in an open class in life estate, the grandchildren have contingent remainders in absolute ownership that will be valid if the class closes within 21 years of lives in being, T's estate has a reversion.

20. *Without RAP.* Essentially the same answer as 19, but the classifications have changed. Katie and Laura have life estates, their children have contingent remainders in fee simple absolute and T's estate has a reversion in fee simple absolute.

Common Law. Essentially the same answer as 19, but the classifications have changed. Katie and Laura have life estates, and T's estate has a reversion in fee simple absolute.

Wait and See. Katie and Laura have life estates; the grandchildren have contingent remainders in fee simple absolute that are valid under the RAP, T's estate has a reversion in fee simple absolute. The grandchildren's contingent remainder will now never be invalidated under the RAP because it will vest in a complete class or fail on the deaths of Katie and Laura, both of whom were lives in being.

APPENDIX

E

A. PARTITION PROBLEM

As illustrated in *Ark Land*, the law has a strong presumption in favor of partition in kind. In many contexts, dividing a 12-acre parcel in kind among three tenants in common would be straightforward—each of the three co-tenants would get a four-acre parcel. The local zoning law, however, presents a problem here because it imposes a five-acre minimum lot size. Under these circumstances, dividing the property into three four-acre parcels would greatly diminish the value of the property because none of the lots would be buildable under the zoning law. John therefore would have a strong argument that partition in kind would be severely economically harmful—the value of the unbuildable four-acre lots together would be *much* less than the value of the whole 12-acre parcel. On the other hand, *Ark Land* held that negative economic impact is not dispositive, especially when there is a long-standing emotional attachment to the property. The court would almost certainly order a partition in kind if Zach and Cathy agreed to take a seven-acre parcel together and give John a five-acre parcel. This would preserve the value of the parcels and would avoid the economic hardship problem caused by the minimum lot size requirement imposed by the zoning law. If Zach and Cathy insisted on dividing the 12 acres into three equal four-acre plots, the court would be forced to decide whether the negative economic consequences would outweigh Zach and Cathy's emotional attachment to the property and the presumption in favor of partition in kind. Note in this context that John is a family member. Unlike Ark Land, he did not buy into the property taking a risk about the outcome in the partition process. Also note that Ark Land was still able to mine coal with the land partitioned in kind, albeit more expensively than if the land was partitioned by sale. *Ark Land* held that economic impact was not dispositive, but it did not hold that it is irrelevant. We set the problem up so that it is a close case, and we could see a court going either way.

The best result here would probably be for Zach and Cathy to buy out John. A buyout would give both parties what they want. Zach and Cathy would keep the property, and John would get the money he needs to start his business. Parties sometimes have a hard time negotiating for the best result, though, especially when they are members of the same family. The buyout procedure set up by the Uniform Partition of Heirs Property Act would help by establishing the fair market value of the property and providing a procedure for the parties opposing partition by sale (here, Zach and Cathy) to buy out the party proposing partition by sale (here, John).

B.   ACCOUNTING FOR COSTS AND RENT PROBLEM

In the accounting proceeding, Angela will be entitled to contribution from Maya for half of the costs of the mortgage and the upkeep. Angela paid $15,000 per year for two years, for a total of $30,000. Maya's share of these costs is $15,000.

Angela occupied the warehouse for one year. Generally speaking, absent ouster, a co-tenant in possession (here, Angela) is not liable to the other co-tenant (here, Maya) for the rental value of the property. In *Esteves*, however, the court noted that if the co-tenant in possession is seeking contribution for operating and maintenance costs, the tenant out of possession should be able to set off her proportional share of the fair rental value against the costs. Here, Angela is seeking contribution for costs, so Maya should be able to claim the fair rental value against Angela for the year Angela was in sole possession. The fair rental value for that year was $12,000. Maya's proportional share of the fair rental value is $6,000. So far, Maya owes Angela $9,000 (the $15,000 in costs, less the $6,000 in fair rental value).

Angela also needs to account to Maya for Maya's share of the rent actually collected from Sidney. Sidney paid $6,000 for the year ($500 per month for one year). Maya's share is $3,000. At the end of the day, Maya owes Angela $6,000 (the $9,000 owed in the last step, less Maya's $3,000 share of the rent collected from Sidney).

If there had been an ouster, Maya's entitlement to her share of fair rental value from Angela for the year that Angela was in sole possession would be even clearer. It does not matter a great deal in this particular context because Maya already has a good claim to the rental value as a set off against the mortgage and upkeep costs paid by Angela. In a different context, Maya's entitlement for her share of fair rental value could be very important.

Also, with an ouster, Maya would be entitled to half of the fair rental value for the year that Sidney rented the property rather than just half of the rent that Angela actually collected from Sidney. The fair rental value for that year was $12,000. Maya would be entitled to half of that, or $6,000. Recall that Maya owed Angela $9,000 before we accounted for the rent from Sidney. If there had been an ouster, we would credit Maya with $6,000 (half of the fair rental value) rather than $3,000 (half of the rent actually collected). So if there had been an ouster, Maya would owe Angela $3,000 ($9,000 less the $6,000 share of the fair rental value).

C.   JOINT TENANCY PROBLEM

At the beginning of the fact pattern, Cathy, John, and Louise are joint tenants:

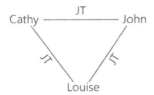

In 1985, Louise sold her share to Ralph. This severed the joint tenancy relationship for Louise's share. Cathy and John remain joint tenants, and they are tenants in common with Ralph:

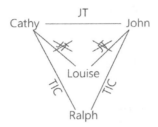

Cathy then mortgages her share to Bill. This leaves us with two possibilities. In a jurisdiction where the unilateral mortgage by one joint tenant severs the joint tenancy, Cathy, John and Ralph are all tenants in common. In a jurisdiction where the mortgage does not sever, Cathy and John are still joint tenants with each other and tenants in common with Ralph. At this point, Bill has a valid mortgage on Cathy's interest in both scenarios:

Cathy now dies, leaving all of her property to Jeremy. In a jurisdiction where the mortgage severs the joint tenancy, Jeremy inherits Cathy's share, and Bill's mortgage survives. Jeremy, John, and Ralph are tenants in common, each with a 1/3 share. Jeremy's share is subject to Bill's mortgage. In a jurisdiction where the mortgage did not sever the joint tenancy, Cathy's interest disappears, leaving John as the sole owner of the 2/3 that they owned as joint tenants. When Cathy's interest disappears, Bill's mortgage disappears. John and Ralph are tenants in common, with John having a 2/3 share and Ralph having a 1/3 share:

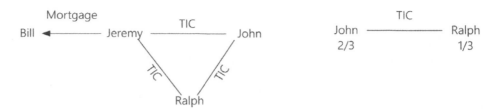

The outcomes between the parties therefore depend on the jurisdiction's approach to whether a mortgage severs a joint tenancy. If yes, then Bill's mortgage survives, and Jeremy, John, and Ralph are tenants in common with 1/3 shares. If no, then Bill's mortgage does not survive, and John (2/3 share) and Ralph (1/3 share) are tenants in common.

D. TENANCY BY THE ENTIRETY PROBLEM

The answer depends on the jurisdiction's approach to whether the creditor of one spouse can reach the property held by the entirety to satisfy the debt. In a Group II jurisdiction, Perry will be successful in attaching Julia's share. Perry will have equal rights to possess and use the property with Larry. Perry will also step into Julia's shoes for the right of survivorship. If Julia dies first, Larry will own the property under the right of survivorship free and clear of Perry's interest. If Larry dies first, Perry will own the property outright. In a Group III jurisdiction, Perry would not be successful because Group III does not allow the creditor of one spouse to attach the property held by the entirety. Perry's mortgage on Julia's share would be ineffective. Julia and Larry would own the property as tenants by the entirety, and the property held by the entirety would be immune from claims by Perry based on the debt Julia owes to him. (Note that this result arguably is fairer here than in *Sawada* because Perry was a contract creditor who voluntarily entered into the transaction with Julia and who could have taken steps to protect himself from this risk in advance.) In a Group IV jurisdiction, Perry will not be able to get access to the property while Julia and Larry were still alive, but Perry will be able to get Julia's right of survivorship. As in Group II, if Julia dies first, Larry will own the property under the right of survivorship free and clear of Perry's interest. If Larry dies first, Perry will own the property outright.

INDEX